D1827794

1 MONTH OF
FREE
READING

at
www.ForgottenBooks.com

By purchasing this book you are eligible for one month membership to ForgottenBooks.com, giving you unlimited access to our entire collection of over 700,000 titles via our web site and mobile apps.

To claim your free month visit:

www.forgottenbooks.com/free185934

* Offer is valid for 45 days from date of purchase. Terms and conditions apply.

ISBN 978-0-483-07031-8
PIBN 10185934

This book is a reproduction of an important historical work. Forgotten Books uses
state-of-the-art technology to digitally reconstruct the work, preserving the original format
whilst repairing imperfections present in the aged copy. In rare cases, an imperfection in
the original, such as a blemish or missing page, may be replicated in our edition. We do,
however, repair the vast majority of imperfections successfully; any imperfections that
remain are intentionally left to preserve the state of such historical works.

Forgotten Books is a registered trademark of FB &c Ltd.
Copyright © 2017 FB &c Ltd.
FB &c Ltd, Dalton House, 60 Windsor Avenue, London, SW19 2RR.
Company number 08720141. Registered in England and Wales.

For support please visit www.forgottenbooks.com

WILLIAM & MARY DARLINGTON
MEMORIAL LIBRARY
UNIVERSITY OF PITTSBURGH

A

GENERAL HISTORY

OF THE

BRITISH EMPIRE

IN

AMERICA:

Containing,

An HISTORICAL, POLITICAL, and COMMERCIAL VIEW
of the ENGLISH SETTLEMENTS; including all the
COUNTRIES in NORTH-AMERICA, and the WEST-
INDIES, ceded by the PEACE of PARIS.

In TWO VOLUMES.

VOL. II.

By MR. WYNNE.

FORTIA FACTA PATRUM, SERIES LONGISSIMA RERUM
PER TOT DUCTA VIROS ANTIQUÆ AB ORIGINE GENTIS.
VIRG. ÆN. I. 641.

LONDON,
Printed for W. RICHARDSON and L. URQUHART, under
the Royal-Exchange.
M DCC LXX.

CONTENTS

OF

VOLUME II.

Affairs

Fort

Defcription

Trade

CONTENTS. v

Remarks

THE

HISTORY

OF THE

BRITISH EMPIRE

IN

AMERICA.

WE concluded our laſt volume with the capture of two French ſhips of war, the Alcide and the Lys, by admiral Boſcawen's ſquadron off Cape Race, in Newfoundland. This was, properly ſpeaking, the commencement of the laſt war; in which, as is well known, Canada, the hiſtory of which we are now writing, was entirely conquered from the French. It is true, the operations of this war were not confined to that province, but extended over the whole continent; notwithſtanding which, we ſhall, in this place, give a connected and uninterrupted hiſtory of it from its firſt breaking out, till its concluſion by the peace of Paris. By this means the reader

Vol. II.   B   will

will have before him, a full and compleat view of thefe great and memorable tranfactions by which fuch mighty and important changes have been wrought in the fyftem and policy of the new world : whereas, were we to purfue that plan which the nature of our work feems to require; were we to be guided in our accounts of the warlike oppe- rations by the geography of the places, or the names of the provinces where they happened, it is manifeft, that the narration would be rendered broken and obfcure, and would convey neither amufement nor inftruction.

This war, which fpread afterwards like a devour ing flame over every quarter of the globe, fo as in a manner to threaten the deftruction of the human fpecies itfelf, begun, and took its rife, from difputes about territory in the immeafurable defarts and wilds of North America, regions which never were cul- tivated, were always thinly inhabited, and many centuries muft of neceffity elapfe before it can be faid that they properly deferve the name of either : yet thefe very circumftances, I mean the immen- fity of the country, its being uncultivated and fcarcely inhabited, which it might have been thought would have kept all quarrels about its poffeffion at an infinite diftance of time, were the very caufes which hurried the conteft on. This part of America (befides the Indians, who feem to be an inferior race of men, certainly deftitute, and, to appearance, incapable of a regular Euro- pean civilization) was inhabited, as far as it can be

faid

faid to be fo, by the French and Englifh : the latter were in poffeffion of the fea-coaft, the harbours, and mouths, and banks of the rivers ; and fome, though a very inconfiderable number, had fettled it may be as far as a hundred, or one hundred and fifty miles back in the country : the former were not in poffeffion of any fea-coaft or harbours on the continent, properly fo called, but had made fettlements on the two great rivers Miffiffippi and St. Laurence, the one running fouth, and the other north nearly, their fources being at no great diftance from one another, and forming a line almoft parallel to the fea-coaft claimed and inhabited by the Englifh. Here furely was extent of territory fufficient for the emigrants of both nations, had they been in numbers infinitely greater than they actually were, and had they attended folely to the avowed purpofes of thofe emigrations, to the planting and fettling thofe uncultivated waftes and forefts, which they either feized as uninhabited, forceably took poffeffion of, or fairly purchafed from the barbarous natives : it muft have been long before their interefts clafhed, or they could have poffibly interfered with one another : but there is no fetting limits to the reftlefs defires and ambitions of men. However, befides this confideration common to all the human race, there was another which involved thefe two nations in wars and bloodfhed more readily perhaps than would have happened to any other two nations in the world ; I mean that hoftile difpofition which has for many centuries, at leaft

ever

ever fince the days of Edward III. fubfifted between
the natives of France and England, and which has
broken out into numberlefs wars, attended with a
greater effufion of blood than in thofe between the
Greeks and Perfians, the Romans and Carthagi-
nians, wherein the empire of the world was difputed and determined.   The French and Englifh carrying their hereditary animofity with them from
Europe, it frequently occafioned the commiffion
of open acts of violence in the new world, when
their refpective ftates were at peace in the old one.
Thus the feeds of a bloody conteft between the
two nations in America were fown with the very
firft fettlement of both in it ; which has at laft happily ended for both in the extirpation of one of them
from that country.   This event was haftened
rather than delayed by the immenfity of the territory for which they were difputing : for this naturally prevented any boundaries being amicably fixed
between them from the firft ; and when once difputes
had begun upon this point, and national honour,
or private intereft, came to be concerned, or which
is the fame thing, were thought to be fo, it was
perhaps impracticable ever after.   Befides the indefinite, and indeed ridiculous and extravagant
charters, or grants of land, made by the fovereigns
of both kingdoms to their refpective fubjects, neceffarily made both look upon each other as mutual
encroachers.   Thefe are the general principles
which rendered an American war inevitable, one
time or other, between the two nations ; and here
follow

follow the particular facts and circumstances which hurried on that which we are now to treat of.

The hasty and ill-digested treaty of Aix-la-Chapelle had finally determined none of the points in dispute between Great-Britain, on the one hand, and the crowns of France and Spain on the other; particularly the boundaries of Acadia, or Nova Scotia, which had long been a bone of contention between England and France; and the property of the four neutral islands in the West Indies, St. Lucia, St. Vincent, Tobago, and Dominica, were left to be settled by the uncertain method of commissaries, wherein it is easy for either party by chicanery, by multiplying memorials, answers, and replies, to protract the decision to an unlimited time. Before the commissaries were appointed on either side, or met for that purpose, and very soon after the conclusion of the peace, the government of Great Britain had established a colony in Nova Scotia, and built the town of Halifax on the bay of Chebucto, where there is one of the finest harbours in the world. The only regular settlement which before this time the English possessed in this province, was at Annapolis Royal, called, when in the hands of the French, Port Royale, where, ever since the peace of Utrecht, they had maintained a small garrison. The rest of the province was inhabited by those called French neutrals, who though by treaty they might rather be deemed subjects of the British crown, yet still retained all the passions and affections of their ancestors, and the people

whose

whofe language they fpoke, and whofe manners and cuftoms were familiar to them. Accordingly upon every difpute or mifunderſtanding between the two crowns, thefe colonifts were extremely alert in harraffing the Britifh fettlers, and inciting the Indians to difturb them by their ufual method of carrying on war by fudden incurfions, ambuf- cades, and fcalping parties. The court of France could not decently take open offence at this new colony eftablifhed on the bay Chebucto, for it was undoubtedly in that part of Acadia which they themfelves never difputed being Britifh property. This fettlement, however, being from the firft powerful and formidable, having met with extra- ordinary encouragement from the Britifh legiflature and government, gave great umbrage to the difaf- fected neutrals, who failed not to renew their ufual practices, and to diftrefs and harrafs the infant co- lony all in their power, with the intention, no doubt, of forcing them to abandon their project.

Much about the fame time the French, in direct contradiction to the moft exprefs treaties, had at- tempted an eftablifhment upon Tobago, one of the neutral iflands. Mr. Grenville, governor of Barbadoes, having received intelligence of this matter, difpatched captain Tyrrel, in one of his majefty's frigates, to enquire into the particulars ; and that officer found above three hundred men al- ready landed, two batteries erected, and two fhips of war lying before them to protect the new fettle- ment, who had befides received promifes of an im-

mediate

mediate reinforcement from the marquis de Cay-
lus, governor of Martinico, who had published an
ordonnance authorizing the subjects of the French
king to settle the island of Tobago, with assurances,
that he would defend them from the attempts of all
who should presume to oppose their undertaking.
This part of the proclamation was in answer to one
issued forth by the governor of Barbadoes, and
affixed in different parts of the island, commanding
all the inhabitants to remove in thirty days under
pain of military execution.

Captain Tyrrel, with a spirit becoming a commander in the British navy, immediately on his arrival gave the French officers to understand, that
their master had no right to settle the island which
had been declared neutral by treaties ; and that, if
they would not voluntarily desist, he should be
obliged to employ force to compel them, and
drive them off. Night coming on, and Mr. Tyrrel's ship falling to leeward, the two French commanders seized that opportunity of making the
best of their way to Martinico, and the English captain returned next day to Barbadoes, having no
power to commit hostilities.

Accounts of this affair, together with a copy of
the French governor's ordonnance, being transmitted
to the court of London, a courier was immediately
dispatched to the English envoy at Paris, with directions to make representations to the court of
Versailles on this subject. The French ministry,
sensible of their weakness, and of the imprudence

of

of hazarding an immediate rupture, and being informed how much the merchants and people of
Great Britain were alarmed and irritated at their
attempts to poſſeſs theſe iſlands, thought proper to
diſown the proceedings of the governor of Martinico, and gave the ſatisfaction required, by ſending him orders to diſcontinue the ſettlement, and
evacuate the iſland of Tobago.

This buſineſs, together with the tranſactions in
Nova Scotia, naturally brought on the meetings
and conferences of commiſſaries, to ſettle the
matters in diſpute. Theſe were held at Paris,
but, as might be foreſeen, were productive of no
deciſion. On the contrary, memorials were heaped on memorials, till they amounted to immenſe
volumes, and rendered the ſubject of altercation
more doubtful and perplexed than ever. The following is the account which a celebrated modern
hiſtorian gives of this tranſaction : " The object
that now employed the attention of the Britiſh miniſtry, was the eſtabliſhment of the preciſe limits
of Acadia, or Nova Scotia, where the new colony
had ſuffered great miſchief and interruption from
the incurſions of the Indians, excited to theſe outrages by the ſubjects and emiſſaries of France.
Commiſſaries were appointed by both crowns to
meet at Paris, and compromiſe theſe diſputes ; but
the conferences were rendered abortive by every
art of cavilling, chicanery, and procraſtination,
which the French commiſſioners oppoſed to the
juſtice and perſpicuity of the Engliſh claims. They
                                                      not

not only misinterpreted treaties, though expreſſed
with the utmoſt preciſion, and perplexed the whole
with difficulties and matter foreign to the ſubject,
but they carried the fineſſe of perfidy ſo far, as to
produce falſe charts and maps of the country, in
which the rivers and boundaries were miſplaced
and miſrepreſented *." Every reader of candor
and reflection cannot but ſuſpect this view of the
matter of prejudice and partiality. Had a French
author given the ſame account of the behaviour of
the Engliſh commiſſioners, it is not improbable, that
after a moſt careful peruſal of all the proofs and
memorials on both ſides, he ſhould be doubtful on
which ſide juſtice lay. And indeed this ſeems unavoidable from the nature of the thing in diſpute,
which was a vaſt extent of country claimed by each
nation, founded on grants and charters of their re-
ſpective ſovereigns, who at the very time they
expedited thoſe charters, were totally ignorant of
the extent and boundaries of that very country they
were thus granting away. Hence it was impoſſible
that thoſe charters, and ſurely both ſovereigns had
equal right to grant them, ſhould not frequently claſh
and interfere, and be inconſiſtent with one another.
And while both parties referred to them, reaſoned
from them, and reckoned them of equal force and
validity, an amicable deciſion was impracticable.

But in all probability, neither this, nor the diſputes about the neutral iſlands, would have been

---

* Smollett's Continuation, vol. I. p. 84, 85.

pro-

productive of national hoftilities, had not differences, proceeding from fimilar caufes, arifen a-
bout matters deemed of infinitely greater importance. As we obferved before, the Englifh were
poffeffed of the fea-coafts, and the French had fettled along the banks of the two rivers St. Laurence
and Miffifippi. The Englifh territory being divided into feveral diftinct and independant provinces, many difputes had arifen between the contiguous ones about their refpective boundaries,
owing to the vaguenefs and want of precifion in
their charters. When fuch things happened between fubjects of the fame parent ftate, it is
no wonder that the like caufes co-operating, they
fhould fpring up, and end at laft in violence between two nations naturally hoftile, and enemies
to one another. We cannot but be very much in
the dark with refpect to the circumftances and extent of the grants of territory made by the French
king to his fubjects; but in all probability, fome
of them were as inconfiftent and extravagant, as
truth and candor oblige us to confefs thofe of our
own fovereign were, refpecting at leaft Virginia
and the two Carolinas. The charters by which
thofe countries were granted to the original proprietors, befides great part of Florida, and St.
Auguftine, long poffeffed and garrifoned by the
Spaniards, comprehended all the country of America lying between certain latitudes, and extending
in longitude from the Atlantic-ocean to the great
South-fea; in which tract muft of neceffity be included,

cluded, not only all the French settlements on the Miffifippi, but the greateft part of New Mexico, poffeffed by the Spaniards long before thefe charters were heard. Hence it is obvious, we are neither to feek for the caufes of the quarrel, nor to form our notions of the juftice, or injuftice of either fide, from any claims founded on thefe grants, or inferences drawn from them; but all this muft depend on other and more eftablifhed principles. And confidering the matter in the real and only point of view it ought to be vieweded in, we hefitate not, without departing from our avowed impartiality, to maintain that the French had long been infpired with intentions of making hoftile encroachments upon the Englifh colonifts, and that they were in the laft war particularly the original aggreffors.

When any members of a civilized people leave their native land to fettle in a wafte uncultivated country, the natural employment of thefe emigrants muft be agriculture, and a confined fort of a commerce. To do juftice to the Englifh colonifts, it muft be confeffed, they have never, but when driven by force, varied from that line of action. It has been quite otherwife with the French: almoft entirely neglecting commerce, looking upon agriculture as only a fecondary confideration, their main politics have been rather to conquer and fubdue, than to plant and fettle; and, inftead of mercantile factories, they have erected military forts. It is from this different genius and bent of the two nations, manifefted by the uniform feries of their conduct

conduct pursued for ages, and not from a few particular accidents, nor from flimzy reasoning on the meaning of terms and the extent of boundaries, and the running of imaginary lines in vague and indefinite charters, which undoubtedly would never furnish an object of dispute, unless people were predisposed to quarrel, and only wanted a pretence for proceeding to hostilities, that we are to form our judgments of the justice or injustice of either side, in the commencement of the last war. This is a new point of view in which we have set this important object ; and we are persuaded it will be found consonant to truth and reason, and that it does ample justice to the moderation and pacific dispositions of our countrymen. It is certain, that the main object of the English was planting and agriculture ; and that they never removed from the sea-coasts, and settled up the country, but when they were straitened for room in the places which they originally occupied. They made no settlements, and built no forts, at a distance from the capitals of their respective colonies ; and which, consequently, could not be maintained and supported, by the natural intercourse of human affairs, in such remote establishments. When such was their invariable practice, it was impossible that they could ever be justly charged with making hostile invasions and encroachments on their neighbours the French ; and had the conduct of the latter been directed by the same motives, many centuries must have elapsed before the two nations could have been,

been, properly speaking, neighbours to one another, in those almost unbounded territories. But
their principles and conduct were quite the reverse :
actuated by the same principles in the new world
which had so long, and so fatally, distinguished that
people in Europe, they have made military establishments, and erected fortifications, at an immense distance from one another, and from their two
capitals, and in situations where they cannot be even
kept up but by unnatural exertions, both of power
and politics, and where they could never serve any
good purpose of commerce, far less of cultivation
and agriculture. Beholding, with the jealous and
envious eyes of a rival, the slow, but sure, advance
and progress of the British colonies in population,
commerce, and cultivation ; mortally dreading the
increase of a power, which must be the more confirmed and stable, because it employed no unnatural or iniquitous means for that purpose, they have
long determined on measures to stop the further
growth of the British settlements, unavoidable because natural, if left to themselves, and to confine
them within narrow limits, within a few leagues of
the sea-coast. With this ambitious view, they had
connected their two colonies of Canada and Louisiana, by a chain of forts from Quebec to New-
Orleans. This, though it could have served no
purpose of colonization, might have been defensi-
ble had they restricted themselves, in these military
establishments, to the banks of the two great rivers,
or their neighbourhood : but not contented with
this,

this, they made military settlements so very near the English frontier, which had been planted by a natural and regular progress, and, what is still more convincing, at so great a distance from any of their own colonies, with such vast tracts of land, either desert or inhabited by hostile savages; lying between them, that a bare inspection of the map is sufficient to demonstrate that it could only be done with a hostile intention, and a view of making encroachments. The most palpable instance they gave of such designs was the building of Fort Frederick, called by us Crown Point, upon Lake Champlain; at a great distance from Montreal, the nearest of their own establishments, and within the territories of the Indians called Mohawks, acknowledged, by treaty, to be friends and allies, and under the protection of the English. This they effected in the year 1716, and though complained of at the time, no notice was taken of it by the British court; and amongst many other articles, perhaps of greater importance, it was utterly forgotten, and consequently left undecided at the pacification of Aix-la-Chapelle. In short, from the whole tendency of the French conduct it appears almost indisputable, that they had fixed their hearts on possessing themselves of one of the English harbours on the Atlantic-ocean, envying their rivals, no doubt, the mighty advantages they reaped, in the way of navigation and commerce, from the most extensive sea-coast in their hands, and regretting their own unfortunate situation with respect to

these

thefe articles, having no other maritime communication for the immenfe territories which they
claimed as their own, but the mouths of two rivers,
the navigation in neither of which was convenient.
To conclude, a very fuperficial reflection on the
different foundations of the French and Britifh colonies, and the different temper and character of
the inhabitants, will enable any impartial man,
without the leaft hefitation, without having recourfe
to partial reprefentations of inconfequential, and,
at beft, doubtful facts, and without lending ear to
vulgar prejudices; equally forcible on both fides,
to determine the important queftion, who were the
aggreffors in the laft war. The Britifh colonies
were bounded by fober, regular, progreffive cultivation; the French by wild, irregular, uncon-
nected enterprize. The Britifh colonifts were peaceable farmers and traders; and the French, if they
deferve that name, turbulent freebooters and adventurers.

A difpute about fettling, or rather trading on
the Ohio, one of the fineft rivers in America, and
watering one of the fruitfuleft countries, and one
of the moft falubrious climates in the world, gave
the firft occafion to regular and national hoftilities;
and thefe, in a due progrefs of things, brought on
a formal war between the two ftates. To enquire
in this place who were the aggreffors, or who had
juftice on their fide in this quarrel, attended with
fuch memorable confequences, would be, after
what has been above faid, fuperfluous. It is ridiculous

culous to think of deciding it by arguments drawn
from grants and charters, for no doubt both parties could produce vouchers of that nature from
their refpective fovereigns, and perhaps from the
Indians, themfelves, equally pointed and explicit,
to appearance of equal validity, and therefore of
no validity at all. The only confideration by which
we can form any judgment, is the fituation and geography of the country in difpute; and from its
eafy communication with the Englifh provinces of
Penfilvania and Virginia, at least infinitely eafier
than with any of the French fettlements which deferved the name, we are well warranted to infer,
that the project of the Englifh was the project of
fober policy and traffic; and that the French, pretending to interfere and difturb them in it, were
influenced by unruly ambition and wild adventure.
Befides, this fettlement was no new project of the
Englifh; fo long ago as the year 1716, Mr. Spotfwood, governor of Virginia, finding the Outa-
wais, now called the Twightees, extremely well
difpofed towards the Englifh, formed the fcheme
of purchafing fome of their lands upon this river,
and opening a trade with them : but the French
being at this time full fraught with their vaft and
vifionary fchemes about the Miffifippi, and there
being, at the fame time, an excellent good intelligence between the two courts, this project was dif-
countenanced. After the peace of Aix-la-Chapelle
it was renewed ; but the moft prudent article in it
was neglected, that of conciliating the natives, by
                                        making

making agreements with them for the purchafes of their lands. Some merchants of Maryland and Virginia, forefeeing the great advantages refulting from the cultivation of this fine country, and an exclufive commerce with the natives, on prefenting a petition to the government, were indulged not only with a moft extenfive grant of thefe lands, but likewife with an exclufive privilege of trade. They forthwith fent a furveyor to take plans of the country, as far as the Falls of the Ohio. The natives, though pacific in their difpofition, were alarmed at this ftep; and this their jealoufy was inflamed by the French, who reprefented the conduct of the Englifh in the moft invidious colours. Befides, this great acquifition of territory, and profpect of an exclufive monopoly, failed not to give umbrage to fome of their own countrymen, who would find their interefts hurt by it. The feparate traders of Virginia and Maryland co-operated with the French, in inflaming and keeping up the animofity of the Indians. Not contented with this, the French continued to ftrengthen themfelves, by building fortifications at Niagara and Lake Erie, inhabited by Indians, if not fubjects, at leaft allies to Great-Britain, as alfo on the Ohio itfelf. Mr. Hamilton, then governor of Penfylvania, laid thefe proceedings before the affembly of that province; and propofed erecting truck-houfes, in the nature of fmail fortreffes, on the Ohio, for the protection of the Britifh traders there. This propofal was approved of, in general, by the affembly; but diverfity of interefts,

and other difficulties which were ſtarted, prevented
the execution of it; while the French were proceeding in ſuch a manner as to become every day
more and more powerful and formidable. Mr.
Dinwiddie alſo, governor of Virginia, was extremely attentive to theſe operations, and tranſmitted
home ſuch ſpirited repreſentations upon them, as
failed not to give the alarm to the Britiſh government.   Reſolved to omit nothing within the ſphere
of his power, he ſent major Waſhington, with a
letter, to the French commandant of a fort on the
river au Beuf, which falls into the Ohio, complaining of the encroachment, and requiring him to evacuate that place, as it was within the Britiſh territory.   The French officer returned for anſwer, it muſt
be confeſſed, with great propriety, that as it was
not his buſineſs to examine into the property of the
lands in diſpute, it could not be expected he ſhould
quit his poſt, but that he would tranſmit the governor of Virginia's letter to the governor-general of
Canada.   Mr. Dinwiddie, ſeeing nothing was to be
expected by the way of amicable negociation, projected the building a fort near the forks of the river,
as a bridle on the French : the colony undertook to
defray the expence, and the materials were actually
provided, and tranſported to the ſpot ; but no
meaſures being previouſly taken to obtain the con-
ſent and good-will of the natives, this attempt
ſerved further to exaſperate them.

While matters in Virginia were thus, by degrees,
ripening into an open rupture, hoſtilities, though
not

not, properly speaking, national ones, were actually commenced in Nova-Scotia. Halifax had been no sooner built, than the French privately stirred up the Indians against the English, whom, agreeable to their barbarous manner of carrying on war, they took every opportunity to waylay and surprize. Many they scalped and murdered, and those whom they took prisoners they sold, for arms and ammunition, to the French; who, on being questioned for this practice, pretended they entered into it with favourable views to the English captives, who would otherwise be tortured and put to death, after their manner, by the Indians: but the disingenuity of this excuse was manifest, from more considerations than one. In the first place, they exacted exorbitant ransoms for the liberty of those whom they had thus pretended to have saved from a worse fate than slavery: in the next place, it was certain, that the scalping parties of the Indians who made these prisoners were headed by Frenchmen, and under their guidance; and, when repeated complaints, on this account, were made to the governor of Louisbourg, his constant reply was, that his jurisdiction did not extend over the Indians, and indeed as little over those Frenchmen who were their conductors, who being inhabitants of the district of Annapolis, and having thought proper to remain there after that country had been ceded to the English, were, in reality, to be deemed subjects of Great-Britain. The futility and evasive intent of this answer were very soon made evident in the sequel.

In

In the spring of the year 1750, general Corn-
wallis, governor of Halifax, sent major Lawrence,
at the head of a small party, to reduce those French
inhabitants of Annapolis, whose practices, and even
whose subjection to France, had been thus dis-
claimed by the governor of Louisbourg, to good
order and obedience. At the major's approach,
they reduced their houses to ashes, forsook their possessions, and threw themselves under the protection
of M. la Corne, whom, even while the conferences for ascertaining the limits of Nova-Scotia
were carrying on at Paris, the governor of Canada
had detached with a party of regular troops, and a
body of militia, to fortify a post on the bay of,
Chiconecto, the possession of which not only secured
to the Indians of the continent a free passage into
the peninsula on which Halifax stands, and a safe
retreat in case of being pursued, but also encouraged
the French inhabitants of Annapolis to break out
into open rebellion against the English government.
In fact, these fugitives were received by La Corne
with all cordiality, who, by means of this reinforcement, saw himself at the head of fifteen hundred men, well appointed, with arms and ammunition. Major Lawrence, finding himself unable
to face a body so greatly superior to his small detachment, and, at the same time, having no orders
to use forcible measures against any but the Indians, and their open abettors, thought proper to demand a conference with the French commander.
This being granted, he desired to know for what
reason

reafon the French inhabitants of Nova-Scotia had thrown off their allegiance to Great-Britain, and broken that neutrality which they had fworn to, and hitherto affected to profefs? La Corne took no notice of this requifition; but contented himfelf with informing the major, in general terms, that he had orders to defend his prefent poft, and thefe orders he was refolved to obey. Mr. Lawrence, it may be prefumed, not extremely well fatisfied with the contemptuous filence obferved with refpect to his principal demand, returned to Halifax, without being able to accomplifh the main end of his expedition. No fooner was his retreat known, than the French neutrals (fo they were ftill called) returned to their habitations, which they had deferted; and, together with the Indians, renewed their incurfions upon the English territories, and made depredations on the inhabitants of Halifax, and their neighbouring fettlements. Juftly incenfed at thefe outrageous hoftilities, and convinced, from repeated experience, that the French inhabitants were irreconcileable enemies to the Englifh name and government, that they would neither fubmit quietly to it themfelves, nor fuffer others to enjoy it with tranquillity, the Englifh governor of Nova-Scotia now took a final refolution of extirpating them from a country which, on account of their turbulence and treachery, they deferved not to poffefs. Major Lawrence, with a thoufand men, was tranfported by fea to Chiconecto, where he found the French and Indians intrenched, and refolved to oppofe his landing. This, however, he effected with a few companies;

and,

and, after receiving and returning a fmart fire,
rufhed into their intrenchments, from which he
drove them in the utmoft confufion, having killed
and wounded a confiderable number of their men.
They fled acrofs a river, by which means they faved
themfelves from further purfuit ; for, on the oppo-
pofite banks ftood La Corne, at the head of
a body of regular troops, who were drawn up
in order of battle, and received the fugitives
as friends and dependants. Before this time, he
had erected a fort, called Beau Sejour ; and now
the Englifh built one likewife, on the other fide
of the river, named, from its founder, St. Lawrence. This, though intended to reprefs the incurfions of the French, and their barbarous allies
the Indians, was far from effectually anfwering the
purpofe. The latter, being always fupplied with
canoes, arms, and ammunition, from the French,
found means, in fpite of the check of this fort, in
which a pretty numerous garrifon was left, to make
feveral incurfions into the interior parts of the peninfula ; in one of which, they furprized the little
town of Dartmouth, oppofite to Halifax, and murdered, fcalped, and carried off prifoners, the greateft part of the inhabitants. The French, under
La Corne, continued to ftrengthen themfelves on
the neck of the peninfula, by fortifying two additional pofts ; one diftinguifhed by the name of
Baye Verte, and another at the entrance of St. John's
river, on the north fide of Fundy Bay.

Reprefentations of thefe outrages and encroachments being tranfmitted home to England, the earl
of

of Albemarle, the British ambassador, presented a memorial to the French court, complaining of them, and demanding satisfaction for them ; and, particularly, that the subjects of Great-Britain who had been made prisoners should be set at liberty, and the losses they had sustained made up to them ; that exemplary punishment should be inflicted on the perfons who had committed these outrages on them ; that the fort of Niagara should be immediately razed ; and, lastly, that positive orders should be sent to De la Jonquiere, the French commander in America, to desist from violence against the British subjects in that country. The French court, not being yet sufficiently prepared for an open rupture, thought proper to return an answer, which might, at least, serve to amuse for a while. They set at liberty six Englishmen, who had been sent prisoners from America to France : this they did immediately, and also promised to send their governor-general of Canada the most express orders to prevent all causes of complaint for the future. But if any such orders were publickly sent, it is most probable they were contradicted by private instructions : for De la Jonquiere paid no regard to them, but continued to encourage the Indians, and permit the French to harrass the English, both on the Ohio and in Nova-Scotia ; as also to compleat their chain of forts to the southward, in order to effectuate their wild ambitious scheme of uniting their two colonies, and confining the English within narrow limits, the sea on one side, and their encroachments on the other.

The

The English fuffered the moft alarming and important violences on the Ohio, and there the firft regular hoftilities, having the fanction of legal authority on both fides, were committed : for the Britifh government, juftly irritated at these manifeft evafions of the moft folemn promifes, and at proceedings as hoftile as they were treacherous, at length difpatched orders to all the governors of the colonies not only to ftand on their defence, but forcibly to drive the French from their fettlements on the Ohio. Much about the fame time, a political confederacy, for their mutual defence, was ftrongly recommended to them all; and the governor of New-York was directed to confer with the chiefs of the Six Nations, called by the French the Iroquoife, and to endeavour, by means of valuable prefents, and promifes of more, to wean them from the French intereft; into which they had been artfully allured by that intriguing people, and attach them to their former friends and allies, the Englifh. But neither of thefe fchemes was attended with the wifhed for fuccefs, at leaft for the prefent: the different views and interefts of the colonies, both religious and political, prevented the one; and tho' the Indians, indeed, came to the conference at Albany, and received the prefents, as ufual, yet they, backward and indifferent, promifed but little, and did ftill lefs.

While the Englifh were only deliberating, and that perhaps with no great unanimity, about executing the orders they had received, the French exe-

executed theirs, and proceeded to action, with great vigour and alacrity. They surprized Logs-town, a fort built by the Virginians on the Ohio: they made themselves masters of the block-house and truck-house adjacent to it, where they found skins and other commodities, to the value of twenty thousand pounds, which they were not contented with plundering, but also murdered all the British traders, except two, who found means to escape: at the same time, M. de Contre-cœur proceeded, in three hundred canoes, from a fort called Venungo, which they had built on the banks of the Ohio, with a thousand men, and eigh-teen pieces of cannon, and, arriving at the conflu-ence of the Monangahela with that river, reduced, by surprize, a considerable fort, which the province of Virginia had there erected. These hostilities were followed by several other skirmishes between the people of the two nations, which were fought with various success.

At last, a most important expedition was under-taken by the government of Virginia. Major Washington, of whom mention has been made be-fore, was dispatched from thence, at the head of a body of four hundred men, to check the hostile operations of the French. He took possession of a post on the banks of the Ohio, at a place called the Great Meadows, where he erected a fort of tempo-rary fort, hoping to be able to defend it till the re-inforcements, which were expected from New-York, should arrive; in which expectation he was,

howe-

however, difappointed. `De Villier, a French offi-
cer, who had under his command no lefs than nine
hundred men, at the fort of Monangahela, lately
taken from the Englifh, being informed of Wafhington's.fituation and ftrength, fent him a formal requifition to relinquifh his poft, which he called an
encroachment on the French territory, by the hands
of one of his fubalterns, called Jamonville, attended by a fmall party. According to the French
accounts, Jamonville and his company were either
killed or taken prifoners by Wafhington, in a manner contrary to all the rules of war eftablifhed among
civilized nations. To avenge this injury and af-
front, De Villier marched, with the remainder of
his troops, to attack Wafhington; who, not difcouraged by the inferiority of numbers, defended
himfelf for a time with fuch intrepidity, that the
French commandant found it expedient to offer
him a very honourable capitulation, which was,
that both parties fhould retire; the Englifh to Will's
Creek, within the acknowledged confines of Virginia, and the French to their former fituation at
Monongahela. Wafhington embraced the propofal, and delivered two officers as hoftages for the
reftitution of the furviving prifoners of Jamonville's
detachment. Thefe terms were no fooner agreed
on, than a body of French Indians appeared; and,
though they were prevented from breaking the capitulation, which they were very earneft to do, yet
the French commander fuffered them to harrafs the
Englifh in their retreat, and plunder their baggage.

                                                Loud

Loud complaints of thefe flagrant and unwarrantable hoftilities were preferred to the court of Verfailles, by the earl of Albemarle, the Englifh ambaffador. But the French miniftry having now conceived a fond, though, as it afterwards appeared, a fallacious notion, that they had tranfmitted reinforcements and fupplies to Quebec fufficient to withftand all the force which the Englifh colonies, with what affiftance the mother-country would chufe to afford, could mufter againft them; fo far from offering any adequate fatisfaction, took not their ufual pains to apologize for them; and thus an open rupture between the two nations became inevitable.

At firft, indeed, the French had greatly the fuperiority over their enemies, owing to the different conftitutions of the two governments in that country. That of Canada, or New-France, moved by one direction, and infpired by one head, faction was unknown in it; all its force was united in one point, and acted with a view to one common end. The Englifh were divided into feparate governments, actuated by diftinct, and fometimes contradictory interefts: they not only had complaints againft each other, the Virginians imputing Wafhington's misfortune to the people of New-York, who had not fulfilled their engagements, but were alfo difcontented among themfelves. Some very immaterial points in difpute raifed a quarrel between the affembly and governor of Virginia, which put a ftop to all bufinefs; an extremity which both parties ought carefully to have avoided, when

4   the

the danger from the common enemy was fo great. The governor and affembly of Penfylvania were, from the like caufes, in the fame fituation; and the inhabitants of New-York were inflamed to the higheft pitch of difcontent, by a difcovery they had made of fome inftructions which Sir Danvers Ofborne, their late governor, who died immediately upon his arrival, had brought over with him. The reft of the colonies were in a very little better fituation, and had agreed on no one plan of action: if they concurred in any thing, it was, in alternately blaming the backwardnefs, and imploring the affiftance, of their mother-country. That affiftance was, at laft, effectually lent them; otherwife, the difpute would have been foon decided, in a different manner than it afterwards was.

The firft ftep taken was the appointing the officers of two regiments, confifting of double battalions, to be raifed in America, and commanded by Sir William Pepperel, and general Shirley, who had enjoyed the fame command in the laft war. A body of Britifh regulars was likewife deftined for the fame fervice, and orders given for their embarkation at Corke, in Ireland: and, as it was forefeen that the national and provincial troops muft frequently act in conjunction, in order to render the fervice more uniform, a claufe was added to the annual mutiny-bill, enacting, that all officers and foldiers being enlifted, and in pay, which are or fhall be raifed in any of the Britifh provinces in America,

by

by authority of the refpective governors or governments thereof, fhall, at all times and in all places, when they happen to join or act in conjunction with his majefty's Britifh forces, be liable to martial law and difcipline, in like manner, to all intents and purpofes, as the Britifh forces are; and fhall be fubject to the fame trial, penalties, and punifhments. At the fame time, a powerful fleet was equipped, which afterwards failed in two feparate divifions, under admirals Bofcawen and Holborn, to North-America; a meafure which was then feverely taxed by a certain anti-minifterial writer. Nor were the French lefs alert in their naval preparations. Befides the different parties of land-forces which they had at various times tranfported to Canada, fometimes in fingle fhips, Mr. Macnamara, an officer of Irifh extraction, failed from Breft, and directed his courfe towards North-America, having under his command a fleet of twenty-five fhips of the line, befides frigates and tranfports, which latter had on board a great quantity of ammunition and warlike ftores, and a body of four thoufand regular troops, commanded in chief by the baron, Diefkau; but before he had proceeded many leagues beyond the chops of the Englifh Channel, he returned to Breft with nine of the capital fhips, and M. Bois de la Mothe continued his courfe to the original place of deftination, with the remainder of the armament.

In fact, the Englifh miniftry do not feem to have poffeffed the beft intelligence; nor, at any rate, to

have

have acted with the prudence requisite in the conducting such an arduous business. They must not have known the original strength of the French fleet; otherwise, they never would have dispatched admiral Boscawen with so small a number as eleven ships, especially as that officer, as it afterwards appeared, had orders to act in an hostile manner. Even when that strength came to be known, the reinforcement they sent after him, under admiral, Holborne, was by no means equal to the purpose; for when they effected a junction, against which, however, there were many chances, they would still have been so far inferior to the French, that the superior skill and alertness in naval operations, which the English boast, and really seem to possess, over the French, could not be expected to compensate for it; whereas, had the French met with them separately, which was by no means impossible, their destruction, in that case, must have been unavoidable: even after the return of Macnamara with nine ships of the line, which our ministry could neither know nor suspect, they enjoyed a very bare superiority over them when joined, and when separated were far out-numbered: so that, in this whole transaction, the English administration were certainly more fortunate than provident.

The earl of Albemarle, the English ambassador in France, had been for some time taken off by a sudden death, and no other minister had been appointed in his room. The duke de Mirepoix, a nobleman endued with an honour and integrity

seldom

feldom found in a ftatefman, particularly a French one, was then ambaffador at the court of London. Seeing the vigorous preparations for war carrying on by the Englifh, and himfelf being deceived, or kept in the dark, with refpect to the real defigns of his own court, he continued to negociate with the Englifh miniftry, made very earneft proteftations to them of the good faith of France, and even fcrupled not to fay, he would be anfwerable for it with his own private honour. But the minifters, being better informed than he imagined, fhewed him copies of the orders fent to the governor-general, and other French officers of Canada, which flatly gave the lie to all he had fo folemnly afferted. Confounded at this, unable to deny the flagrant proofs that were laid before him, and not a little difgufted at the infincere part, fo derogatory to his honour, which he had been induced to act, he returned to Paris, and warmly upbraided the French miniftry not only for their fallacy, but alfo for the deception they had impofed upon himfelf. Unable to give a fatisfactory anfwer to his juft reproaches, they referred him to the king ; who immediately fent him back to London with orders to affure the court of England, from himfelf, of his pacific intentions. But fuch affurances were now of no avail, nor in the leaft attended to : both the French and Englifh fleets being by this time arrived at North-America, the Britifh miniftry made no fcruple of declaring to the duke de Mirepoix, that admiral Bofcawen had orders to attack the French

fhips,

fhips, wherever he fhould meet them. To which
the duke replied, that his mafter would confider
the firft gun that fhould be fired in an hoftile manner as an actual declaration of war. Far from being intimidated by this menace, the preparations
for war were continued with redoubled ardour,
powerful fleets were equipped, new fhips were put
on the ftocks, an hot prefs for feamen fet on foot,
and the land-forces augmented.

In the mean time, news were impatiently expected from America, where it was known the firft warlike operations would commence. At laft, accounts arrived that admiral Bofcawen had taken
two French fhips of the line. It feems this officer
had reached the American coaft a few days before
M. Bois de la Mothe, the greateft part of whofe
fhips, being favoured by the impenetrable fogs fo
familiar to that part of the world, effectuated, un-
noticed by their enemies, their paffage to Canada;
fome by the ufual way, between Cape-Breton and
Newfoundland; and the others by the ftraits of
Belleifle, on the north of the latter ifland, a navigation hitherto unattempted by large fhips of war:
two of them only, being feparated from their con-
forts in the fog, the Alcide and the Lys, both
pierced for fixty-four guns, but the latter actually
mounting no more than twenty-two, were intercepted by the Englifh fleet. Two Englifh fhips
of the fame ftrength, the Dunkirk and Defiance,
commanded by the captains Howe and Andrews,
bore down upon, engaged, and took them, after a
fhort,

fhort, but vigorous refiftance. As foon as the French king received authentic accounts of this hoftility, which were firft publifhed in the London Gazette, on July 15, 1755, he recalled his two ambaffadors, the duke de Mirepoix, from the court of London, and M. Buffy, from Hanover; being now fenfible, for the firft time, that a war with Great-Britain was unavoidable. This event occafioned not greater confternation to the French miniftry, who had hitherto, perhaps on grounds not altogether improbable, flattered themfelves, that the adminiftration in England would continue to be amufed with fruitlefs unmeaning negociations about the limits of Nova-Scotia, and fuffer them, without material interruption, to proceed in their encroachments, and in compleating their great plan, of eftablifhing a regular chain of fortifications upon the back of the Englifh American fettlements; than it raifed joy and exultation among the people of England, ever fond of war, efpecially with France: not fo much on account of the fplendor and importance of the action, but becaufe it convinced them, which many ftill affected to doubt of, that the government were now thoroughly in earneft.

We fhall now, agreeable to our plan, confine ourfelves to the civil tranfactions and warlike operations of North-America, taking no notice of what happened in Europe, but only fo far as it has a reference to our main fubject.

The CAMPAIGN of 1755.

IN the beginning of this year, the assembly of the province of Massachuset's Bay had prohibited all commerce, or intercourse of any sort, with the French at Louisbourg: they had likewise raised, early in the spring, a body of provincial troops, which they sent to Nova-Scotia, to assist major-general Lawrence, now governor of that province, in his enterprizes against the French. We have already given an account of the attempts made last year to subdue the French neutrals, which were far from being so successful as was expected, owing to the assistance they received from the French regular troops from Canada. This project was resumed with great vigour this year, and the execution of it entrusted to lieutenant-colonel Monckton. Accordingly, in the beginning of May, this officer, at the head of a large detachment, set out on his march by land, while captain Rous, with three frigates, and a sloop of war, sailed up the bay of Fundy, to assist his operations, by water. Colonel Monckton met with no resistance till he arrived, with his little army, on the banks of the river, on which he found a large body of regular troops, neutral French or Acadians, and Indians, drawn up to great advantage, and ready to oppose his farther progress. Four hundred and fifty of them were posted in a block-

house

houſe mounted with cannon, and ſituated on the oppoſite ſide of the river; the reſt were intrenched behind a ſtrong breaſt-work of timber, raiſed, by way of an outwork, on this ſide the river, to defend the block-houſe. The Engliſh provincials attacked the breaſt-work with great vivacity, and carried it; after an obſtinate diſpute, which laſted about an hour, ſword in hand. The garriſon in the block-houſe, beholding the fate of their companions, deſerted it, and betook themſelves to flight, leaving the paſſage of the river free to the Engliſh.

Colonel Monckton proceeded directly againſt the French fort of Beau Sejour; which he inveſted as well as the ſmall number of his troops would permit him: for the ſpace of four days he continued to bombard it; and, juſt as he had mounted his cannon, and was ready to begin battering the body of the place, the French demanded a capitulation; which was granted them, on condition that the garriſon ſhould be ſent to Louiſbourg, and not ſerve in America for ſix months. The garriſon accordingly was tranſported thither, to the number of one hundred and fifty; and the Acadians, who, to the number of three hundred, were found in the place, received a pardon, having, as they aſſerted, been forced into the French ſervice.

The next day, after leaving a garriſon in Beau Sejour, and changing its name to that of Fort Cumberland, colonel Monckton attacked the other French fort upon the river Gaſperau, which runs into Bay Verte: it immediately fell into his hands;

and

and here he found a large quantity of provifions,
and all manner of warlike ftores, this being their chief
magazine for fupplying the neighbouring Indians
and Acadians with arms, ammunition, and other
requifites. In the mean time, captain Rous, with
the frigates under his command, failed to attack a
fort which the French had built at the mouth of
the river St. John : but the enemy abandoned it
at his firft appearance, after having burfted their
cannon, blown up their magazine, and demolifhed
all the works they had raifed, as much as time
would allow them to do. The French now poffeffed no place of ftrength in Nova-Scotia. The
reduction of this country was thus effected, with
the lofs only of twenty men killed, and about the
fame number wounded ; and fifteen hundred A-
cadians were difarmed, who fome time afterwards,
to the irreparable lofs of this province, were, with
their wives and children, ravifhed from their habitations, and difperfed, in fmall bodies, over different parts of Englifh America, (a ftep which nothing but the moft abfolute neceffity could juftify)
where they fettled, during the continuance of the
war ; and, ftill retaining their former habit of fobriety and induftry, applied themfelves, the women to
houfhold employment, and the men to fifhing : and
being extremely frugal, foon became more affluent
than the Englifh inhabitants of the fame rank in life.
At the conclufion of the peace, having then liberty
to retire to any part of the French dominions, tho'
every indulgence was offered them, they all deferted to a man, and were tranfported to Cape Francois,

cois, in the ifland of Hifpaniola. From thence they were fome time afterwards removed to Tibe-ron Bay, near Cape Nicholas in the fame ifland, where Count d'Eftaing, the governor, was then projecting a new fettlement : here the greateft part of them miferably perifhed of difeafes, contracted from the unwholefomenefs of the climate, and a vertical fun, which they were unufed to. Such was the deplorable end of thefe poor people, who, befides their remarkable fobriety, induftry, and or-derly behaviour, were in their perfons extremely vi-gorous and robuft, and the women fair and ele-gant, to a degree feldom feen among their European country-women. Could they have been prevailed on to become Englifh fubjects, and to continue quiet and peaceable, the moft fruitful part of No-va-Scotia, which they inhabited, inftead of being, as it is at prefent, a depopulated defert, would have had its vallies cropped with corn, and its hills co-vered with herds and flocks.

While the New-England people were thus em-ployed in reducing the French in Nova-Scotia, preparations were made in Virginia for attacking them on the Ohio. A camp was formed at Will's Creek, and a fort built, called Fort Cumberland. Major-general Braddock, having been conftituted by his majefty generaliffimo of all the troops which were in, or fhould be fent to America, arrived in Virginia before the end of February, and, as foon as he poffibly could, fummoned the feveral gover-nors to meet him, in order to confult on the bufi-nefs of the enfuing campaign. The meeting was

held

held at Alexandria, in Virginia. After much debate, it was agreed, that for the prefervation of Ofwego and reduction of Niagara, Shirley's and Pepperel's regiments fhould be fent to Lake Cntaric, on which lake an armed veffel or. two fhould be built, of about fixty ton each, to command it ; the execution of which was entrufted to Mr. Shirley, while general Braddock attacked Fort du Quefne, a poft lately built on the river, near the conflux of the Monangahela, and general Johnfon, with the provincial troops, was directed to inveft Crown-Point, on the frontiers of New-York.

In confequence of thefe refolutions, general Braddock, at the head of two thoufand two hundred men, began his march againft Fort du Quefne, though, being difappointed by the Virginia contractors, he had neither provifions nor a fufficient number of carriages for fo long a march, and arrived at Fort Cumberland, in his way thither, the 1cth of May. From thence to Fort du Quefne the diftance is at leaft an hundred and forty miles : the general fhould, therefore, have certainly landed in Penfylvania, and the contract for fupplying his troops fhould have been made with fome of the principal people there, who could eafily have performed their contracts ; and had he encamped at Franks-Town, or fome where on the fouth-weft borders of that province, his road to Fort du Quefne would have been more practicable, and fifty miles nearer than from Will's Creek.

Innumerable were the difficulties he had to furmount, in a country rugged, pathlefs, and un-

known,

known, acrofs the Alleghanny mountains, through unfrequented woods and dangerous defiles; and thefe dangers were doubled by the difappointments which he met with in almoft every thing which he had to do with the provinces: out of two thoufand five hundred horfes, and two hundred waggons, on which he was affured he might depend, he only received twenty waggons, and two hundred horfes. In like manner, his other expectations came to nothing, through the negligence of all the perfons with whom he had any dealings. We may conceive the difficulties which general Braddock met with in this terrible march, when we confider that he was obliged (to make ufe of his own expreffions) to be continually employed in making a road as he proceeded, with infinite labour, acrofs mountains and rocks of an exceffive height, vaftly fteep, and divided by torrents and rivers.

Notwithftanding thefe difcouragements and hardfhips, the general, being informed that the French were expecting a reinforcement of five hundred regular troops, to prevent fuch an increafe of ftrength in the enemy, determined to pufh forward by forced marches. But the impetuofity of his temper, and the too contemptible opinion that he entertained of the enemy, prevented his paying a proper regard to the reprefentations of his officers, and the hazard of entering woods without reconnoitring the enemy, which proved his ruin; he therefore, without farther lofs of time, marched from Fort Cumberland, on the 10th of June, (leaving a garrifon

D 4

there under the command of captain Innes) againſt Fort du Queſne, with his little army in two divi- ſions: at the head of the firſt, conſiſting of fourteen hundred men, was the general himſelf, with the greateſt part of the ammunition and artillery; the ſecond, with the proviſions, ſtores, and heavy bag- gage, was led by colonel Dunbar, with about eight hundred men, with orders to follow as faſt as the ſervice would admit. Having, by this means, leſ- ſened his line of march, he careleſsly proceeded with great expedition, inſomuch that his rear was left near forty miles behind; and being ſo incautious as ſel- dom to beſtow time to reconnoitre the woods he was to paſs through, though earneſtly intreated by Sir Peter Halket to proceed with caution, and to em- ploy the Indians that were with him in ſcouting the woods, ſuffered himſelf, when he had advanced within ten miles of the fort, to be ſurprized by an ambuſcade of French and Indians. The attack was begun with hideous howlings, and a quick and heavy fire upon the vanguard, under colonel Gage, and all along his left flank, from the Indians, ſo art- fully concealed under the trees and buſhes that not a ſingle man of them could be perceived. Immedi- ately the main body, in good order, advanced to ſuſtain them. Orders were then given to halt, and form. At this juncture, the van falling back upon them in great confuſion, in an inſtant the panic be- came general; but, being rallied by their officers with much difficulty, they were brought to give one fire: after which, they again fell back; but

were

were once more, with inconceivable difficulty, rallied by their officers, and ftood one fire from the enemy; but then, without returning it, they fled, particularly the regular troops, with the ut-moft terror and precipitation, in fpite of their officers, moft of whom behaved very gallantly: but they were equally deaf to commands and in-treaties. Braddock himfelf difcovered at once the greateft intrepidity, and the higheft imprudence; for inftead of ordering a retreat till he could fcour the avenues, lined with the enemy, with grape-fhot from the ten pieces of cannon, which he had with him; or ordering his Indians to advance in flanking parties againft the invifible enemy, he obftinately continued on the fpot where he was, and gave orders to the few brave officers and men who remained with him, to form and advance. In the mean while the French Indians, who always take aim when they fire, fingled out the officers by their drefs, and killed or wounded moft of them. At laft, having had five horfes fhot under him, he received a wound in his lungs through his right arm, of which he died in four days, having been carried off the field by the bravery of lieutenant-colonel Gage and another officer. His fecretary, eldeft fon of general Shirley, Sir Peter Halket, colonel of the forty-fourth regiment, with fe-veral other officers of diftinction, were killed, and above feven hundred private men; all the ammunition, artillery, baggage of the army, and

and the general's cabinet, containing his inftructions, and other papers of confequence, fell into
the hands of the enemy : and had not the provincial militia, which the general had always defpifed,
bravely formed, and advanced againft the Indians
in the woods, though equally expofed to the fire
of the enemy, the whole army had certainly been
cut off. The panic among the troops continued
till they met the rear divifion ; when the army retreated, without ftopping, till they arrived at Fort
Cumberland, though the enemy never attempted
to purfue, or even appeared in fight, either during
the battle, or after the defeat.

   The real ftrength of the enemy is uncertain ;
but it is fuppofed that they had upwards of two
thoufand regular troops, including the Canadian
militia, which in this country is equal in ufefulnefs
to the regular troops from Old France, befides
great numbers of Indians, who were planted in
ambufcade, and from whom our foldiers fuffered
far the moft. The lofs of the enemy was very inconfiderable by their own account, which in all
probability was the cafe, as they were concealed
behind trees and bufhes in fuch a manner, that our
men knew not whither to point their mufkets.

   Thus ended this unhappy expedition, whofe bad
confequences to the Britifh intereft were rendered
worfe by its increafing the fpirit and activity of the
French, and riveting the Indians more firmly in
the intereft of their new allies. On the contrary,
                                          the

the Indians in the Englifh intereft defpifed us, for not being able to protect ourfelves; and fuch an univerfal panic feized all the colonies, that they feemed for fome time to give up all for loft.

Nothing could now prevent the outrages and encroachments of the Indians and French on the back of Virginia, Maryland, and Penfylvania, except a ftrong garrifon at Fort Cumberland; where, if the remains of Braddock's army had fortified themfelves during the reft of the fummer, they would have been a fufficient check upon the French and their fcalping parties of Indians: but inftead of purfuing fo prudent a meafure, colonel Dunbar, on whom the command devolved, left only the fick and wounded under the care of two companies of provincial militia at Fort Cumberland, and with fixteen hundred men marched, on the fecond of Auguft, for Philadelphia, where their prefence could be of no immediate fervice; from whence they were ordered by general Shirley, now com-mander in chief in America, to Albany, in the province of New-York.

Virginia, Maryland, and Penfylvania, were, by thefe means, left entirely defencelefs and deftitute of protection from their cruel enemies; and the ufual difputes between their governors, affem-blies, &c. ran fo high, that every falutary propo-fal, for the public fafety, was rejected. Penfylva-nia, the moft powerful of the three, was at laft induced to vote fifty thoufand pounds for the de-fence

fence of the frontier; but even this sum, ridicu-
loufly fmall as it was, compared with the flourifhing ftate of the province, could not be procured,
the governor refufing to give his affent to the act
of the affembly for raifing that fum, becaufe they
had taxed the proprietors eftate in proportion to
thofe of the inhabitants.

Our colonies to the northward were more active
and fuccefsful in their preparations for war. The
affembly of New-York prohibited the fending
provifions to any port, fettlement, or ifland, belonging to the French on the continent of America,
or any of the adjacent iflands; and voted forty-five
thoufand pounds for the defence of their province,
which lay moft expofed to an invafion of the French
from Crown Point. With this fmall fupply, and the
affiftance of the eaftern colonies, together with the
few regular troops ordered thither by general Shirley, from Penfylvania, the province of New-York
planned two expeditions, one againft the French
fort of Crown-Point, and the other againft Niagara,
fituated between the lakes Ontario and Erie. General Johnfon, by birth an Irifhman, who had long
refided on the Mohock river, in the weftern parts
of New-York, where he had gained the univerfal
love of both the inhabitants, and the neighbouring
Indians, whofe language he had learned, whofe
manners he was perfectly acquainted with, and
whofe affections he had gained by his juftice, generofity, and humane behaviour towards them,
was

was appointed commander of the firft; and general Shirley himfelf undertook the latter expedition *.

Albany was appointed for the rendezvous of the troops for both expeditions, where moft of them arrived before the end of June. This army confifted of near fix thoufand men, exclufive of Indians, raifed by the governments of Bofton, Connecticut, New-Hampfhire, Rhode-Ifland, and New-York, and foon marched forwards, about fixty miles from Albany, under the command of major general Lyman; and as foon as the artillery, battoes, provifions, and other neceffaries were ready, on the eighth

---

* It may be neceffary here to remind the reader of the fituation and ufes of the three great French forts in North-America : Niagara, Du Quefne, and Crown-Point, were three forts built by the French in confequence of their fcheme to poffefs all the paffes of the back countries, and fecure them by ftrong garrifons, to reftrain us from penetrating farther into the continent than the part which we poffeffed, and to exclude us from all commerce with the Indians, and engrofs the fur trade to themfelves. Crown-Point was built about the year 1730, by the Canadians, in the territories of New-York, little more than one hundred miles from Albany. From this advanced garrifon they could eafily annoy all the upper-parts of New-York and New England, and prevent the fettlement of any lands north of Hudfon and Connecticut rivers. Fort du Quefne was built in 1752, on the forks of the river Monongahela, on the territories of Penfylvania, and enabled the French to harrafs that as well as the neighbouring provinces of Maryland and Virginia. Niagara was fituated between the lakes Erie and Ontario, and fecured the communication between Canada and Louifiana. It lay in the country of the Scnegas, the moft powerful of the Five Nations, and was built fince the year 1721.

of

of Auguft general Johnfon fet out with them for the Carrying-Place, where he joined and reviewed his army, that had been employed in building a fort at the landing place, on the eaft fide of Hudfon's-River, called Fort Edward. Towards the latter end of the month he advanced about fourteen miles farther north, and encamped in a ftrong fituation, both his flanks being covered by a thick wooded fwamp, his rear by Lake George, and his front by a breaft-work of trees felled for that purpofe, to wait for his battoes; and then intended to proceed to Ticonderoga, at the other end of the lake, about fifteen miles diftant from the fort, at the fouth end of Lake Champlain, called Fort Frederic by the French, and by us Crown-Point. While he continued in this camp, fome of his Indian fcouts, of whom he took care to fend out numbers along both fides, and to the farther end of Lake George, before called Lake Sacrament, brought him intelligence, that a confiderable number of the enemy were on their march from Ticonderoga, by the way of the South-Bay, towards the fortified encampment, fince called Fort Edward, which general Lyman had built at the Carrying-Place, and where four or five hundred of the New-York and New-Hampfhire troops had been left as a garrifon. General Johnfon gave notice thereof to colonel Blanchard, the commander, with orders to call in all his out-parties, and to keep his whole force within the entrenchments. He was further informed by his fcouts, about

twelve

twelve o'clock at night, that they had seen the enemy within four miles of the camp at the Carrying-Place, which they fcarcely doubted their having by that time attacked. Early in the morning general Johnfon called a council of war, wherein it was unadvifedly refolved to detach one thoufand men, in order either to fuccour Fort Edward, or intercept the enemy in their return from that poft, whether victorious or repulfed, though they had no account of the number or ftrength of the enemy, nor could obtain any certain information in that refpect from the Indians ; becaufe they have no diftinct words or figns whereby to exprefs large numbers, otherwife than pointing to the ftars in the firmament, or to the hairs of the head, which fometimes may denote a number lefs than a thoufand, as well as at another time ten thoufand.

Accordingly this body of men, with about two hundred Indians, marched about nine o'clock in the morning under the command of colonel Williams, an officer much efteemed for his perfonal bravery and good conduct ; but they had not been gone two hours, when thofe in the camp began to hear a clofe firing, as they imagined at about three or four miles diftance. As it approached nearer and nearer, they rightly fuppofed that their detachment was overpowered, and retreating towards the camp ; which was foon confirmed by fome fugitives, and prefently after by whole companies, who fled back in confufion. The general therefore detached lieutenant - colonel Cole, with

three

4

three hundred fresh men, to stop the enemy's pursuit, and to cover the retreat of the English, who might otherwise have been entirely cut off: and this alarm gave him time to strengthen his front with heavy cannon, to take possession of some eminencies on his left flank, and to fix a field piece in a very advantageous situation.

About eleven the enemy appeared in sight, and flushed with this advantage, marched forwards in a very regular order towards the centre of the English camp, till they were within one hundred and fifty yards of the breastwork; when, to the astonishment of the general, baron Dieskau made a halt for some time, which proved his ruin: the English army was in some consternation, and had the breastwork been immediately attacked before the army recovered their spirits, the fortune of the day would, in all probability, have been decided in his favour. However, at length Dieskau began the attack at such a distance, with platoon firing, that it did little execution against troops who were defended by a strong breast-work; and this ineffectual fire so raised the spirits of the English forces, that having prepared their artillery during the time that the French halted, they soon dispersed the Indians and Canadians by a brisk discharge of grapeshot, who fled into the woods on each side of the camp, and there squatted behind bushes, or skulked behind trees, from whence they continued firing with very little execution, most of their shot being intercepted by the brakes and thickets, for they

never

never had the courage to advance to the verge of the woods.

The French commander, thus deserted by his Canadians and Indians, instead of retreating as prudence directed, fell into another error; finding he could not make a close attack upon the front of the camp, which he found well fortified, and lined with cannon, contrary to his intelligence; with his small number of regulars, moved first to the left, and then to the right, in both which places he in vain attempted to force the breastwork, but was repulsed, being unsupported by his irregulars. These several attempts served only to weaken and dispirit his troops, who suffered greatly by the fire from the camp, and were. about four in the afternoon, thrown into confusion; which was no sooner perceived by general Johnson's men, than they, without waiting for orders, jumped over their breastwork, attacked the enemy on all sides, and after, killing a considerable number of them, entirely dispersed the rest.

The French, whose numbers at the beginning of this engagement amounted to about two thousand men, including two hundred grenadiers, eight hundred Canadians, and the rest Indians of different nations, had near eight hundred men killed, and thirty taken prisoners * : among these last was

---

* Amongst whom was Monf. St. Pierre, who commanded their Indians, the most useful officer the French had in all their expeditions in those parts, and in their treaties with the Indians.

general Dieſkau himſelf, who was found at a little
diſtance from the field of battle, dangerouſly wounded, leaning on the ſtump of a tree for his ſupport.
Our loſs did not exceed one hundred and thirty
killed, and ſixty wounded, and thoſe chiefly of the
detachment under colonel Williams ; for we had
very few either killed or wounded in the attack
upon the camp, and none of diſtinction, except
colonel Titcombe killed, and the general himſelf, and major Nicholls, wounded. Among
the ſlain of the detachment under colonel Williams,
which would probably have been almoſt entirely
cut off, had not lieùtenant-colonel Cole been ſent
out from the camp with three hundred men, with
whom he ſtopped the enemy's purſuit, and covered
the retreat of his friends, were colonel Williams,
major Aſhley, captains Ingerſal, Puter, Terral,
Stoddart, M'Gimes, Stevens, and ſeveral ſubalterns,
beſides private men, with forty Indians, and old
Hendric, the brave Mohawk ſachem or chief captain †.

When baron Dieſkau ſet out from Ticonderoga,
his deſign was only to ſurprize and cut off the intrenched camp, now called Fort Edward, at the
Carrying-Place, where there were but four or five

---

† It is to be remarked, that in this engagement the Indians,
ſome of the Mohawks excepted, retired from the camp, and
did not join the army till after the battle ; which plainly ſhews,
they were determined to join the conqueror, whether French
or Engliſh.

hundred

hundred men. If he had executed this scheme, our army would have been thrown into great difficulties; for it could neither have proceeded farther, nor have subsisted where.it was, and he might have found an opportunity to attack it with great advantage in its retreat: but when he was within four or five miles of that fort, his people were informed that there were several cannon there, and none at the camp; upon which they unanimously desired to be led on to this last, which he the more readily consented to; as he himself had been told by an English prisoner, who had left this camp but a few days before, that it was quite defenceless, being without any lines, and destitute of cannon: which, in fact, was true at that time, for the cannon did not arrive, nor was the breastwork erected, till about two days before the engagement. To this misinformation, therefore, must be imputed this step, which would otherwise be inconsistent with the allowed character and abilities of baron Dieskau. A less justifiable error seems to have been committed by general Johnson, in not detaching a party to pursue the enemy when they were routed and fled. Perhaps he was prevented from so doing, by the ill fate of the detachment which he had sent out in the morning under colonel Williams. However that may be, this neglect had like to have proved fatal the next day to a party sent from Fort Edward, consisting of an hundred and twenty men of the New-Hampshire regiment, and ninety of the New-York regiment, under the

com-

command of captain M'Ginnes, as a reinforcement to the army at the camp. The Indians and Canadians, who had escaped from the slaughter of the French army in the morning, having collected themselves into a body of about four hundred, and rendezvoused at the place where Williams was defeated the day before, intercepted this detachment about four in the morning; but M'Ginnes made such a disposition, and behaved with such bravery, that he not only repulsed the assailants, but after a sharp engagement, which lasted two hours, defeated and dispersed them entirely, with the loss only of two men killed, eleven wounded, and five missing. He himself unfortunately died of the wounds which he received in this engagement, a few days after he arrived at the camp with his party.

This victory, though very honourable for Mr. Johnson, and the provincial troops under his command, yet as it was gained late in the season, and as the army was in no very good condition, it had no consequences. The principal intention of this expedition was to reduce Crown-Point; but the year was now too far advanced for an undertaking of that kind, they therefore erected a small stockaded fort at the hither end of Lake George, and then returned to Albany. When the account of this victory reached England, great rejoicings were made in the capital, his majesty created general Johnson a baronet, and the parliament presented him with five thousand pounds.

The

The other expedition, under general Shirley, was attended with very little advantage : he arrived at Oſwego on the eighteenth of Auguſt, but the reſt of the troops, badly provided with proviſions, and artillery, did not reach that place till the thirty-firſt, too late to make an attempt on Niagara, though it was weil known, that even the poſſibility of his ſuccefs muſt, in a great meaſure, depend upon his ſetting out early in the year, as will appear to any perſon who conſiders the ſituation of our fort at Oſwego, this being the only way by which he could proceed to Niagara.

. Oſwego lies on the ſouth-eaſt ſide of the Lake Ontario, near three hundred miles almoſt due weſt of Albany, in New-York. The way to it from thence, though long and tedious, is the more convenient, as the greateſt part of it admits of water carriage, by what the inhabitants call battoes, a kind of light flat bottomed boats, wideſt in the middle, and pointed at each end, of about fifteen hundred weight burden, managed by two men, called battoe-men, with paddles and ſetting poles, the river being in many places too narrow to admit of oars. From Albany to the village of Shenectady, which is ſixteen miles, is a good waggon road. From thence to the Little-Falls in the Mohawk-river, being ſixty-five miles, the paſſage is by water carriage, up that river, conſequently, againſt the ſtream, which in many places is rapid, and in others ſo ſhallow, that when the river is low, the watermen are obliged to get out and draw their battoes over the rifts. At the Little-Falls is a land-

E 3　　　　　　　　　　carriage

carriage for about a mile, over ground fo marfhy, that it will not bear any wheel-carriage; but a colony of Germans, fettled there, attend with fledges, on which they draw the loaded battoes to the next place of embarkation on the fame river. From thence they proceed by water up that river for fifty miles to the Carrying-Place, near the head of it, where there is another land-carriage, the length of which depends upon the drynefs or wetnefs of the feafon, but is generally fix or eight miles over in the fummer months. Here the battoes are again carried upon fledges, till they arrive at a narrow river called Wood's-Creek, down which they are carried by a gentle ftream for about forty miles into the Lake Oney-ada, which ftretches from eaft to weft about thirty miles, and is paffed with great cafe and fafety in calm weather. At the weftern end of this lake is the river Onondaga, which, after a courfe of between twenty and thirty miles, unites with the river Cayuga or Sene-ca; and their united ftream runs into the Lake On-tario, at the place where Ofwego Fort is fituated. But this river is fo rapid as to be fometimes dange-rous, befides its being full of rifts and rocks; and about twelve miles on this fide of Ofwego, there is a fall of eleven feet perpendicular, where; of courfe, there is a poftage, which, however, does not exceed fifty yards. From thence the paffage is eafy, quite to Ofwego.

The Lake Ontario, on which this fort ftands, is near two hundred and eighty leagues in circumfe-rence: its figure is oval, and its depth runs from twenty to twenty-five fathoms. On the north fide

are

are several little gulphs. There is a communication between this lake and that of the Hurons, by the river Tanaswate; from whence it is a land-carriage of six or eight leagues to the river Toranto, which falls into it. The French had two forts of consequence on this lake; Fort Frontignac, which commanded the river St. Laurence; where the lake communicates with it; and Niagara, which commanded the communication between the Lake Ontario and the lake Erie.

Though we had long been possessed of Fort Oswego, and though it lay greatly exposed to the French, upon any rupture between the two nations, no care had ever been taken to put it in a tolerable state of defence, or even to build a single vessel fit for navigating the lake, until the beginning of this year, when, at the meeting which general Braddock had with the governors of the colonies at Alexandria, it was resolved to strengthen both the fort and garrison, and to build some large vessels there. Accordingly, a number of shipwrights and workmen were sent thither in May and June; and, at the same time, captain Bradstreet marched thither with two companies, consisting each of an hundred men, to reinforce the hundred that were there before under captain King. The fort consisted only of a stone wall, mounting but five cannon, three or four pounders, and was otherwise in a very defenceless condition, when general Shirley arrived there. The Indians of the Six Nations, to whom he had sent invitations, and by great num-

E 4 bers

bers of whom he had expected to be joined, instead
of complying with his desire, absolutely declared
against all hostilities on that side of the country,
insisting that Oswego, being a place of trade and
peace, ought not to be disturbed by either party;
so that he was joined by very few Indians. The
season was not only now too far advanced, but,
tho' the general waited till the 26th of September,
when he received a supply of provisions, it was so
small, that it was scarcely sufficient to subsist the
six hundred men that he intended to carry with
him against Niagara, and to support the troops he
was to leave at Oswego, for twelve days. But, by
this time, the rainy boisterous season had begun;
and the few Indians who had joined him declared,
that there was no crossing the lake Ontario in battoes at that season of the year, or at any time before the ensuing summer. The expedition was therefore, in a council of war, unanimously agreed to be
deferred till the next year; and the forces were employed in erecting barracks, and two new forts, one
on the east, and the other on the west side of the river Onondaga. Having settled these matters, he set
out on his return to Albany, on the twenty-fourth
of October, leaving colonel Mercer, with a garrison
of no more than seven hundred men, at Oswego,
though he had received repeated advice, that the
enemy had then above a thousand men at Fort
Frontignac, and the new forts were not yet near compleated. Thus ended this unsuccessful expedition,
and the campaign, for this year, on the side of the

English;

Englifh ; for the French, and their Indian allies, during the whole winter, committed the moſt horrid ravages on the weſtern borders of Virginia and Penſylvania : they murdered, ſcalped §, or carried into captivity, the miſerable inhabitants ; and burnt and deſtroyed all the farms they met with in their incurſions.

The AMERICAN CAMPAIGN of 1756.

General Shirley, being diſmiſſed from his military command, was ſucceeded by general Abercrombie, who aſſembled, in the month of June, the Engliſh forces at Albany, conſiſting of two regiments which had ſerved under Braddock, two battalions raiſed in America, two regiments he had juſt brought with him from England, four independant companies maintained many years in New-York, the New-Jerſey regiment, four companies levied in North-Carolina, and a body of provincial forces,

§ The operation of ſcalping is performed by the Indians in the following manner : the unfortunate victim being diſabled, or diſarmed, the Indian, with a ſharp knife worn for the purpoſe, makes a circular inciſion to the bone, round the upper part of the head, and tears off the ſcalp with his fingers. Previous to this execution, he generally diſpatches the priſoner by repeated blows on the head, with the hammer-ſide of a weapon called a tomahawk : but ſometimes they ſave themſelves the trouble, and ſometimes the blows prove ineffectual ; ſo that the miſerable wretch is found alive, groaning in the utmoſt agony of torture. The Indian ſtrings the ſcalps he has procured, to be produced as teſtimonies of his prowefs ; and receives a premium for each ſcalp from the nation under whoſe banners he has enliſted.

raiſed

raifed by the government of New-England. As to
the fettlements towards the fouthward, Penfylvania,
Maryland, and Virginia, they had fuffered, and
were daily fuffering, fo much from the incurfions
of the enemy, that it was with the utmoft difficulty
they could defend themfelves. And in South-Carolina the difproportion of negroe flaves to the number
of white inhabitants was fo great, that the government could not, with fafety to the province, fpare
any reinforcement for the general enterprize. The
plan for the campaign was to reduce Fort Niagara,
as being the moft effectual means for difabling the
French from maintaining their forts on the Ohio,
or keeping up their communication between Canada and Louifiana. Ticonderoga and Crown-Point
were likewife to be reduced, for the fecurity of New-
York. All the convenient paffes upon Lake Champlain were to be feized by the Englifh ; Fort du
Quefne was to have been befieged ; and Quebec itfelf
to have been alarmed by a body of troops detached
up the river Kennebec. This plan of operations
was promifing, and not impracticable, even by the
Britifh troops that were in readinefs ; but it feemed
as if the general had no inftructions to enter upon
any decifive meafures till the arrival of lord Loudon,
who had been appointed commander in chief of all
his majefty's forces in America, with powers that
were fuppofed fufficient to remove all the delays, and
the caufe of thofe obftructions, which had defeated
moft of the former operations and falutary meafures propofed for their common defence. But
his lordfhip did not arrive till the feafon was too

far

far advanced for their being executed; occasioned, as was said, by the unsettled state of the English ministry. Besides, the provincial officers were so divided in their opinions, that his authority was necessary for bringing the troops into the field. And thus another year was lost, the provinces left exposed to the invasions and barbarities of the enemy, and the French, who received a reinforcement of near three thousand men, under the command of general Montcalm, an excellent officer from Europe, at liberty to strengthen their posts, and distress the English settlements, with impunity.

During this state of inactivity, the army received the disagreeable news of the enemy's entering the country of the Five Nations, our antient allies, where they reduced a small post, occupied by twenty-five Englishmen, whom they put to the sword, and butchered in a most cruel manner. Soon after, having received intelligence that a considerable convoy of provisions and stores, for the garrison at Oswego, was ready to set out from Schenectady, and be conveyed in battoes up the river Ononda_ga, they formed an ambuscade, among the woods and thickets, on the north side of that river; but finding that the convoy had passed before they reached the place, they determined to wait the return of the detachment. Their design, however, was frustrated by the vigilance and bravery of colonel Bradstreet, who expected such an attempt, and had taken his measures accordingly. In his return down the river Onondaga, while he stemmed the stream with his battoes, formed into three divi-

fions,

fions, he was faluted by a party of Indians, fecreted
amongft the bufhes and trees on the north fhore,
with the war-whoop, and a general difcharge of
mufketry. Bradftreet immediately landed his men
on the oppofite banks, and with a few of the fore-
moft, took poffeffion of a fmall ifland, where he
was forthwith attacked by a party of the enemy,
who had forded the river; but thefe he foon repulfed. Then, quitting the ifland, and collecting
together the whole of his ftrength, amounting to
about two hundred men, he advanced, and fell
fword in hand, upon another body, which had
paffed the river a mile higher, with fuch vigour,
that many were cut in pieces, and the reft driven into the river with fuch precipitation that a confiderable number of them were drowned. He then
boldly attacked the main body of the enemy, confifting of above fix hundred men, which had forded
the river ftill higher, and purfued them to the other
fide, where they were entirely routed and difperfed ;
and, receiving afterwards a reinforcement under
captain Patten, who was on his march to Ofwego,
and another of two hundred men from that garrifon, he in all probability would have deftroyed the
whole Prench detachment, confifting of feven hundred men, had not an heavy rain fell, and fwelled
the river and rivulets fo much as to render it impracticable to purfue the enemy. The action lafted
near three hours. Our chief lofs was among the
battoe-men, by the firft fire from the bufhes ; but
the enemy had about two hundred killed, and feventy taken prifoners.

The

The parties therefore separated, Patten and his men accompanied the detachment to Ofwego, and Bradftreet marched to Schenectady ; from whence he repaired to Albany, and acquainted general Abercrombie with the intelligence he had received from the prifoners, that the French had affembled a confiderable force on the eaftern fide of Lake Ontario, with a numerous artillery, and all other implements, to befiege the fort of Ofwego, the garrifon of which, by this time, had been reinforced to the number of about fourteen hundred men, befides three hundred workmen and failors, either in the fort, or pofted in fmall parties between the fort and a place called Burnet's Field, to fecure a paffage through the country of the Six Nations, who were no longer to be relied on. Upon this information, major-general Webb was ordered to march with a regiment to the relief of Ofwego. But notwithftanding the advantage which the lofs of this place would give the enemy in all their future operations, and although the army at Albany could mufter twenty-fix hundred regulars, and near feven thoufand provincials, under the command of general Winflow, at Fort William-Henry ; their march was ftopped by the arrival of Lord Loudon, tho' the neceffaries were providing for their fubfiftence on the road. His prefence did not at all contribute to the unanimity of the provincials ; for, notwithftanding the imminent danger of Ofwego, the province of New-York, and the northern governments, infifted upon the reduction of Crown-
Point,

Point, previous to all other operations, as being moft dangerous for their country ; and that fome regiments of regulars fhould join general Winflow, who was marching with feven thoufand provincials to attempt that conqueft ; while the remainder of the army fhould remain at Albany; for the defence the frontier, in cafe Winflow fhould be defeated ; and, though they were at laft prevailed with to confent to the march of general Webb, with the regiment firft ordered by general Abercrombie, it was the 12th day of Auguft, before this fupply could fet out from Albany ; but on his arrival at the Carrying Place, between the Mohawks River and Wood's Creek, he met with the difagreeable news that Ofwego was taken, and the garrifon made prifoners of war. General Webb, apprehending himfelf in danger of being attacked by the enemy, therefore, returned to Albany, after having rendered Wood's Creek impaffable to canoes, by felling trees, and throwing them into the ftream.

By this misfortune, the two forts, Ontario and Ofwego, were loft. The garrifon, as has been already obferved, confifted of fourteen hundred men, under the command of lieutenant-colonel Mercer, a brave experienced officer ; but the fituation of the forts was ill chofen, the materials moftly logs of wood, the defences badly contrived and unfinifhed, and, in fhort, the place quite untenable againft a regular approach. The marquis de Montcalm, fucceffor to Diefkau, an enterprizing officer, was charged with this expedition, having under his

com-

command thirteen hundred regulars, seventeen hundred Canadians, and a confiderable body of Indians. In the mean time, notwithftanding his precautions, lieutenant-colonel Mercer, who commanded the garrifon, received repeated intelligence that the enemy were encamped about thirty miles to the eaftward of Ofwego, and particularly, on the 6th of Auguft, that there was a large encampment of French and Indians about twelve miles eaft of the fort : he difpatched an exprefs-boat to the commanding officer upon the lake, who was then out on a cruize to the weftward, with a brigantine and two floops, to acquaint him, that he intended next day to fend four hundred men, in whale-boats, to vifit the enemy, and defiring him to keep to the eaftward as much as poffible, in order to cover the men in the boats, and hinder the enemy from approaching nearer ; but, by fome ftrange neglect, the veffels returned next day to Ofwego, and, in endeavouring to enter the harbour, the brigantine was driven on rocky ground by a gale of wind, where fhe lay, beating about, for eighteen hours, and was afterwards forced to be hove down.

Monfieur Montcalm, who had proceeded with the utmoft caution, to prevent a furprize, having gained intelligence of the fituation of the Englifh veffels, that the brigantine was ftranded and the other two returned into the harbour, took the opportunity of tranfporting his ftores and artillery from Fort Frontignac, where he had arrived the 6th of July ; over the lake, to the bay of Nixouri, within

within a mile and an half of Fort Ontario, the place of general rendezvous; having made admirable difpofitions to fecure a retreat, in cafe of a mifcarriage. His firft care was to block up the fort by water with two large armed veffels, and to poft a ftrong body of Canadians on the road by land, to cut off all communication and fuccours from the befieged. At another creek, within half a league of Ofwego, he erected a battery for the protection of his veffels ; and on the 12th day of Auguft, at midnight, having made the neceffary difpofitions, he opened the trenches before Fort Ontario, with thirty-two pieces of cannon, from ten to eighteen pounders, befides feveral brafs mortars and howitzers. The garrifon kept up a brifk fire till fix o'clock the next evening, and killed their principal engineer in the trenches ; but the colonel finding the place untenable, and having fired away all his fhells and ammunition, ordered the cannon to be fpiked up, evacuated the fort, and croffed the river to Little-Ofwego Fort, which was effected without the lofs of a fingle man.

The French general immediately took poffeffion of the deferted fort ; and, early the fame night, began a grand battery, formed in fuch a manner that it could not only batter Fort Ofwego, diftant about two miles Englifh, and fecure the way from thence to Fort George, fituated on a hill about four miles and an half up the river ; but alfo annoy the entrenchment of Ofwego.

The

The troops, to the number of three hundred and feventy, or thereabouts, which had retreated from Fort Ontario, were ordered immediately to join colonel Schuyler, who was charged with the defence of the fort on the hill, to the weft of the old fort, under the direction of Mr. Mackellar, the engineer: but the advantages propofed by a communication between thefe two forts ,were foon fruftrated, from a bold action of a body of twenty-five hundred Canadians and Indians, who fwam acrofs the river in the night between the thirteenth and fourteenth, and cut off the communication between the two forts. The next day, colonel Mercer was unfortunately killed by a cannon-ball; and the fort being deftitute of all cover, the garrifon left without a commander of equal abilities, demanded a capitulation the following day; and furrendered prifoners of war, upon condition of their being exempted from plunder, carried to Montreal, and treated with humanity. To the eternal ftain of Montcalm's reputation, and the French name, thefe articles were violated. Under the fhameful pretence that he could not reftrain the Indians, they were fuffered not only to rob, but to murder feveral of the Englifh officers and foldiers, after they had given up their arms, and moft inhumanly to fcalp the fick and wounded who were in the Englifh hofpital: they affaffinated lieutenant de la Court, as he lay wounded in his tent, under the protection of a French officer: finally, Montcalm, in direct violation of the articles, and in contempt of common

humanity,

humanity, delivered twenty of the garrifon into the hands of the Indians ; who, in all probability, were put to death with the moft excruciating tortures, according to the cuftom of thofe favages, (a circumftance that he could be no ftranger to) in revenge of the fame number of Indians killed during the fiege.

The French, having thus made themfelves mafters of Ofwego, inftantly demolifhed the two forts, in which they found one hundred and twenty one pieces of artillery, fourteen mortars, a great quantity of ammunition, warlike ftores, and provifions, befides two floops, and two hundred battoes ; and embarked with the utmoft fpeed for Fort Frontignac, with their prifoners and booty, in their way back to Montreal and Quebec. Perhaps the depofiting fuch an important magazine in a place altogether indefenfible, is as palpable an inftance of folly, temerity, and mifconduct, as any to be met with in hiftory.

Thus fell the key of the Lake Ontario, by the neglect of the managers, the impropriety and infufficiency of the means made ufe of to defend it from the attacks of an enemy, from the delays that prevented a timely relief, and from too great a fear for the prefervation of New-York and New-England. But the lofs of this poft, the garrifon, and implements of war, which had been fo indifcreetly lodged there, was not the worft effect of fuch fatal mifconduct. The ftopping up Wood's Creek, the only communition from the Mohawks River to Oneyada ; and deferting and deftroying the forts at the Great Carrying

rying Place, which, after the lofs of Ofwego, was our 'moft advanced poft in the country of the Six Nations; a poft fo ftrongly fortified, and fo inacceffible to the enemy's artillery, that it might have defied the whole French army in America to take it; together with general Webb's retreat to the German Flats, about fixty miles nearer to Albany; expofed the Six Nations, and all the adjacent country, to the mercy of the enemy, who were at liberty to over-run the fine country on the Mohawk's River almoft to Albany, and to penetrate into the provinces of Penfylvania, New-Jerfey, Maryland, and Virginia. It alfo encouraged the Indians to join our enemies, or obferve a ftrict neutrality, when they found we were not able to protect them, and the French had performed their promife to deftroy Ofwego.

The earl of Loudon, finding the feafon too far advanced to admit of any enterprize againft the enemy, applied himfelf to make preparations for an early campaign in the fpring, to form an uniform plan of action, and to promote a fpirit of harmony among the different governments. He caufed comfortable barracks to be built at Albany; where he put his forces into winter-quarters; and provided the forts Edward and William-Henry with numerous garrifons.

Fort Granville, on the confines of Penfylvania, an inconfiderable block-houfe, was furprized, plundered, and burnt, by the enemy, who drove into captivity the fmall garrifon, confifting of twenty-

two

two foldiers, with a few women and children; and in their incurfions perpetrated many fhocking murders upon the defencelefs inhabitants of the frontiers. In revenge, colonel Armftrong, with a party of two hundred and eighty provincials, marched from Fort Shirley, on the Juniata River, one hundred and fifty miles weft of Philadelphia, to Kittanning, an Indian town, the rendezvous of the Morian Indians, who had been concerned in deftroying Fort Granville, fituated twenty-five miles above Fort du Quefne, on the Ohio, a rout of one hundred and forty miles, through the woods; with whom he came up in the morning early of the fifth day, while the Indian warriors were regaling themfelves with a dance. The colonel difcovered their fituation by their whooping; and, halting about one hundred perches below the town, on the bank of the river, prepared his men, and attacked them as foon as the day broke. Captain Jacobs, the chief of the Indians, defended his houfe bravely, through loop-holes in the logs. The colonel offered them quarter; but they, fearful of his fincerity, refufed to fubmit. By this obftinacy, their houfes having been fired, many were fuffocated and burnt, and captain Jacobs, his fquaw, and a boy called the king's fon, were fhot, as they were attempting to efcape through a window, and the reft, to the number of near forty, perifhed in the affault. Eleven Englifh prifoners were releafed, who had been taken in a fkirmifh by the Indians, the night before.

To

To prevent, as much as poffible, the incurfions of the Indians for the future, a ftrong fort was built at Winchefter, called Fort Loudon. The governor of Penfylvania concluded a treaty of peace with the Delawar Indians, who inhabit the banks of the river Sufquehanna; as the governor of Virginia did another with the Cherokees and Catawbas, two powerful neighbouring Indian tribes, capable of bringing three thoufand warriors into the field, four hundred of whom joined the Englifh forces at Fort Cumberland.

No action of great importance diftinguifhed the naval tranfactions of this year. On the coafts of America, in the beginning of June, captain Spry, who commanded a fmall fquadron cruizing off Louifbourg, in the ifland of Cape Breton, took the Arc en Ciel, a French man of war of fifty guns, having on board fix hundred men, with a large quantity of ftores and provifions, for that garrifon; as alfo, another fhip with feventy foldiers, two hundred barrels of powder, two large brafs mortars, and other warlike ftores. And on the twenty-feventh of July, Captain Holmes, being in the fame latitude, with two fhips of the line, and a couple of floops, engaged two French fhips of the line of fuperior force, and four frigates, and obliged them to fheer off, after a fharp engagement.

The

The C A M P A I G N of 1757.

THE long meditated attack on Crown-Point being for the prefent laid afide, an expedition to Louifbourg was fubftituted in its place. On the ninth of July, admiral Holborn arrived at Halifax, with a ftrong reinforcement of men and fhips*; by which the earl of Loudon, who waited his arrival at that place, was put at the head of the greateft European army that had ever appeared in North-America. Several fmall veffels were now difpatch-

---

* The fleet confifted of the following fhips, including one fhip of the line and twelve frigates before in North-America.

Ships.	Men.	Guns.	Ships.	Men.	Guns.
Newark	700	80	Succefs	150	22
Invincible	700	74	Port Mahon	150	22
Grafton	590	68	Nightingale	150	22
Terrible	630	74	Kennington	150	20
Northumberland	520	68	Elphingham	150	20
Captain	580	68	Ferrit floop	120	16
Orford	520	68	Furnace bomb	100	16
Bedford	480	64	ditto	100	16
Naffau	480	64	Vulture floop	100	14
Sunderland	400	64	Hunter	100	14
Defiance	400	64	Speedwell	90	12
Tilbury	400	64	Hawke	100	12
Kingfton	400	60	Gibraltar's Prize	80	12
Windfor	350	54	Jamaica	100	14
Sutherland	306	50	Lightning firefhip	50	
Winchelfea	160	24			
				10200	1350

ed

ed to difcover the ftrength of the enemy at Louifbourg; which returned with the unwelcome news,
that there was at that time in the ifland of Cape
Breton fix thoufand regular troops, and three thoufand militia, befides Indians, together with feventeen
fhips of the line, and three frigates, moored in the
harbour of Louifbourg, commanded by M. de Bois
de la Mothe, who had failed from Breft in May;
which intelligence was confirmed by letters found
on board a packet, bound from Louifbourg to
France, taken by one of the fhips ftationed at
Newfoundland : the expedition, therefore, was deferred till fome more convenient opportunity.

The departure of Lord Loudon, with all the regular troops to Halifax, gave the French general,
Montcalm, an opportunity of improving the fucceffes
of the former campaign. In the very opening
of the feafon, he had made three different attacks
on Fort William-Henry, in all which he had been
repulfed by the bravery and vigilance of the
garrifon. Colonel Parker, in attempting with
about four hundred men, in whale and bay
boats, to diflodge a French advanced guard at
Ticonderago, was outwitted by the enemy, who
having waylaid three boats which he had fent
to the main land to make difcoveries, and procured information of the colonel's defigns from the
prifoners, placed three hundred men in ambufh behind the point where he propofed landing, and
fent three battoes to the place of rendezvous. Colonel Parker, miftaking thefe for his own boats,
eagerly put to fhore, and was furrounded by the

F 4 enemy,

enemy, reinforced with four hundred men, who attacked him with fuch impetuofity that only two officers and feventy foldiers, efcaped of the whole detachment. Montcalm flufhed with this fuccefs, and animated by the abfence of Lord Loudon, drew his forces together, and made frefh preparations for the fiege of Fort William-Henry, fituated on the fouthern coaft of Lake George, with a view to command that lake, and protect the Englifh colonies. The fort was garrifoned by about three thoufand regulars, and general Webb was pofted at no great diftance with an army of four thoufand men. Montcalm brought againft it near ten thoufand troops, including Canadians and Indians, and a good train of artillery; and invefted the fort, which he immediately fummoned to furrender; out of humanity, as he pretended, it being, as he faid, yet in his power to reftrain the cruelties of his Indians, and oblige them to obferve a capitulation, as none of them were yet killed; which would not be in his power in other circumftances. The garrifon of the fort, depending on being relieved by general Webb, made a brave defence; but being difappointed in their expectations, were obliged on the ninth of Auguft, the fixth day of the fiege, to capitulate. The terms were, that the garrifon and troops in the retrenched camp fhould march out with their arms, the baggage of the officers and foldiers, and all the ufual neceffaries of war, efcorted by a detachment of French troops, or interpreters, attached to the Savages. It was agreed, that the

the gate of the fort ſhould be delivered to the
French troops immediately after the capitulation
was ſigned, and the retrenched camp on the departure of the Engliſh forces : that the artillery,
warlike ſtores, proviſions, and in general every
thing, except the effects of the officers and ſoldiers,
ſhould, upon honour, be delivered to his Moſt
Chriſtian majeſty's troops ; for which purpoſe, it
was agreed there ſhould be delivered with the capitulation an exact ſtate of the troops, and an inventory of the ſtores : that the garriſon of the fort,
and the reſt of the troops, ſhould not ſerve for the
ſpace of eighteen months againſt his Moſt Chriſtian
majeſty, or his allies : that the officers and ſoldiers,
Canadians, women, and Indians, made priſoners by
land, ſince the commencement of the war in America, be delivered within three months at Carillon;
in return for which, an equal number of the garriſon ſhould be capacitated to ſerve : that an officer
ſhould remain as an hoſtage, till the ſafe return of
the eſcort ſent with the Engliſh troops : that the
ſick and wounded, not in a condition to be tranſported to Fort Edward, ſhould remain under the
protection of the marquis de Montcalm, who engaged to uſe them with tenderneſs and humanity,
and to return them as ſoon as recovered : that proviſions for two days ſhould be iſſued out for the
Engliſh troops : and that, in teſtimony of his
eſteem and reſpect for colonel Munro and his garriſon, on account of their gallant defence, the

mar-

marquis de Montcalm; fhould return one cannon, a fix-pounder.

Thefe articles were perfidioufly broke through, in almoft every point. The Indians in the French intereft were permitted to commit the moft inhuman cruelties : they plundered the Englifh troops as they marched out, dragged the Indians in the Englifh fervice out of their ranks, and tomohawked and fcalped them ; they ripped up the bellies of the women, and acted over again the tragedy at Ofwego, in fight of the French army. However, the greateft part of the army got fafe, though in a wretched condition, to Fort Edward, after having been purfued above feven miles by the Indians ; and the remainder, flying for protection to the French general, were by him fent home. The enemy demolifhed the forts, carried off the effects, provifions, and artillery, together with the veffel that had been conftructed on the lake, and then returned to Montreal, without making any further attempts on the colonies *.

* In the month of July, the enemy were very near furprizing Fort Johnfon by a ftratagem. Their intention was to rufh into the fort in the evening, when the gate was opened to admit the women, fent out every day to milk the cattle. But being a few minutes too late, the gates were luckily fhut before they arrived ; upon which they knocked for admiffion, were challenged, and fired upon by the centinel. Immediately, the cannon were fired, to alarm the country ; and the enemy, perceiving their fcheme baffled, retired precipitately.

The

· The expedition to Louifbourg being laid a-
fide,: admiral ·Holbourne, no longer embarraf-
fed with the care of tranfports, failed for Louifbourg with fifteen fhips of the line, four frigates,
and a firefhip. On the twentieth of Auguft he appeared before the harbour, and faw the French admiral make the fignal to unmoor ; but being great-
ly.inferior in ftrength to the enemy, did not chufe
to rifk an engagement, and therefore returned to
Halifax : but being reinforced about the middle
of September with four fhips of the line, he again
failed to Louifbourg, with an intention to draw the
enemy to a battle. · La Mothe, the French admiral, was however too prudent to hazard an engagement, the lofs of which muft have expofed all the
French colonies to the attempts of the Englifh.
The fquadron continued cruizing before the harbour of ·Louifbourg until the twenty-fifth, when
they were overtaken by a terrible ftorm. In about
twelve hours, they were driven within two miles of
the breakers on the coaft of that ifland, when
the wind providentially. fhifted, and faved the
whole fquadron from inevitable deftruction, except
one, which was loft on the rocks, and about half
the crew perifhed. Eleven fhips were difmafted,
others threw their guns overboard, and the whole
returned to England, in a fhattered condition.
Thus ended the third campaign in America,
by fea and land, where, with twenty thoufand
regular troops, and a navy of twenty fhips of
the line, nothing was done againft the enemy ;
our forts were taken from us, our Indians left

defence-

defencelefs to the mercy of the enemy, and a large tract of country relinquifhed, to the eternal reproach and difgrace of the Britifh name.

The CAMPAIGN of 1758.

THE Englifh miniftry, being greatly diffatisfied with the conduct of the war in America, lord Loudon was recalled; and the command there, of courfe, devolved upon general Abercrombie. The army then in America confifted of fifty thoufand troops, of whom twenty-two thoufand were regulars, exclufive of the fleet and marines. The troops being divided into three detached bodies, as the objects of operation were various, were headed by three diftinct leaders. Twelve thoufand men were deftined for an attempt upon Louifbourg, under the command of major-general Amherft; fixteen thoufand, under the general himfelf, were referved for the reduction of Crown-Point; and eight thoufand, under the direction of brigadier-general Forbes, were allotted for the conqueft of Fort du Quefne.

The reduction of Louifbourg, being an object of immediate confideration, was undertaken with all poffible difpatch. On the twenty-eighth of May, general Amherft embarked his troops at Halifax, in Nova-Scotia, and failed for Louifbourg, with the Englifh fquadron, confifting of twenty-one line of battle fhips, and twenty frigates, commanded by admiral Bofcawen, that had arrived from England fome

time

time before ; the whole fleet, including transports, amounted to one hundred and fifty fail. On the fecond of June, the fleet came fafely to an anchor in Gabarus Bay, about feven miles to the weftward of Louifbourg. The garrifon of this place was compofed of two thoufand five hundred regular troops, and three hundred militia, formed of the burghers, under the command of the Chevalier Drucour ; and, foon after the landing of the Englifh forces, the enemy was reinforced by three hundred and fifty Canadians, including fixty Indians. The mouth of the harbour was guarded by fix fhips of the line and five frigates; three of which were funk acrofs the harbour's mouth, in order to render the paffage impaffable to the Englifh fleet. The governor had taken every precaution in his power to prevent a landing : he had drawn entrenchments in every part where he fuppofed it poffible to land, fupported them with batteries in convenient places, and lined them with a numerous infantry. But though this chain of pofts extended two leagues and an half along the moft acceffible parts of the beach, fome fpots ftill remained unfortified ; and on one of thefe the Englifh forces were difembarked.

Upon the firft appearance of the Englifh fleet, the French governor, Drucour, fent out feveral detachments to obferve their motions ; but general Amherft, by fending feveral floops, under a ftrong convoy, towards Lorembec, beyond the mouth of the harbour, drew the enemy's attention to that

I

part

part of the ifland, while a landing was actually effected on the other fide of the town; on the eighth
of June, under the command of brigadier-general
Wolfe ; feveral floops and frigates having previoufly fcoured the beach with their fhot.' The
difembarkation, however, was attended with many
difficulties, from a violent furf which rolled impe-
tuoufly on the beach, and a fevere fire of cannon
and mufquetry from the enemy, who referved their
fhot till the boats were almoft clofe to the fhore.
Wolfe, however, purfued his point, with admirable
courage and deliberation ; and the foldiers, though
the fire of the enemy did great execution, and
many boats were overfet and broke to pieces,
fupported and encouraged in all difficulties, by the
example, fpirit, and conduct, of their truly gallant
commander, leaped into the water, gained the
fhore, (the general himfelf being among the firft
who landed), and fell upon the enemy with fuch order and refolution, that they foon obliged them to
fly in confufion.   But the difficulty of landing artillery and ftores in boifterous weather, added to
the nature of the ground, which, being marfhy,
was unfit for the conveyance of heavy cannon, retarded the operations of the fiege, which were carried on with great circumfpection by general Amherft.

The firft thing done was to fecure a point called
the Lighthoufe-Battery, from whence they might
play upon the French fhips in the harbour, which
were capable of bringing all their guns to bear upon
the

the approaches of the befiegers, and on the batteries on the other fide, of the harbour. General Wolfe performed this fervice with his ufual conduct, activity, and bravery ; and took poffeffion of this and all the other pofts in that quarter. His fire from this poft, on the twenty-fifth, filenced the ifland battery, which was that moft immediately oppofed to his. In the interim, the befieged made feveral fallies, but with very little effect : but the fhips in the harbour ftill continued to bear upon him, until the twenty-firft of the following month, when one of them blew up, and communicating the fire to two others, they alfo were, in a fhort time, confumed to the water edge. The regular approaches conducted by the engineers, under the immediate command and infpection of general Amherft, were now carried on with vigour, and drew near the covered way, and things were in a good condition to make a lodgment on it ; the enemy's fire was confiderably flackened ; the town was confumed to the ground, in many places ; and the works had fuffered much, in every part. Yet the enemy ftill delaying to furrender, the admiral, who had, during the whole fiege, co-operated with the general with remarkable harmony, chearfully affifting him with cannon and other implements, with detachments of marines to maintain pofts on fhore, with parties of feamen to act as pioneers, and affift in working the guns and mortars ; notwithftanding the feverity of the weather, refolved on a ftroke, which, by being decifive of the poffeffion of the

harbour,

harbour, might make the reduction of the town a matter of little difficulty. He accordingly fent fix hundred feamen in boats, to take or burn the two fhips of the line which remained ; and, if fuccefsful in this attempt, he propofed the next day to fend in fome of his great fhips, to batter the town on the fide of the harbour. This fcheme was fuccefsfully executed by captains Laforey and Balfour, who entering the harbour, in the night between the twenty-fifth and twenty-fixth days of the month, in fpite of the fire from the French fhips and batteries, boarded them, fword in hand, and made themfelves mafters of both the fhips ; one of which was fet on fire and deftroyed, being aground, but the other was towed out of the harbour in triumph.

This ftroke, in fupport of the fpirited endeavours of the land forces, was conclufive ; the French governor, finding it impoffible to ftand an affault, and divers practicable breaches being effected, capitulated on the next day, by which he and his garrifon became prifoners of war. Thus, at the expence of about four hundred men, killed or wounded, the important ifland of Cape Breton, and ftrong town of Louifbourg, were taken ; in which the victors found two hundred and twenty-one pieces of cannon, and eighteen mortars, with a very large quantity of ftores and ammunition. The inhabitants were fent to France in Englifh fhips ; but the garrifon, fea-officers, failors, and marines, amounting, in the whole, to five thoufand fix hundred and thirtyfeven, were carried prifoners to England.

As

As this ifland, and the town of Louifbourg, were
of the greateft importance to France, and the centre of their valuable fifhery, a conftant repofitory
for their privateers, who from thence in great
numbers infefted the colonies, and the key to their
fettlements on the continent of North-America; a
defcription of both, while they remained in the
hands of the enemy, will not, we hope, prove
difagreeable to the reader, efpecially as the ifland
is now ceded to England, the fortifications demolifhed; and the ftrong forts and batteries
rendered a confufed heap of ruins.

The town of Louifbourg, in the ifland of Cape
Breton, was fituated in the latitude of 45 deg. 50
min. north, and 58 deg. 35 min. weft, of the me-
ridian of London. It was of a middling fize;
the houfes of wood, on ftone foundations, which
were carried about fix feet above the ground.
The town was walled; and extremely well fortified
in the modern manner; there was, indeed, one part
without any wall, for about an hundred yards; but
it would have been here quite unneceffary, the fea
flowing clofe to the town, and therefore a pallifadoe
was judged a fufficient defence. Even fmall barks
could not approach it, for want of a fufficient depth
of water; and fhips were obliged to keep at a very
confiderable diftance, on account of rocks and
fhoals. Befides, there were two collateral baftions,
which flanked this part very advantageoufly. In
the centre of one of the chief baftions was a ftrong
building, with a moat on the fide towards the town,

VOL. II.   G   which

which was called the citadel, though it had neither artillery nor a ftructure proper to receive any : the entrance to it, indeed, was over a draw-bridge ; on one fide of which was a corps de garde, and advanced centinels on the other. Within this building were the apartments for the governor, the barracks for the garrifon, and the arfenal ; and under the platform of the redoubt, a magazine, always well furnifhed with military ftores. The parifh church alfo ftood within the citadel ; and without it was another, belonging to the hofpital of St. Jean de Dieu, an elegant, fpacious ftructure, though founded long fince.

The harbour is large and fafe, but the entrance very narrow ; being confined between an ifland, on which was a ftrong fort, and the oppofite fide, where was a very high tower, made ufe of as a lighthoufe. Here was a large fortification, called the Royal Battery, which defended the mouth of the harbour ; and beyond it another fort, built farther within the harbour. From this fort the coaft winds inward, and forms a large bay, with a good depth of water, defended from all winds ; and here the large veffels were laid up in winter ; but in fummer they anchored before the town, at about a quarter of a league diftance ; though fmaller fhips might come within a cable's length of the fhore, and lie quiet from all winds except the eaft, which blows right into the harbour's mouth.

The entrance of the harbour is very fafe, there being only one rock, which is under water ; but the

fands

fands near it are dry. In winter, however, the harbour is entirely frozen over : that feafon begins here towards the end of November, and lafts till May or June. Sometimes the frofts fet in fooner, and are more intenfe; it not being uncommon for the harbour to be wholly frozen over in October.

The ifland produces a great quantity of timber; particularly oaks of a prodigious fize, pines fit for mafts, cedar, afh, plane-trees, and afpins, and contains excellent coal-mines. The great length, and intenfe cold, of the winters, being a great impediment to agriculture, the inhabitants made fifhing their fole occupation; and their example was followed by the inhabitants of St. John's, a fmall adjacent ifland in the gulph of St. Laurence, which fubmitted immediately, upon the reduction of Louifbourg.

In the mean time, the military operations on the continent were carried on with equal vigour. The forces under the immediate conduct of general Abercrombie, confifting of near feven thoufand regular troops and ten thoufand Provincials, embarked, in the beginning of July, on the Lake George, in the neighbourhood of Lake Champlain, on board of nine hundred batteaus, and one hundred and thirty-five whale-boats, with provifions, artillery, and ammunition; feveral pieces of artillery being mounted on rafts to cover the intended landing, which was effected without oppofition. The general then formed his troops into three columns, and marched againft Ticonderoga, a fort, fituated on a

point

point of land between Lake George and a narrow gut communicating with Lake Champlain,
fecured by a morafs in front, and on the other three
fides furrounded with water.

The enemy's advanced guard fled on his approach, with great precipitation, deferting a logged
camp, after having burnt their tents, &c. The country was all a thick wood, thro' which the Englifh
forces continued their march, but found it impaffable, with any regularity, for fuch a body of men;
and the guides proving extremely unfkilful, the
troops were bewildered, and the columns broken,
falling in one upon another. Lord Howe, at the
head of the right centre column, fell in with a party
of French regulars, of about four hundred men,
who had loft their way in their retreat from their
advanced poft: a fkirmifh enfued, in which the
enemy were routed, with confiderable lofs; one
hundred and forty eight being taken prifoners,
including five officers. This trifling advantage
was dearly bought with the lofs of lord Howe,
who fell in the beginning of the action, unfpeakably
regretted; having diftinguifhed himfelf, in a peculiar manner, by his courage, activity, and rigid
obfervation of military difcipline, and acquired the
efteem and love of the foldiery by his generofity,
fweetnefs of manners, and engaging addrefs. The
troops were now fo greatly fatigued and difordered,
from want of reft and refrefhment, that general
Abercrombie thought it advifeable to march back
to the landing place. As foon as the men were recovered

covered from their fatigue, lieutenant-colonel Bradftreet was detached with a regiment of regulars,
fix companies of Royal Americans, and a body
of Rangers, to take poffeffion of a faw-mill in
the neighbourhood of Ticonderoga, which had
been deferted by the enemy.

Abercrombie having fecured this poft, advanced
to Ticonderoga, where the enemy had made a very
ftrong line, upwards of eight feet high, on that
part of the front where the morafs failed, defended
by cannon, and near fix thoufand men, including
Canadians and Indians. A great number of felled
trees, with their branches outward, were fpread
before the entrenchment, which projected in fuch a
manner as to render it almoft inacceffible.

Neverthelefs, the engineer who was fent to reconnoitre the place, made fo favourable a report of the
entrenchment, that it appeared practicable to force
it by mufquetry alone; and, in confequence thereof, the fatal refolution was taken not to wait the arrival of the artillery, which could not be eafily
brought up, on account of the badnefs of the
ground; but to attack the enemy, without lofs of
time. The general was confirmed in this precipitate refolution, by the account he received from his
prifoners, that a body of three thoufand men, under
Monf. de Levy, were on their march to join the
enemy, and were very fhortly expected to arrive.
This officer had been detached to make an irrup-
tion through the pafs of Oneyada, on the Mohawks
River, but had been recalled, before he could exe-

G 3 cute

cute this defign, upon intelligence of general Abercrombie's approach to Ticonderoga *.

When the attack began, the ftrength of the
enemies lines; which had been fo little forefeen,
was but too feverely felt. Though the troops
behaved with the utmoft fpirit and gallantry, they
fuffered fo terribly in their approaches, and made
fo little impreffion on the intrenchment, that the
general feeing their repeated and obftinate efforts
fail of fuccefs, (being upwards of four hours expofed to a moft terrible fire from the enemy, who
were fo well covered, that they could with the
greateft deliberation direct their fire without the
leaft danger to themfelves), thought it neceffary to
order a retreat. The army retired unmolefted to
their former camp, to the fouthward of Lake
George, the evening after the action, with the
lofs of about eighteen hundred men, killed or
wounded, including a great number of officers.
Every corps behaved on this unfortunate occafion,
with the greateft intrepidity; but the greateft lofs
was fuftained by lord John Murray's highland regiment, of which above half of the private men,
and twenty-five officers were either killed or defpe-
rately wounded.

To repair this misfortune, general Abercrombie detached colonel Bradftreet with three thou-

* Brigadier Stanwix was afterwards fent thither, with a
confiderable body of Provincials; and this important pafs fecured by a fort built at that juncture.]

sand

fand Provincials, againſt Fort Frontenac, ſituated on the north ſide of the river St. Laurence, where it takes its riſe from the Lake Ontario. The colonel had ſome time ſince formed a plan for making himſelf maſter of this place; he accordingly, after having ſurmounted great difficulties, penetrated with his army, to the eaſtern bank of the Lake Ontario, where embarking on board ſeveral ſloops and batteaus, provided for that purpoſe, he landed within a mile of Fort Frontenac, the garriſon of which, conſiſting of one hundred and ten men and a few Indians, ſurrendered at diſcretion in leſs than two days after it had been attacked, without the loſs of a ſingle man on our ſide. The fort itſelf was inconſiderable and badly conſtructed, being only a ſquare of one hundred yards; and though it contained ſixty cannon, only half of them were mounted, and ſixteen ſmall mortars. Nine armed ſloops were taken and burnt, and an immenſe quantity of proviſions and merchandize, deſigned for their troops on the Ohio, and their garriſons to the ſouthward and weſtward. The fort poorly fortified and weakly garriſoned for a poſt of ſuch importance, being the magazine for all their weſtern and ſouthern garriſons and Indian allies, was demoliſhed, agreeable to general Abercrombie's inſtructions. Colonel Bradſtreet having performed this important ſervice, returned ſafely to Oſwego. This was a ſevere blow to the enemy, whoſe troops to the ſouthward were now in danger of ſtarving; but it is

not

not eafy to conceive the general's reafon for giving orders to abandon a poft fo ftrong by nature, that if it had been properly fortified and garrifoned, and the veffels preferved and kept cruifing on the lake, it might have rendered the Englifh mafters of Lake Ontario, and have terribly harraffed the enemy, both in their commerce and expeditions to the weftward.

However, in all probability, the fuccefs of colonel Bradftreet greatly facilitated that of the expedition againft Fort du Quefne, under general Forbes; who with his little army of fix thoufand men, began his march from Philadelphia for the River Ohio, in the beginning of July, through a prodigious tract of country; very little known, and rendered almoft impaffable by woods, mountains, and moraffes, being continually harraffed on his route by the French Indians. Having penetrated with the main body as far as Ray's-town, diftant ninety miles from Fort du Quefne, and advanced colonel Bouquet with two thoufand men, to Lyal Henning, fifty miles farther; that officer detatched major Grant, at the head of eight hundred men, to reconnoitre the fort and its outworks; but the enemy fuddenly fallying out, on his approach, with a large body of forces, the colonel, after a fevere engagement that lafted three hours, being overpowered with numbers, was obliged to retreat with the lofs of three hundred men, killed or taken prifoners, including major Grant, who was carried prifoner to Fort du Quefne, and

nineteen

nineteen officers. But this was the enemy's last success, for the main body of the army being conducted with greater skill and circumspection, baffled all their attempts; so that being now convinced by several skirmishes, that all their attempts to surprize the troops and interrupt their communication were in vain; and their Indians wavering in their obedience, in proportion as the English army advanced, they dismantled and abandoned the fort, and fell down the Ohio, on the twenty-fourth of November, towards their more southern settlements on the Mississippi. The next day general Forbes erected the English flag on Fort du Quesne, which he named Pitsburgh: and having repaired its works, left a garrison of Provincials there, and concluded a treaty of friendship and alliance with the Indian tribes; and on his march back to Philadelphia built a blockhouse, near Lyal Henning, for the defence of Pensylvania; but his constitution being delicate, died of fatigue, before the army arrived at that province. Thus, without the least resistance, in the third year after the commencement of hostilities, we became masters of the fortress, the contention for which had kindled up the flames of so destructive and general a war; and, notwithstanding the unhappy affair at Ticonderoga, the campaign proved highly advantageous, and honourable to the English interest. Louisbourg, St. John's, Frontenac, and Du Quesne reduced, removed from the colonies all terror of the Indian

incur-

incurfions, drew from the French thofe ufeful allies, freed the frontiers from the yoke of their enemy's forts, made their fupplies difficult, their communications precarious, and all their defenfive,
or offenfive operations ineffectual; while their country, uncovered of its principal bulwarks, laid open
to the heart, and afforded the moft pleafing profpects of fuccefs from the vigorous meafures intended to be purfued in the enfuing campaign.

The French, as has been already feen, by artful
infinuations, had drawn moft of the Indian nations
from their alliance with Great Britain, and infti-
gated thofe favages to commit the moft horrid
acts of barbarity on the innocent inhabitants of
the back fettlements: but the time was now come
when their perfidious falfities loft their prevailing
power. A grand affembly of the Indian nations
was held at Eafton, about ninety miles from Philadelphia, and a formal treaty concluded between
Great Britain and fifteen Indian tribes, inhabiting
the vaft tract of country lying between the Apalachian mountains and the lakes. The Twightees,
an Indian tribe, fettled between the Ohio and the
lakes, did not, however, affift at this affembly,
though fome fteps had been taken towards an alliance with them. The conferences were managed
by the governors of Penfylvania and New Jerfey,
accompanied by Sir William Johnfon's deputy for
Indian affairs, four members of the council of
Penfylvania, fix members of the affembly, two
agents for New Jerfey, and a great number of
                                        planters

planters and citizens of Philadelphia, chiefly Quakers.
The names of the Indian nations which affifted at
this treaty were the Mohawks, Oneidoes, Onon-
dagoes, Cayugas, Senecas, Tufcaroras, Nantico-
gues, Conoys, Tuteloes, Chugnuts, Delawares,
Unamies, Minifinks, Mohicons, and Wappingers,
the whole number of Indian deputies and chiefs
amounting to five hundred, including their women
and children. The deputies of the Six Nations
expreffed their refentment on the occafion, for
fome exceffes committed by the Englifh on their
people. The Delawares and Minifinks complained,
that the Englifh had encroached on their lands, and
given the firft occafion for hoftilities. There was
alfo a mifunderftanding between the Indians themfelves, the chiefs of the Six Nations taking umbrage
at the importance affumed by Teedyufcung, one of
the Delawares, over whom, as their defcendants, they
exercife a kind of parental authority; fo that the
principal bufinefs of the Englifh governors, was to
afcertain the limits of the lands in difpute, reconcile the Six Nations with the Delawares their ne-
phews, remove every caufe of complaint againft the
Englifh, detach them from the French intereft, and
induce them to exert their influence in perfuading
the Twightees to accede to this treaty. Thefe
favages, though poffeffed of few ideas, their
mental faculties circumfcribed within very narrow bounds, and their behaviour brutal and fero-
cious, yet conduct themfelves in matters of importance to the community, by the general maxims

of

of reafon and juftice; and their treaties, though managed in a ridiculous manner, are founded upon good fenfe and found reafon. Their language is harfh, guttural, and polyfyllabical; and their fpeech confifts of hyperbolical metaphors and fimiles, that give it an air of dignity, and heighten the expreffion. They manage their conferences by means of wampum, a kind of beads formed out of a hard fhell, and either ftrung in fingle rows, or fewed on broad belts of different dimenfions, according to the importance of the fubject. Thefe belts are exchanged whenever a propofition is offered, an anfwer made, a promife corroborated, a declaration attefted, or a treaty confirmed. The conferences lafted eighteen days; and the precifion with which the Indians treated was wonderful; for they required fatisfaction for, and mentioned every life their countrymen had loft, and the fmalleft damage they had fuftained. At length, every article being fettled, to the approbation of all parties, the Indians were gratified with valuable prefents, and returned the next day to their refpective places of abode, feemingly with a hearty deteftation of the French.

The CAMPAIGN of 1759.

THE Indians being once more united to the Englifh intereft, inftead of employing the whole ftrength of our arms, againft one object, which would have rendered our natural fuperiority

of

of litttle ufe, by fuffering the enemy to collect, as they had hitherto done, their ftrength into one fingle point; it was propofed, this year, to fall as nearly as poffible at the fame time upon Crown Point, Niagara, Quebec, and the forts to the fouth of Lake Erie: that by thus diftracting and weakening the enemy, all Canada might fall in one campaign. The different expeditions were planned in fuch a manner as to affift each other. General Wolfe, who had fo eminently diftinguifhed himfelf at the fiege of Louifbourg, was to proceed up the river St. Lawrence as foon as the navigation fhould be free from ice, with a body of eight thoufand men, and a ftrong fquadron of fhips from England, to befiege Quebec, the capital of Canada. General Amherft, the commander in chief, at the head of twelve thoufand troops, was to reduce Ticonderoga and Crown Point, then crofs Lake Champlain, and proceeding along the banks of the river Richlieu, to the river St. Lawrence, join general Wolfe before Quebec. Brigadier-general Prideaux with a third body of troops, affifted by a confiderable number of Indians, affembled by the influence and under the command of Sir William Johnfon, had orders to attack the French fort near the fall of Niagara, which commanded in a manner all the interior parts of North America, and was a key to the whole continent. As foon as this fort was carried, the general was to embark on the Lake Ontario, fall down the river St. Lawrence, make himfelf mafter of Montreal,

treal, and then join general Amherſt. General Stanwix commanded a ſmaller detachment for re-ducing the forts on the Ohio, and ſcouring the banks of the Lake Ontario. It was imagined that if general Prideaux's ſcheme, in addition to its own end, ſhould not facilitate either of the other two capital undertakings, it would probably, as Nia-gara was the moſt important place the French had in that part of the world, make them draw together all the troops they had upon the lakes, to attempt its relief, which would leave the forts on thoſe lakes expoſed. In reality it had that effect.

The army under general Amherſt was the firſt in motion. Lake George, or, as the French called it, Lake Sacrament, is a long, but, in propor-tion, narrow body of water, about forty miles in length, and incloſed on either ſide with marſhy grounds, which communicates by another long, and very narrow ſtreight, with Lake Champlain. This ſtreight was ſecured at each ſide by a fort; that to the ſide of Lake George was called Ticon-deroga, that towards the Champlain Lake was call-ed Fort Frederic, or Crown Point, both extremely ſtrong by their ſituation; and the former had re-pulſed our troops with conſiderable loſs laſt year, as has been already related. The general paſſed Lake George without the leaſt oppoſition from the ene-my; though the progreſs of his operations had been ſo greatly retarded by impediments thrown in his way by certain individuals of great influence

in

in America, that the season was far advanced before he crossed the lake. On his arrival before
Ticonderoga, the French at first seemed determined
to defend the place ; but perceiving the English
general both prudent, cautious, and resolute, and
being perfectly acquainted with the strength of
our forces, having also orders to retreat from
place to place towards the centre of their operations
at Quebec, rather than run the least risque of being
made prisoners of war ; they abandoned this strong
post in the night of the 27th of July, after having
damaged its fortifications as much as the time
would possibly admit, and retired to Crown Point.

General Amherst immediately set himself about
repairing the works of this strong post, which effectually secured Lake George, covered the frontiers of New York, and was of such vast importance to enable him to push forward his offensive
operations, or to favour his retreat if unsuccessful.
In the mean time he continually detached scouting
parties into the neighbourhood of Crown Point, in
order to watch the motions of the enemy ; and although he had room to imagine that the same reasons which had induced them to abandon their lines
at Ticonderoga, would induce them also to evacuate Crown Point, he took all his measures with
the same care and caution as if he had expected an
obstinate defence, and an attempt to surprize him
on his march ; mindful how fatal too much security had proved to us in this part of the world
on many occasions. One of his scouting parties
brought

brought intelligence, on the firſt of Auguſt, that the French had abandoned Crown Point, as he had foreſeen, after ſetting the fort on fire, a body of rangers were immediately diſpatched to take poſſeſſion of the place; and the general himſelf embarked with the reſt of the army, and on the 4th day of the month, arrived at the fort, where the troops were immediately encamped. Being thus in poſſeſſion of the moſt important poſt in this part of the country, he immediately laid the foundations of a new fort for the farther ſecurity of the Britiſh dominions on that ſide, and to prevent the incurſions of ſcalping parties, by whom the frontier plantations had ſo dreadfully ſuffered: Hitherto the French had been actually eſtabliſhed in the heart of our territories, ſo that during a war of three years we had in fact been only acting on the defenſive; but now the ſcene was changed.

The general, ſoon after his arrival at Crown Point received information, that the enemy, to the number of three thouſand five hundred men, under the command of Monſieur de Bourlemaque, with a ſtrong train of artillery, had retired to Iſle au Noix, ſituated near the north eaſt extremity of Lake Champlain; and that the lake was occupied by four large veſſels mounted with cannon, and manned with piquets from different regiments, under the direction of Monſ. le Bras, a captain in the French navy, aſſiſted by Monſ. de Rigal and other ſea officer; with which they hoped

hoped to prevent the progrefs of the Englifh into
the interior parts' of Canada.' In confequence of
this advice,'' general. Amherft, who had for fome
time employed captain Loring in building of veffels at Ticonderoga, being fenfible of the confequence of a naval fuperiority on the lake, directed
him to launch, as expeditioufly as poffible, a floop
of fixteen guns, and a float of timber eighty-four
feet in length, capable of carrying fix large cannon, together with a brigantine. Thefe veffels
being ready for fea by the 11th of October, the
general embarked with the whole army in batteaus,
in order to attack the enemy; but the weather
growing tempeftuous, he was forced to take fhelter
in a bay on the weftern fhore, where the men were
landed for refefhment. In the interim, captain
Loring, with his fmall fquadron, failed down the
lake, chaced a French fchooner, and drove three
of their veffels into a bay, where two of them were
funk, and one run aground by their own crews,
who by that means made their efcape: the laft,
however, was repaired and brought off by captain
Loring, fo that now the enemy had only one
fchooner remaining. General Amherft, after having remained fome days wind-bound, reimbarked
his troops and proceeded on his voyage; but the
ftorm that had abated, beginning to blow again
with redoubled fury, fo as to render it impoffible
for boats to live on the lake, the feafon for action
being over, and winter fetting in with the moft rigorous feverity, he found it was impoffible to ac-

VOL. II.   H   complifh

complish his defign, and therefore returned to the fame bay where he had before taken fhelter, relanded his troops, and marched back to Crown Point, which he reached the 21ft of October. Having fecured a fuperiority on the lake, his attention was now wholly employed in erecting the new fortrefs at Crown Point, and three fmall out-forts for its better defence ;- in opening roads of communication between Ticonderoga and the provinces of New Hampfhire and Maffachufets.Bay ; and in making difpofitions for the winter quarters of his troops, fo as to protect the back colonies from the inroads of the enemy.

During this whole fummer he received not the leaft intelligence of general Wolfe's operations, except a few hints contained in fome letters relating to the exchange of prifoners, fent from the French general, Montcalm, who gave him to underftand, that Mr. Wolfe had landed in the neighbourhood of Quebec, and feemed refolved to befiege that city : that he had honoured him (the French general) with feveral notes, fometimes filled with threats, fometimes couched in a foothing ftrain ; adding, that they were determined to give him battle foon, and that a few days would determine the fate of Quebec. But his communication continued open with the army under general Prideaux, and he received advice before he left Ticonderoga, that the expedition againft Niagara had proved fuccefsful.

General Prideaux, reinforced by the Indian auxiliaries under Sir William Johnfon, advanced

to

to the cataract of Niagara, without meeting with
the leaft· obftruction, and invefting the fort about
the middle of July, carried on his approaches with
great vigour, until the 20th of that month, when
vifiting the trenches, he was unfortunately killed
by the burfting of, a cohorn. As foon as this accident happened, an exprefs was difpatched to general
Amherft, who, without lofs of time, fent brigadier-
general Gage from Ticonderoga to affume the
command. of the army : .but the command, which
in the interim had devolved upon Sir William
Johnfon, could not have been betterbeftowed. He
omitted nothing to continue the vigorous.meafures
adopted by the deceafed general ; and pufhed
on the fiege with fo much alacrity, that in a few
days the approaches were brought within one hundred yards · of the covered way.

The enemy, alarmed at the imminent danger of
this important place, collected all the regular
troops, and Canadians which they could draw from
Detroit, · Venango, Prefque Ifle, and all their
pofts about the lakes, and a large body of Indians, in· order to reinforce the garrifon at Niagara. ·The whole detachment amounted to feventeen hundred men, under the command of Monf.
d'Aubry. General Johnfon, being informed of
their approach, made the neceffary difpofitions for
intercepting them in 'their march. The light infantry and piquets were pofted, in the evening, to
the left, on the road leading from the Fall of Nia-

H 2 gara

gara to the fortress; and were reinforced in the morning early with the grenadiers, and part of the forty-fixth regiment, commanded by lieutenant colonel Maffey; whilst another regiment, under the command of lieutenant-colonel Farquhar, was posted at the tail of the works, in order to support the guard of the trenches. The Indians in the English service were placed on his flank. In the mean time, the French continued their march, and about eight in the morning difcovered the English army, drawn up in order of battle. The Indians, under the command of Sir William Johnfon, advanced to fpeak with their countrymen who ferved in the French army; but they declined this conference, and immediately uttered the horrible fcream called the war-whoop, which had now loft its effect among the Britifh forces; and began the attack with the greateft impetuofity. But the enemy were fo well received, that in about half an hour their whole army was routed. The purfuit was hot and bloody; it continued for five miles, and the French general, with all his officers, were taken prifoners.

This action, which happened on the 24th of July, was fought in fight of the French garrifon at Niagara; and was no fooner decided in our favour, than the general fent major Harvey, with a trumpet, to the governor of the fort, with a lift of the feventeen officers taken prifoners, to exhort him to furrender, while he had it ftill in his power to

reftrain

reftrain the Indians ; adding, that he was at liberty
to fend a perfon to fee the officers, and fatisfy himfelf with refpect to the fact. Accordingly, an officer was difpatched from the fort, and fuffered to
converfe with Mr. d'Aubry, and the other prifoners. On his return, the governor agreed to treat,
and the capitulation was figned that very night.
The garrifon furrendered prifoners of war, and, to
the number of fix hundred and feven men, were
conducted to New-York. Sir William Johnfon,
by his influence over the Indians, protected them
from their favage infolence and cruelty, fo that the
foldiers kept their baggage ; all the women, at
their own requeft, were fent to Montreal ; and the
fick and wounded were treated with the utmoft
care and humanity. Thus, for a fecond time, this
felf-taught general obtained a compleat victory
over the boafted difcipline of the French arms ;
and a fecond time had the good fortune to make
the commander in chief his prifoner. But this was
his leaft praife. Though eleven hundred Indians
followed him to the field, he reftrained them within
regular bounds, and their example demonftrably
proved, that the exceffes which the other favages
had been guilty of againft the Englifh, had been
prompted and directed by the French. It muft
not be omitted, to the honour of this gentleman,
that, though he was not regularly bred a foldier,
the moft compleat officer could not have made
more excellent difpofitions for the battle, or have

H 3   conduct-

conducted the fiege, from the beginning to the end, with a more cool and fteady refolution, or with a more compleat knowledge of all the neceffary manœuvres of war. The taking of Niagara broke off effectually the communication fo much talked of, and fo much dreaded, between Canada and Louifiana; and by this ftroke, one of the capital political defigns of the French, which occafioned the war, was defeated in its direct and immediate object *.

How-

* Niagara is, without exception, the moft important poft in America, and fecures a greater number of communications, through a more extenfive country, than perhaps any other pafs in the world; for it is fituated at the very entrance of a ftreight by which the Lake Ontario is joined to that of Erie, which is connected with the other three great lakes by the courfe of the vaft river St. Lawrence, which runs through them all, and carries off their fuperfluous waters to the ocean. A little above the fort is the Cataract of Niagara, the moft remarkable in the world, for the quantity of water and the greatnefs of the fall; the perpendicular fall of the water being exactly one hundred and thirty-feven feet. This fall would interrupt the commerce between the two lakes, but for a road made by the French up the hilly country that lies by the ftreight; fo that, after travelling about eight miles, perfons may reimbark, and proceed, without further interruption, to the Lake Erie.

Thofe who travel by land are alfo obliged to crofs the ftreight; the lakes being fo difpofed, that without an hazardous voyage the Indians cannot otherwife pafs from the north-weft to the fouth-eaft parts of North-America, for many hundred miles. The fort of Niagara thus naturally commands the Six Nations, and all thofe Indian tribes that lie to the northward of the lakes, as well as thofe that are fcattered along the banks of the Ohio,

However defirable the reduction of Niagara and Crown-Point might be to the colonies, the conqueſt of Quebec was of ſtill greater importance, and the attempt far, more dangerous. Few enterprizes were ever attended with more difficulties, or conducted with greater caution, prudence, and intrepidity. The fleet deſtined for this expedition, ſailed from England in the middle of February, under the command of the admirals Saunders and Holmes, who had both given evident proofs of their conduct and courage in the ſervice of their country. By the 21ſt of April they were in fight of the iſland of Cape Breton ; but the harbour of

Louiſ-

Ohio, Ouabache, and Miſſiſippi, and, according as it was poſſeſſed by the French or Engliſh, connected or disjointed Canada and Louiſiana.

From the time the French were acquainted with this place, they were fully ſenſible of its importance, both with reſpect to trade and dominion. They made ſeveral attempts to eſtabliſh themſelves here ; but the Indians conſtantly oppoſed it, and obliged them to relinquiſh a fort which they had built ; and guarded this ſpot, for a long time, with a very ſevere and prudent jealouſy.

But whilſt we neglected to cultivate the love of the Indians, the French omitted no endeavours to gain theſe ſavages to their intereſt ; and prevailed at laſt, under the name of a tradinghouſe, to erect a ſtrong fort at the mouth of the ſtreight. A French officer, of an enterprizing genius, had been a priſoner among the Iroquois a long time ; and, according to their cuſtom, having been naturalized, grew very popular amongſt them, and at laſt regained his liberty. He communicated to the then governor of Canada a plan for an eſtabliſhment at Niagara, and undertook to execute it himſelf. He returned among the Iro-

H 4

quois,

Louifbourg was blocked up with ice in fuch a manner, that they were obliged to bear away for Halifax
in Nova-Scotia. From hence rear admiral Durell
was fent with a fmall fquadron up the river St. Laurence, as far as the Ifle de Coudres, in order to intercept any fupplies that might be fent from France to
Quebec. He took three fmall fhips, befides fome
fmall craft, laden with flour and other provifions;
but had the mortification to find, that the frigates,
and the tranfports, loaded with provifions, had already reached that city ; and having taken poffeffion
of the Ifland de Coudres, proceeded to the Ifle of
Orleans. Meanwhile, admiral Saunders arrived at
Louifbourg ; and the troops being embarked,
                                                which

quois, and pretending great love for their nation, which was
now his own, told them; he would gladly vifit his brethren
frequently ; but it was proper for that purpofe, that they fhould
allow him to build himfelf an houfe, where he might live according to his own manner ; at the fame time, propofing to
them advantages in trade for this eftablifhment. His requeft
was eafily granted. The houfe was built, and by degrees extended and ftrengthened by various additions, and at laft became a regular fortrefs, which had ever fince awed the Six Nations, and checked our colonies.

As to thofe immenfe lakes, which are all in a manner commanded by this fort, the reader need only caft his eyes on the
map of North-America to be convinced of their importance.
They afford by far the moft extenfive inland navigation in the
whole univerfe. Whoever is mafter of them, muft fooner or
later command that whole continent. They are all furrounded
by a fine fruitful country, in a temperate pleafant climate.
The day may poffibly come when this noble country, which
feems calculated for univerfal empire, will fufficiently difplay its
own importance.

which did not exceed feven thoufand men, regulars and provincials, though the original plan
intended nine thoufand for this expedition, exclufive of thofe under general Amherft, (whofe
affiftance on the occafion was taken for granted) proceeded up the river St. Laurence without further delay. The land-forces were commanded by major general Wolfe, whofe military
abilities had fhone with fuch fuperior luftre at
the fiege of Louifbourg; and under him were
the brigadiers Monckton, Townfhend, and Murray.

The whole embarkation arrived in the latter end
of June at the Ifle of Orleans, about two leagues
below Quebec, a large fertile ifland, about twenty
miles in length, and between feven and eight in
breadth, well cultivated, producing plenty of grain,
and populous, without any accident whatever, notwithftanding the reports of the dangerous navigation of the river St. Laurence, probably
fpread for political purpofes. This ifland extends almoft quite up to the bafon of Quebec,
its moft wefterly point advancing towards an
high point of land on the continent, called
Point Levi. Thefe two points fhut up the view
of the northern and fouthern channels, which
environ the Ifle of Orleans; fo that the harbour of Quebec appears to be a bafon land-locked
upon all fides. The poffeffion of both thefe points
was therefore abfolutely neceffary, as they might be
employed either with great advantage againft the
town,

town, or much to the annoyance of the befiegers; for whilft the enemy continued mafters of thofe, it was impoffible for a fhip to lie with fafety in the harbour of Quebec. General Wolfe no fooner landed on this ifland than he diftributed a manifefto among the inhabitants importing, That the king his maf-ter, juftly exafperated againft France, had fet on foot a confiderable armament by land and fea, to humble the pride of that crown, and was deter-mined to reduce the moft confiderable French fet-tlements in America. He declared, it was not againft the induftrious peafants and their families, nor againft the minifters of religion, that he de-figned to make war: on the contrary, he lament-ed the misfortunes to which they muft be expofed by the quarrel, offered them his protection, and promifed to maintain them in their temporal pof-feffions, as well as in the free exercife of their reli-gion; provided they would remain quiet, and take no part in the difference between the two crowns, directly or indirectly. He obferved, that the Englifh being now mafters of the river St. Laurence, all fuccours from Europe muft be intercepted; and that they had befides, a powerful army on the con-tinent, under the command of general Amherft. He affirmed, that the refolution the Canadians ought to take was neither difficult nor doubtful; as the utmoft exertion of their valour would be ufe-lefs, and only ferve to deprive them of the advan-tages which they might reap from their neutrality. He reminded them, that the cruelties exercifed by

the

the French on the fubjects of Great-Britain in America, would excufe the moft fevere reprifals; but Englifhmen were too generous to follow fuch barbarous examples. He again offered them the fweets of peace, amidft the horrors of war, and left it to themfelves to determine their own fate. But whatever refolution they might take, he flattered himfelf the world would do juftice to his conduct, which fhould be regulated by the ftricteft rules of juftice. He concluded with laying before them, the ftrength and power as well as generofity of England, which thus humanely ftretched out her hand to them; a hand ready to affift them on all occafions, even when France, by her weaknefs, incapable of affifting, abandoned them in the moft critical moment.

This humane manifefto produced no effect; the Canadians thought they could place no dependance on the promifes and fincerity of a nation, whom their priefts had induftrioufly reprefented as the moft favage and cruel enemy on earth. Poffeffed with thefe notions, which prevailed even among the better fort, they chofe to abandon their habitations, and expofe themfelves, and their families, to certain ruin, by provoking the Englifh with the moft cruel hoftilities, rather than remain quiet, and confide on the general's promife of protection. Inftead of fuch a prudent conduct, the Canadians joined the fcalping parties of Indians, who fkulked among the woods, and falling on the Englifh ftragglers by furprize, murdered

them

them with the moft inhuman barbarity.; fo that Wolfe, whofe generous nature revolted againft fuch wanton and perfidious cruelty, after having in vain expoftulated on this head with the French general, was obliged to connive at fome retaliations, in order to intimidate the enemy, and effect by punifhment, what the lenient hand of kindnefs had attempted in vain.

The conduct of Montcalm, the French commander in chief, did honour to his judgment; though his army was greatly fuperior to that of the Englifh, he carefully avoided an engagement, and prudently refolved to depend on the natural ftrength of the country, which feemed almoft unfurmountable. The city of Quebec was ftrongly fortified, fecured with a numerous garrifon, and plentifully fupplied with provifions and ammunition. The troops of the colony were reinforced with five regular battalions, formed of the principal inhabitants; all the Canadians in the neighbourhood capable of bearing arms, and feveral tribes of Indians, were completely difciplined; and with this army Montcalm took the field, and incamped in a very advantageous fituation, along the fhore of Beaufort, between the river St. Charles, and a bank of fand of great extent, which prevents any confiderable veffel from approaching the fhore, in his front, and thick impenetrable woods on his rear. There never was a ftronger poft; it was impoffible to attack him in it, and whilft he

re-

remained there it was in his power to throw fuccours into the city whenever he pleafed.

Wolfe faw all the difficulties that muft attend
his undertaking the fiege of Quebec, almoft inacceffible by its fituation, and defended by a fuperior army; but he knew at the fame time,
that he fhould always have it in his power to
retreat, while the Englifh fquadron maintained
its ftation in the river; nor was he without hopes
of being joined by general Amherft. Receiving
advice, that a detatchment of the enemy, with a
train of artillery, was pofted at Point Levi, on
the fouth fhore, oppofite the city of Quebec, he
determined to diflodge them before they had
intrenched themfelves. Accordingly he detatched
brigadier Monckton with four battalions, who paffed
the river in the night; and next morning, after
a flight fkirmifh with fome of the enemy's irregulars, obliged them to quit that poft, which was immediately occupied by the Englifh *. At the fame
time

---

* Monf. Montcalm forefaw the great advantages that would
refult to us over their capital, from being poffeffed of Point
Levi; and propofed, before the Englifh armament came up
the river, that four thoufand men fhould be ftrongly entrench-
ed here, with fome cannon, and that other works fhould alfo
be conftructed higher up the country, at certain diftances, for
the troops to retire to, in cafe their lines fhould be carried at
the Point. But Monf. Vaudreuil over-ruled this propofal in
a council of war, and infifted, that though we might demo-
lifh a few infignificant houfes with fhells, yet we could not
bring

time colonel Carleton, with another detatchment, took poffeffion of the weftern point of the Ifle of Orleans, and both pofts were directly fortified, in order to anticipate the enemy, who, as has been already obferved, if they had kept poffeffion of either, might have rendered it impoffible for fhips to lie at anchor within two miles of the city. Befides, Point Levi was within cannon-fhot of the city; a battery of cannon and mortars was of courfe immediately erected there. Montcalm, fore-feeing the effect of this battery, detatched a body of fixteen hundred men crofs the river, to attack and deftroy the works before they were compleated: but the attempt mifcarried. The battery being fi-nifhed without further interruption, a continual fire was kept up againft the city with fuch fuccefs, that in a little time the upper town was confiderably damaged, and the lower town reduced to an heap of rubbifh. In the mean while the fleet, one divi-fion of which, under admiral Saunders, was ftationed below in the north channel of the Ifle of Orleans, oppofite to Montmorenci; the other under admiral Holmes, above the town, at once to divert the ene-my's attention, and to prevent any attempts againft the batteries that played againft Quebec, fuffered great damage from a ftorm, which blew with fuch violence, that many of the tranfports ran foul of

bring cannon to bear upon Quebec a-crofs the river; and was firmly of opinion, that it was their duty to ftand upon the defenfive, with their whole army on the north fide of the bafon, and not divide their force on any account whatfoever.

one

one another and were driven on shore, a number of small craft and boats foundered, several of the flat-bottomed boats were rendered unfit for farther service, and divers large ships lost their anchors. The enemy, in order to take advantage of the confusion which they supposed this disaster must have occasioned, at midnight, sent down five fire ships and two rafts to destroy the fleet. The scheme, though well contrived, was happily defeated by the prudence of the English admiral, and the resolution and alertness of the sailors, who resolutely towed the fire ships and rafts fast aground, where they lay burning to the water's edge, without doing the least damage to the English squadron. A second attempt of this kind was made on the very same day of the succeeding month, which proving equally ineffectual, the French general thought proper to lay aside his design.

As soon as the works for securing the hospital and stores were finished, the English forces crossed the river St. Laurence in boats, and landing under the cover of two sloops, encamped on the side of the river Montmorenci, with a view of passing that river, and bringing the enemy to an engagement. The next morning a party of rangers, posted in a wood to cover some fascine makers, were attacked by the French Indians, and defeated; but the nearest troops advancing, the enemy were in their turn repulsed with considerable loss. The reasons that induced general Wolfe to choose this situation by the falls of Montmorenci, in which

he

he was feparated from Quebec by this and another river named St. Charles, were, that the ground which he had chofen was high, and in fome meafure commanded the oppofite fide where the enemy was pofted: that there was a ford below the falls paffable every tide for fome hours at the latter part of the ebb and beginning of the flood; and he was in hopes that means might be found to pafs the river higher up, fo as to fight Monf. Montcalm on lefs difadvantageous terms than directly attacking his intrenchments. Accordingly, on reconnoitring the river Montmorenci, a ford was difcovered about three miles above; but the oppofite bank, which was naturally fteep and covered with woods, was rendered fo ftrong by intrenchments, as to be almoft inacceffible. The efcorte was twice attacked by the French Indians, who were both times repulfed; thefe fkirmifhes coft the Englifh about forty men killed and wounded, including officers. Wolfe therefore deferred his intended attack on the French army, till he had furveyed the river St. Laurence above Quebec, in hopes of difcovering a place more favourable for a defcent.

Accordingly, the admiral, at his requeft, on the 18th of July, fent two men of war, two floops, and fome tranfports, with troops on board, up the river; and they paffed the city of Quebec, without fuftaining the leaft damage. The general being himfelf on board this little armament,

care-

carefully obferved the banks on the fide of the enemy, which were extremely difficult from the nature of the ground, and the works of the enemy. Though a defcent feemed impracticable between the city and Cape Rouge, where it was intended, general Wolfe, in order to divide the enemy's force, and procure intelligence, fent a detachment, under colonel Carleton, to land higher up at Point au Tremble, where he had been informed a good number of the inhabitants of Quebec had retired with their moft valuable effects. This fervice was performed with little lofs, though the colonel at landing met with fome oppofition from a body of Indians: feveral prifoners were brought off, but no magazine was difcovered.

The general, thus difappointed in his expectations, returned to Montmorenci, where Brigadier Townfhend had, by maintaining a fuperior fire acrofs the river, prevented the enemy from erecting a battery, which would have commanded the Englifh camp; and now refolved to attack the French army, though pofted to great advantage.

As the men of war, for want of a fufficient depth of water, could not come near enough to the enemy's entrenchments, to annoy them in the leaft, the admiral prepared two flat bottomed armed veffels, which might on occafion be run aground to favour a defcent. With the affiftance

of

of thefe veffels, Wolfe propofed to make himfelf mafter of a detached redoubt near the water
edge, fituated, according to all appearance, out of
mufquet fhot of the enemy's entrenchments on
the hill.   If the French fupported this work it
muft neceffarily bring on an engagement, a circumftance which he earneftly wifhed for; and if
they tamely beheld its reduction, he would have
it in his power to examine their fituation at leifure,
fo as to be able to determine where they might be
attacked with the greateft profpect of fuccefs.
Preparations were accordingly made for the attack; on the laft day of July, in the forenoon,
the boats of the fleet were filled with grenadiers,
and part of Brigadier Monckton's brigade from
Point Levi.   The two brigades under Brigadiers
Townfhend and Murray were drawn out, in order to be ready to pafs the ford, when judged
neceffary.   To facilitate their paffage, the admiral
ftationed the Centurion, of fifty-four guns, in the
channel, to check the fire of the lower battery,
which commanded the ford: a numerous train
of artillery was placed upon the eminence, to en-
filade the left of the enemy's entrenchments;
and the two armed veffels prepared for this purpofe were ran aground near the redoubt, to favour
the defcent of the forces.   The manifeft confufion produced among the enemy by thefe previous
meafures, and the fire of the Centurion, which was
well directed and fuftained, determined the ge-

neral

neral to ftorm this intrenchment without further delay.

At a proper time of tide the fignal was made, but in rowing towards the fhore, many of the boats from Point Levi ran aground upon a ledge that runs off a confiderable diftance from the fhore; and this accident occafioned fo much time to be loft in remedying the diforder, that Wolfe was obliged to ftop the march of brigadier Townf-hend's corps, which he perceived to be in motion. In the mean time, the boats were floated and ranged in proper order, though expofed to a fevere fire of fhot and fhells; and the general in perfon, affifted by feveral fea officers, founding the fhore, pointed out the place where the troops might land with the leaft difficulty. Thirteen companies of grenadiers, and two hundred men of the fecond Royal American battalion, were the firft on fhore, and obliged the enemy to abandon the redoubt below the precipice. They had received orders to form in four diftinct bodies, and begin the attack, fupported by brigadier Monckton's corps, as foon as the other troops fhould have paffed the ford, and be near enough to contribute their affiftance. But unfortunately the grenadiers, impatient to acquire glory, without waiting for any reinforcement, or forming themfelves as directed, in great confufion ran up the hill, and made many efforts to gain the fummit, which they found lefs practicable than had been expected: in this fituation they received a general difcharge of mufquetry

from

from the enemy's breaft works, which was continued without any return ; our brave foldiers
referving their fire, until they fhould reach the top
of the precipice, which was inconceivably fteep :
to perfevere any longer they now found was to
little purpofe, their ardour was checked by the
repeated heavy fire of the enemy, which did fuch
execution among them, that at length they were
obliged to retire in diforder, and fhelter themfelves
under the redoubt which the French had abandoned at their approach. The general feeing the
fituation of affairs, night drawing on, and the
ammunition of the army damaged by a moft
dreadful ftorm, ordered them to retreat and form
behind Monckton's brigade, which was by this
time landed and drawn up upon the beach, in good
order. They accordingly retreated, leaving a
confiderable number lying on the field expofed to
the barbarity of the Indians. The enemy did not
attempt to purfue ; fo, the whole repaffed the
river without moleftation, and returned to their
former camp at Montmorenci.

The two armed veffels, which were aground,
were burnt to prevent their falling into the enemy's hands. The lofs of our forces this day,
killed, wounded, and miffing, including all ranks,
amounted to four hundred and forty-three, among
whom were two captains and two lieutenants killed
on the fpot ; colonel Burton of the forty-eighth
regiment, fix captains, nineteen lieutenants, and
three enfigns wounded,

The

The general, immediately after this mortifying check, detached brigadier Murray, with twelve hundred men, in transports, above the town, to co-operate with admiral Holmes, whom admiral Saunders had sent up the river, to destroy the French ships if possible. The brigadier was also instructed to seize every opportunity of fighting the enemy's detachments. In pursuance of these directions, he twice attempted to land on the north shore; but these attempts were unsuccessful: his third effort was more fortunate; he made a descent at Chambaud, and burned a considerable magazine, filled with arms, cloathing, provision, and ammunition. By the prisoners he learned that Fort Niagara had surrendered; and discovered by intercepted letters, that the enemy having abandoned Ticonderoga and Crown Point, were retired to Isle au Noix; and that general Amherst was making preparations to pass Lake Champlain, and attack the corps commanded by Monf. Bourlemaque. The enemy's ships being secured in such a manner as not to be approached, and nothing else occurring that required the brigadier's longer stay, he returned to the camp at Point Levi.

But this intelligence, otherwise so pleasing, brought no prospect of any assistance from that quarter. The season wasted apace. The general fell violently ill, from care, watching, and fatigue, too great to be supported by a delicate constitution, and a body unequal to the vigorous and enterpriz-

ing

ing foul that it lodged. His own high notions, the public expectation, the fuccefs of other com-manders, oppreffed his fpirits, and converted dif-appointment into difeafe. During his illnefs he defired the general officers to confult together for the public, utility ; and it was their opinion that any farther attempts at Montmorenci were to little purpofe ; and that the points Levi and Or-leans being left in a proper ftate of defence, the reft of the troops fhould be conveyed up the river, and the future principal operations fhould be above the town, in order, if poffible, to draw the enemy to an action. This meafure, however, was not a-dopted until the general and admiral, affifted by the principal engineer, had reconnoitred the town of Quebec, with a view to a general affault. But after a careful furvey, it was unanimoufly agreed that fuch an attack was impracticable : for though the men of war might have filenced the batteries of the lower town, they could not affect the up-per works, from which they muft have fuftained confiderable damage. The camp at Montmorenci was therefore broke up, and the troops encamp-ed at Point Levi. The fquadron under admiral Holmes made movements up the river for feveral days fucceffively, in order to amufe the enemy pofted on the north fhore.

On the 5th and 6th of September, the general embarked the forces ; but the tranfports being ex-tremely crowded, and the weather bad, one half of
the

the troops were landed for refreshment on the south
shore. As soon as matters were ripe for action, he
directed admiral Saunders to make a feint with his
squadron, as if he proposed to attack the French in
their entrenchments on the Beauport shore, below the town, and by his motions to give this
feint all the appearance of reality possible. This
disposition being made below the town, Wolfe embarked his forces about one in the morning, and
admiral Holmes's division failed three leagues further up the river than the place where he intended
to land, in order to conceal his real design. He then
embarked the troops, and fell down silently with
the tide; but by the rapidity of the current, and
the darkness of the night, the boats were carried a
little below the intended place of attack. The
ships followed them, and arriving just at the time
that had been concerted, to cover their landing,
the troops were disembarked without loss, or
indeed the knowledge of the enemy.

This remarkable success was, in some measure,
owing to the following accident : two French de-
serters had been carried the evening before on board
the English fleet, and from them the general learned, that the garrison expected that night to receive
a convoy of provisions in boats, from the detachment above the town, commanded by Monf. Bougainville. The knowledge of this circumstance
was of the utmost consequence, and tended to deceive the centinels posted along-shore to challenge
boats and vessels, and give an alarm, if necessary.

The

The firſt Engliſh boat being queſtioned accordingly, captain Donald M'Donald, of Fraſer's Highland regiment, who was perfectly acquainted with the French language, anſwered without heſitation, to their challenging word, *Qui va la ?* (Who is there) *La France.* When the centinel aſked, *Au quel regiment ?* (To what regiment do you belong ?) The captain replied, *De la Reine,* (To the queen's) which he accidentally knew to be one of thoſe that were under the command of Bougainville. The ſoldier took it for granted that this was the expected convoy, and allowed the boats to proceed, without further interruption. The other centries were deceived in the ſame manner; though one more wary than the reſt, ran down to the water's edge, and called, *Pour quoi ne parlez vous plus haut ?* (Why don't you ſpeak with an audible voice ?) To this queſtion, which implied doubt, the captain anſwered with admirable preſence of mind, in a low voice, *Tais tois, nous ſerons entendües,* (Huſh ! we ſhall be overheard, and diſcovered). Thus cautioned, the centinel retired without farther altercation.

As the troops could not be landed at the place intended, when they gained the ſhore, an high precipice appeared before them, extremely ſteep, and almoſt perpendicular. A little path winded up this aſcent, ſo narrow that two perſons could not go a-breaſt ; and even this path, by which alone the forces could poſſibly reach the ſummit, was ſtrongly intrenched, and defended by a captain's guard. Such great difficulties did not abate the hopes of

the

the general, or the ardour of the troops. Colonel Howe's light infantry, laying hold of ſtumps and boughs of trees, pulled themſelves up, diſlodged the enemy, and cleared the path ; then gained the top of the hill, without further interruption, and as faſt as they aſcended formed themſelves ; ſo that the whole army was in order of battle by day-break.

Montcalm, when the news was brought him, could ſcarcely credit the report ; but ſtill believed it to be a feint, to induce him to abandon that ſtrong poſt, which had been the object of all the real attempts that had been made ſince the beginning of the ſiege. But no ſooner was he undeceived, and found that the Engliſh army had really gained the Heights of Abraham, which in a manner commanded the town of Quebec on its weakeſt part, than he determined to riſk a battle ; and accordingly quitted his intrenched camp, and having collected his whole force from the ſide of Beauport, marched towards the Engliſh army, without delay.

General Wolfe, perceiving the enemy croſſing the river St. Charles, began to form his own line, which conſiſted of ſix battalions and the Louiſbourg grenadiers ; the right commanded by brigadier Monckton, and the left by brigadier Murray. Colonel Howe, who was juſt returned with his light infantry from taking a four-gun battery, was poſted in the rear of the left. M. de Montcalm advancing in ſuch a manner as ſhewed his intention was to flank the left of the Engliſh, briga-

dier

dier Townfhend was ordered thither with Amherft's regiment, which he formed *en potence*, prefenting a double front to the enemy : he was afterwards reinforced with two battalions, and the referve, confifting of one regiment, formed in eight fubdivifions, with large intervals, was pofted behind the right. The right wing of the enemy was compofed of half their colony troops, two battalions of regulars, and a body of Canadians and favages : their center confifted of a column formed by two other regular battalions; and their left of one battalion, with the reft of the colony troops : the bufhes and corn-fields in their front were lined with fifteen hundred of their beft markf-men, who kept up an irregular galling fire, which proved fatal to many brave officers, thus fingled out for deftruction. This fire was indeed in fome meafure checked by the advanced pofts of the Eng-lifh line, who picqueered with the enemy for fome hours before the battle began. Both armies were almoft entirely deftitute of artillery ; the French having only two pieces, and the Englifh two fix-pounders, which the feamen had with great diffi-culty drawn up from the landing-place ; but thefe were extremely well ferved, and galled their co-lumn feverely, obliging them to alter their dif-pofition.

About ten in the morning the enemy advanced brifkly to the charge in three columns, two of them inclining towards the left of our army, and the third to our right, firing obliquely at the two ex-

tremities

tremities of our line, from the diftance of one hundred and thirty yards, until they came within forty yards, which our troops withftood with the greateft intrepidity and firmnefs, referving their fire. This uncommon fteadinefs, together with the havock which the grape-fhot from our field-pieces made amongft them, threw them into fome diforder. The Englifh, who had been ordered to load with double-ball, now poured in a terrible difcharge, and continued their fire with fuch deliberation and fpirit, that the enemy immediately gave way, and fled with precipitation. General Wolfe himfelf was ftationed on the right, at the head of Bragg's regiment and the Louifbourg grenadiers, where the attack was warmeft, and ftanding confpicuous, in the very front of the line, had been aimed at by the enemy's markfmen, and at laft received a fhot in the wrift, which did not oblige him, however, to quit the field. Having wrapped an handkerchief round his arm, he continued giving orders without the leaft emotion, and advanced at the head of the grenadiers, with their bayonets fixed, when another ball unfortunately pierced the breaft of this young hero *, juft as the enemy gave

way,.

---

* When the general was carried off wounded to the rear of the front line, he defired thofe who were about him to lay him down ; being afked if he would have a furgeon ? he replied, " It is needlefs, it is all over with me." An officer prefent cried out, " They run, fee how they run." " Who run !" demanded our hero, with great earneftnefs, like a perfon roufed from fleep ? The officer anfwered, " The enemy, Sir, egad,

they

way, and victory was crowning all his labours with
fuccefs. General Monckton, the next in command,
fell immediately after, and was conveyed out of the
line. While the right and center of the front line
preffed on with their bayonets, the Highlanders with
their broad-fwords, fupported by the 58th regiment, fell on the enemy with irrefiftible impetuofity,
and drove them with great flaughter into the town,
and the works they had raifed at the bridge, over
the river St. Charles. The action was lefs violent
on the left and rear of the Englifh. Some of the
light-infantry had thrown themfelves into houfes,
where being attacked, they defended themfelves
with great courage and refolution, being fupported
by colonel Howe, who taking poft with two companies behind a fmall copfe, and frequently fallying
out on the flanks of the enemy during their attack,
often drove them into heaps, while brigadier
Townfhend advanced platoons againft their front;
fo that the right wing of the French was totally
prevented from executing their firft intention.
The brigadier himfelf remained with Amherft's regiment, to fupport this difpofition, and over-awe a
body of Indians pofted oppofite the light-infantry,

they give way every where." Whereupon the general rejoined,
" What do the cowards run already ? Go one of you, my lads,
to colonel Burton—tell him to march Webb's regiment with all
fpeed, down to Charles River, to cut off the retreat of the
fugitives from the bridge." Then turning on his fide, he
added, " Now, God be praifed, I will die in peace ;" and
thus expired.

waiting

waiting for an opportunity to fall on the rear of the English army.

'General Wolfe being flain, and general Monckton dangeroufly wounded, the command of courfe' devolved on general Townfhend, who, upon this information, haftened to the center, and formed the' troops again, that were fomewhat difordered in the purfuit, with all poffible expedition. He had fcarce performed this neceffary duty, before Monf. Bougainville, with a body of two thoufand frefh' men, appeared in the rear of the Englifh army. He had marched from Cape Rouge the moment he received advice that the Englifh troops had gained the Heights of Abraham ; but did not arrive time enough to have any fhare in the action.

General Townfhend immediately ordered two battalions, with two pieces of artillery, to advance a-gainft this officer; but he retiring among the woods and fwamps, the general prudently declined pur-fuing. He had already gained a complete victo-ry, taken a great number of French officers, and was in poffeffion of a very advantageous fituation, which it would have been highly imprudent to ha-zard for the fake of defeating Bougainville's de-tachment. Monf. de Montcalm was mortally wounded in the battle, and conveyed to a convent' of Auguftine nuns, about a mile from Quebec; from whence, before he died, he wrote a letter to general Townfhend, recommending the prifoners to' that generous humanity which diftinguifhes the
British

Britifh nation. Monf. de Senefergue, and Monf. de St.Ours, the two next in command, were alfo flain. About a thoufand of the enemy were made prifoners, including a great number of officers; and about eight hundred were killed in the action. The fhattered remains of their army, after having reinforced the garrifon of Quebec, retired to Point au-Tremble, from whence they continued their retreat to Jacques Quartier, where they remained intrenched till the feverity of the weather forced them to make the beft of their way to Trois Rivieres and Montreal.

This important victory, though gained at the expence of only fixty-one men killed, including nine officers; and of five-hundred and ninety-eight wounded, was dearly bought. The death of general Wolfe was a national lofs, and univerfally lamented: foldiers may be raifed, officers will be formed by experience, but the lofs of a genius in war is not eafily repaired. By nature formed for military greatnefs, his memory was retentive, his judgment deep, and his comprehenfion furprifingly quick, clear, and extenfive; his conftitutional courage not only uniform and daring, perhaps to an extreme, but he poffeffed alfo that higher fpecies of it, a ftrength, fteadinefs and activity of mind, which no difficulties or dangers could deter. Generous, gentle, friendly, affable, and humane, he was the pattern of the officer, and the darling of the foldier; his fublime genius foared above the pitch of ordinary minds; and had his faculties been

exercifed

exercifed to their full extent, by opportunities and
action, and his judgment been fully ripened by
age and experience, he would have rivalled the moft
celebrated heroes of antiquity.

General Townfhend employed his time, from the
day of action, in fecuring his camp with redoubts;
in making a road up the precipice for his cannon,
in getting up the artillery, in preparing batteries,
and cutting off the enemy's communication with
the country. _ And admiral Saunders, who had all
along co-operated heartily with the land forces for
the advantage of the fervice, on the feventeenth
day of the month failed up with his whole fleet,
in a difpofition to attack the lower town, while
the upper part fhould be affaulted by the general.
But at noon, the fame day, before any battery was
finifhed, a flag of truce was fent from the town,
with propofals of capitulation, which, after mature
confideration, were accepted and figned, by the
general and admiral, the next morning. By thefe
articles it was agreed, that the garrifon of the town
fhould march out with all the honours of war, and
be embarked for France as conveniently as poffible:
that the inhabitants fhould lay down their arms,
and be maintained in the poffeffion of their houfes,
goods, effects, and privileges; nor fhould be
molefted on account of their having bore arms
in defence of the town, as they had been forced to
it, and it was cuftomary for the inhabitants of the
colonies of both crowns to ferve as militia: that
the effects belonging to abfent officers fhould not
be

be touched : that the faid inhabitants fhould not be removed, nor compelled to quit their houfes, until their condition fhould be fettled by a treaty of peace between their moft Chriftian and Britannic Majefties : that the exercife of the Roman Catholic religion fhould be permitted ; and fafeguards granted to all religious houfes and perfons, as well as to the bifhop, who fhould be at liberty to excercife freely, and with decency, all the funcions of his office wherever he fhould think proper, till the poffeffion of Canada fhould be determined between their Britannic and moft Chriftian majefties : that the artillery and warlike ftores fhould be delivered up *bona fide*, and an inventory taken thereof : that the fick, wounded, commiffaries, chaplains, phyficians, furgeons and apothecaries, and other perfons employed in the hofpitals, fhould be treated according to the cartel fettled between the belligerant powers on the fixth day of February, 1759 : that before delivering up the gate and entrance of the town to the Englifh forces, their general fhould fend fome foldiers to be placed as fafe-guards at the churches, convents, and chief habitations : that the governor of the city fhould be permitted to fend advice to the Marquis de Vaudreuil, governor general, of the reducion of the town ; and alfo to be allowed to write to the French miniftry to inform them thereof : and, laftly, that the prefent capitulation fhould be duly and puncually executed, without being liable to non-execution, under pretence of reprifals, or the non-execution of any preceding capitulation.

The

Thus the capital of the French America was
furrendered to the Englifh upon honourable and
advantageous terms, after a moft fevere campaign
of three months ; and perhaps if the whole be
confidered, there never was an enterprize of fuch
difficulty carried on with more gallant perfeverance,
or accomplifhed with more vigour and ability. A
city, ftrong in its fituation and fortifications, was
to be attacked; an army, greatly fuperior to the
befiegers, was pofted near the walls of the city in an
impregnable fituation ; and that army was to be
forced to battle, againft the inclinations of a wife,
cautious commander. A theatre of more than five
leagues was to be filled, and operations of that extent were to be carried on, in the face of the fuperior
army, by fewer than feven thoufand men. In this
conteft, attended with fo many difficulties, it may
be faid with juftice, the natural genius of the commander fhewed itfelf fuperior to every thing. All
the difpofitions to that daring but judicious attempt
near Sillery, which at laft drew Montcalm from his
entrenchments, were fo many mafter-pieces in the
art of war. Yet notwithftanding the extraordinary
abilities of the general, thefe things could never
have been accomplifhed had not the marine co-operated with an unanimity, diligence, activity, and
fkill, which never could have taken place but from
that perfect love to their country, which animated
all concerned in the expedition.

Several circumftances concurred to induce the
general to grant fuch advantageous terms : the ene-

my were affembling in the rear of the Englifh army, the feafon was become wet, ftormy, and cold, threatening the troops with ficknefs, and the fleet with accidents; and befides, he confidered the advantage that would refult from taking poffeffion of the city while the walls were in a ftate of defence. Indeed the capitulation was a fortunate ftroke for the Englifh general, who afterwards received information from deferters, that the enemy had rallied, and were reinforced behind Cape Roufe, under Monfieur de Levy, arrived from Montreal for that purpofe, with two battalions of regulars; and that Monfieur de Bougainville, at the head of eight hundred men, with a convoy of provifions, was on his march to throw himfelf into the town on the eighteenth, the very morning on which it was furrendered: for the place was not then compleatly invefted, as the enemy had broke down their bridge of boats, and pofted detachments in very ftrong works on the other fide of the river St. Charles.

As foon as the capitulation was ratified, the Englifh troops took poffeffion of Quebec on the land fide, and guards were pofted in different parts of the town to preferve order and difcipline; at the fame time captain Pallifer, with a body of fea-men, entered the lower town, and took the fame precautions. The next day the prifoners, who were about a thoufand in number, were embarked on board tranfports for France: in the mean time, the inhabitants of the country came in great num-bers to deliver up their arms, and take the oath of

fidelity

fidelity to the English government; and a garrison of seven thousand men was placed in the city, under brigadier-general Murray, with plenty of provisions and ammunition. Soon after, the fleet set sail for England; fearing left the setting in of the frost should lock them up in the river St. Laurence during the whole winter.

The death of general Montcalm, which was doubtless an irreparable lofs to France, in all probability, overwhelmed the enemy with confternation, and confounded all their councils; as we cannot otherwise account for the tame surrender of Quebec, while the garrison had still a communication with their army, to an handful of troops, even after the victory they had gained; for though the place was not regularly fortified on the land fide, and moft of the houfes were in ruins, yet the walls and parapets had not fuftained the leaft damage: the befiegers were hardly fufficient to inveft it, entirely; a frefh army was affembled in the neighbood, with which their communication continued open; and the feafon was fo far advanced, that the Englifh forces muft foon have been obliged to defift by the feverity of the weather, and even retire, with their fleet, before the approach of winter, which always freezes up the river St. Laurence.

The city of Quebec * confifts of two towns, diftinguifhed by the High and Low Town: they are

separated

---

* Derived from *kep beis*, an old Algonquin expreffion, which fignifies *what is ftreight*, according to the French hiftorians,

who

separated from each other by a steep cliff, which is
a natural fortification to near two-thirds of the Upper Town, at the same time that it serves for a shel-
ter to the Lower Town from the keen, penetrating,
north-west winds. The buildings were in general
very good, until destroyed by our artillery during
the siege ; and consisted, besides dwelling-houses,
of several churches, colleges, convents, and other
public edifices, which in this city, as well as in the
rest of Canada, are built of a durable greyish stone,
whereof there is great plenty in this province. The
streets of the Higher Town are broad, but uneven,
running upon a declivity from the south, where
they are highest, to the north. Those of the Lower
Town are narrow, standing on a confined spot of
ground, which is commonly overflowed by the
tide to the foot of the precipice, and, by the retiring
of the waters, pointed out a place at the head of a
spacious and most delightful bason, commodious
in all respects for merchants to build on and inhabit
for the conveniency of trade, the tide rising here
eighteen feet and an half. The principal public
buildings were, the cathedral, of which only the
walls remain ; the bishop's palace ; the colleges of
the Jesuits and Recollects ; the convents of the Ur-
sulines, and Hotel de Dieu, with their churches ; a

advance, that the Aborigines first expressed themselves to that
effect, with admiration, upon their first discovering the streight,
formed in that part by Cape Diamond, and some eminencies
jutting into the river from the south shore.

seminary

feminary for the education of youth, almoft beat to pieces, with a neat chapel adjoining; a ftately unfinifhed houfe, for the Knights Hofpitallers; the intendant's magnificent palace, in the fuburbs of St. Roch; and the church of Notre Dame de la Victoire, in the Low Town, of which the walls only are ftanding*. According to report, there was a fine painting in this church, reprefenting a town in flames, with this infcription, " That in the year 1711, when this capital was threatened with a fiege by Walker and Hill, one of their pious women, pretending to be infpired, prognofticated, that this church, and the Lower Town, would be deftroyed by the Englifh in a conflagration, before the year of our Lord 1760; which made fo great an impreffion on all ranks of people, that they dedicated two days every year to fafting and worfhip, and implored the interceffion of their patronefs with the Almighty, to protect that church and city, from fire and fword." In the corner-houfes of the ftreets are niches in the walls, with ftatues as large as the life, of St. Jofeph, St. Urfula, St. Auguftine, and other faints, with the like figures in the fronts of their churches and religious houfes, which have an agreeable effect to the eyes of paffengers. The citadel, the refidence of the governor, fituated on the grand parade, a fpacious fquare, furrounded with fair buildings, is curioufly

---

* This church was built to commemorate the raifing the fiege of this city, when attacked by Sir William Phips, in 1694, who was obliged to retire with confiderable lofs.

erected

erected on the top of a precipice fouth of the epif-
copal palace, and overlooks the Lower Town and
bafon ; whence you have a moft delightful and extenfive profpect of the river downwards, and the
country on both fides. There is alfo another citadel on the fummit of Cape Diamond, with a few
guns mounted on it ; but excepting its commanding an extenfive view of the circumjacent country,
and of the Upper and Lower River, is in other refpects mean and contemptible. Moft of the other
public buildings make a ftriking appearance, particularly the intendant's fuperb palace, the Jefuits
college, Urfuline and Hotel de Dieu convents, and
the bifhop's palace, which, as well as the citadel,
being built of brick, and fituated on the top of the
precipice between the Higher and Lower towns,
fuffered very confiderably from our batteries during
the fiege.

On the right of the defcent leading to the Lower
Town ftands a ftately old houfe, faid to be the firft
built of ftone in this city ; and over the front door
is carved a dog, gnawing a large flefhy bone, with
the following whimfical infcription :

Je fuis le chien qui ronge l'os,
Sans en perdre un feul morceau :
Le temps viendra, qui n'eft pas venu,
Je mordrai celui, m'aura mordu.

Thus tranflated :

" I am the dog that gnaws the bone, without
lofing a fcrap of its meat. The time will arrive,

3   though

though it has not yet come, when I shall bite him who has bit me."

The first proprietor of this house was possessed of a plentiful fortune, which he, after many disappointments and losses in trade, had scraped together with the most indefatigable industry. Whether the foregoing device alluded to these particulars of his own private life; or whether the bone meant Canada, and the dog, the emblem of fidelity, the French settled there, as if determined faithfully to defend that colony against the savage natives, or the English, who may perhaps be alluded to by the two last lines of the inscription, is submitted to the more penetrating capacity of the curious reader.

The custom-house is also in the Low Town, where the collector is splendidly lodged, and, by its particular situation, is the only house in that quarter, which escaped being damaged by our shells during the siege.

The general hospital stands near a mile distant from the town, on the W. N. W. side, and is a stately building; it is agreeably situated on the south side of the river Charles, which meanders under its walls, and consists of a spacious dome, with two great wings, one fronting the north, the other the south. In this house is a convent of Augustine nuns, who have lands appropriated for their maintenance: these sisters, from religious motives, have assigned the principal parts of this dwelling for the reception of sick and wounded officers and sol-

K 4   diers,

diers, whom they attend with the greateſt humanity and tenderneſs. This hoſpital was endowed by the French king with a handſome ſalary, for the ſupporting of a phyſician, ſurgeon, and other neceſſary officers. The nuns perform every menial office about the ſick, with the ſame indifference that one man would attend another ; making it a point of conſcience ſo to do. Each patient has his bed, with curtains, allotted to him, and a nun to attend him. The beds are ranged in galleries on each ſide, with a ſufficient ſpace between each for a perſon to paſs : theſe galleries are ſcraped and ſwept every morning, and afterwards ſprinkled with vinegar ; ſo that ſtrangers are not ſenſible of the leaſt unſavoury ſcent in ſummer. The patients are allowed a kind of fan, to cool themſelves in ſultry weather, or to keep off the gnats, which at that ſeaſon, by reaſon of the vicinity of ſome marſhes, and the river Charles, are very troubleſome. Every officer has an apartment to himſelf. The nuns are courteous, rigidly reſerved, and very reſpectful : their dreſs conſiſts of a black gown, with a bib and apron ; a cloſe cap on their head, with a forehead-cloth down to their eyebrows ; their breaſts entirely covered ; their ſleeves are made ſo long as to reach almoſt to their wriſts ; their cloaths ſweep the ground ; on the top of the head is pinned a ſquare piece of black ſhalloon, which ſerves as a cloak, flowing careleſsly over their ſhoulders, below their waiſt : they wear a ſilver crucifix about three inches long, which hangs by a black ribbon from the neck to the girdle, and makes a very decent, grave appearance. In the

the south wing of the edifice is a superb church, and
in the other wing a neat chapel ; in both are several
images and Scripture paintings, as large as life :
that of St. Peter, in an attitude of contrition for
having denied his Master, is the best, and is truly
expressive. The altar of the church is sumptuously
gilded, with a tolerable painting behind it. Over
it is a large clumsy representation of God, carved in
wood, with a long grey beard, and flaxen hair,
cloathed in white, and surrounded with angels ; in
his right hand is a globe, his left points ungrace-
fully to something invisible to the spectator. The
altar-cloths and hangings are of curious needle-
work, wrought on silk in different colours, by the
nuns. The walls are wainscotted with oak to half
their height ; and the pannels painted in dark
shaded landscapes, representing the adjacent country. On the south side of the chancel is a pair of
large, folding, grated doors, before which the nuns
sit on benches one above another, as in the theatre,
to attend divine service. To the west of them are
two confessional boxes ; and over the west door a
very neat gallery for music, to which they ascend
by a pair of stairs, on the right and left of the entrance. On the north side of the church is a sa-
loon, with a curious monument, and an altar over
it, elegantly arched, and ornamented with small
figures of wax, personating our Saviour and the
Virgin Mary ; on each side are two images, one of
St. Augustine, the patron of this order, which is a
venerable figure, cloathed in purple and white,
bare-

bareheaded, and a long grey beard, with a flaming heart in his right hand, which feems to engrofs his attention; and a fmall book in his left. The other reprefents St. Charles, archbifhop of Milan, who liberally endowed this church and hofpital: he ftands upright, with his hands acrofs; and an open book laid upon them, which he feems to read very attentively; his filver hair flows down his fhoulders, and he is dreffed in fcarlet and white.

This monument is erected in memory of John, fecond bifhop of Canada, the principal founder of this charity, whofe epitaph, perhaps, may not be unacceptable to the inquifitive reader; we fhall therefore give a faithful tranflation of it.

EPITAPH *of the moft illuftrious, and moft reverend Father in God, meffire* * *John Baptift de la Croix, chevalier de St. Valier, fecond bifhop of Quebec, founder of this houfe.*

Grenoble was the place of his high birth,
His piety was in his infancy early confpicuous;
Engaged in the church, almoner to the king,
His merit fhone forth in that illuftrious employ,
Whilft, by his hands, Lewis diftributed his bounty.
His morals infpired the courtiers with wifdom:
His example moved many abbès of the court;
To him they owed their fincere return to God.
Far from being ambitious of court-favours or titles,
He perfevered in refufing a bifhopric in France,
Whofe mitre would have fat too light upon him;
Preferring that of Canada, on account of its feverity,

* A title of honour among the French, applied only to perfons of quality.

This

This mitre was made for the head of a faint,
Who, for its fake, chofe to encounter difficulties,
And came here, in fpite of billows, winds, and monfters,
To acquire it in the country of the fwarthy Americans,
Acrofs hundreds of fhelves of pointed rocks.
This mitre prefented itfelf, and pleafed his fancy:
The defire of fuffering made him accept of it,
And he croffed the boifterous feas in order to wear it.
Like a brilliant ftar in the prime of life,
He was feen to land in this favage country:
He came here fucceffor to the illuftrious Laval,
Apparently the rival of all his virtues;
He imitated his faith, his prudence, and zeal,
In many refpects, perhaps, he exceeded his pattern.
His ability for eftablifhing and maintaining good order,
Will ferve for an example to future prelates.
His majeftic air and venerable afpect;
Every thing was great and refpectable in him.
Bifhop of a country he had made choice of,
He bore, according to his wifh, the moft weighty croffes.
He fhewed on all occafions invincible courage,
And was infenfible to all earthly difafters.
A prifoner with the Englifh five years detained,
His virtue triumphed in his captivity.
In the greateft dangers a ftranger to fear;
His fole dread was that of infringing God's laws,
Of feeing them violated, of failing in his duty
Towards the flock, committed by Heaven to his care.
He loved his fheep dearer than his own life;
And for them all had the tendernefs of a father.
He omitted nothing for their increafe in holinefs.
He diftributed amongft them more than a million of livres,
Amiable charity formed his character:
Senfibly feeling for the miferies of the poor,
He always relieved them, Heaven feconding his endeavours;
Witnefs the three hofpitals, which he himfelf founded.
His heart burning with the moft ardent flame for God,
He lived and died employed in the converfion of fouls;

And

And religion is indebted to him for the progress
It has made in this country these forty-three years.
These virgins, to whom he was the tenderest father,
Preserve, as a treasure, his most precious ashes.
These ashes maintain the heavenly ardours,
Kindled in their hearts by their holy founder;
         And, when distracted,
Their souls make this tomb resound with their lamentations;
Groaning to think their father is no more.
These ashes tell them, that he lives in his virtues;
That he ought to be imitated; and their most delightful study
Should be to demonstrate their gratitude, by following his
         example:
That all he desired, in return for his bounties,
Was to see peace and holy fervour reign within this place.
Here reposes the model of holy prelates,
Whose uncommon piety was always matter of admiration.
By an hundred noble works he testified his zeal:
Three hospitals founded point out his great charity.
His genius, talents, and illustrious birth,
Must have procured him a bishopric in Old France.
His prince, who esteemed him, would have kept him there;
But, contemning pomp and human grandeur,
Mindful how vain they would one day appear,
He came to Canada, to encounter hardships.
During forty-three years, the faith, through his means,
Has made in this country a marvellous progress.
His love, his reverence, towards the Supreme Being,
His care and extreme affection for his flock,
Will for ever render him worthy of our regret.

Ye virgins, whom dying he made his legatees,
And trustees of his heart and his ashes,
Preserve tenderly this precious treasure:
Though he bequeathed you no large revenues,
      He left you a great example;
Infinitely more valuable than silver or gold.

Here lies the moſt illuſtrious prelate John Baptiſt de la Croix de St. Vallier, &c. &c. of Grénoble, moſt nobly deſcendéd ; firſt almöner to Lewis XIV. and afterwards ſecond biſhop of Canada : for piety and zeal, for ſouls, another Borromeo * ; for ſweetneſs of manners, and mildneſs of his government, a ſecond de Sales † : while he lived the father of the poor, he died -in the arms of the poor, to whom he had devoted himſelf and his whole fortune. He deſired to be laid in this hoſpital, founded by him with great trouble and expence. He breathed his laſt on the 28th of December 1727, in the ſeventy fifth year of his age, and forty-third of his epiſcopate. This monument was erected by the nuns of this religious houſe, in grateful remembrance of their moſt beloved father, and munificent founder. *May he reſt in peace.*

In this ſaloon lie alſo the remains of general Montcalm, to whoſe memory, by permiſſion of the Engliſh government, a monument was erected in 1761, with a Latin inſcription, by the academy of Belles Lettres at Paris, of which the following lines are a faithful tranſlation :

Here lieth,
In either hemiſphere to live for ever,
Louis Joſeph de Montcalm Gozon,
Marquis of St. Veran, baron of Gabriac,

---

* St. Francis de ſales, biſhop of Geneva, who was expelled that country by Calvin, the famous reformer.

† Called St. Charles, formerly archbiſhop of Milan.

Com-

Commandatory of the order of St. Louis,
Lieutenant-general of the armies of France;
Not lefs an excellent citizen than foldier,
Who knew no defire but that of true glory:
Happy in a natural genius, improved by literature,
Having gone through the feveral fteps of military honours
With uninterrupted luftre,
Skilled in every branch of military fcience,
The juncture of times, and the crifis of dangers.
In Italy, in Bohemia, in Germany,
An indefatigable general;
He fo difcharged his important trufts,
That he feemed always equal to ftill greater.
At length, grown bright with perils,
Sent to fecure the province of Canada,
With an handful of men,
He more than once repulfed the enemy's forces,
And made himfelf mafter of their forts,
Replete with troops and ammunition.
Inured to cold, hunger, watchings, and labour,
Unmindful of himfelf,
He had no fenfation but for his foldiers;
An enemy with the fierceft impetuofity,
A victor with the tendereft humanity.
Adverfe fortune he compenfated with valour,
The want of ftrength with fkill and activity;
And with his counfel and fupport,
For four years, protracted the impending fate of the colony,
Having by various artifices,
Long baffled a great army,
Headed by an expert and intrepid commander,
And a fleet furnifhed with all warlike ftores:
Compelled at length to an engagement,
He fell in the firft rank, in the firft onfet,
With thofe hopes of religion which he had always cherifhed,
To the inexpreffible lofs of his own army,
And not without the regret of the enemy's,
XIV. September, A. D. MDCCLIX, of his age XLVIII.

His

His weeping countrymen
Depoſited the remains of their excellent general
In a grave
Which a fallen bomb, in burſting, had excavated for him,
Recommending them to the generous faith of their enemies.

The chapel is ſmall, and extremely neat, free from all ſuperſtitious pageantry. Within the chancel ſtands a table with a green cloth over it, as in the church of England ; the walls are wainſcotted, and with the rails of the chancel, ſeats, and a compact gallery for ſingers, are painted an olive colour. Here, as well as in the church, are lamps burning both by day and night, according to the Romiſh cuſtom. But whatever deficiency, in point of ornament, may be in this chapel, is amply compenſated in that of the Urſulines within the city, where no art has been ſpared to render it throughout as oſtentatiouſly ſhowy and captivating as poſſible. This convent is dedicated to St. Urſula, whoſe deſcent the nuns have traced to Scotland. She is ſaid to have been killed by the Indians, while labouring for their converſion. In commemoration of this pious woman, and her martyrdom, her ſtatue is erected againſt the wall of the edifice, with an arrow transfixed through her breaſt.

The Hotel de Dieu is a ſpacious fair building, with an attic ſtory, and ſeems as if intended to be enlarged in the form of a ſquare: at preſent it conſiſts of two wings only, making a ſaliant angle. It was conſtructed, as appears by an inſcription, in the year 1639, at the ſole expence of Mary de Vigne-

not,

rot, dutchefs of Aiguillon, of whom there is a tolerable portrait on her knees, in a praying pofture.
This houfe is dedicated to St. Jofeph, the patron of
Canada. The fifters of this convent are in general
elderly women, lefs polite and complaifant than in
the other two nunneries, which may be attributed
to their remarkable aufterity. There is fuch a fame-
nefs in all the churches and chapels of the different
religious houfes, that a farther defcription of them
feems unneceffary.

The principal ftrength of Quebec confifts in its
lofty fituation: fhip-guns cannot have fufficient
elevation to do it any confiderable damage, and it is
too hazardous an undertaking for bomb-ketches to
attempt to deftroy it, becaufe they muft be expofed to a furious fire from the feveral batteries
erected above each other down to the water's edge;
and any fhips brought againft it muft run up with
the flood, ftand off and on until the tide of ebb,
and then retire. For thefe and other obvious reafons, the immortal Wolfe poffeffed himfelf of Point
Levi, on the fouth fide of the river, whence only
he could have cannonaded the town with fuch fuccefs.

The communications between the Low and
High Town, from their prodigious natural fteep-
nefs, are always difficult to be afcended, and were
refpectively defended (when the place furrendered)
by traverfes, batteries, and flank-fires, that fcoured
all thofe paffages, fo as to render them entirely inacceffible in cafe a defcent had been made below.
Befides

Besides these occasional flank-fires, to scour the
avenues throughout the city, its defences consisted
of twelve batteries, designed for an hundred and
fifty pieces of cannon, but did not mount above
one hundred and six ; the greatest number of them,
particularly that called Le Clerge en Barbette,
pointed to the bason and the south shore, to defend
the anchoring-ground, and the channel to the Upper River : these were mostly thirty-six pounders ;
the rest, except a few eighteen pounders, were
composed of twelves, and from that size downwards
to four and three pounders ; besides several mortars
of different calibres, lodged in various places, for
the annoyance of shipping. The'ramparts, or line
of fortification towards the country, consists of an
entire wall of masonry, of a modern construction,
and seems to be part of a design intended to be can-
non-proof : there are no batteries here, except a
few flank-fires about the works of St. Louis, St.
Jean Palais, and one or two other places. This
line of stone-work extends from the south-south-
west corner, behind the citadel of Cape Diamond,
to the north corner, near the lower road, leading
from the country to St. Roch, where, by the assistance of nature, it forms a strong angle, and runs
away in a long curtain eastward, excluding that
whole suburb to Port Palais, and a little beyond it ;
whence it terminates to the Low Town with the
dicing slope of the rock, and with no other defence
than a regular piquet-work on its summit, with
loop-holes for musketry, and two nine pounders
pointed to the strand, at the entrance of the Little

River. At the eaft end of the Upper Town is a wall of mafonry, which joins to the piquet-work before-mentioned on the north-eaft, and runs fouth; being intended to cover a fteep byeway leading to the fally-port from the Lower Town, and may be effectually protected by mufketry, as it is of a good height, with a foot-bank, fupported by fcaffolding, which gives fmall arms a great command over that quarter, the men being well covered from above. On the flank oppofite the fouth fhore, from the fouth-weft angle all round Cape Diamond, is another ftockade-work, that runs down to the dock-yard in the Low Town, with loop-holes for mufketry. There is no ditch round the town, nor any kind of outworks. The line of mafonry encompaffing the city on the weft, is revefted on the infide with a great body of earth, in which are two fpacious vaults, with fally-ports. At fome diftance, within the line, are a chain of redoubts of mafonry, extending from Cape Diamond down to the Hangman's Redoubt, which is near the ftrong angle before defcribed. Thefe were the antient limits of the city; and originally there was a common garden wall between each of the redoubts, for the defence of the town againft the incurfions of the Indians. The ground to the north-weft of Cape Diamond, within the walls, is high, and an excellent fpot whereon to erect grand batteries, which would range the adjacent country for a vaft extent, and even the Upper River, as far as Sillery. Upon the whole, it is in the power of art to render this

city

city as impregnable on the land fide, as it is naturally, by its fingular fituation, inacceffible towards
the river.

Nor were the Biitifh arms lefs fuccefsful in the
American iflands. A fquadron of nine fhips of the
line, under captain Hughes, with fixty tranfports,
containing fix regiments of foot, had failed from
England in the month of November 1758, for the
Weft-Indies, to reduce the French Caribbee iflands.
General Hopfon commanded the land forces, and
Commodore Moore, then in the Weft-Indies, was
to take the command of the fleet deftined for this
expedition, on its arrival at Barbadoes. The firft
object of their orders was Martinique, fituated about
twenty leagues north-weft of that ifland, the feat
of government, and the center of all the trade
which France carries on with thefe iflands; a place
extremely ftrong, both by nature and art; the
fhore, on every fide, indented with very deep bays,
called cul de facs, and the fands only difcoverable
at low-water, forming in many places a hidden and
almoft infurmountable barrier. A ridge of lofty
and almoft impaffable mountains runs north-weft
and fouth-eaft, quite through the ifland; and both
fides of the country are interfected at inconfiderable
diftances with deep gullies, through which, in the
rainy feafon, the water rufhes down with great impetuofity. In other refpects, the ifland is pleafant
and fruitful, well watered, well cultivated, and populous. The two principal places are St. Pierre
and Port Royal; both confiderable towns in this

part

part of the world, for their magnitude, trade, and ftrength.

From this fhort defcription, the reader will eafily conceive how defirable fuch a conqueft muft be, and the difficulties that naturally oppofed themfelves to it ; the greater, as at this time there was a confiderable number of regular troops in the ifland, which has a numerous and well difciplined militia, excellently adapted to the fervice of the country, and can bring into the field -a large body of negroes, accuftomed to arms, and, in general, well affected to the intereft of their mafters.

The men of war having filenced the batteries on fhore, and driven the enemy from their entrenchments, the forces were landed without oppofition on the weft fide of Port Royal harbour ; but the deep gullies, inclofed by fteep precipices, proved an infurmountable obftacle to the regular march of the troops, or the conveyance of artillery. The enemy had broken up the roads ; and the troops had to march five miles through fuch roads, and fuch an impaffable country, before the town of Port Royal could be attacked by land. General Hopfon, therefore, judged the difficulties on the land fide infurmountable, and commodore Moore declaring it was impoffible to land the cannon nearer to the fort, the forces were reimbarked on the next day after their landing.

As nothing could be done againft Port Royal, the fleet failed for St. Pierre, where, upon examining the coaft, new difficulties arofe ; and it was determined

termined in a council of war, at which both the principal land and fea officers affifted, that the fort could
not be reduced without fuch lofs to the troops and
fhips as would entirely difable them from profe-
cuting any further attempt: it was therefore agreed
to abandon their enterprize againft Martinique.
But though foiled in this their firft attempt, they
refolved not to return home with the difgrace of having done nothing worthy of the greatnefs of the armament; and confidering that the ifland of Guadaloupe, another of the Caribbees, lying at the diftance
of thirty leagues to the weftward, was an object
of almoft as much real confequence as Martinique,
though neither fo ftrongly fortified or garrifoned,
immediately failed to attack that ifland.

Guadaloupe is about fifteen leagues in length, and
twelve in breadth; and obtained its name from a chain
of mountains in Old Spain, fo called. To fpeak
with accuracy, it is rather to be confidered as two
iflands, divided from each other by a fmall arm of
the fea, not above three hundred feet over in the
wideft part. One of thefe iflands is called Grande
Terre, the other Guadaloupe; and are together in
circuit about ninety leagues. Grande Terre is almoft
deftitute of frefh water; but in Guadaloupe, not lefs
than fifty rivers empty themfelves into the fea, many of them navigable for boats nine miles up the
country, not to mention the numberlefs fprings
which rife among the rocks, and after a thoufand
beautiful meanders, lofe themfelves in the larger
ftreams. No place in all the Weft-Indies affords

L 3   more

more agreeable and romantic fcenes, being full of high mountains; one of which, that far overtops the reft, is a volcano, and produces confiderable quantities of fulphur. The ifland alfo contains hot-baths, of great ufe in medicine. The land in the vallies is extremely fertile, and produces the ufual Weft-Indian commodities, fugar, indigo, coffee, cotton, ginger, &c. and the mountains abound with game. The air is more temperate and falubrious than it is in general between the tropics, and the country populous and flourifhing. The government comprehends two fmaller iflands, viz. All Saints, and Defeada, which appear at a fmall diftance from the coaft, on the eaftern fide of the ifland.

The French began to fettle in this ifland as early as 1632. But, like their other colonies, this continued long in a languifhing condition, and did not emerge from its difficulties till after the peace of Utrecht, when France turned her attention ftrongly to thefe iflands. However, Guadaloupe partook lefs of its care than Martinique; and yet from its natural advantages, it does not fall fhort of that ifland, either in the quantity or quality of its produce. Hitherto the importance of this ifland was little known to England; the people of Guadaloupe being forbid, by an old regulation, to trade directly with Europe, and only allowed to fend their produce to Martinique, from whence they were fupplied with European commodities. Attempts had been made upon this ifland in 1691

and

and 1703; but the armaments being neither powerful enough, nor the operations conducted with sufficient abilities to produce any permanent effects,
our troops only laid waste the country, and retired
with their booty : but on the present occasion, we
were more able, strong, and successful.

On the 23d of January the fleet arrived before
the town of Baffe Terre, the capital of the island,
a place of considerable extent, large trade, and defended by a strong fort, which, in the opinion of the
chief engineer, was not to be reduced by the
ships. Notwithstanding which, commodore Moore
brought four ships of the line to bear against the
citadel; the reft of the fleet were disposed of so as
to act against the town, and the batteries which ob-
structed the landing. About nine in the morning
captain Trelawney, in the Lion, began the engagement, by attacking a battery of nine guns, and
the firing soon became general, and was continued,
with the utmost fury, until night, when the citadel,
and all the batteries, were effectually silenced.
During this cannonade the bombs, that were in-
cessantly thrown into the town in vast quantities,
set it on fire in several places; and the fire continued burning the whole of this and the following
day, when the town was almost wholly reduced to
ashes. In this sharp action, the loss on the side of
the English was very inconsiderable. The next
day the forces landed without opposition, and took
possession of the town and citadel. The island was,
however, far from being reduced; the country be-

ing

ing rugged, mountainous, and abounding with difficult and dangerous paffes and defiles ; and the inhabitants had retired with their armed flaves into
the mountains, determined to defend their poffeffions to the laft extremity.

General Hopfon died at Baffe-Terre, on the
27th of January, and was fucceeded in the command by general Barrington, who refolved to profecute the final reduction of the ifland with vigour,
and accordingly ordered part of the troops to embark for Grande Terre, under colonel Crump, who
attacked and reduced the towns of St. Ann and
St. Francois. Whilft this manœuvre diverted the
enemy's attention, the general himfelf attacked and
carried the ftrong poft of Gofier ; and thus Grande
Terre was in a manner reduced, and difabled from
fending any fupplies to Guadaloupe.

A great part of the enemy had retired to a confiderable mountain, not far from the town of Baffe
Terre, called Dos d'afne, or the Afs's Back ; a
poft of great ftrength and importance, as it commanded the town, and at the fame time formed the
only communication between it and the Capes-terre,
the moft level, pleafant, and fruitful part of the whole
ifland. It was judged impracticable to force a paffage into the Capes-terre, by this way, and all the
reft of Guadaloupe was in the poffeffion of the
French : a plan was therefore formed to furprize
Petit-bourg, Gonoyave, and St. Mary's, and from
thence to march into Capes-terre, the reduction of
which might be eafily accomplifhed. But this de-

2   fign

fign failing, it was neceffary to attempt thofe places by open force: accordingly, colonel Clavering and colonel Crump landed, with a detachment of fifteen hundred men, in a bay near Arnonville, without oppofition, and attacked the enemy, who were ftrongly intrenched at Le Corne, a place ftrong by nature, and of the utmoft importance, as it covered the whole country as far as the Bay of Mahaut, where provifions, and fupplies of all forts, were landed from the Dutch ifland of St. Euftatia. This poft, after a fhort difpute, was forced; another entrenchment, at Petit-bourg, met with the fame fate; and a third, near St. Mary's, was alfo carried. The troops having thus, at laft, penetrated into Capes-terre, the ifland capitulated on the 1ft of May, on the following terms: " The regular troops to be fent to Martinique, and allowed the ufual honours of war; and the inhabitants to be protected in their poffeffions, and in the free enjoyment of their civil and religious liberties." The capitulation was juft figned, when the French fquadron, commanded by M. Bompart, appeared off the ifland, and landed at St. Ann's, in Grande Terre, the general of the French Caribbee iflands, with fix hundred regular troops, a confiderable number of free-booters and negroes, with a large quantity of arms and ammunition; but finding that the ifland had capitulated, reimbarked his troops and ftores with all poffible expedition, and returned to Martinique. Had this reinforcement arrived a few hours fooner, in all probability, the

reduc-

reduction of Guadaloupe would have been found impracticable; the Englifh army having fuffered vaft lofs by ficknefs, from the intolerable heat of the climate. The fmall iflands near Guadaloupe, Defeada, Santos, Petite Terre, and Marigalante, furrendered a few days after, on the fame terms.

Thus this valuable ifland came into the poffeffion of Great-Britain, after a campaign of near three months, in which the Englifh troops perfevered with the utmoft firmnefs and courage. Continual fatigue, the air of an unaccuftomed climate, pofts ftrong by nature and art, defended by men who fought for every thing that was dear to them; all thefe difficulties only increafed the ardour of our forces, who thought nothing impoffible under commanders not more diftinguifhed for their intrepidity and military fkill, than their zeal for the fervice of their country, and the perfect harmony that fubfifted between them. It ought not to be omitted, to the honour of the inhabitants, that in general they exerted themfelves very gallantly in the defence of their country; Madame du Charmey, a confiderable planter, particularly diftinguifhed herfelf, heading her fervants and negroes, and acquitting herfelf in a manner not unworthy of the braveft foldier, in the defence of her property.

The

The CAMPAIGN of 1760.

A Strong fquadron of fhips was ftationed at Halifax, in Nova-Scotia, under the command of Lord Colville, an able and experienced officer, with inftructions to revifit Quebec in the fummer, as foon as the river St. Laurence fhould be navigable; and general Amherft, commander in chief of the forces in America, wintered in New-York, that he might be at hand to affemble his troops early in the fpring, and recommence his operations for the entire reduction of Canada. General Murray, who was left governor of Quebec, with a garrifon of feven thoufand men, neglected no ftep that could be taken by the moft vigilant and able officer, for the maintaining the important conqueft of Quebec, and fubduing all the Lower Canada, the inhabitants of which actually fubmitted, and took the oath of allegiance to the king of Great-Britain. He accordingly was no fooner fettled in his government, than he began repairing the ruins of the city, built eight redoubts of wood without the city, made foot-banks along the ramparts, opened embrafures, placed cannon, blocked up all the avenues of the fuburbs with a ftockade, caufed eleven months provifions to be carried up to the Higher Town, and formed a magazine of four thoufand fafcines. As foon as thefe, and feveral other neceffary labours were in fome meafure executed, he

fent

fent out two detachments to take poffeffion of St. Foix and Loretto, two pofts of great confequence, as they fecured eleven parifhes in the neighbourhood of the city. Another detachment, confifting of feveral hundred men, marched to St. Auguftine, brought off the enemy's advanced guard, with a great number of cattle, and difarmed the inhabitants. A third detachment of two hundred men, being fent to the other fide of the river, difarmed the inhabitants there alfo, and compelled them to take the oath of allegiance. By this ftep, the Englifh became mafters of the fouthern fide of the river St. Laurence, and were fupplied with good quantities of frefh provifions. During three whole months in the winter, the troops were employed in dragging wood for fuel into the city : this conftant hard labour, together with the exceffive cold, and the want of vegetables and frefh provifions, greatly diminifhed their number ; and before the end of April a thoufand foldiers were dead, and double that number rendered unfit for fervice.

In the mean time, the chevalier de Levis, the French general, got intelligence of the low ftate of the garrifon, and refolved to attempt carrying the city, in the depth of winter. In purfuance of this fcheme, he made all the neceffary preparations for this enterprize. His advanced pofts were eftablifhed at Point au Tremble, St. Auguftine, and Le Calvaire, and the main body of the army quartered between Trois Rivieres and Jaques Quartier. He alfo took poffeffion of Point Levi, where he formed

a ma-

a magazine of provifions, great part of which fell
into the hands of the Englifh; for as foon as the
river was frozen over, general Murray fent thither
a body of two hundred men, at whofe approach
the enemy abandoned their magazines, and retreated with precipitation; whilft the detachment
took poft in a church, until they could build two
wooden redoubts, and fortify them with artillery.
The enemy foon returning with a greater force, to
recover this poft, fome battalions, with the light
infantry, marched to cut off their communication;
but they fled in great confufion, and afterwards
took poft at St. Michael, a confiderable diftance
farther down the river. M. de Levis now refolved to defer the fiege of Quebec, that it might
be carried on in a more regular manner. He ordered the French fhips up the river to be rigged,
repaired the fmall craft, built gallies, caft bombs
and bullets, and prepared fafcines and gabions;
while general Murray employed his garrifon in
making preparations for a vigorous defence. He
fent out a detachment, which furprized the enemy's
pofts at St. Auguftine, Maifon Brulee, and Calvaire, where they took ninety prifoners. The light
infantry were ordered to poffefs themfelves of and
fortify Cape Rouge, to prevent the enemy's landing
at that place, and to be nearer at hand to obferve
their motions; but when the froft broke up, fo that
their fhips could pafs down the river, the enemy
landed near St. Auguftine.

The

The general, confidering Quebec as no other than a ftrong cantonment, had projected a plan of defence, by extending lines, and intrenching his troops on the Heights of Abraham, which, at the diftance of eight hundred paces, entirely command the ramparts of the city, and might have been defended by a fmall force againft a confiderable army. Neceffaries of all kinds for this work had been provided, and in the middle of April the general intended to execute the intended lines, but found it impracticable, as the earth was ftill covered with fnow in many places, and every where rendered impenetrable by the froft. Being informed, on the 26th at night, that the enemy had landed at Point au Tremble, to the number of fifteen thoufand, including five hundred Indians, he ordered all the bridges that lay in their way to be broke down, fecured the landing-places at Sillery and the Foulon, and next day marched out, at the head of the grenadiers of the army, five regiments, and the piquets for the garrifon, with ten fix pounders, to fuftain the light infantry and Rangers, who were already advanced, took poffeffion of an advantageous fituation, and thus defeated the fcheme which the French commander had formed for cutting off the Englifh pofts. Thefe being all withdrawn, the general, the fame afternoon, marched back to Quebec, with little or no lofs, though his rear was harraffed by the enemy.

Monf. de Levis and his army occupied the village and neighbourhood of St. Foy the following
night,

night, and his advanced pofts poffeffed the coppice
contiguous to the General Hofpital ; but early in
the morning of the 28th, the Englifh light troops
fallied out, and, with little difficulty, drove them
to a greater diftance. General Murray confidering, that though the enemy were greatly fuperior in
number, yet the Englifh forces were habituated to
victory, and were provided with a fine train of artillery, and that by fhutting them up at once within the walls of the city, he fhould rifk his whole
ftake on the fingle chance of defending an indifferent fortification ; a chance that could not be much
leffened by an action, though the event fhould
prove unfortunate, determined to hazard an engagement, and if unfuccefsful to defend the place to the
laft extremity ; then retreat to the Ifle of Orleans
or Coudres with the remains of the garrifon, and
there wait for a reinforcement.

In purfuance of this refolution, about feven
o'clock, he marched out to the Heights of Abraham with his little army, confifting of about three
thoufand one hundred and forty men, with eighteen
pieces of cannon, viz. ten twelve-pounders and fixteen fix-pounders, and two howitzers : the troops
alfo carried out their intrenching tools, the general's intention feeming to be to intrench his army,
and cover the town. Upon his arrival at thefe
Heights, he defcried the enemy's van on the eminencies of the woods of Syllery, and the bulk of
their army to the right, marching along the road
of

of St. Foy, inclining as they advanced, in order to conceal themfelves. On this difcovery, his line of battle being already formed, the troops were ordered to throw down their intrenching tools, and march forward; this being judged the decifive moment to attack the enemy, in hopes of reaping every advantage that could. be expected over an army not yet thoroughly arranged. The Englifh troops accordingly advanced with the greateft alacrity; the right wing, commanded by colonel Burton, confifted of the fortieth regiment, the eighteenth, and the fecond battalion of Royal Americans; the left, under colonel Frafer, was formed of the twenty-eighth and feventy-eighth regiments, with the Highlanders; the fifty eighth was the right center corps; and the forty-third, the left center, was commanded by colonel James; the fecond line was compofed of the thirty-fifth, and the third battalion of Royal Americans, drawn up two deep, to appear more numerous; major Dalling's corps of light infantry covered the right flank; the left was fecured by captain Hazen's company of Rangers, and an hundred volunteers, commanded by captain Macdonald; the artillery were placed occafionally in front, in the intervals, or on the flanks, as circumftances required, under the command of major Godwin, affifted by major M'Kellar, the principal engineer. The field-pieces were extremely well ferved, and did amazing execution; and as foon as the army came within reach

were

of mufketry, the light infantry attacked the French, grenadiers on the left of their army, and routed them. At the fame inftant, the volunteers and Rangers engaged their right, repulfed them in like manner, and poffeffed themfelves of a redoubt oc-cupied before by the enemy. Their center-pofts, feeing their right and left give way, fled without firing a fhot. Whilft the Englifh troops gained this advantage over their van, the main body of the French army advanced with great expedition, compleatly formed in columns, in fpite of the ut-moft efforts of the Englifh. One of thefe columns came, without lofs of time, to fuftain their flying grenadiers, now purfued by the Englifh light infan-try, who being overpowered, were obliged, with great lofs, to retire to the rear, and were of little fervice af-terwards; the enemy profiting thereby, inftantly wheeled round fome rifing grounds, and charged the right wing of the Englifh army vigoroufly in flank; while Monf. de Levis, with another divi-fion, made a like movement on the left, and then the action became obftinate on both fides. General Murray immediately ordered the thirty-fifth regi-ment from the fecond line, to fupport the right wing; and the third battalion of Royal Ame-ricans to fupport the left, who acquitted them-felves with great honour. Quebec being the grand object, the enemy feemed regardlefs of the center of the Englifh army, hoping, if they could outflank the wings, they fhould be able to get between

Vol. II.   M   the

the Englifh army and the city. With this view, they fuftained their right and left wings with frefh reinforcements ; and fortune, at length, inclined to the more numerous army. The enemy poffeffed themfelves of two redoubts on the left of the Englifh army, which gave them a great advantage ; but by an excellent movement of the forty-third regiment, ordered by colonel James, from the center, to fupport the third battalion of Royal Americans on the left ; both thefe corps made a vigorous effort to recover thofe works, and fucceeded ; but at laft being reduced to an handful, were compelled to yield to fuperior numbers. In the courfe of the action, the Englifh were infenfibly drawn from their advantageous fituation into low fwampy ground, where the men fought almoft knee-deep in melted fnow : under thefe unhappy circumftances, it was impracticable to draw off the artillery, and after having performed prodigies of valour, our enfeebled army, having the whole force of the country to contend with, and its communication with the town being in danger of being intercepted, after an engagement of two hours, was obliged to give up the conteft. The troops were accordingly ordered to fall back, a command they were hitherto unacquainted with : the retreat was conducted with great regularity, and the enemy did not purfue with the fpirit which the importance of their victory required, having been very roughly handled. Tho' the Englifh had eleven hundred, of all ranks,

i   killed,

killed, wounded, and made prifoners, and loft the greateft part of their artillery : the French, whofe loffes fell moftly upon the flower of their army, loft double that number, and reaped no effential advantage from their victory.

General Murray, far from being difpirited by his defeat, as foon as he retired within the walls of Quebec, profecuted the repairs of the fortifications, which had been interrupted by the feverity of the winter; and the foldiers exerted themfelves with incredible alacrity, not only in labouring at the works, but alfo in the defence of the town, before which the enemy had opened trenches on the very evening of the battle. Their fleet, confifting of three fhips, anchored at Foulon by Sillery, below their camp, and for feveral days their boats were employed in landing ftores, artillery, and provifions. Mean while they worked inceffantly at their trenches before the town, and on the 11th of May opened one bomb battery, and three batteries of cannon. The garrifon made the neceffary difpofitions to defend the place to the laft extremity, two cavaliers were raifed, fome outworks contrived, and one hundred and thirty-two pieces of artillery were placed on the ramparts, moftly dragged there by the foldiery. Though the enemy cannonaded the place brifkly the firft day, their fire foon flackened, and their batteries were, in a manner, filenced by the fuperior fire of the garrifon; yet, notwithftanding this formidable artillery, had a French fleet from Europe appeared

M 2   firft

firſt in the river St, Laurence, in all probability Quebec would have reverted to its former owners,

Lord Colvil had ſailed from Halifax, with the fleet under his command, on the 22d of April; but was retarded in his paſſage by thick fogs, contrary winds, and great ſhoals of ice floating down the river, Commodore Swanton, who had ſailed from England with a ſmall reinforcement, arrived in the beginning of May with two ſhips at the iſle of Bic, in the river St. Laurence, where he propoſed to wait for the reſt of his ſquadron, which had been ſeparated from him in his paſſage; but one of theſe, the Leoſtoffe, commanded by captain Dean, had entered the harbour of Quebec, on the 9th of May, and acquainted the governor that the Engliſh fleet was at hand. And the commodore no ſooner received intelligence that Quebec was beſieged, than he ſailed up the river with all poſſible expedition, and on the 15th, in the evening, anchored above Point Levi.

The governor expreſſing an earneſt deſire that the French ſquadron, above the town, might be removed, commodore Swanton in the Vanguard, with the frigates, worked up with the tide of flood, early in the morning of the 16th, to attack the French ſquadron. At firſt Mr. Vauguelin, the French commodore, ſhewed an appearance of engaging, but ſoon made off: the Pomona was forced on the rocks above Cape Diamond, and burnt; the reſt were purſued: the Atalanta was drove aſhore near Point au Tremble about ten

leagues

leagues above the town, and fet on fire ; and the remainder were all taken or deftroyed, except La Marie, a fmall floop of war, which threw her guns over-board, and efcaped to St. Peter's Lake, above Trois Rivieres, After having performed this notable fervice, the commodore fell down to the channel off Sillery, and enfiladed the right flank of the enemy's trenches for feveral hours fo warmly, that between his fire, and that of the garrifon, they were entirely driven from their works. The French general fent a party, with two field-pieces, to play upon the Vanguard, but without any effect; for by the fhip's fheering in the current, fhe brought fome of her guns to bear on thofe of the enemy, and obliged them to retire.

This difafter, and the arrival of a ftrong Englifh fleet in the river St. Laurence, fo difpirited the enemy, that in the following night they raifed the fiege, and retreated with great precipitation, leaving behind them their artillery, ammunition, camp-equipage, implements, and provifions. As foon as the governor received this intelligence, he ordered the batteries to fire _a ricochet_, in hopes the fhot might over-take them in their flight, and fcour the circumjacent country*, and marched him-

* This method of firing is by elevating the guns at leaft ten degrees above their level, fo that the fhot may bound and roll after they ftrike. This is a very advantageous invention, and is afcribed to marfhal-Vauban; for guns are loaded with a fmaller quantity of powder, and confequently lefs damaged.

M 3   felf

felf, at the head of his forces, in purfuit of them; but they had paffed the river at Cape Rouge, before he could come up with their rear: however, he took fome prifoners, and a great quantity of baggage. The enemy, who had fuftained great lofs during the fiege, having one hundred and fifty-two officers killed and wounded, now retired as expeditioufly as poffible to Jaques Cartier, where they were abandoned by the greateft part of the Canadians, and having loft all hopes of fucceeding againft Quebec, began to take proper meafures for the prefervation of Montreal, againft which general Amherft, notwithftanding all his difappointments, was now meditating an expedition.

At this place Mr. de Vaudreuil, governor-general of Canada, fixed his head-quarters, and propofed to make his laft ftand againft the efforts of the Englifh general. He not only levied troops, collected magazines, and erected new fortifications in the ifland of Montreal, but even had recourfe to feigned intelligence, and other delufive arts, to fupport the fpirit of the Canadians, and their Indian allies, and acted with the fpirit and forefight of an able and experienced general, determined to exert himfelf to the utmoft for the prefervation of the colony, even though very little profpect of fuccefs remained. His hopes, fmall as they were, were founded on the natural ftrength of the country, almoft inacceffible to an army by woods, mountains, and moraffes, which might retard the progrefs of the Englifh, and, perhaps, protract the

war

war until a general pacification. In the mean time general Amherft conveyed inftructions to governor Murray, to advance by water towards Montreal, with all the troops that could be fpared from the garrifon of Quebec, and detached colonel Haviland with a body of troops from Crown Point, to take poffeffion of the ifle Aux Noix, in the Lake Champlain, and from thence penetrate the neareft way to the river St. Laurence; while he himfelf, with the main body of the army, amounting to about ten thoufand men, including Indians, proceeded from the frontiers of New York, by the rivers of the Mohawks and Oneida, to the Lake Ontario, and fell down the river St. Laurence to the ifland of Montreal: by thefe means he propofed to hem in, and entirely furround the enemy. In purfuance of this plan, two armed floops were provided to cruize on the Lake Ontario, under the command of captain Loring, as well as a great number of battoes for the tranfportation of the troops, artillery, ftores, baggage, and provifions; feveral regiments were ordered to proceed from Albany to Ofwego; and the general leaving Schenectady in the latter end of June, arrived there himfelf on the ninth of July with the remainder of the forces.

Two French veffels having appeared off Ofwego, fome battoes were difpatched to Niagara, to inform captain Loring thereof, who immediately failed in queft of them; but they efcaped his purfuit, though they had been twice

M 4 feen

seen in the neighbourhood of Oswego since the arrival of the general, who endeavoured to amuse them by sending battoes to different parts of the lake. The army being assembled, and joined by upwards of thirteen hundred Indians under Sir William Johnson, colonel Háldimand was detached with the grenadiers, the light infantry, and a battalion of Highlanders, to take post at the bottom of the lake, and assist the armed vessels in finding a passage to La Galette. On the tenth of August the army embarked on board battoes and whale boats, and proceeded towards the source of the river St. Laurence. Learning that one of the enemy's vessels had run aground, and was disabled, and that the other lay off La Galette, he determined to make the best of his way down to Sweegatchie, and attack the French fort of Isle Royale, farther down the river St. Laurence, the source of which it in a great measure commands. On the 17th the row-gallies fell in with the French sloop commanded by Mr. de Broquerie, which struck, after a warm engagement. The general having detached some engineers to reconnoitre the coasts and islands near L'Isle Royale, made a disposition for the attack of that fort, which was accordingly invested, after he had possessed himself of the islands. Some of these, viz. the islands Galot and Picquet, the enemy abandoned with such precipitation, as to leave behind a number of scalps they had taken on the Mohawk River, two swivel guns, a quantity of tools and utensils, iron, and some barrels of pitch.

3 ·   The

The Indians were fo exafperated at finding the fcalps, that they fired all the houfes, not fparing even the chapel. Batteries being erected on the neareft iflands, within fix hundred yards of the fort, it was cannonaded not only by them, but by the armed floops, which had anchored before it, and a difpofition made for making an affault, when the governor, Mr. Pouchot, beat a parley, and furrendered the fort.: the garrifon, confifting of near three hundred men, were made prifoners of war. The enemy, during the fiege, had a lieutenant of marines, with twelve men, killed, and thirteen wounded. The whole lofs on the fide of the befiegers, was twenty-one men killed, and twenty-three wounded. The fort mounted twelve twelve pounders, two eight pounders, two fix pounders, thirteen four pounders, four brafs fix pounders, and four of one pound each. The general finding the fort well fituated for commanding Lake Ontario and the Mohawk River, employed fome days in repairing the fortifications; and placed a garrifon in it of two hundred men, under the command of captain Ofborne.

Fort Levis or L'Ifle Royale, as has been obferved, is very advantageoufly fituated: the ifland is fmall, and entirely comprehended within the works, which are carried on in the fame irregular manner as nature has formed the infulary fhores about it; but the area of the fort is a regular fquare, within four baftions only, which feems to have been the firft intention on fortifying the
ifland;

ifland; fo that, in all appearance, the other defences have been occafionally added, to render the
place more refpectable, and cut off our communication with Montreal, to which it is an excellent
barrier. The country, north and fouth, inhabited
chiefly by Indians, is level, rich, and capable of
great-improvements, which, with the uncommon
fertility of the adjacent iflands, producing Indian
and other corn in great plenty, and the profpect of
an immenfe fur trade, induced the government of.
Canada to eftablifh a ftrong fettlement in this diftrict.

·From this place the navigation down the river
St. Laurence was extremely difficult and dangerous, owing to a great number of violent rapids
and falls; among which forty-fix battoes, feventeen whale-boats, a row-galley, and above fourfcore
men, with fome artillery, ftores, and ammunition,
were loft. At length, after a tedious, fatiguing, dangerous voyage, of two months and feventeen days,
fince their departure from Sheneсtady, on the
6th of September the troops were landed on the
ifland of Montreal, without oppofition, except from
fome flying parties, which exchanged a few fhot,
and then retired with precipitation. The fame day,
the general repaired a bridge which the French had
broke down in their retreat, and, after marching
two leagues, formed his army on a plain before the
city of Montreal, where they lay all night on their
arms, the advanced centries being doubled; and
the fame precautions were taken at La Chine, the
place

place where the troops landed, and where a strong body of forces had been left to guard the battoes, &c.

Immediate orders were issued for some pieces of artillery to be brought up from La Chine. General Amherst being determined to commence the siege in form, without the least delay; but in the morning of the seventh, the marquis de Vaudreuil sent two officers, to demand a capitulation; which, after some letters had passed between the two generals, was granted, upon favourable terms, considering that they were hemmed in on all sides. General Murray, with the troops from Quebec, who in his passage had disposed the inhabitants of the south shore of the river St. Laurence to submit, and deliver up their arms, having burned the village of Sorel, the inhabitants of which were in arms; lord Rollo, with the reinforcement from Louisfbourg, made himself master of Trois Rivieres, without opposition, disarmed the inhabitants on the north side, and obliged them to take the oath of neutrality, had by this time both landed on the island of Theresa; and colonel Haviland, with the corps under his command, who had sailed from Crown-Point on the 11th of August, without meeting the least opposition, till he came to Isle aux Noix, which, as soon as he had, broke ground and erected batteries, the enemy abandoned, as well as Fort Chambley, and every other post in proportion as he advanced, until he reached Longeil, on the south side of the river, opposite to Montreal, where he arrived also at

the

the next day. This critical junction of our three armies, effected in the space of forty-eight hours, was a circumstance equally favourable and furprizing, if we reflect on the different routs they purfued through an enemy's country, where they had no intelligence of each other's motions, the immenfe difficulties they had to encounter every where, from a numerous and wary enemy, ftill infinitely heightened by the fingular nature of the country, and the danger of an unknown navigation. All Canada now furrendered, on condition of preferving their civil and religious liberties, and properties. As foon as the capitulation was figned, colonel Haldimand took poffeffion of Montreal with the grenadiers and the light-infantry, and brought off in triumph the colours of Shirley's and Pepperel's regiments, that had been taken at Ofwego, and depofited here as trophies. Brigadier-general Gage was appointed governor of the place, with a garrifon of two thoufand men ; and general Murray returned to Quebec, where the garrifon was augmented to four thoufand. The mild, though determined method, which general Amherft purfued in negociating with the marquis Vaudreuil, does him great honour ; while his moderation and humanity, to an ungenerous enemy, reflects the greateft reproach on them for their paft cruelties, and repeated breaches of faith, adds a tenfold luftre to his conqueft, proclaiming him the *hero* and *Chriftian*, and demonftrates to the whole world, the truth of what was fo fenfibly advanced by the
immor-

Immortal Wolfe, in his firft manifefto. " The unparalelled barbarities exerted by the French in America, might juftify the bittereft revenge; but Britons breathe higher fentiments of humanity, and liften to the merciful dictates of the Chriftian religion."

Montreal, fituated on the ifland of that name, the fecond place in Canada, for extent, buildings, and ftrength, befides poffeffing the advantages of a lefs rigorous climate, for delightfulnefs of fituation, is infinitely preferable to Quebec. It ftands on the fide of a hill, floping down to the river with the fouth country, and many gentlemen's feats thereon, together with the ifland of St. Helen, all in front; which form a charming landfcape, the river St. Laurence here being about two miles acrofs. Though the city is not very broad from north to fouth, it covers a great length of ground from eaft to weft, and is nearly as large and populous as Quebec. The ftreets are regular, forming an oblong fquare; the houfes well built, and in particular the public buildings, which far exceed thofe of the capital in beauty and commodioufnefs; the refidence of the Knights Hofpitallers being extremely magnificent. There are feveral gardens within the walls, in which, however, the proprietors have confulted ufe more than elegance: particularly thofe of the Sifters of the Congrègation, the Nunnery Hofpital, the Recollects, Jefuits, feminary, and governor. Befides thefe, there are many other gardens and beautiful plantations without the gates; as the garden of the

General

General Hofpital, and the improvements of Mr.
Liniere, which exceed all the reft, and are at an
agreeable diftance on the north fide of the town.
The three churches and religious houfes are plain,
and contain no paintings, nor any thing remarkably
curious, but carry the appearance of the utmoft
neatnefs and fimplicity. The city has fix or
feven gates, large and fmall; but its fortifications are mean and inconfiderable, being encompaffed by a flight wall of mafonry, folely calculated
to awe the numerous tribes of Indians, who reforted
here at all times from the moft diftant parts, for the
fake of traffic, particularly at the fair held here
every year, which continued from the beginning of
June till the latter end of Auguft, when many folemnities were obferved, and the governor affifted,
and guards were placed to preferve good order, in
fuch a concourfe of fo great a variety of favage
nations. There are no batteries on the walls, except for flank fires, and moft of thefe are blinded
with planks and loop-holes, made at the embrafures
for mufketry. Some writers have reprefented thefe
walls to be four feet in thicknefs, but they are miftaken : they are built of ftone, the parapet of the
curtains does not exceed twenty inches, and the
mertins, at the flank-fires, are fomewhat thicker,
though not near three feet. A dry ditch furrounds
this wall, about feven feet deep, encompaffed with
a regular glacis.

On the infide of the town is a cavalier, on an ar-
tificial eminence, with a parapet of logs or fquared
timbers,

timbers, and fix or eight old guns, called the citadel. Such were the fortifications of Montreal, the
fecond place of confequence in Canada, until the
enemy raifed the fiege of Quebec; and then, in
expectation that the Englifh forces would follow
them, a battery was erected, with two faces for nine
guns, but had only four twelve-pounders mounted,
two pointing to the navigation of the river, and the
others to the road leading from Long-Point to the
town, with a traverfe for mufketry, elevated on the
infide of the battery, for the defence thereof, together with fome piquet-works, forming a barrier
to the entrance of the place, with loop-holes for
their markfmen; and thefe, with two advanced
redoubts, were all the temporary works made
for its defence. The inhabitants, in number
about five thoufand, are gay and lively, more attached to drefs and finery than thofe of Quebec;
and from the number of filk facks, laced coats, and
powdered heads that are conftantly feen in the
ftreets, a ftranger would imagine, that Montreal
was wholly inhabited by people of independent fortunes. By the fituation of the place, the inhabitants are extremely well fupplied with all kinds of
river fifh; fome of which are unknown to Europeans, being peculiar to the lakes and rivers of this
country. They have likewife plenty of black cattle, horfes, hogs, and poultry: the neighbouring fhores fupply them with a great variety of
game in the different feafons; and the ifland
abounds

abounds with well tafted foft fprings, which form a multitude of pleafant rivulets.

The ifland of Montreal itfelf is near forty miles in length, and about thirteen in breadth, where wideft. The foil is exceedingly rich and good, producing all kinds of European grain and vegetables, in great abundance, with variety of garden fruits. The fouth fide is the moft inhabited, of courfe beft cultivated ; and befides the fettlements, which are numerous, the ifland is adorned with villas, for the retirement of the more wealthy merchants during the fummer feafon. No Indians are fettled here ; nor are, they fond of fettling on iflands, from an hereditary diftruft left they fhould be cut off by the Europeans. The religious community of St. Sulpice, at Paris, were proprietors of this ifland, which they had by grant from the crown, and which produced them a confiderable revenue.

The French miniftry had made an attempt to fuccour Montreal, by fending in the fpring a confiderable number of tranfports, laden with ftores, under the convoy of fix frigates : three of thefe were taken in the Englifh Channel ; but the reft which efcaped learning, that the Englifh fquadron had failed up the river St. Laurence, took fhelter in the Bay of Chaleur, on the coaft of Acadia, from whence they immediately difpatched an exprefs by land to Montreal, for orders from M. Vaudreuil. Captain Byron, who commanded the fhips of war that were left at

Louif-

Louisbourg, having received intelligence of them from brigadier Whitmore, governor of Louisbourg, failed thither with his squadron*, and found them lying at anchor. The whole French fleet confisted of the Machault, a frigate of thirty-two guns, Le Bienfaisant of twelve guns, pierced for thirty, the Marquis de Malo's of sixteen guns, and nineteen small vessels, which were all deftroyed, together with two batteries that had been raised for their protection, and sixty-seven English prisoners released, who had been taken by this fleet in small vessels bound for Quebec. The French town, consisting of two hundred houses, was also demolished, and the settlement totally ruined.

All the French subjects inhabiting the territories from the Bay of Fundy to the banks of the river St. Laurence, and all the Indians throughout that tract of country, were now subjected to the English government. In the month of December the preceding year, the French colonists of Miramichi, Rickebuctou, and other places along the gulph of St. Laurence, made their submission, by deputies, to colonel Frye, who commanded in Fort Cumberland, at Chignecto. They afterwards renewed this submission in the most formal manner, by subscribing articles, by which they obliged themselves, and the people whom they represented, to repair in the

* The Fame of seventy-nine guns, Dorsetshire seventy, Achilles sixty, Repulfe thirty-two, and the Scarborough twenty. The channel being difficult, and little water, the large ships could not possibly reach higher than the first battery.

spring to Bay Verte, with all their effects and shipping, to be disposed of according to the direction of colonel Laurence, governor of Halifax in Nova-Scotia. They were accompanied by two Indian chiefs of the Micmack nation, a powerful and numerous tribe, now become intirely dependent on his Britannic majesty.

The CAMPAIGN of 1762.

THE French being thus expelled from all their settlements on the continent of North-America, except that of Louisiana, bordering on the river Mississippi, which was deemed an object of little or no importance, it was resolved, towards the close of the last year, to transfer the seat of war to the French islands in the West-Indies, against which nothing had been attempted since the reduction of Guadaloupe, except that in the month of June last, the neutral island of Dominica, which the French had settled, was reduced by a small detachment from Guadaloupe, and four ships of the line, with a few frigates, in the following mannner: On the first appearance of the English squadron off Roseau, two deputies came off in order to treat of surrendering; but their first fears subsiding, the inhabitants refused to submit, and manned their intrenchments. The ships immediately anchored close to the shore; the troops landed in the evening,

ing, and formed on the beach, under the fire of the
squadron. : Lord Rollo, seeing the forces galled by
an irregular fire from trees and bushes, considering
that the intrenchments commanded the town, which
he had already taken possession of; that the country was naturally strong, and the enemy might be
reinforced before morning, resolved to attack their
intrenchments, without delay; which was immediately executed with such vigour and success, that
the enemy were soon driven from all their batteries
and intrenchments, and Mr. Longprie, the governor, with some other officers, were taken at their
head-quarters. Next day the inhabitants delivered
up their arms, and took the oath of allegiance to
his Britannic majesty.

The miscarriage of the former expedition a-
gainst Martinique, did not discourage the English ministry from making it the object of
another attempt. A strong squadron was accordingly equipped, under rear-admiral Rodney,
which sailed from Spithead in the month of
October, 1761, with a number of transports,
on board of which were four battalions from
Belleisle, which were to be joined at Barbadoes
by eleven battalions from New-York, together
with some regiments and volunteers from the Leeward Islands; so that the whole of the land-forces
did not fall much short of twelve thousand men,
the chief command of whom was vested in general
Monckton, who had acquired so much reputation
in North-America.

The

The English fleet, which now confided. of eighteen ships of the line, besides frigates, bomb-veſſels, &c. (having been reinforced by the ſquadron on the Barbadoes ſtation) anchored in St. Ann's Bay, on the eaſtern ſide of the iſland, on the 8th of January, after ſilencing ſome batteries which the enemy had erected on that part of the coaſt. In the courſe of this ſervice, the Raiſonable, a ſhip of the line, was by the ignorance of the pilot loſt, upon a reef of rocks, though the men were ſaved, toge-ther with her ſtores and guns. The general, however, judging this an improper place for diſembarkation, the troops were landed on the 16th, at a creek called Caſ-navire, without the loſs of a man ; the fleet having been diſpoſed ſo properly, and having directed their fire with ſuch effect, that the enemy was obliged, in a ſhort time, to abandon the batteries that had been erected to defend this inlet. The troops being landed, and reinforced with two battalions of ma-rines from the ſquadron, the general reſolved to beſiege the town of Fort Royal ; but, in order to make his approaches, he found it neceſſary to at-tack Morne Tortenſon and Morne Garnier, two conſiderable eminencies, which commanded the town and citadel, and were protected, like the other high grounds in this iſland, with very deep ravines, and this great natural ſtrength improved by every contrivance of art. Morne Tortenſon was firſt to be attacked. To favour this operation, a body of regular troops and marines were ordered to ad-vance on the right along the ſea-ſide, towards the town, in order to take poffeffion of the redoubts which lay in the lower grounds. A thoufand feamen, in flat-bottomed boats, were to row clofe in fhore, to affift them in their enterprize ; and the light in-fantry, fupported by the brigade of Walfh, was to advance on the left towards the country, and if pof-fible to turn the enemy, whilft the grenadiers and the body of the army attacked their center, under the fire of the batteries, which had been erected on the oppofite fide, with great labour and perfe-verance, the cannon having been dragged upwards of three miles by the feamen. Thefe judicious difpofitions were executed with fpirit and refolution : the attack fucceeded in every quarter, and the enemy's works were fucceffively carried, until, af-ter a fharp conteft, the Englifh troops remained mafters of the whole eminence ; fome of the ene-my efcaping into the town, to the very gates of which they were purfued, and the reft to Morne Garnier, which was as ftrong and much higher than Morne Tortenfon, and of courfe commanded it.

Thus far the operations had proved fuccefsful; but nothing could be done decifive without the poffef-fion of the other eminence, our troops being much molefted by the enemy from that fuperior fituation. Whilft proper difpofitions were making for the at-tack of Morne Garnier, the enemy's whole force def-cended from that eminence, and attacked the Eng-lifh advanced pofts, but they were immediately re-pulfed ; and the ardour of the Englifh troops was

fo

fo great, that they improved a defenfive advantage into an attack, paffed the ravine with the fugitives, fcaled the hill, feized the batteries, and polted themfelves on the fummit of Morne Garnier; the French regular troops efcaping into the town, and the militia difperfing themfelves in the country. Thefe fignal fucceffes were obtained at the fmall expence of four hundred men, including a few officers, killed and wounded, in the different attacks; but the lofs of the enemy was much more confiderable.

The fituations which commanded the town and citadel being now fecured, the enemy capitulated, as foon as the batteries were compleated, and furrendered this important place, the fecond in the ifland, on the 4th of February; and next morning the garrifon, to the number of eight hundred, marched out with the honours of war, in order to embark for France, agreeable to the articles of capitulation.

St. Pierre, the capital, a place of no contemptible ftrength, ftill remained to be reduced: and it was apprehended, that the refiftance here might be confiderable, if the ftrength of the garrifon, in any degree, correfponded with that of the fortifications, and the natural advantages of the country; but the reduction of Fort Royal had fo greatly abated the enemy's confidence, that, defpairing of making any effectual defence, they refolved to hold out no longer; and general Monckton, juft as he was ready to embark in order to reduce St. Pierre, was

fortu-

fortunately prevented by the arrival of deputies, who came with propofals of capitulation for the whole ifland, from M. de la Touche, the go- vernor-general, who had retired with his forces to this town. On the 14th the terms were fettled, and the capitulation figned, which was nearly the. fame as that granted to Guadaloupe; and on the 16th, the Englifh general took poffeffion of St. Pierre, and all the pofts in that neighbourhood, and M. de la Touche, the governor-general, with M. Rouille, the lieutenant-governor, the ftaff-officers, and about three hundred and twenty grenadiers, were embarked in tranfports for France.

The furrender of Martinique naturally drew on the furrender of all the dependent iflands. Grena- da, a fertile ifland, and poffeffed of fome good har- bours, was given up without oppofition; St. Lucia and St. Vincent, the right to which had fo long been a bone of contention between the two na- tions, followed its example. Thus the Englifh now became the fole and undifturbed poffeffors of all the Caribbees, that chain of innumerable iflands, which forms an immenfe bow, extending from the eaftern point of Hifpaniola almoft to the continent of South-America; and though fome of thefe iflands are barren, none of them very large; and but few of them well inhabited, they boaft of more trade than falls to the lot of many refpectable kingdoms.

The time in which Martinique was reduced, was a circumftance of almoft as much confequence as

the

the reduction itfelf ; for war having been declared againft Spain in the beginning of the year, it became advifable to ftrike early fuch an effective blow againft that nation as might incline their miniftry to a fpeedy peace, or influence the fortune of the whole war, if it fhould continue. In order to execute this plan, it was neceffary to employ a very great force, and of courfe to recall a very confiderable part of the troops from Martinique, whilft the feafon permitted them to act.

The British adminiftration having determined to transfer the war into the Spanifh Weft-Indies, with great judgment, fixed their eyes at once upon the capital object, and refolved to commence their operations where others of lefs ability would have chofen to conclude. The plan of the war in 1740, in the Spanifh Weft-Indies, in which we began with Porto-bello, and fo proceeded to Carthagena, &c. was mean, and founded on wrong principles ; becaufe the fuccefs of one attempt did nothing towards infuring fuccefs in the others. But the prefent plan was great and juft; the whole trade and navigation of the Spanifh Weft-Indies centering at the Havannah, the conqueft of which would enable us effectually to intercept the enemy's refources, and lay all Spanifh America open to our future attempts.

This expedition was intrufted to the earl of Albemarle, as commander of the land forces, recommended for this fervice by the late duke of Cumberland, under whofe aufpices he had been formed to war; and the fleet deftined to co-operate in the attack,

attack, was commanded by admiral Pocock, who
had already diftinguifhed himfelf by his gallant behaviour in the Eaft-Indies. They failed from Portf-
mouth on the 5th of March, and on the 27th of
May following were joined off Cape Nicholas, on
the north-weft point of Hifpaniola, by a detachment of the fleet from Martinique, under Sir James
Douglas ; and in confequence of this junction, their
whole force confifted of nineteen fail of the line,
eighteen fmaller veffels of war, including bomb-vef-
fels, &c. and about one hundred and fifty tranfports, having on board near ten thoufand land-
forces. A reinforcement of four thoufand men had
been ordered from New-York, and it was expected would arrive time enough to bear a part in their
military operations.

The common courfe of failing from Europe to
the Havannah is to keep to the fouth of the ifland
of Cuba, and fall into the track of the galleons-
but this, though far the fafeft, being the moft tedious paffage, and the fuccefs of the whole enterprize depending upon its being in forwardnefs before the hurricane-feafon came on, the admiral chofe
the neareft courfe, through the Old Straits of Bahama, a narrow paffage, amidft a vaft number of
fmall iflands, not lefs than feven hundred miles in
length, from eaft to weft : this paffage, through
almoft its whole extent, is bounded on the right
and left by the moft dangerous fands and fhoals,
which render the navigation fo hazardous, that
it has ufually been avoided by fingle, and even
fmall

small vessels. However, the admiral being provided with a good chart of lord Anson's, resolved to trust to his own sagacity, conduct, and vigilance, to carry safely through those streights a fleet of near two hundred sail. Every precaution was taken to guard so bold an attempt from the imputation of temerity : a vessel was sent to reconnoitre the passage, and when returned was ordered to take the lead, some frigates followed; sloops and boats were stationed on the right and left, on the shallows, with well adapted signals, both for the day, and the night. The fleet moved in seven divisions, and being favoured with good weather, through the admirable dispositions which were made, got through the streghts in eight days, without the smallest loss or interruption; and on the 6th of July lay to, about five leagues to the eastward of the Havannah, after having taken a Spanish frigate and a storeship in the passage.

St. Jago, situated at the south-east part of the island, is indeed the capital of Cuba : but the Havannah, tho' the second city in rank, is the first in wealth, extent, and importance. Its harbour is in every respect one of the best in the West-Indies, and perhaps in the world. The entrance is by a narrow passage, upwards of half a mile in length, which afterwards expands into a large bason, forming three cul de sac's, capable of containing a thousand sail of the largest ships, having almost throughout six fathom water, and being sheltered from every wind. In

this

this bay the rich fleets from the several parts of the Spanish West-Indies, called the galleons and the flota, affemble, before they finally fet out on their voyage for Europe; which circumftance has rendered the Havannah, fituated on the weft fide of the harbour, in a beautiful vale, with the fea in front, and furrounded on the oppofite fide by the river Sagida, one of the moft opulent, flourifhing, and populous cities in this part of the globe. Great care was taken to fortify and fecure a place, which, being the center of fo rich a commerce, would naturally become the faireft mark for the attempt of an enemy. The narrow entrance into this harbour was fecured on one fide by a very ftrong fort, called the Moro, built upon a projecting point of land; on the other it was defended by a fort, called the Puntal, which joined the town. The town itfelf, which ftands oppofite to the Moro, was alfo furrounded by a good rampart, flanked with baftions, and fecured with a ditch.

The Spaniards, who for fome time had been preparing for war, had formed a confiderable navy in the Weft-Indies. This fleet, which amounted to twelve fail of the line, befides frigates, lay now in the bafon of the Havannah, not having received, when the Englifh armament appeared before the port, any authentic account from their court of the commencement of hoftilities between the two nations. But though the Spaniards were very far from being deficient in taking proper meafures for

their

their defence, in every other refpect, almoft the only ufe they made of their fhips was to fink three of them behind a ftrong boom, which they laid acrofs the mouth of the harbour.

As foon as all things were in readinefs for a general difembarkation of the troops, the admiral, with part of the fleet, bore away to the weftward, and made a feint of attempting to land upon that fide, about four miles from the town ; while commodore Keppel, with another part of the fquadron, approached to the eaftward of the harbour, and effected a landing without oppofition, between the rivers Bocanao and Coxemar, about fix miles from the Moro, having previoufly filenced a fmall fort. The principal body of the army was deftined to act upon that fide : it was divided into two corps, one of which, commanded by general Elliot, was advanced a confiderable way up the country, towards the fouth-eaft of the harbour, in order to cover the fiege, and to fecure the parties employed in watering, and procuring provifions ; the other, under general Keppel, was immediately employed in the attack on the Moro, to the reduction of which the efforts of the Englifh were principally directed, as the Moro commanded the town and the entrance of the harbour. To make a diverfion in favour of this grand operation, a detachment of two thoufand men, including eight hundred marines, under colonel Howe, were landed at Chorera river, four miles to the weftward of the town. Such was the difpotion of the land-forces during the fiege.

The

The hardships which our troops encountered in carrying on the siege of the Moro are almost inexpressible: the earth was every where so thin, that it was with the greatest difficulty they could cover themselves in their approaches. There being no spring or river near, it was necessary to bring water from a great distance; and so precarious and scanty was this supply, that they were frequently obliged to procure it from the ships. Roads for communication were to be cut through thick woods, and the artillery was to be dragged a vast way over a rough rocky shore. But such was the resolution of our people, that no difficulties, no hardships, slackened for a moment the operations against this important place. Batteries were, in spite of all difficulties, raised against the Moro, and along the hill upon which this fort stands, in order to force the enemy's ships farther into the harbour, and thus prevent them from disturbing the approaches.

The garrison in the Moro had still a communication with the town, from which they received reinforcements and supplies; and on the 29th of June made a sally with a thousand chosen men, and a detachment of armed negroes and mulattoes, in order to destroy the works of the besiegers: but were repulsed by the piquets, and advanced posts, with the loss of above two hundred men killed or taken.

Whilst the works were vigorously carrying on ashore, the admiral, not contented with the great assistance which he had before lent to every part of the land service, resolved to try something further,

and

and which was more immediately within his own
province, towards the reduction of the Moro.
Accordingly, on the 1ft of July, the day the
Englifh batteries were opened, three of the largeft
fhips of the line, the Dragon, the Cambridge,
and the Marlborough, commanded by captains
Hervey, Gooftrey, and Burnet, were fent to attack that fort, which they cannonaded for feven hours without intermiffion; but the Moro
being fituated upon a high and very fteep rock,
was proof againft all their efforts: befides, the fire
from the oppofite fort the Puntal, and the batteries of the town, galled them extremely, infomuch,
that in order to fave the fhips from abfolute deftruction, Commodore Hervey was obliged at length,
though unwillingly, to difcontinue the attack, as
the fhips were very much fhattered in this long
and unequal conteft. We had one hundred and
fifty men killed and wounded, including captain Gooftrey, of the Cambridge, a brave and experienced officer, who fell in the beginning of the
engagement. This bold attempt was neverthelefs
of confiderable fervice, by diverting the enemy's
attention to that fide: the Englifh, in the mean
time, pouring in their fire with redoubled fury from
the batteries, it foon became much fuperior to that
of the enemy, and greatly damaged their works:
but the moment the fhips retired, the Spaniards
returned again to the eaftern face of the fort, and
made as vigorous a defence as before, and both
fides kept up a conftant fire for feveral days. It
now

now became evident, that the reduction of this fortrefs muft be a work of time.

In the midft of this fharp and doubtful conteft, the capital battery againft the fort unfortunately took fire, and was almoft wholly confumed; and the labour of fix hundred men, for feventeen days, deftroyed in a moment.

This mortifying ftroke was felt the more feverely, becaufe the other hardfhips of the fiege were become by this time almoft infupportable. The reinforcement from North-America had been in vain expected; ficknefs had reduced the army to half its number, at the fame time that it doubled the fatigue of the few who ftill preferved fome remains of ftrength; and no lefs than three thoufand of the feamen were in the fame miferable condition: befides, as the feafon advanced, the profpect of fucceeding grew fainter; and the fleet riding on an open fhore, muft to all appearance, be expofed to inevitable ruin, if the hurricane-feafon fhould come on before the reduction of the place. But in the midft of thefe diftreffes, the fteadinefs of the commanders infufed life and activity into the troops, and roufed them to incredible exertions. New batteries were erected in the place of the old; and their fire now foon became fuperior to that of the enemy: by degrees the cannon of the fort were filenced, all the upper works beaten to pieces, and at length, on the 20th of July, the troops made a lodgement on the covered way. Some days before they gained this great advantage, the Jamaica fleet appeared in its

passage

paſſage to Europe, from which the army procured
bags of cotton, and ſeveral conveniencies for the
ſiege. Not many days after, a conſiderable part
of the troops from New-York arrived. Some of
the tranſports, in their paſſage through the Old Bahama ſtreights, were loſt; but the men were ſaved,
and brought off in five ſloops, detached by the
admiral on that ſervice: five other tranſports, having on board three hundred and fifty of Anſtru-
ther's regiment, and an hundred and fifty provincials, were taken by a French ſquadron near the
paſſage between Máya Guanna and the North
Caicos.

In this advanced ſtate of the ſiege a new difficulty appeared; an immenſe ditch, eighty feet long and
forty feet wide, more than forty feet of that depth
cut in the ſolid rock. The ſoil of the neighbouring country being very thin, it appeared impoſſible
to fill it up. To undermine it was the only expedient, which might have proved impracticable, if
fortunately a thin ridge of rock had not been left
in order to cover the ditch towards the ſea. Along
this ridge the miners paſſed, without cover, to the
foot of the wall, where they made a lodgment with
little loſs. In the night of the 21ſt a ſerjeant, and
twelve men, ſcaled the walls by ſurprize; but, the
garriſon being alarmed before they could be ſuf-
tained, were obliged to make a precipitate retreat.
Next day, at four in the morning, a body of twelve
hundred men, chiefly compoſed of the country militia, mulattoes, and negroes, were tranſported a-
croſs

cross the harbour, climbed the hills, and attacked
the besiegers in three different places, under cover
of a warm fire from the Fort Puntal, the west bastion, the lines and flanks of the entrance, and the
shipping in the harbour. But after a warm difpute, which cost the English about fifty men, killed and wounded, all the three parties were repulsed, and driven down the hill with great slaughter, a confiderable number being drowned in the
hurry of their retreat. The Spaniards loft in this
well concerted but unfuccefsful fally, upwards of
four hundred men. On the 30th, about two in the
morning, a floating battery was towed out into the
harbour, and fired with grape-fhot and fmall arms
into the ditch, though without any great interruption to our miners; and the clofe fire of the cover-
ing party foon compelled the enemy to retire.

This was the last effort for the relief of the Moro,
which, though abandoned by the city, did not offer to capitulate. In the afternoon of the fame day
two mines were fprung with fuch effect, that a practicable breach was made in the bastion; and orders
were immediately given for the affault. The troops
mounted the breach with great intrepidity, and drove
the enemy from every part of the ramparts, after a
short, tho' warm difpute, in which about one hundred and thirty Spaniards were killed, including feveral officers of diftinction, in particular Don Louis
de Velafco, the governor of the fort, (the marquis
Gonzales having been blown up when the mine
was fprung) who had diftinguifhed himfelf from

beginning of the fiege by his courage and activity;
and in this laft action, after performing every thing
that could be expected from the moft romantic
gallantry, fell by a.fhot he received in defending
the colours of Spain. About four hundred of the
garrifon threw down their arms, and were made
prifoners; the reft were either killed, or drowned
in attempting to efcape to the Havannah. In this
attack the Englifh loft but two lieutenants and
twelve men'; and one lieutenant, four ferjeants,
and twenty-four men only, were wounded.

The governor of the Havannah now directed
his chief fire againft the fortrefs which he had loft,
and fent down a large fhip of the line to the entrance of the harbour, from whence fhe could batter it with more effect: her efforts, however, were
fruitlefs. In the mean time general Keppel erected a line of batteries, confifting of forty-three pieces
of cannon and twelve mortars, along the hill of the.
Cavannos, on the extremity of which the fort ftands,
in order to command the whole eaftern fide of the
city, from one end to the other; and a plan was
formed for making a new attack to the weftward of
the town. On the 10th of Auguft the batteries on
the Cavannos being finifhed, the earl of Albemarle
fummoned the governor to furrender, who refo-
lutely anfwered, that he would defend the place to
the laft extremity. Next morning, at day-break,
the batteries began to play againft the town and the
Puntal with fuch continued and irrefiftible fury,
that the Puntal fort was filenced in fix hours, and in

ano-

another hour the north baſtion was almoſt diſabled. Flags of truce now appeared from every quarter of the town, which were followed by a capitulation, whereby the eſtabliſhed religion, their former laws, and private properties, were ſecured to the inhabitants. The garriſon, which was reduced to about ſeven hundred men, was conveyed to Old Spain, and on account of its brave defence, was allowed the honours of war. A diſtrict of one hundred and eighty miles weſtward was included in the capitulation. The Spaniards ſtickled hard to ſave the men of war, and to have the harbour declared neutral; but after two days altercation, hoſtilities being about to be renewed, they thought proper to recede from their demands; and the Engliſh troops were put in poſſeſſion of the Havannah on the 14th of Auguſt, after a ſiege of two months and eight days, at the expence of five hundred men, including fifteen officers, killed; and about ſeven hundred, comprehending thirty-nine officers, cut off by contagious diſorders, which raged with redoubled violence after the reduction of the place.

The acquiſition of the Havannah was not only a military advantage of the higheſt claſs, but equal to the greateſt naval victory, by its effect on the marine force of Spain; and the plunder equalled the produce of a national ſubſidy. Nine ſail of Spaniſh ſhips of the line, ſome of the fineſt veſſels in the world, were taken, with four frigates; and two more, that were in forwardneſs on the ſtocks, were deſtroyed. Three of their capital ſhips had been,

as

as has been already mentioned, funk by themfelves at the beginning of the fiege. In ready money, tobacco collected at the Havarnah on account of the king, and other valuable merchandize, the plunder did not fall much fhort of three millions fterling, exclufive of great quantities of artillery, fmall arms, and warlike ftores, that fell into the hands of the conquerors; fo that the Britifh nation was more than indemnified for the expedition, and the lofs to Spain was irreparable.

M. de Ternay having efcaped from Breft in a fog, with four fhips of the line and a bomb-ketch, with a proportionable number of land-forces, arrived on the 24th of June at the Bay of Bulls, in Newfoundland, where he landed fome troops without oppofition; and finding the ifland unprepared to make a refiftance, took poffeffion of two fmall Englifh fettlements, Trinity and Carbonear, which he deftroyed, as likewife the ftages for curing cod, and implements of the fifhery, took feveral veffels, and did confiderable damage to the Englifh fettlers on different parts of the coaft. The town of St. John's, being in no condition of defence, alfo capitulated; and the garrifon, confifting of one company of foldiers, were made prifoners of war, together with the officers and crew of his majefty's floop the Gramont, which was in that harbour.

This petty triumph was but of a very fhort duration. The armament fitted out in England to retake Newfoundland, the moment the news arrived,

rived, was rendered unneceffary by the vigilance and
activity of general Amherft, commander in chief in
North-America. Having received advice of the
progrefs which the French armament had made on
the coaft of Newfoundland, he detached colonel
Amherft with a body of land forces, and lord Colville, who commanded the Englifh fquadron in A-
merica, to recover this valuable ifland. Lord Colville
accordingly failed from Halifax, and blocked up the
harbour of St. John by fea, even while M. de Ternay, the French commodore, lay at anchor in it with
a fuperior fquadron. On the 11th of September
he was joined by colonel Amherft, who had touched at Louifbourg, and taken on board fome troops,
which, with thofe embarked at Halifax, amounted
to about eight hundred, chiefly Highlanders and
light infantry. The troops landed, after a fhort
refiftance, in Torbay, about feven miles to the
northward of St. John's; and though this part of
the country was rendered difficult by mountains
and paffes, occupied by the enemy, the Britifh
forces advanced to the ftrong poft of Kitty-vitty,
which they took fword in hand, and likewife drove
the enemy from two other heights, which they had
fortified, and did not abandon without bloodfhed.
On the 16th of September they encamped in the
neighbourhood of St. John's Fort, and next day a
mortar-battery was compleated. The French commodore had funk fome fhallops in the entrance of
the harbour, which was commanded by a breaft-

O 3   work

work and an unfinifhed battery. Thefe being taken, and the channel opened, colonel Amherft received his artillery and ftores by water conveyance. Unfortunately lord Colville, with his fquadron, was drove by contrary winds to fome diftance from the coaft. In his abfence, M. de Ternay took advantage of a thick fog, and made his efcape, not being difcovered by the Englifh fleet till he had got at a confiderable diftance. On the 10th, in the morning, M. de Haufonville, the commander of the French forces at St. John's, who had already been fummoned, but had refufed to furrender, thought proper to demand a capitulation, and furrendered himfelf, with his garrifon, prifoners of war, on condition of being conveyed to Breft the firft opportunity. They were a fine body of troops, and nearly equal in number to the befiegers. Thus the town and fort of St. John's, with all the other petty places which the French had taken on this coaft, were recovered with very little lofs, by a handful of troops, who acted with moft remarkable refolution, and furmounted many difficulties, by dint of indefatigable labour and perfeverance. In this fhort expedition, lieutenant Schuyler, of the Royal Americans, was killed : captain M'Donald died of the wounds he received in attacking one of the enemy's fortified pofts : the captains Bailie and M'Kenzie were wounded, but recovered : and not above twenty men were loft in all the different actions.

Such

Such were the principal events of the late moſt glorious war in every part of America; and having omitted no care to render our narrative as perfect as the nature of the work would permit, we flatter ourſelves, it has proved as entertaining as the ſubject is intereſting to the reader.

THE

THE

HISTORY

OF THE

BRITISH EMPIRE

IN

AMERICA.

✶✶✶✶✶✶✶✶✶✶✶✶✶✶✶✶✶✶✶✶✶✶✶✶✶

CANADA.

BOUNDARIES, NATURAL HISTORY, PRODUCTIONS, and TRADE.

THE extent or boundaries of Canada are variously fixed by the French geographers, and perhaps yet remain undiscovered, as well as the source of the river St. Laurence, which runs through this country, and is pretended to be derived from remote north-western lakes, as yet unknown to Europeans. Leaving these matters to more competent judges, we shall confine our account of this

country

country from Lake Ontario, lying between 41 and 43 deg. north latitude, weft longitude 79 deg. which feems to be the moft natural fource of this noble river, to its gulph or entrance at Cape Raye, on the ifland of Newfoundland; and to the lands and fettlements immediately in view of this navigation, being the moft interefting parts of this colony: the extenfive forefts backward of them, being, to this day, chiefly in their rude primitive ftate, uninhabited and ùnfrequented, except by the native favages, and the coureurs du bois or hunters, whofe accounts are extravagant and erroneous. The entrance of the river St. Laurence is formed by Cape Raye, before-mentioned, on the north-eaft and north; by the ifland of Cape Breton on the fouth-weft, fituated about one hundred leagues from Quebec, the capital, which lies about the center of the province; thence to Trois Rivieres, reputed half-way to Montreal, thirty-three leagues; and from Montreal to the north-eaft point of Lake Ontario the diftance is, by computation, near feventy leagues. But there is another entrance into the river from the fea, north-about through the Streights of Belleifle, an ifland of no great extent, on the eaftern coaft of New-Britain, which gives name to thefe ftreights, and feparates the north part of Newfoundland: this paffage, however, being very unfafe, is feldom frequented.

The iflands in this long extenfive river are almoft innumerable, and many of them are fertile, inhabited, and well cultivated; particularly the ifles of

Coudre

Coudre and Orleans, below Quebec; thofe of St. Ignatius, Therefa, Montreal, and Jefus, with fome of leffer note in that diftrict ; and feveral others to the fouth-weft of them in the Lake St. 'Francis, the principal of which is St. Peter's. Montreal and Orleans are the moft confiderable ones : but the former having been already defcribed, we fhall proceed to give a fhort defcription of the Ifle of Orleans only. This ifland, though not above twen‧ ty-one miles in extent, and not above four broad in its wideft part, is divided into five parifhes, and contains feveral gentlemen's feats. Its fituation is delightful, on a noble river, in the heart of a charming country, and furrounded by a great number of natural curiofities, and pleafant villages. The north-weft and north fides of the ifland are woody ; but all the reft of it is laid out in compact farms, and very well cultivated. The foil is fertile, producing every fpecies of grain and vegetables, the fame as in England.

There are a great variety of fafe and commodious harbours in this river, after clearing the iflands of Cape Breton and St. John ; of which the principal are Chaleurs, Gafpee, Tadoufac, and Chaudiere ; but the haven of Quebec exceeds all the reft, where an hundred fhips of the line may ride in the greateft fafety.

The navigation of this river, from its entrancce to Quebec, is not fo difficult as reprefented by the French, for political reafons ; but with refpect to the upper part, from that capital to Montreal, tho'

there

there is water enough for veffels not drawing more than eleven feet ; yet the navigation is difficult and perplexing, and in tacking from one fhore to another, obftructions are frequently met with, and which, according to the Canadians, are often moved from one part of the river to another, by the immenfe floats of ice that roll up and down the currents, at the breaking up of the winters : and, as the currents are extremely rapid in moft places, veffels fhould be well provided with fufficient ground-tackle. There are no cataracts between the capital and Montreal, as fome writers have advanced, except a ftrong ripple between Jaques Cartier and Chambaud, called the Rapids of Richlieu ; where, at high water, though the channel runs ferpentine, there is a fufficient depth for a forty-gun fhip. In the navigation from Montreal upwards, frequent interruptions are met with, particularly between that ifland and lake St. Francis ; but the others, between the lake and Ifle Royale, are more frightful than dangerous. Sloops cannot work higher up than Montreal, nor come farther down from Lake Ontario than to Ifle Royale ; but the intermediate difficulties may be furmounted by flat-bottomed-boats or canoes. Upon the whole, this is a moft valuable river, and, except at its very entrance, free from thofe fogs fo endemial to the coafts of Nova-Scotia, Cape Breton, and Newfoundland.

The lower part of the country, from the mouth of the river St. Laurence, is wild, uncultivated,

and

and on the fouth fide covered with impenetrable
woods, moftly of pine and dwarf-fpruce, with ftu-
pendous rocks and barren mountains, which form
a moft difmal profpeft; while the north, for feveral
leagues, is low, marfhy, and covered with ftrong
reeds, rufhy grafs, with clofe forefts, appearing at
fome diftance.   The firft fettlement after clearing
the frontiers of Nova-Scotia, is St. Barnaby, on
the fouth fhore, about thirty leagues within the
gulph, where the fight is entertained with a profpeft of an open, feemingly fertile, civilized country; and the numerous parifhes from thence upwards, though fome fpots are barren, are in general
fertile, open, and well cultivated, producing corn,
flax, and vegetables, ftocked with horned cattle,
fheep, fwine, poultry, and horfes, and exceedingly
well watered by innumerable rivers and rivulets,
which empty themfelves into the river St. Laurence, and are plentifully ftored with falmon, eels,
and other fifh peculiar to thefe waters *.   The
                                              north

* The principal fifh inhabiting the river St. Laurence, from
its gulph to the lakes, are a great variety of fmall whales,
particularly the fouffleur, fo called from his blowing the
water after diving, as whales do, through an hole behind
his head. Porpoifes, dolphins, and fea-cows, innumerable.
This laft is an amphibious animal, as large as fome oxen,
which has a fkin like that of a fea-dog, and a mouth like
a cow, with two projecting teeth, crooked downwards, about
half a yard long: thefe tufks are as valuable as ivory, and are
applied to the fame ufes: the fore-feet are like thofe of a cow,
the hinder-feet webbed, like thofe of a goofe. This animal
                                              has

north country does not make so promising an appearance; the first settlements being the king's farms at Mal Bay, near the river Saguenny, and haven of Tadousac. Where the lands have undergone cultivation, the soil is kind; but the country east and north-east of these farms remains in its original state, with lofty and steep banks to the river. The lands on the south side also rise gradually high and steep, after clearing the woody island of Anticosti, with trees and underwoods on the sides of the declivities, and continue so for the most part on both coasts, all the way upwards. From Mal Bay to Cape Tourmente, not less than thirty miles, is mountainous and barren; but then the eye is agreeably surprized with a pleasant settlement, called St. Paul's; where, and from which parish upwards, the country is in general clear, fertile, and well improved, in like manner as the lands on the south coast, and intersected by numerous rivers and streams, that run into the river St. Laurence. However, neither coast is uniformly fruitful; there are several exceptionable tracts on both

---

has seldom more than one or two young ones, is strong, wild, and very difficult to be taken on shore. It is said to eat neither flesh nor fish; but that its food consists of a submarine weed, known by the name of sea-sorrel. The inhabitants catch them by the following stratagem: they tie a bull to a stake, fixed on the shore, in the depth of two feet water: they then beat and torment him, by twisting his tail, until they make him roar; as soon as these creatures hear his cries, they crawl to the bull, and are easily taken. Salmon, eels, bass, mackarel, gusperot, her-both fides, and in many parifhes fmall forefts are met with, perhaps defignedly.left for fuel, fhelter, and other purpofes.   The lands on the coafts, from Montreal to Lake Francis, are very woody, with a cold and fpungy foil ; but from this lake to Lake Ontario, north and fouth, the ground is much better, producing variety of excellent timber for fhip-building, good grafs, and little or no underwood. The French had no fettlements farther weft than the Cedars, about half-way between Lake Ontario and Lake St. Francis ; the country round the former, and on the principal rivers flowing into it, being inhabited by the Iroquois, whofe chief employment, when not at war, is hunting and fifhing.

The winter-climate, for above fix months, is feverely cold, four of which are truly rigorous : the vaft river St. Laurence is early frozen over, to a great depth ; but the atmofphere is generally clear and ferene, except when a fnow-ftorm fets in, which

herrings, gold-fifh, (fome near fifteen inches in length) chad, feveral fpecies of cod, haddock, pike, turbot, hallibut, plaice, lampreys, perch, fprats, thornback, a particular fpecies of tench, congar, fmelts, and roach. The fhell-fifh are, fmall lobfters, crabs, oyfters, cockles, winkles, and mufcles, larger and better flavoured than in Europe, but fo coated with a pearly kind of fand, that it is difficult to open and clean them.

The lakes abound with fturgeon, armed fifh, divers forts of trout, in particular a fpecies of falmon-trout, fome of which weigh near fixty pounds, and are five feet and a half in length, and about one foot diameter ; eels, white-fifh, a fpecies of herring, mullet, carp, gulfifh, gudgeons, and many other forts, whofe names are unknown to Europeans.

feldom

feldom continues above twenty-four hours, during which time it is inceffant *. The fummers, tho'. fhort, are pleafant, except in July and Auguft, when it is exceedingly hot, with violent thunder-ftorms; but this feafon is fo prolific, that, as in other northern climates, the farmer reaps the fruits of his labour within four months after the feed is fown, and the quicknefs of vegetation in gardens is furprizing.

This country produces various kinds of timber; fuch as, red, white, and evergreen oak; black and white birch, fir and pine trees of different fpecies, maple †, alder, cedar, bitter-cherry, afh, chefnut, beech, hazel, black and white thorn, apple, pear, plumb trees, and an infinite number of nondefcripts; befides a great variety of fhrubs, particularly the capillaire, which grows like fern, and

is

---

* The ftoves that are ufed in this country are excellently adapted to the climate. They are made of caft iron, at a foundery contiguous to Trois Rivieres, and ftand upon a frame of the fame metal, about eight inches from the ground; and if the floor is boarded, the place where the ftove is to be fixed fhould firft be covered with leaves of fheet iron, as fhould likewife the edges of the holes in wooden partitions; thro' which the pipes are conveyed from one room to another, to render them perfectly fafe.

† The fap of this tree has an exceeding pleafant tafte, and makes a very wholefome drink in fevers. This liquor is drawn by cutting a gafh in the tree two inches deep, and about a foot long: at the lower end of this wound is fixed a fmall trough, made of reed or cane, fix inches long, with a veffel placed underneath to receive the fap. Some trees yield five or fix bottles of this liquor in a day, of which the Americans make a fugar of a grey fandy colour, but fo hard and folid as not to be eafily

broken

is found in great plenty in the woods : the merchants of Quebec exported great quantities of its fyrup annually to France.

The Canadians have variety of game, both fowl and quadrupeds, in the greateſt plenty ; fine poultry, vaſt flights of wild pigeons, and an excellent breed of black cattle, ſheep, ſwine, and horſes, with which the farms in general are plentifully ſtocked.

They have hitherto raiſed no ſtaple commodity, to anſwer any conſiderable demand : ſome tobacco has been planted, indeed, which is uſed by the meaner ſort of people ; but from not being properly manufactured, is wretched inſipid ſtuff, and unfit for ſale. Their trade with the Indians produces all their returns for the European market ; which conſiſt principally of the furs of beavers, foxes, and racoons, with deer ſkins, and all the branches of the peltry. Furs, indeed, are more plenty to the ſouth, but not of ſo good a ſtaple. Theſe, with what corn and timber they ſend to the Weſt-India iſlands, furniſh ſufficient to render life eaſy and agreeable in a plentiful country.

broken : this ſugar is an excellent pectoral. In the ſame manner they bleed the ſpruce fir, (but the inciſion does not require to be made ſo deep or long) whence a fine fragrant balſam is extracted, known by the name of Canada balſam, leſs heating than balſam capivi, and of infinite benefit taken internally, in ulcerations of the lungs, as well as externally applied to bruiſes or green wounds. The time for drawing the ſap from both theſe trees is from the middle of February to the middle of April.

The

The beaver is an amphibious quadruped. The largest are somewhat less than four feet in length, and fifteen inches in breadth over the haunches. In the most northern parts their skins are generally quite black, though there are sometimes found beavers entirely white. In the more temperate countries they are brown, their colour becoming lighter in proportion as they advance farther southward. The lighter the colour, the less quantity of fur they yield, and consequently are less valuable. The beaver is said to live fifteen or twenty years, and the female to carry her young four months: her common litter is four, having only four teats. The muscles of this animal are exceeding strong, and in appearance thicker than its size requires. Its bowels are extremely slender, its bones very hard, and its jaws surprizingly strong, each of which is furnished with ten teeth, two incisive, and eight double teeth. The incisives of the upper jaw are two inches and a half long; those of the under jaw upwards of three, following the bending of the jaw, which gives them surprizing force for so small an animal. The jaws do not exactly correspond; the upper advances considerably over the under jaw, so that they cross like the blades of a pair of scissars. The head is like that of a mountain-rat; the snout is pretty long; the eyes little; the ears short, round, hairy on the outside, and smooth within; the legs short, particularly the fore-legs, which are not above five inches long, and much like those of a badger; the nails are

VOL. II. P made

made obliquely, and hollow like quills ; the hind-feet are different, being flat, and furnished with membranes between the toes. Thus the beaver can walk, though flowly, and fwims with the fame eafe as any other aquatic animal. Its tail is almoft four inches broad at the root, five in the middle, and three at the extremity ; in large beavers about an inch thick, and a foot in length. Its fubftance is a firm fat, and is covered with a fcaly fkin ; the fcales are hexagonal, half a line in thicknefs, and from three to four lines long, and reft on each other, like thofe of fifhes. The tefticles of this animal lie concealed within the loins. The drug called caftor is an infpiffated fecretion, contained in two fmall bags, of the form of a pear, near the anus of both male and female, and not the tefticles of this animal, as formerly wrongly fuppofed.

The manner in which they build their habitations is extremely curious. They firft pitch on a fpot where there is plenty of provifions, and all materials neceffary for building : above all things water is abfolutely neceffary ; and in cafe they can find neither lake nor pool, they fupply that defect by ftopping the courfe of fome rivulet with a dyke, to effect which they fell trees with their teeth, but above the place where they intend to build, and take their meafures fo well, that the trees always fall towards the water ; and cut them into proper lengths with their teeth, roll them towards the water, and thus navigate them to the place where they are to be employed. This dike confifts of piles, nearly as thick

as

as one's thigh, fupported by ftrong ftakes, inter-
woven with fmall branches, and the vacant fpaces
are filled with fat earth fo exactly, as rot a drop
of water paffes through. They prepare this earth
with their feet, and their tail ferves for a trowel for
building, as well as for a wheelbarrow for tranfporting this mortar, which is done by trailing themfelves along on their hinder feet. When they have
arrived at the water-fide, they take this earth up
with their teeth, apply it with their feet, and then
plaifter it with their tail. The foundation of thefe
dikes is generally about twelve feet thick, diminifh-
ing upwards gradually, till at laft they come to be only about three feet in thicknefs, the ftricteft proportion being exactly obferved ; the fide towards the
current of the water is always made floping, and
the other fide quite upright.

The conftruction of their cabbins is equally curious. They are round, about ten or twelve feet
in diameter on the flooring, according to the number of inhabitants, and are built on piles, in the
middle of the fmall lakes formed by the dikes, on
the bank of a river, or at the extremity of fome
point that projects into the water. Their roofs are
arched like the bottom of a bafket; the partitions
are two feet thick, and made of the fame materials,
though lefs fubftantial than thofe in the dike, and
the whole is fo well plaiftered with clay within,
that not the leaft air can enter. The flooring is
placed about a foot above the water; but as the
upper part runs to a point, the under is much

larger

larger than the flooring, which the reader may figure to himself by fuppofing all the upright, pofts to refemble the legs of a great A, whofe middle-ftroke is the flooring; canes, leaves, and fmall branches of pine-trees compleat this flooring, which has a hole in the middle to go out, at when they pleafe, and into this all the cells open.

. There is alfo in this country a little animal, of much the fame nature with the beaver, called the mufk-rat. It has almoft all the properties of the beaver; the ftructure of the body, and particularly of the head, is fo very like, that the mufk-rat might eafily be miftaken for a fmall beaver, were it not for its tail, which is like that of a common rat, and his tefticles, which contain a moft exquifite mufk. They live upon vegetables during the fummer; but at the approach of winter conceal themfelves in hollow trees, and remain in that ftate without food, during the whole winter. They build cabbins in form like thofe of the beaver, but far from being fo well executed.

The climate, as has been obferved, being intenfely cold in winter, and the people manufacturing nothing, fhews what the natives want from Europe; wine, fpirituous liquors, tobacco, cloths, (chiefly coarfe) linen, wrought iron, &c. The Indian trade requires fpirituous liquors, tobacco, a fort of duffil blankets, guns, powder and ball, kettles, hatchets, tomohawks, toys, and trinkets. The Indians exchange their peltry for thefe articles; and the French Indian traders, in the manner of the original

ginal inhabitants, traverfe the vaft lakes and rivers that divide this country, in canoes of bark, with incredible induftry and patience, and carry their goods into the remoteft parts of America.

⁂⁂⁂⁂⁂⁂⁂⁂⁂⁂⁂⁂⁂⁂⁂⁂⁂⁂⁂⁂⁂⁂⁂

VIRGINIA.

THE country, which ftill bears this name, is now reduced to that tract which has the river Potomack upon the north; the bay of Chefapeak upon the eaft; and Carolina upon the fouth. To the weftward, the grants extend it to the South-fea; but our planting goes no farther than the great Allegany mountains, which boundaries leave this province in length two hundred and forty miles, and in breadth about two hundred, lying between the fifty-fifth and fortieth degrees of north latitude.

In our account of the firft expeditions of the Englifh to America, the hiftory of this colony has been given to the year 1620, when its government was fettled, and the colony in a flourifhing ftate, owing to the care of the earl of Southampton, one of the company for attempting new fettlements in Virginia, through whofe means Sir George Yardley brought with him to Virginia, thirteen hundred men in twenty-eight fhips. Negroes were

P 3

this

this year firft imported into this colony by a Dutch
fhip, and new fettlements were now formed, in the
room of thofe which had been deferted. The boundaries of James-town were marked out; the borders
of James and York rivers were peopled, and public and private property was afcertained with precifion. A fait-work was alfo fet up at Cape Charles,
and iron-works at Falling Creek. Sir George was
fucceeded in his government, in 1621, by Sir
Francis Wyatt, who carried with him from England a frefh fupply of people. The market was
now fo over-ftocked with tobacco, that the planters
were great lofers : to remedy which James I. ordered, that no planter fhould raife above one hundred pounds worth of tobacco, but apply themfelves to other manufactures.

At this time the colony was fo populous, that the
affembly found it neceffary to appoint inferior courts
for the trial of fmall caufes; but as yet no proper
police fubfifted for regulating matters between the
planters and native Indians, who appeared fo tract-
able and fubmiffive, that the Englifh admitted
them into their houfes, and they thus became mafters of the myftery of fire-arms, the knowledge of
which ought to have been carefully concealed from
them. Their chief Sachem was at this time Oppecancanough, one of whofe favourites had been
executed by the Englifh for murdering a colonift;
whofe death haftened the execution of a fcheme
which that Prince had long formed for a general
maffacre of the Englifh, which was fixed to the 22d
of

of March, 1622. Fortunately some of the natives, who were become converts to Christianity, discovered the conspiracy to one Mr. Pace, a few hours before the time fixed on for its execution, who gave the alarm to his fellow colonists. The discovery, however, did not reach the remoter plantations time enough to prevent three hundred and thirty-four English from being cut off. The manufacturers near Iron-Creek were all destroyed, except a boy and a girl who concealed themselves, an inexpressible loss to the colony ; for those works never could be restored, and all knowledge of the late discovered lead mines was lost. It also frustrated the project for erecting a glass house at James-town. The planters having recovered themselves, destroyed all the natives who fell into their hands, and drove the remainder into the woods. Even the authority of the government could not put a stop to their revenge : so that after the governor, by promising the Indians peace and pardon, had prevailed with them to return to the cultivation of their lands, the English massacred them, destroyed Oppecancanough's palace, and drove the poor natives from all the cultivated parts of Virginia.

New measures were now pursued for the benefit of the colony, the natives were reinstated in their possessions ; but the tyrannical disposition of the English settlers still continuing, the Indians formed another conspiracy, and massacred all they could meet with. The differences and disputes that prevailed among the colonists, encouraged

the

the natives in their insurrections; and when Charles I. came to the crown, the English property, in Virginia, was reduced to so low a pass, that his Majesty dissolved the company, and commanded all patents and processes should issue in his own name, reserving a quit rent of two shillings for every hundred acres. The assembly was continued on its former basis, and the government vested in a governor, assisted with twelve council. Sir John Harvey was the first governor after the dissolution of the company; who behaved in such an arbitrary a manner, that the inhabitants, in 1639, sent him prisoner to England; a measure so disagreeable to the arbitrary principles of Charles I, that though the Virginians sent over two gentlemen to support their charge against him, he was reinstated in his government, without their being admitted to an audience; and several planters were sent for to England, and subjected to much inconveniency, by being frequently obliged to attend upon the council-board. But matters growing very serious between that king and his parliament, Harvey was at last removed from his government, and Sir William Berkeley appointed in his place.

These disputes between the governor and the colonists, rendered the English despicable in the eyes of the natives, and encouraged Oppecancanough, a man of uncommon abilities, both of body and mind, to meditate a fresh war. Having complained of many encroachments upon his lands, contrary to the public faith, without the least regard being

paid

paid to his remonftrances, he ordered his fubjects to attack the out-fettlements, where they maffacred near five hundred Englifh, while he himfelf cut off thofe who were fettled about York River, near his capital. But advancing in profecution of his fcheme into the Englifh territories, fome diftance from his own refidence, Sir William Berkeley furprized him in Henrico county with a party of horfe, and propofed to have fent him to England; but a brutal Englifhman wounded him mortally in the back. Though at that time fo far advanced in years, that he was unable to move without affift-ance; yet he behaved with a magnanimity worthy of the greateft heroes of antiquity. Underftand-ing, by means of a fervant, that he was expofed to the diverfion of the populace, " Had it been my fortune (faid he to Berkeley) to have taken thee prifoner, I would not have expofed thee to the in-fults of the rabble."

Berkeley improved this incident, by making a peace with the Indians, who could find none to fup-ply the place of their deceafed fachem : but there is reafon to believe that the colonifts did not make a very warrantable ufe of their advantages. At the time the civil war broke out in England, the Englifh fettlers in Virginia were computed to a-mount to fifteen thoufand, exclufive of women and children; but a fatal difference then arofe between the governor and planters : Berkeley, a man of great refolution, fided with the king, and prohibit-ed all intercourfe between the Virginians and the ing party in England, to the infinite prejudice of the colony. Their ftaple commodity, tobacco, of which vaft quantities were at that time taken off in England, lay upon their hands; and though they did not want for provifions, yet being deftitute of manufacturers, and the benefits of commerce, they were unable to fupply themfelves even with tools for agriculture. The Englifh parliament refolved to reduce this colony, as well as the other American plantations, to their fubjection. Accordingly, Sir George Ayfcough being fent with a fleet to reduce Barbadoes, detached, agreeable to his inftructions, a fmall fquadron, on board of which were fome land forces, againft this province. The Dutch being then on bad terms with England, Berkeley engaged fome of their fhips to affift him againft this armament; which they did fo effectually, that Dennis, who commanded the Englifh fquadron, defpairing of fuccefs, was obliged to have recourfe to ftratagem. He acquainted the colony, that he had on board a valuable cargo, the property of two leading men of the country, which he would detain if they did not furrender. The intereft of the colony directed them to a fubmiffion, which Berkeley being unable to prevent, retired to his own plantation; and thus Virginia fell into the poffeffion of the Englifh parliament, which made a very moderate ufe of its fuccefs, and perfecuted none of the Virginian Royalifts, for their principles or refiftance.

The

The Englifh parliament appointed colonel Digges to fucceed Berkeley in the government, during whofe adminiftration nothing remarkable happened. Afterwards, the unfettled ftate of affairs in England feems to have introduced fome confufion into the government of this colony, to which one Mr. Bennet and one Mr. Matthews fucceeded, by Cromwell's orders. On the death of Matthews, the people of Virginia applied to Sir William Berkeley to refume the government, who refufed to comply, unlefs the people would ftand by him in their allegiance to their lawful fovereign, againft the power of the ufurpation, which they confented to do, and Charles II. was accordingly proclaimed all over the province; but luckily for them, during thefe tranfactions, Cromwell died, and Charles II. was reftored. However, Berkeley received no other reward than being continued in his government, and made one of the proprietors of Carolina. Berkeley going over to England, to congratulate the king on his reftoration, fubftituted colonel Morrifon in his government, who collected the laws into one body, procured others for the encouragement of manufactures of all kinds, and regulated parifh-fettlements fo well, that the clergy were all comfortably provided for.

The welfare of this colony being at this time a favourite meafure with the king, Berkeley had many audiences on this bufinefs. In 1662, Sir William returned to Virginia, and procured an act of the affembly for enlarging James Town, by each county

build-

building a certain number of houfes : a wife provifion, had it been followed; but the planters were
fo fond of living upon their own eftates, that it
proved of little effect.

The reftoration having taken place, many of
the Republicans were, in their turn, banifhed to
Virginia, and their principles gaining ground, almoft ruined the colony ; for the fervants formed a
confpiracy to murder their mafters, and ufurp the
government of the colony themfelves. One of the
confpirators, named Birkenhead, difcovered the
plot to the government; and the confpirators were
intercepted by a party of militia-horfe, as they were
marching towards Poplar-fpring, the place fixed
on for their rendezvous. Four of the ringleaders
were hanged; and Birkenhead obtained his free-
dom, with the reward of two hundred pounds.
In confequence of this confpiracy, orders were fent
from England to build forts, and a citadel, at James
Town, for the protection of the government; but
no money being ordered for thefe purpofes, the
Virginians forgot their danger, and the meafure was
neglected, only a fmall battery of cannon being
raifed for the protection of James Town.

The government in England, thinking they had
a right to all the advantages that could arife from
their colonies, enforced the navigation act with rigour, fo that no foreign goods could be imported
into this colony, unlefs they were firft landed in
England; which raifing the price of European
goods, and lowering that of tobacco, created great
difcontents

difcontents among the Virginians, efpecially as the planters were undermined, on all occafions, by the people of Maryland, who being under a feparate government, underfold them in their tobacco, as they were not bound by any of the acts which the province of Virginia paffed for difcontinuing the planting of that ftaple, till its value fhould rife ; againft which oppofition of the Maryland planters they remonftrated, to no purpofe. A project was adopted in England, to oblige fhips trading to this colony to ride under certain forts, to be built upon rivers, which alone were to be deemed the forts of trade, an excellent means for fortifying the province in fpeculation ; but little regard was paid to it by the planters, who, regardlefs of every thing but their own interefts, carried on their trade in fuch places as beft fuited themfelves, which weakened the colony ; and during the Dutch war, the enemy frequently infulted its coafts, and fometimes even cut fhips out of its harbours. About this time fourteen Englifh, and an equal number of Indians, were fent to make difcoveries upon the continent. They travelled feveral days, under the command of captain Batt, when arriving at a certain boundary, the Indians refufed to proceed farther ; afferting, that thofe nations murdered all ftrangers.

Upon Batt's return, Berkeley, who ftill continued governor, refolved to go in perfon, and improve his difcoveries ; but was prevented, by an unexpected rebellion. The infurgents complained of mifmanagements in the government, the decay

of

of their trade, of exorbitant grants, which included the fettled property of many people, and
the moleftation they met with from the Indians;
all which they attributed to the feverity of the Englifh governor, who paid no regard to the intereft
or condition of Virginia. Colonel Park, and Mr.
Ludwell, fecretary of the colony, had been fent to
England to petition for redrefs; but were forced to
return, without the leaft profpect of relief. At
length, the depredations committed by the Indians

governor refufed, thinking it illegal for the people to judge of their own intereft; and the governor being flow in his preparations againft thofe

man, of a graceful prefence and winning carriage,
who had been bred to the law, and had a lively
and fluent expreffion, fit to fet off a popular caufe,
and to influence men who were ready to hear whatever could be faid, to colour in a proper manner
what was already ftrongly drawn by their own feel-
ings, by a fpecious or perhaps real, though ill-
judged regard, took up arms, without any commiffion, to act againft the enemy; and being now at
the head of near feven hundred men, found himfelf in a condition to give law to the governor,
and forced him to give a fanction, by his authority,
to thefe proceedings.

Bacon, thus armed with the commiffion of a general, and followed by the whole force of the colony, was preparing to march againft the Indians,
when

when the governor, freed from the immediate terror of his forces, revoked his commission, proclaimed him a traitor, and issued a reward for apprehending him. This brought matters to extremities. Bacon adhered to what he had done; the people adhered to Bacon: and the governor, not in the least inclined to temporize, fled over the river Potowmack, proclaimed Bacon's adherents traitors, put himself at the head of a small body of troops, which he had raised in Maryland, and of such Virginians as continued faithful to him, and wrote to England for supplies. On the other hand, Bacon marched to James Town, and in his march treated the governor's friends and abettors as rebels, destroying their plantations; by his own authority, and that of four of the council, summoned the assembly, and for six months disposed of all things according to his own pleasure. A civil war seemed now unavoidable, and by this time the colony was almost entirely ruined; for the Indians, taking advantage of the distractions among the English, under pretence of assisting the governor, fell upon the frontiers, gave no quarter to age or sex, and indiscriminately destroyed the plantations of both parties, when all was quieted in a sudden manner, as it had begun, by the natural death of Bacon. The people, unable to act without a head, now proposed terms of accommodation, which Berkeley accepted; and peace was restored and preserved, not so much by the removal of the grievances complained of, as by the arrival of a regiment from England,

which

which remained a long time in the country. It muſt be remarked, in honour of the moderation of the government, that no perſon ſuffered in his life or eſtate for this rebellion ; a circumſtance the more extraordinary, as at that time many people were very importunate in ſoliciting grants of land in Virginia.

Sir William Berkeley, reſolving to viſit England, appointed Herbert Jeffreys, Eſq; deputy-governor ; but died himſelf, ſoon after his arrival in his native country. Jeffreys ſummoned an aſſembly to meet at Middle Plantation, now called Williamſburgh, and invited the Indians there to treat of a peace, which they joyfully accepted. To render this meeting as ſplendid as poſſible, and to impreſs the Indians with a high idea of the Engliſh nation, it was fixed for the 29th of May, the birth and re-ſtoration day of Charles II. The princeſs Pa-munke attended at the head of her chiefs, and ſilence being proclaimed, the articles of peace, which the deputy-governor had drawn up, were read, and explained by interpreters ; and the queen, being admitted within the bar of the court, chearful-ly ſigned them ; the whole ceremony was con-cluded by a general diſcharge of all the artillery : after which, her majeſty and the Indian chiefs were nobly entertained by the governor, and returned home highly ſatisfied with their treatment.

The following year deputy-governor Jeffreys died, and was ſucceeded in his poſt by Sir Henry Chicheley (lord Colepepper having been appointed

3 chief

chief governor) who built forts at the head of the four great rivers, in order to curb the Indians; and paffed an act for preventing the fhipping off tobacco from Virginia, by the people of Carolina and Maryland, to the manifeft prejudice of the colony. In 1679, lord Colepepper arrived in Virginia himfelf, and not only brought over with him a commiffion for trying Bacon's followers, but alfo fuch inftructions from the Englifh miniftry as unhinged the conftitution of the colony, and rendered it wholly dependent on the crown. The affembly, fenfible of the vaft powers with which he was invefted, paffed many of his bills without oppofition; and he, in return, agreed to thofe which feemed conducive to the intereft of the colony. But inftead of refting fatisfied with a thoufand pounds a-year, the falary ufually paid to his predeceffors, he prevailed on the affembly to grant him double that fum, befides one hundred and fifty pounds for his houfe-rent; and as prefents of wine, &c. had been generally made to the governor by captains of fhips, he obliged every captain to pay him twenty fhillings for each veffel under an hundred tons, and thirty fhillings for all above that burthen; which impofition has fubfifted ever fince, though founded on no act of affembly.

As he propofed to make but a fhort ftay in the colony, he determined to make the moft of his powers for his own intereft: accordingly, the current coin of Virginia being in value far lower than the fame pieces in the neighbouring governments, he firft

bought

bought up all the light dollars which he could procure at five fhillings each, and then raifed their value
to fix by proclamation. But his avarice was difappointed; for though he iffued his dollars at the
advanced price, and obliged the regiment brought
over by Sir John Berry to receive them at that rate,
yet in his own falary, his duty on fhipping, and
other parts of the revenue, he was a confiderable
lofer by thofe light pieces; and this ftep occafioned
a mutiny among the troops.

Befides this arbitrary proceeding, his lordfhip
daily gave the Virginians frefh provocation, by re-
pealing the acts of affembly, and giving them to underftand, that their validity depended alone on his
pleafure. His conduct would certainly have occafioned a rebellion, if the common people had not
fuffered fo much lately by Bacon's infurrection, that
they had neither ability nor fpirit to engage in
another: and the governor, in whatever did not
concern himfelf, was always ready to promote the
welfare of the colony. However, thefe confidera-
tions did not prevent the affembly from coming to
fome very vigorous refolutions againft his arbitrary
meafures. On his return to England, he appointed Sir Henry Chicheley deputy-governor,
having refided in Virginia not above twelve months.
The colony having recovered its late loffes, the
planters made more tobacco than they could vend,
and the poorer fort, perceiving the commodity
fall in its value confiderably, entered into a combination to deftroy their own and their neighbours
crops,

crops, which frantic refolution they in part executed; but many of them being apprehended, were
tried, and executed for felony.

An incident that now happened gives us an opportunity of animadverting on the arbitrary dif-
pofal of American lands by the crown.   It is true,
the firft adventurers being under contract with the
government, the crown had a right to infift upon
the due performance ; but after the lands fo difcovered were cultivated and fettled at their expence,
and under thofe grants, none but themfelves could
have any property in thofe lands: yet this obvious
maxim of juftice was frequently violated, under various frivolous pretences.   A large tract
of land in Virginia, called the Northern-neck,
which had been granted to the earl of St. Albans
and other proprietors, was now regranted to lord
Colepepper.   This tract contained feveral counties, which had a right to fend reprefentatives to
the affembly ; but the inhabitants being of opinion, that they muft fuffer by being under a proprietary direction, brought an appeal before the affembly againft his lordfhip's claim.   This was a tender
point ; but to do lord Colepepper juftice, he acted
in the affair with great equity and caution: and
fatisfied all the juft demands of the former proprietors, though he perceived, that, without fome frefh
authority from England, he could never bring the
affembly over to his views.   He therefore fomented a difpute between the affembly and council,
by encouraging the affembly to infift upon the fole

right

right of judging appeals; but reprefented matters
fo at home as to procure an order vefting that
right folely in the governor and council. However, far from taking any undue advantage of a
circumftance fo much in his favour, he endeavoured, by every method, to reconcile the inhabitants
of the Northern Neck to his proprietaryfhip, but
in vain: for the majority of them carried their
complaints before the affembly, and petitioned the
king, tho' having no agent in England, without
fuccefs.   At laft, finding their caufe defperate, they
compounded with lord Colepepper, and paid him
their quit-rent; and the eftate is now in the poffeffion of the Fairfax family, one of whofe anceftors
married the daughter of lord Colepepper, that nobleman leaving no male heir.

   Lord Colepepper omitted nothing that could
contribute to the profperity of the province.   He
banifhed from the courts of law the low practices which had long oppreffed the fuitors, and are
a difgrace to the profeffion; reduced the public expences, efpecially by demolifhing the forts erected
by Chicheley, which were found very expenfive,
and inadequate to the intended purpofes, and in
their room fubftituted fome troops of light-horfe,
in order to fcour the country, and check the Indians, who were now too much reduced to make any
dangerous attempts againft the colony.   Having,
by his own authority, appointed Mr. Spencer refident of the council, in preference to elder members,
by which the adminiftration of the colony devolved

on

on him in the abfence of the governor and his deputy, he returned to England, in 1682, and was fucceeded by lord Effingham, who is accufed of having outdone him in all his arbitrary meafures, tho' the province did not receive the like benefits from his adminiftration. Equally mean as imperious, he compelled the clerks and under-officers of his courts to fhare their fees with him ; obliged attornies and fchoolmafters to take out licences ; introduced exorbitant expences into all teftamentary affairs ; imprifoned the people by his own authority, without bringing them to a trial ; fubftituted proclamations in the room of laws, and even pretended he could repeal ftanding laws. The judges, however, paid no regard to thefe proclamations. · In his patent, he had a power of infifting on the quit-rent in money ; but by an act of affembly, the planters were allowed to pay it in tobacco, at twopence per pound : when that commodity fell in its value, he by proclamation repealed this law, and demanded the quit-rents, either in money, or tobacco at one penny per pound : a hardfhip to which the Virginians were obliged to fubmit, from the exprefs words of the patent. They, however, fent colonel Ludwell to England, as their agent, to petition his majefty for redrefs of their grievances ; but were fo far from obtaining any, that upon the acceffion of James II. the duties on tobacco were increafed to fuch a degree as muft have wholly ruined that trade, if other colonies, both Spanifh, French, and Englifh, had not difcontinued raifing that ftaple.

As

As the ftate-houfe at James Town had not been
rebuilt, fince it was burnt down by col. Laurence,
one of Bacon's officers, the governor prevailed on
the affembly to lay a duty on all liquors imported
from other colonies, for rebuilding it. He erected
a court of chancery, under pretence that he was by
his patent invefted with a chancery power, in which
he fat himfelf, employed his council as mafters in
chancery, exacted moft exorbitant fees, and wholly
fet afide the chancery jurifdiction that had always refided in the general court hitherto; who neverthelefs refumed it on his lordfhip's departure for England, which happened foon after the Revolution;
when he appointed colonel Nathaniel Bacon, father
of the before-mentioned Nathaniel Bacon, refident
of the province. During his adminiftration, the
project of a college was approved of by the council,
and referred to the affembly.

Soon after, Francis Nicholfon, Efq; was made deputy-governor; a gentleman well qualified for this
poft, who formed a plan of government far more liberal and public-fpirited than any that the Virginians
had ever yet experienced. He refumed the propofed
plan for a college, which feemed to have been fufpended for want of money, and, by his affiftance,
twenty five hundred pounds were foon fubfcribed,
and confiderable donations received from the Virginian merchants in London. The affembly now drew
up an addrefs to king William and queen Mary,
praying for a charter to found it, which met with
all imaginable encouragement. The Rev. Dr.
Thomas

.Thomas Bray was appointed president of the future college, who purchased a handsome library for its use, and engaged several other learned gentlemen as fellows and professors. But the money subscribed being insufficient for the purpose, occasioned a fresh delay : at length, this inconveniency was removed, their majesties, the nobility, clergy, and gentry of England, generously contributing their aid ; and the buildings were erected upon a very noble plan drawn by Sir Christopher Wren, with large gardens, and all the conveniences to be met with in similar European institutions, and salaries appointed for the professors, among whom is a master for instructing Indian youths. The college has been since greatly improved, and at present bids fair to be one of the seats of science and the polite arts.

Mr. Nicholson omitted no means to ingratiate himself with his people, encouraged all schemes that were laid before him for improving the colony, and bestowed prizes on such as excelled in athletic exercises ; a most excellent policy in a country surrounded by savage nations. But notwithstanding all his endeavours, the Virginians could never be brought to live together in large towns, because every one chose to cultivate the spot of ground that lay most convenient for his own ease and interest. During his government, a cohabitation act indeed passed ; but was so far from having effect, that the greatest part of James Town continued in ashes and uninhabited, and no new towns were built. After all, though cohabitation

Q 4

may be commodious for great traders; yet many have doubted whether it would contribute to the real intereſt of the colony, as living ſeparately keeps the price of labour low, and prevents the luxury and vices that prove ſo deſtructive to individuals in large cities. He likewiſe paſſed ſeveral acts for the encouragement of the linen, leather, and other manufactories, and acquired the eſteem of the, inhabitants, by his affability, and great attention to the intereſt of the colony.

Lord Effingham being removed from his government in 1692, was ſucceeded by Sir Edmund Andros, a man extremely obnoxious for his arbitrary behaviour as governor in other American provinces, during the late reigns; and who, in the public opinion, was thought to deſerve capital puniſhment, inſtead of being rewarded with the government of Virginia. This extraordinary ſtep can only be accounted for by ſuppoſing, that the Engliſh miniſtry was then compoſed of Tories, as was frequently the caſe in king William's reign; and that he poſſeſſed ab.lities for a governor, which he had proſtituted only to their intereſt; for he was far from being a bad governor of Virginia. As the Engliſh merchants and captains of ſhips diſliked the cohabitation act, which in the end would have reſtricted them to particular ports, Sir Edmund, who arrived in February, brought with him inſtructions to procure its repeal, in which he ſucceeded. A patent was laid before the ſame aſſembly for making one Mr. Neale poſtmaſter-general of Virginia, and the other American provinces;

vinces; but though an act was paffed in his favour, the fcheme was dropped, it being found impoffible to carry it into execution, from the ftraggling fituation of the provincial houfes. In the
following year a dreadful ftorm happened, which
ftopping up fome rivers, and opening channels for
others, which were even navigable, feemed to reverfe the courfe of nature.

The great objection to his government was,
his attempts to reduce the conftitution of the province to a nearer conformity with that of England;
which the Virginians ftrongly oppofed, thinking it
would leffen the authority of their affembly, whofe
acts they confidered as their beft fecurity for their
eftates. In other refpects, Sir Edward was a
good governor : he encouraged all kinds of manufactures ; the propagation of cotton ; erected
fulling-mills ; regulated the public offices, into
which great abufes had crept ; put in order the
regifters and public papers ; fhortened the expence
of time in law and commercial proceedings ; and was
in a fair way of retrieving his character, when he
was recalled in 1697. About this time the Englifh
fquadron commanded by admiral Neville, which had
been in purfuit of the French admiral, De Points,
arriving at Virginia, brought with it an infectious
diftemper, of which the admiral himfelf died, and
moft of his principal officers ; which communicating itfelf to the Virginians, made great havock,
efpecially at James Town. The Whig intereft now
prevailing in England, Mr. Nicholfon, who was

2   in

in Maryland, was appointed governor of Virginia, who immediately removed the courts of juftice, his own refidence, and the feat of provincial bufinefs, to Middle Plantation, which he chriftened Williamf-burgh ; and laid out the town in the form of a W, perhaps from the low conceit of paying a compliment to the initial letter of that monarch's name, fince which James Town is dwindled into an infignificant village. The college had been erected here, and oppofite to it the governor now built a ftately ftructure, which he ftiled the Capitol, and laid the foundations of many new handfome buildings. All this could not be done without great expence, and the planters, who had no idea of public magnificence, repined at the fums levied ; the more, becaufe the crops this year were remarkably fhort, and their fervants fickly ; a tax of fifteen fhillings having been laid upon every white fervant, and twenty upon every negro : and thefe grievances grew ftill more infupportable by the war then ready to break out between France and England, and the fwarms of privateers that infefted the coaft.

Among others, in 1700, a French privateer arrived at the mouth of James River, and intercepted fome fhips bound for London ; but a fmall veffel flipping by him, acquainted captain Paffenger, of the Shoreham man of war, who came up with the privateer, and forced him to furrender. About this time a fort was projected at New-York, to be provided with a regular garrifon. The people of New-York, unable to bear the expence, reprefent-

ed

ed by their agents, that as Virginia would be greatly benefited by the said fort, which would secure
them against the invasions of the French and Indians, they ought to contribute at least nine
hundred pounds towards the expence. Governor
Nicholson, being of the same opinion, undertook
to carry this affair through the assembly; but he
was disappointed in his expectations; for the af-
sembly remonstrated, " That neither the forts then
existing, nor any other that might be built in the
province of New-York, could in the least avail to
the defence and security of Virginia; for that either
the French or Indians might invade that colony,
and not come within an hundred miles of any such
fort." Notwithstanding his ill success in the af-
sembly, the governor, zealous for the good of the
province, considering himself, in some measure,
answerable for the money, went immediately
to New-York, and gave bills for that sum, re-
lying entirely upon the generosity of queen Anne
for his indemnification. He was equally generous and public-spirited in every other part of his
conduct, having laid it down as a principle, that
all the English provinces on the continent of America, ought to be leagued in one common interest,
and contribute jointly, according to their abilities,
to defend each other against their enemies *.

About

* During his government, the Virginians entertaining a notion that prodigious benefits would arise to the province from

the

About this time a war breaking out between France and England, the governor laid an embargo upon the fhipping, to prevent their falling into the enemy's hands.   Some time after a terrible hurricane happened, which did prodigious damage to the fhipping and plantations ; in other refpects, Virginia, at this time, experienced a greater degree of tranquility than any of the neighbouring colonies. Mr. Nicholfon was recalled in 1704, and fucceeded by the earl of Orkney, who held the nominal commiffion above thirty-fix years.   In fact, as this province was lefs expofed than many others to the attacks of the enemy, the miniftry, from this time, appropriated twelve hundred pounds of the two thoufand granted to the governor, as a penfion for fome nobleman, whom they could not conveniently provide for otherwife.   That this government is fuch appears plainly ; for the deputy-governor, who refides in the province, has his commiffion from the crown, under the great feal, the fame as the governor, and is invefted with the fame powers.   The earl of Orkney's firft deputy-governor was Edward Notte, Efq; during whofe adminiftration nothing memorable happened ; except that he prevailed on the affembly to vote a fund for erecting a houfe for the governor at Williamfburgh. Upon his death, brigadier Hunter was appointed to this poft, a gentleman of great abilities, though

the introduction of camels, beafts able to carry twelve hundred weight each, imported feveral ; but this climate, as well as that of Barbadoes, difagreeing with thofe animals, the project proved aboitive.

he

he had no opportunity of diftinguifhing himfelf in this government, from whence he was removed to that of Jamaica. He was fucceeded by colonel Alexander Spotfwood, who thoroughly underftood the interefts and nature of the Virginians, and being a good mathematician, laid out new plantations and roads, which rendered the province far more commodious and fecure than before. Obferving the great difadvantage of trading with the Indians, without proper regulations, he formed fuch as proved of infinite fervice to the colony; and raifed a fund for educating the children of the Indians, as a means to render them well inclined and ufeful to the colony.

Tobacco being the ftaple produce of Virginia, Mr. Spotfwood obferved, with concern, that through the abufes practifed in that trade it had fallen into fome difrepute at market; and as the province muft have foon been ruined if thefe practices had continued, he paffed a law, which, though repealed afterwards, was certainly well intended, providing, that all tobacco to be carried from Virginia fhould be lodged in warehoufes, and examined as to its quality and goodnefs. After the peace of Utrecht, it being thought highly neceffary that the Virginians, if poffible, fhould acquire fome knowledge of the country beyond the Apalachian mountains, the French having made it a capital maxim in their American policy, to conceal all the country between thofe mountains and the Miffiffippi from the Englifh, he refolved to profecute in perfon this im-

portant

portant difcovery.   On his return from this expedition he tried eight pirates, who were difcovered in the
province in the difguife of traders, four of whom
were executed.   A war breaking out with Spain,
a fcheme was adopted for raifing a great continental Englifh force to attack the weftern Spanifh fettlements; and Spotfwood was intended to head that
important expedition.   But a peace being concluded,
Spotfwood, who had drawn up an excellent plan for
that purpofe, it was fuppofed, hurt his intereft, by
infifting on the practicability of the plan, and requiring, that thofe he had employed fhould be indemnified for their expence and trouble ; and fome
of the Virginians themfelves, thinking him too
converfant in their affairs, practifed feveral low arts
to obtain his removal, whence Hugh Dryfdale, Efq;
was appointed in his room, who arrived in 1723.
Spotfwood remained in America, and upon the
breaking out of the Spanifh war in 1739, his project was adopted by government, and orders iffued for affembling a great force on the American
continent, the command of which was intended to
have been conferred on him, had he not died in the
mean time.   But France entering into the war, and
new alterations happening in the affairs of Europe,
this expedition was alfo dropped, that the war might
be more vigoroufly carried on againft our natural
enemy.

Mr. Gooch, who fucceeded Dryfdale, bore a
great fhare, in his own perfon, of the Spanifh and

French

French war, terminated by the peace of Aix-la-Chapelle, in 1748 *, during which period this province affords nothing worth recording. Under the government of Mr. Dinwiddie, who behaved with great addrefs and fpirit in the late war, Virginia took the lead in alarming the Englifh miniftry about the incroachments of the French; and the vigorous meafures that were purfued in confequence, terminated, as has been already feen, in the reduction of all the French fettlements in North-America, Louifiana excepted, and their ceffion to the crown of England, by the peace of Paris, in 1763.

The CLIMATE, SOIL, and NATURAL HISTORY of VIRGINIA.

The whole face of the country is fo extremely low towards the fea, that even within fifteen fathom foundings, land can hardly be diftinguifhed from the maft head. However, all this coaft of America has one ufeful particularity ; the foundings uniformly and gradually diminifh as veffels approach the land, by which the diftance from fhore may be exactly known. The trees appearing as if they arofe out of the water afford a very uncommon, but not difagreeable view. In failing to Virginia or Maryland, mariners pafs a ftreight between two points of land, called the Capes of Virginia, which opens into the Bay of Chefapeak, one of the largeft and

* See Vol. I. page 513.

fafeft

safest bays in the world ; and enters the country near three hundred miles from the south to the north, having the eastern side of Maryland and a small part of Virginia on the same peninsula, to cover it from the Atlantic Ocean. This bay is for a considerable length about eighteen miles in breadth; and seven in the narrowest part, the water being nine fathoms deep in most places. It receives through its whole extent, both on the eastern and western side, a vast number of navigable rivers ; from the side of Virginia, James River, York River, Rapahannock, and the Potowmack, not to mention those of Maryland.

All these great rivers in the order set down, from south to north, discharge themselves, with several smaller ones, into the Bay of Chesapeak, and are not only navigable themselves for very large vessels a prodigious way into the country, but have so many creeks, and receive such a number of small and navigable rivers, as renders the communication between all parts of this country infinitely more easy than that of any other in the world. The Potowmack is navigable near two hundred miles, being nine miles broad at its entrance, and for a vast way not less than seven. The other three rivers are navigable above eighty miles, and in their several windings approach each other so nearly, that the distance between one and the other is in some parts not more than ten, nay sometimes five miles ; whereas, in others, the same rivers are fifty miles distant from each other. Hence the planters load

and

and unload veffels of great burthen at their cwn doors : a very fortunate circumftance, as their commodities are bulky, and of fmall value in proportion to their bulk ; for elfe they could never afford to fend their tobacco to market at its prefent low price, charged as it is in England with a duty of fix times its original value.

The foil in the low grounds is a dark fat mould, which for many years, without any manure, yields plentiful crops. The foil at a diftance from the rivers is light and fandy, fooner exhaufted than the low country ; but is yet of a warm and generous nature, and, by the help of a kindly fun, yields tobacco and coin extremely well. There is no better wheat than what this province and Maryland produce ; but the culture of tobacco employing all their attention, they fcarcely cultivate wheat enough for their own ufe.

The heats in fummer are exceffive, though not without the allay of refrefhing fea-breezes. The weather is changeable, and the changes fudden and violent. The winter frofts come on without the leaft warning : after a warm day, towards winter, fo intenfe a cold frequently fucceeds, as to freeze over the broadeft and deepeft of the great rivers in a night's time ; but thefe frofts, as well as the rains, are rather violent than of long continuance. Though terrible thunder-ftorms frequently happen in fummer, they feldom do any mifchief. In general the fky is clear, and the air thin, pure, and penetrating.

From the above defcription of the climate and foil, the reader may judge in what excellence and plenty every kind of fruit is produced in Virginia. The forefts are full of all kinds of timber-trees, and the plains are covered almoft the whole year with a prodigious number of flowers and flowering fhrubs, fo rich in colour and fo fragrant, that they occafioned the name of Florida to be originally given this country. It produces various medicinal herbs and roots, particulaily the rattle fnake root, excellent in the pleurify, and all diforders arifing from a vifcidity of the blood, and a fpecific for the bite of that animal ; as alfo the celebrated gin-feng of the Chinefe.

Horned cattle and hogs have multiplied incredibly, tho' the country was totally deftitute of thefe animals at its firft fettlement. The animals natural to the country are, deer, which are very numerous ; a kind of tigers, bears, wolves, foxes, racoons, fquirrels, wild cats, and the opoffum, a very uncommon animal, about the fize of a cat, which befides the belly common to all other animals, has a falfe one beneath it, with an aperture at the end, towards the hinder legs. Within this bag, on the ufual part of the common belly are a number of teats, upon which, when the female conceives, the young are formed, and there hang, like fruit, upon a ftalk, until they grow in bulk and weight to their appointed fize ; then they drop off, and are received into the falfe belly, from which they go

out

out at pleafure, and in which they take refuge, when they apprehend any kind of danger.

The Virginians have all our forts of tame and wild fowl, in equal perfection with us, and fome which we have not; as alfo an immenfe number of birds of various kinds, valuable for their beauty or fong. The white owl of this country is much larger than the fpecies which England produces, and is all over of a bright filver-coloured plumage, except one black fpot upon his breaft; the nightingale, named after the country, is a beautiful bird, whofe feathers are crimfon and blue; the mocking-bird imitates the notes of every other bird, and is judged to excel all in his own fong; the rock-bird, very fociable and agreeable, from the fweetnefs of his melody; the humming-bird, the fmalleft and moft beautiful of the whole feathered race, arrayed in fcarlet, green, and gold: this bird, fuppofed to live by fucking the dew that adheres to the flowers, is too delicate to be brought alive to England. The fea-coafts and rivers abound with feveral of the fpecies of European fifh, and with moft of thofe kinds which are peculiar to America. The reptiles are many. It would be tedious to enumerate all the kinds of ferpents bred here; the rattle-fnake being the principal, we fhall therefore content ourfelves with the defcription of that venomous creature only.

The rattle-fnake, when arrived at its full growth, is nearly as thick as a man's leg; the neck is flat, and very broad; the head fmall; the colour lively, though not dazzling; a pale yellow, with very beautiful fhades, is the moft predominant. But the moft remarkable part of this animal is its tail, which is fcaly, like a coat of mail, fomewhat flattifh, and produces every year a frefh row of fcales; thus, the age of the fnake may be known by thefe rows. When it ftirs, it makes a rattling noife with its tail, from which it has obtained its name. This animal rarely attacks any paffenger who gives him no provocation, but if trod on, certainly bites; and if purfued, folds himfelf up in a circle, and darts with great force againft his enemy.' The bite is mortal, if the rattle-fnake root, bruifed or chewed, a never-failing antidote againft its poifon, be not immediately applied to the wound, in the nature of a pultice; but happily this poifonous animal is feldom met with. The Indians, however, chace this ferpent, and efteem his flefh excellent food.

TRADE, GENIUS of the INHABITANTS, &c.

Tobacco, an aboriginal plant in America, of very antient ufe, though neither fo generally cultivated, nor fo well manufactured, as fince the arrival of the Europeans, is the great ftaple commodity of this country, as well as of Maryland. When at its full height, it is as tall as a common fized man; the ftalk ftrait, hairy, and clammy; the

leaves

leaves alternate, of a faded yellowiſh green, and towards the lower part of the plant very large. The ſeeds of tobacco are firſt ſown in beds, from whence they are tranſplanted, the firſt rainy weather, into a ground diſpoſed into little hillocks, like a hop garden. In a month's time from the tranſplantation, they become a foot high ; they are then topt, and the lower leaves pruned off, and carefully cleared from weeds and worms twice a week ; in about ſix weeks after they obtain their full growth, and begin to turn browniſh, by which mark the tobacco is judged to be ripe. The plants are cut down as faſt as they ripen, heaped up, and laid all night to ſweat ; the next day they are carried to the tobacco-houſe, which is built to admit as much air as is conſiſtent with keeping out rain; where they are hung ſeparately to dry, for four or five weeks, and are then taken down in moiſt weather, otherwiſe they would crumble to duſt. After this they are laid upon ſticks, and covered up cloſe to ſweat for a week or two longer ; and are then ſtript and ſorted, the top being the beſt, the bottom the worſt tobacco ; and are then made up in hogſheads, or formed into rolls. Wet ſeaſons muſt be carefully laid hold on for all this work, elſe the tobacco will not be ſufficiently pliable.

Traders diſtinguiſh two ſorts of tobacco ; Aranookoe, from Maryland and the northern parts of Virginia, is ſtrong and hot in the mouth, but ſells well in the markets of Holland, Germany, and the North. The other ſort is called ſweet ſcent-

ed,

ed, the beft of which comes from James's and York river, in the fouthern parts of Virginia. The revenue is obliged to no commodity fo much as to this: it produces a vaft fum, yet appears to lay but a very inconfiderable burden upon the people of England; all the weight, in reality, falls upon the planter, who is kept down by the lownefs of the original price: and as another province deals in the fame commodity, if the Virginians were to ftraiten the market, and raife the price, the people of Maryland wou'd certainly take the advantage of it; as the Virginians, no doubt, would of the Marylanders in a like cafe. Thus they have no profpect of ever bettering their condition, and are the lefs able to endure it, as they live, in general, to the full extent of their fortunes; and any failure in the fale of their tobacco, of courfe, brings them heavily in debt to the London merchants, who get mortgages on their eftates, which are confumed to the bone with the canker of an eight per cent. ufury. Yet, however the planters may complain of the tobacco trade, the revenue draws near three hundred thoufand pounds a-year from this fingle article; and the exported tobacco, the greater part of the profits of which falls to the fhare of the Englifh merchant, brings almoft as large a fum annually into the kingdom; to fay nothing of the great advantage which England derives from being fupplied by one of its own colonies with a commodity for which the reft of Europe pays ready money; befides the employment of two hundred large fhips, and a proportionable num-

ber

ber of feamen, in this trade. The colony exports annually above forty thoufand hogfheads of tobacco, each hogfhead containing eight hundred weight. It likewife carries on a large trade with the Weft-Indies, in lumber, pitch, tar, provifions, &c. and fends to England flax, hemp, iron, ftaves, and walnut and cedar plank. Their manufactures are fo infignificant as not to deferve mentioning ; for the Virginians take every article for convenience or ornament from the mother-country.

The number of white people in this province amounts to about feventy thoufand ; fo that Virginia is not as populous as might have been expected from fo ancient and flourifhing a colony ; though the number of inhabitants is every day increafing, by the migration of the Irifh from Penfylvania, who fell their lands in that province to the more frugal and induftrious Germans, and take up new ground in the remote counties of Virginia, Maryland, and North-Carolina. A confiderable number of French refugees are likewife fettled in Virginia ; but the negroe flaves, who cannot be fewer than an hundred thoufand fouls, as between three and four thoufand are annually imported into the two tobacco colonies, are much the larger part of the inhabitants ; and the negroes here rather increafe than diminifh, from moderate labour, wholefome food, and a healthy climate.

The Virginians are a chearful hofpitable people, though vain and oftentatious, and for the greater part members of the church of England. There are fome few meeting-houfes of Prefbyterians and

R 4　　　　Quakers ;

Quakers; there being both in Virginia and Mary-land, a general toleration for ministers of all persua-sions, legally qualified, to officiate in places proper-ly licenfed. The country between James River and York River is the beft inhabited and culti-vated. Lunenburgh, the remoteft fettlement, is about an hundred miles fouth-weft from Hanover, which is fixty miles diftant from Williamfburgh, the metropolis.

COURTS of JUDICATURE.

The frontier or fartheft back counties, being of great extent, no navigation, and little foreign trade, hold quarterly county courts only; all the others have monthly courts: variations happen from time to time. In 1752 they were as follows:

QUARTERLY COUNTY-COURTS.

Brunfwick, } Laft Tuefday in March, June,
Fairfax. } September, December.

Lunenburgh. Firft Tuefday in January, April, July, October.

Frederick, } Second Tuefday in February,
Albermarle. } May, Auguft, November.

Augufta. Fourth Tuefdays in faid months.

MONTHLY COUNTY-COURTS

Henrico,
Richmond, } Firft Monday in every
Williamfburgh. } month.

James

James City, Northumberland, Nanfemond.	Second Monday.
York.	Third Monday.
Prince William, Cumberland.	Fourth Monday.
Middlefex, Elizabeth City, Spotfylvania.	First Tuefday.
Prince George, King and Queen, Northampton, Stafford.	Second Tuefday.
Effex, Gooch-land, Princefs Ann, Surry,	Third Tuefday.
Louifa, Weftmoreland, Accomack.	Fourth Tuefday.
Charles City.	First Wednefday.
Warwick, Ifle of Wight, Hanover.	First Thurfday.
New Kent, Southampton.	Second Thurfday.
Norfolk, Colepepper.	Third Thurfday.
Gloucefter, Orange.	Fourth Thurfday.
Chefterfield, King George.	First Friday.

Lancafter

| Lancaster, Carolina. | } | Second Friday. |
| King William, Amelia. | } | Third Friday, in each month. |

Thus the government is divided into forty-five counties; fix of which hold quarterly courts; and thirty-nine hold monthly courts; and the laws by which this province is governed, are, as near as possible, conformable to those of England.

✳✳✳✳✳✳✳✳✳✳✳✳✳✳✳✳✳✳✳✳✳

CAROLINA.

THE whole coast of North-America was formerly known by the name of Virginia. The province now properly so called, with Maryland and the two Carolina's, was known by the name of South-Virginia. The Spaniards consider-ed it as part of Florida, which they made to ex-tend from New-Mexico to the Atlantic Ocean. But as the country shewed no marks of producing gold or silver, it remained entirely neglected by Europe, until, as we observed in the history of Vir-ginia, Sir Walter Rawleigh projected an establish-ment there. It was not in the part now called Vir-ginia, but in North-Carolina, that the first English settlements were made, and unhappily destroyed.

After-

Afterwards, the adventurers entered the Bay of Chefapeak, and fixed a permanent colony to the northward. Thus, though Carolina was the firft part of the weftern coaft of America which had an European colony, yet, by a ftrange caprice, it was long deferted by the European nations, who fettled, with infinitely greater difficulty, in climates much lefs advantageous or agreeable; and it was not until the year 1663 that the Englifh formally fettled this country, when king Charles II. granted by patent to Edward earl of Clarendon, then lord high-chancellor of England, George duke of Albemarle, William lord Craven, John lord Berkeley, Anthony lord Afhley, Sir George Carteret, Sir William Berkeley, and Sir George Colleton, all that territory in his American dominions from the north end of Lucke ifland, in the Southern Virginian Sea, and within 36 deg. of north latitude, to the weft as far as the South Seas, and foutherly as far as the river St. Matheo, bordering on the coaft of Florida, within 31 deg. of north latitude, and fouth-weft, in a direct line, as far as the South Seas aforefaid; with full power to fettle and govern the country, together with the ufual inveftiture of fifheries, mines, power of life and limb, &c. Accordingly, thefe gentlemen had the model of a conftitution framed, and a body of fundamental laws compiled, by the celebrated philofopher Locke; by which the lords proprietors themfelves ftood in the place of the king, gave their affent or diffent to all laws, appointed all officers, and beftowed all titles

tles of dignity. A palatine was to be chosen out of the proprietaries, who was to hold that post during life, and was to be succeeded by the eldest of the other proprietaries. This palatine was to act as president of a court, composed of himself and three other proprietors, who were vested with the execution of the whole powers of the charter: each member was authorised to nominate a deputy, who might act for him in Carolina, but according to his directions. They appointed also two other branches, in a great measure analogous to the old Saxon constitution. They made three classes of nobility: the lowest, composed of those who had grants of twelve thousand acres of land, were to be called barons; the next order were to possess twenty-four thousand acres, or two baronies, with the title of caciques, and were to answer our earls; the third were to possess two caciqueships, or forty-eight thousand acres, and were to be entitled landgraves, a title in this province analogous to that of duke. This body was to form the upper-house, and their lands were not to be alienable by parcels. The lower-house was to be formed, as in the other colonies, of representatives from the several towns or counties; and the whole was not to be called an assembly, as in the rest of the plantations, but a parliament; which was to sit once in two years, oftener, if necessary.

To make this government approach still nearer to the antient feodal constitution, the white inhabitants, from sixteen to sixty years of age, if called

upon

upon by, the grand council, were obliged to take the field with proper arms. Every planter was to pay annually one penny, per acre quit-rent to his proprietary; and each county was to have a sheriff, and four justices of the peace. All free persons who came over, were to have fifty acres of land for themselves, fifty for each man-servant, and as many for each woman servant who was marriageable, and forty for each of either sex who was not marriageable; and every servant, after the expiration of his or her servitude, was to be deemed free, and be intitled to fifty acres, subject only to the above quit-rent. But the proprietaries, in all their leases, carefully excepted all mines, minerals, and quarries of precious stones, as well as when the colonists bought off their quit-rents, which many of them did.

Though the proprietors expended twelve thousand pounds in attempting to settle their grant, the province owed its establishment to the humane disposition of that excellent man who formed the model of their government, which allowed an unlimited toleration to people of all religious persuasions, whereby a great number of dissenters, whom the government at home treated with more rigour than was consistent with justice or good policy, were induced to transport themselves, with their fortunes and families, into Carolina. About 1670, colonel William Sayle was appointed by the lords-proprietors governor of the province. At this time, the lands about Albemarle and Port-Royal rivers, being most convenient for trade, were the

most

moſt frequented; but the colonists ſoon learned, from experience, that paſturage and agriculture were neceſſary for their eſtabliſhment; whence Aſhley and Cooper Rivers drew thither ſuch numbers, that the country thereabouts ſoon became the beſt inhabited part of the colony. In 1671, captain Halſtead arrived with a ſupply of proviſions of all kinds from the proprietaries in England, who created James Carteret, Sir John Yeomans, and John Locke, Eſq; landgraves. Some deviations were made about this time from the original conſtitutions. The number of landgraves and caciques required by the original conſtitution to conſtitute the upper-houſe not being to be found, a governor was nominated by the palatine, whoſe council was to conſiſt of ſeven deputies of the proprietaries, as many choſen by the parliament, and an equal number of the eldeſt landgraves and caciques; to whom were added, (all nominated by the proprietaries) an admiral, a chamberlain, chancellor, chief-juſtice, ſecretary, ſurveyor, treaſurer, high-ſteward, regiſter of births, burials, and marriages, regiſter of writings, and marſhal of the admiralty. The quorum of the council was to conſiſt of the governor and ſix of the members, three of whom were to be proprietary-deputies; and the parliament was to be compoſed of the governor, the deputies of the proprietaries, ten members to be choſen by the freeholders of Berkeley county, and ten by thoſe of Colliton county; but the number of thoſe repre-

ſentatives

3

fentatives was to be increafed, in proportion to the growth of the colony.

On the deceafe of the duke of Albemarle, the firft palatine, the earl of Craven fucceeded to this poft, in 1671, when the above temporary laws were enacted. The proprietors now feem to have conceived very fanguine expectations of the colony; for they ordered captain Halftead to fail up Afhley river to make difcoveries, and fent over the model of a magnificent town, to be built upon a point of land between Afhley and Cooper rivers, as the metropolis of the province, to be named Charles Town. The promifing afpect of the colony invited over many of the old cavalier principles, and others, whofe libertine manners gave great offence to the original planters, who were chiefly diffenters. Thefe new fettlers gaining a majority in one of the affemblies, by attempting to exclude all diffenters, produced a kind of civil war in the colony, and hindered it, for many years, from making that progrefs which might have been expected from its great natural advantages. Sir John Yeomans fucceeded colonel Sayle as governor; but the diforders of the colony ftill increafed, the people fell into difputes of no lefs violent a nature with the lords-proprietors *; and provoking the Indians, by a feries of unjuft actions, gave occafion

* The two parties often came to blows with each other, and one Culpepper was fent prifoner to England by the governor, and tried for high treafon in Weftminfter-hall, for raifing a rebellion in Carolina; but was acquitted,

to two Indian wars, in which however they were at laft victorious, and fubdued almoft all the Indian nations within their limits, on this fide the Apalachian mountains.

To remedy thefe diforders, the proprietaries appointed colonel Weft governor, a wife, moderate, and courageous man, who, at his acceffion to the government, found great licentioufnefs prevailing, party difputes at a great height, and the Indian war ftill raging : however, by fiding with the popular party, (for the proprietaries, in the exercife of their power, had deviated greatly from the original conftitution) he healed the public divifions fo much, that the colony united in repelling the Weftoes, an Indian nation, which had committed great ravages. In 1682, he held a parliament in Charles Town, where feveral good laws paffed ; particularly, an act for fettling the militia. Thefe, and other popular acts of the governor, difpleafing the lords-proprietaries, Weft was removed from his government, and fucceeded by Jofeph Moreton, Efq;

The differences between the Indians and the colony ftill continuing, the proprietaries iffued a commiffion to Maurice Matthews, William Fuller, Jonathan Fitz, and John Boon, Efqrs. to hear and determine all differences between both parties ; which was foon diffolved, the commiffioners being accufed of unfair practices Notwithftanding thefe difcouraging diforders, three counties, viz. Berkeley, Craven, and Colliton, were laid out. Mr. Moreton, during his fhort government,

ment paſſed ſeveral excellent acts for the benefit of individuals, as well as of the colony; but he was ſoon removed, and Sir Richard Kyrle appointed in his room, who ſurvived his nomination but a few months; in conſequence of which, Mr. Weſt was again made governor, whoſe adminiſtration was of vaſt ſervice to the colony, by bringing over many induſtrious planters, moſt of whom were diſſenters. Lord Cardroſs, a Scotch nobleman, ſettled at Port Royal, with ten Scotch families; but diſagreeing with the government, returned home, and the ſettlement came to nothing. Weſt was ſucceeded by James Colleton, Eſq; one of the proprietaries, whoſe government was ſo unpopular, that the repreſentatives of the people thwarted every meaſure he propoſed, even to ſettling the militia, on which their own ſafety depended. Diſputes about tenures and quit-rents ſtill continuing, in 1687 he called a parliament, in which he and his party ſubſtituted, in the room of the original conſtitutions, other articles, under the title of ſtanding laws and temporary laws; a proceeding equally diſagreeable to both proprietaries and planters; ſo that Mr. Colleton was not only obliged to quit his government, but the province alſo. The adminiſtration ſeems now to have been put into the hands of gentlemen of the greateſt intereſt in the colony, without any intention of their being continued; colonel Quarry, Mr. Southwell, colonel Ludwell, and Mr. Smith, were ſucceſſively governors. The laſt, finding it impoſſible to gratify the people in all their de-

mands, in 1694, ingenuoufly informed the proprietaries, that it was impoffible to fettle the country,
except one of the proprietaries was fent over with
full power to redrefs their grievances. Upon
which, lord Afhley, eldeft fon to the earl of Shaftef-
bury, was pitched on for this purpofe; but he declined accepting the government, which was conferred on Mr. Archdale, to whofe printed account
of Carolina the public is chiefly indebted for its information concerning this province.

Mr. Archdale arrived in Auguft 1695, furnifhed with very ample powers, and immediately called
a parliament, in order to redrefs the grievances of
the colony, in which, with good management and
patience, he at laft fucceeded fo well, that the
affembly voted him an addrefs of thanks. He
was fucceeded by Jofeph Blake, Efq; a proprietary,
nephew to the famous admiral Blake. Many inconveniences having accrued from a ftrict adherence
to the letter of the original conftitutions, a fet of
forty-one articles, figned by the proprietaries, under the title of the laft fundamental conftitutions,
were fent from England, which allowed a liberty
of confcience as amply as the former; but were
never confirmed by the affembly. Mr. Blake was
a man very well qualified for adminiftration; for,
though a diffenter, fuch was his moderation, that
he prevailed with the affembly to fettle one hundred and fifty pounds per annum, for ever, on the
clergyman of Charles Town, with a good houfe, a
glebe, and two fervants. Upon his death, in 1700,
the

the deputies of the proprietaries in Carolina, in consequence of their powers in such cases, chose the
eldest landgrave, Joseph Moreton, Esq; who had
been governor before; whose election was objected
to as injurious to the proprietaries, because he had
accepted of a commission from the king to be judge
of the admiralty, though he had before accepted
of a like commission from them. A most ridiculous objection, as no admiralty jurisdiction was expressed in the original patent; yet Mr. Moore, his
competitor, had interest enough to get the election
set aside, and himself chosen, without Moreton's receiving the least redress.

The earl of Bath, son to the late earl, was now
palatine, an enthusiast to the church of England,
whose great ambition was to establish that worship
in the colony, exclusive of all others; a doctrine
at that time enforced in England by the bill against
occasional conformity. Moore was quite pliant to
his views; but was disappointed by the assembly,
in an attempt he made to get the Indian trade into
the hands of the government, which he therefore
dissolved. Towards the latter end of the year 1701,
he called a new assembly, and, according to his enemies, so influenced the sheriff, that strangers, ser-
vants, aliens, nay, mulattoes and negroes, were
polled, and returned; complaints of which, and
many other abuses in his office, were sent to the
palatine; but no redress obtained; perhaps the
charges against him were aggravated.

Upon

Upon the acceffion of Philip V. a war between England and Spain feemed inevitable; and the Carolinians were firmly of opinion, that the Spaniards in Florida were ufurpers upon their original charter; a notion of great fervice to Moore in promoting a fcheme he formed, for engroffing to his government and himfelf the profits of the flave-trade, by felling, in the Britifh iflands, the Spanifh Indians, at a lefs price than negroes could be imported for from Africa. He accordingly, to avoid an enquiry into his own conduct, propofed an expedition againft St. Auguftine; but as war was not yet declared againft Spain, the motion was thrown out of the affembly. But though the oppofition was very ftrong, he foon obtained a majority, and defeated every attempt for having the laft fundamental conftitutions agreed to by the affembly, which produced frefh remonftrances againft his government.

In all probability, Moore could not have got the better of the diffenting intereft, had he not been befriended by the palatine, the proprietaries, and the war with Spain, which gave him a handle for renewing his project againft St. Auguftine. The wealthy planters, in vain, remonftrated againft the inability of the province to undertake fuch an expedition; the affembly voted two thoufand pounds for this fervice. Six hundred Indians were immediately raifed, and colonel Daniel was fent up the river with a party in boats, to make a defcent upon the land fide, while the governor attacked the place by sea. At first success crowned their arms : they defeated the Spanish Indians, and killed or took prisoners about six hundred of them. They next plundered the town of St. Augustine, as they had already done all the open country ; but the inhabitants had retired with their best effects to the castle, which was well fortified, and contained provisions for four months. The English being unprovided with bombs and mortars, and having a very inconsiderable train of artillery, could only blockade the place, until they should receive a supply from Jamaica, for which purpose, a sloop was dispatched thither ; but the commander of it proving dilatory, colonel Daniel, on whose abilities the success of the expedition seems wholly to have rested, went himself to Jamaica, and procured the necessary stores for the siege.

During his absence, two Spanish ships appeared in the offing of St. Augustine, which struck Moore, who had lain there three months, with such a panic, that he raised the siege, burnt his ships, (though some say, they fell into the hands of the Spaniards) and made a precipitate retreat ; and Daniel, on his return to St. Augustine, with great difficulty escaped being taken. Thus Moore shamefully abandoned a certain conquest : for the two Spanish ships were only frigates, one of twenty-two, the other of sixteen guns ; and had he continued the siege a little longer, the place must have infallibly surrendered.

Moore

Moore got fafe to Carolina, after a long fatiguing march by land, which he conducted in a
very unfoldier-like manner; yet, which is very
extraordinary, the Englifh loft no more than two
men in this laborious expedition. The Carolinians
were greatly difpirited with the bad fuccefs of the
expedition; efpecially, as it had entailed upon them
a debt of fix thoufand pounds. When the affembly met, the lower-houfe paffed a bill for the better
regulating elections, which the governor and council, who wanted to raife money to pay off the provincial debt, difdainfully rejected. The affembly
confifted of but thirty members, fifteen of whom
entered a proteft againft the governor's proceedings. In fhort both parties feem to have been in
fault; the governor, with fome of his riotous
friends, infulted the protefters in the moft grofs
manner; and the latter wanted to evade the payment
of the provincial debts.

At laft, Sir Nathaniel Johnfon, governor of the
Leeward Iflands in the reign of king James, who
had afterwards retired to Carolina, was appointed
governor; but he acted upon the principles of the
late governor, Moore, who was appointed attorney-
general, and one of his creatures, Trott, chief
juftice of the common-pleas, then a poft of vaft
power in the province. Notwithftanding the black
colours in which the diffenters have reprefented
Moore, it ought to be remembered, that the colony of Georgia chiefly owes its birth to him. In

1703

1703 he marched against the Spanish Apalachians, eight hundred of whom he killed or took prisoners, with Don Juan Mexia, their commander ; in consequence of which, the whole province of Apalachia submitted, and he transported from thence to the country now called Georgia, fourteen hundred Apalachians, who put themselves under the protection of the English crown.

The remonstrances of the Carolinians, against the riotous proceedings encouraged and abetted by the governors Moore and Johnson, and their illegal practices in procuring returns to be made to the house of representatives, met with a very cold reception in England ; and the assembly meeting in Carolina, a bill, in express violation of the fundamental constitution, was passed, for the more effectual preservation of the government, requiring all persons elected members of the common house of assembly, to conform to the church of England, and receive the sacrament, according to the rites and usage of the said church. Thus all dissenters were disqualified, though legally elected, from sitting in the assembly, and the candidate who had the next majority of votes was to be admitted. The dissenters, alarmed at this illegal oppressive act, instructed Mr. Ash, their agent, to represent their grievances to lord Granville, which he did ; but died before he saw any effect of his representations : indeed his lordship, from his temper and principles, was very unlikely to afford them relief.

The

The diffenters were thus left without redrefs ;
and, to compleat their grievances, a bill paffed,
figned by the governor and deputies, for eftablifhing religious worfhip in this province, according to
the church of England ; and for the erecting
churches, for the public worfhip of God ; and alfo
for the maintenance of minifters, and the building
convenient houfes for them : and commiffioners
were appointed to fee the act put into execution. In
confequence of this act, many oppreffive things
were done by the government of Carolina againft
the diffenters ; and, at laft, the merchants trading
thither petitioned lord Granville for its repeal.
A board of proprietaries was, with great difficulty affembled ; but notwithftanding all the reprefentations of Mr. Archdale, who was himfelf a
proprietary, and Mr. Boone, agent for the diffenters, no redrefs could be obtained.   The bill, however, was of fuch pernicious confequence to the
colony, that the lower-houfe paffed a vote for re-
pealing it ; but the governor diffolved them.   Reprefentations fignifying nothing, Mr. Boone, by
the affiftance of the Carolina merchants in London, carried an application into the houfe of lords
for the relief of the Carolinians ; where the matter
was fully debated ; and the houfe being of opinion, that the proprietors had forfeited their charter, addreffed the queen in behalf of the colonifts,
who referred the matter of the petition to the commiffioners of trade and plantations ; and their opinion coinciding, the attorney and follicitor-general
were

were ordered to proceed againſt the proprietors by *quo warranto.* At length, in 1728, the lords proprietors, making a virtue of neceſſity, accepted ſeventeen thouſand five hundred pounds for their property and juriſdiction, together with five thouſand pounds due to them from the province; except earl Granville, who kept his eighth, which comprehends near half of North-Carolina, on that part which immediately borders on the province of Virginia: and this ſurrender was confirmed by an act of the Britiſh parliament, whereby the province was put under the immediate care and inſpection of the crown. The conſtitution, in thoſe points where it differed from other colonies, was altered; and the country, for the more commodious adminiſtration of affairs, divided into two diſtinct independent governments, called North-Carolina and South-Carolina.

Colonel Johnſon was ſucceeded in the government by major Tynte; to whom ſucceeded Gibbs, Craven, Daniel, Johnſon, and Moore, during whoſe governments nothing material happened. In 1718, Francis Nicholſon, Eſq; was governor, during whoſe time the province was terribly haraſſed by pirates. In 1722, four Indian nations ſent deputies to make peace with the Engliſh; who were well received, and in return owned themſelves ſubjects of Great-Britain.

The province being now under the immediate protection of the crown; by the aſſiſtance received from England, the Indians were expelled, and forced

forced to accept of equitable terms of peace * ; and Robert Johnson, Efq; was appointed governor by the crown, who arrived in Carolina in 1731, and brought over with him a confiderable prefent for the chiefs of the Cherokees, to confirm them in their good difpofition towards the crown of Great-Britain. The Cherokee chiefs being invited to Charles Town, were received in the moft brilliant manner, and ratified a treaty approved of by the affembly, with the utmoft cordiality. Unfortunately, the Virginians and Carolinians purfued feparate interefts among the Cherokee traders ; and the Carolinians frequently complained that the Virginians underfold them. Mr. Johnfon did all in his power to remove every grievance.

---

* It being judged neceffary to bring over the Cherokee Indians, from whom the province had moft to apprehend, to the Englifh intereft, Sir Alexander Cumming, a native of Scotland, undertook this arduous tafk; and on the firft of March, 1729, arrived at Keowee, diftant about three hundred miles from Charles Town Learning from an Englifh trader, that the Lower Creeks had invited the Cherokees to join the French intereft, he, without lofs of time, repaired to the houfe where near two hundred of the Cherokee chiefs were affembled, and was by them received with the greateft marks of refpect. He then requefted a general meeting of the nation, to confer with him at Nequaffee, on the third of April following. In the interim, he travelled a vaft way into their country, was every where received with the greateft cordiality, and upon his return to Nequaffee, the Cherokees folemnly fwore allegiance to the king of England; and made Sir Alexander the compliment of receiving from his hands Moyty, one of their head-men, as chief of all their nation ; and prefented him with their fovereign diadem, together

with

grievance. On the 25th of Auguſt 1732, he had an interview with Mingo-be-Mingo, a Chickeſaw chief, attended by eight men and two women, with two Natchee Indians, who, in his ſpeech to the governor, whom he called father, ſaid, " He had undertaken a very long journey to ſee him; that he hoped the path between them would never be ſhut up; that in his way thither one of his men was killed by the Cherokee Indians, allies to the Engliſh; that he was ſent down by the other head men of the nation to receive a talk from him; and that he would faithfully carry it back." The governor made the beſt apology he could for the Cherokees, and underſtanding that the Chactaws were at variance with the Chickeſaws, on account of their friendſhip to the Engliſh, preſented Mingo with

with five eagles tails, and four ſcalps, requeſting him to lay them at the feet of his majeſty. Moyty would have attended him to England himſelf, had not his wife been very dangerouſly ill; and ſent the head warrior of the Tepetchees, and other chiefs, to England with Cumming, where they arrived at Dover, on the 5th of June, 1730. They were preſented to the king, beheld all the magnificence of the Engliſh court, and bore witneſs to the truth of Sir Alexander's ſpeech, when he declared the ſubmiſſion of their nation to the crown of England. But this idle pageantry was ſoon forgot by them; for the Indians do not ſeem to have the leaſt idea of any grandeur of government out of the verge of their own country. They received no benefit from their ſubjection, whatever might have been the motive; nor was any care taken after Mr. Johnſon's government, to keep up our intereſt among them, though it might have been done at a very trifling expence.

twelve

twelve cags of gunpowder, and twenty-four bags
of bullets; and the two Natchee Indians, and his attendants, with a coat, gun, and hat each; and, after recommending a good understanding between
the Nactees and Chickesaws, and advising the latter to demand satisfaction of the Cherokees in a
friendly manner, dismissed them, highly satisfied
with their treatment. The province of Georgia
was planned during the time of this governor, who
published an advertisement in the Carolina gazette for subscriptions towards its establishment;
gave a most hospitable reception to him, upon
his first arrival at Charles Town, in his way to
Georgia; and procured a vote of the general-
assembly for furnishing him, at the public expence, with an hundred and four head of breeding cattle, twenty-five hogs, and twenty barrels of
rice; and, exclusive of small craft for their conveyance, ordered the scout-boats, with ten rangers *,
under the command of captain Macpherson, to attend him, in order to protect the new settlers
from any insults. The governor, at the same time,
recommended the infant colony to all the friendly
Indians, and would have accompanied Mr. Oglethorpe himself, had not the assembly been sitting :
however, at his request, colonel Bull, a gentleman
extremely conversant in those affairs, went to
Georgia, where he was of infinite service to Mr.

* Rangers, in Carolina, are light-horsemen, kept in pay
to discover the motions of the Indians.

Oglethorpe.

Oglethorpe. Before this time, we find the Carolinians were at war with the Yamaffee Indians ; and
with a hundred whites, and as many Indian allies,
attacked the Yamaffee village, killed thirty-two
of its inhabitants, with a friar, and drove both the
Spaniards fettled there, and the Yamaffees, into St.
Auguftine, which they, blockaded, and demanded
the Yamaffees. to be delivered up to them. The
governor refufed to comply with this demand, afferting, the Yamaffees were fubjects of Spain ; but
offered to make good whatever damage the Englifh
had received. Whereupon the Carolinians retreated, after lying three days before the town. This
Indian war brought a confiderable expence to many individuals, who very juftly complained of the
extravagant grants made by the proprietaries to the
landgraves and caciques, by which thofe who had
defended the province againft the Spaniards and Indians, were prevented from making any advantagi-
ous fettlements at the original quit-rents. The attorney-general, and follicitor-general, in England,
gave their opinion againft the validity of thefe exorbitant grants ; and the difpute was at laft ended,
by an act of affembly to remedy the grievance.

The fituation and fertility of Carolina, with the
intereft the crown took in its profperity, now rendered it a moft flourifhing province. In 1732, Mr.
Purry, a native of Neufchatel, in Switzerland, entered into a treaty with the Englifh government
for fettling, with Switzers, the fpot where lord Car-
drofs had heretofore made a fmall fettlement, which
he

he abandoned, as has been already mentioned. An hundred and feventy-two Swifs accordingly arrived, and in a few months built upon the northern back of the river Savannah a new town, called Purryfburgh, where they were foon joined by more of their countrymen. In confequence of a very laudable fcheme for raifing a barrier of hardy induftrious people on the fouthern frontier of South-Carolina, the affembly voted Mr. Purry four hundred pounds for every hundred effective men he fhould import, and promifed to find provifions and tools for three hundred of them for one year. Purry, in 1734, brought over two hundred and feventy more of his countrymen; fo that above fix hundred Swifs were now fettled at Purryfburgh.

To defray this expence, the crown remitted to the affembly the negroe-duty. A noble fcheme for the benefit of the colony was about the fame time recommended to the governor by his majefty. Eleven new townfhips were to be eftablifhed, to confift each of twenty thoufand acres of land, laid out in a fquare plat; fifty acres, part thereof, to be granted to every inhabitant at his firft fettling; and that land might not be wanting for the conveniency of the inhabitants as their fubftance increafed, no perfon was allowed to take up any land within fix miles of the faid townfhips, refpectively. At the fame time, forty-eight thoufand acres were granted to Mr. Purry, for the ufe of the fix hundred Swifs whom he had imported. Some mifmanagement, however, having crept into

the

the new Swifs plantation, the government iffued a proclamation informing the public, that no grants would pafs of any lands in any of the townfhips laid out in this province, but to thofe only in whofe names the original warrant was made out, and who fhould fettle there.

In 1735, foon after this proclamation, governor Johnfon died, and was fucceeded by Thomas Broughton, Efq; The Englifh government, at this period, was too negligent in the appointment of American governors, who, in general, being men of ruined fortunes, were fent to retrieve them in America, and the fortifications were in a deplorable condition in this, as well as in the other provinces; the legiflature of Great-Britain, then at peace both with France and Spain, neglecting the means of obliging the colonifts to contribute towards their own defence. However, this mifmanagement did not damp the zeal of the Proteftant Swifs and Vaudois; and the latter, accuftomed to the manufacture of filk in their own country, underftanding that Carolina was proper for the culture of filk worms, ftill continued, as well as the Swifs, to flock there; fo that, in a few years, another foreign town, called Wilton or New London, rivalled Purryfburgh. This competition was of fome detriment to the province; the foreigners in general complaining, that the terms upon which they fettled in the province were not fulfilled. The government of England having now determined to fubdivide the great

American

American provinces, Carolina was divided into two diftinct governments, viz. South· and North Carolina.

Nothing further occurs in the hiftory of Carolina, till the government of Mr. Glenn, excepting the common fhare the province took in the war between Great-Britain, France, and Spain. In 1752, South-Carolina was in fo thriving a condition, that upwards of fixteen hundred foreign proteftants arrived in the colony. On the 26th of May 1753, Malachty, attended by the Wolf king, the Ottafee king, with about twenty chiefs, and upwards of an hundred Creek Indians, came to Charles Town, efcorted by three troops of horfe, by the governor's order; to whom his excellency made a fpeech, in their own manner, to perfuade them to ratify their treaties with the Englifh, and make peace with the Cherokees, then under our protection, fome of whom had been murdered by the Creeks, even in the neighbourhood of Charles Town, and expreffed his defire, that there might be a good underftanding among all the Indian nations in alliance with the Englifh. Malachty made a prefent of fkins to his excellency, and accounted for the conduct of his people towards the Cherokees, and the other Englifh Indians; and, upon the whole, promifed every thing which the governor required, excepting an alliance with the northern Indians; which, he faid, was a matter of fo great confequence, that he and his nation muft deliberate upon it. In confequence

fequence of this interview, four hundred Cherokees and Creeks joined the Englifh forces after the taking of Ofwego.

In 1759, during the government of William Henry Lyttleton, Efq; the French in Louifiana, by their infinuations, prevailed upon the Cherokees to attack the Englifh and their Indian allies, many of whom they plundered and fcalped. Mr. Lyttleton having received information of thefe outrages, raifed, with great expedition, a confiderable body of forces, and penetrated, at their head, in the beginning of October, into the heart of the country of the Cherokees, who were fo much intimidated by his vigour and difpatch, that they fent a deputation of their chiefs to fue for peace, which was re-eftablifhed by a new treaty, dictated by the Englifh governor, at Fort Prince George, where he then was, at the head of eight hundred militia, and three hundred regulars *. However, this fubmiffion was only to avoid the ftorm that feemed

ready

* Treaty of peace and friendfhip, concluded by his excellency William Henry Lyttleton, Efq; captain-general and governor in chief of his majefty's province of South-Carolina, with Attakullakulla, or the Little Carpenter, depuiy of the whole Cherokee nation, and other head men and warriors thereof, at Fort Prince George, Dec. 26, 1759.

ARTICLE I. There fhall be a firm peace and friendfhip between all his majefty's fubjects of this province, and the nation of Indians called the Cherokees; and the faid Cherokees fhall preferve peace with all his majefty's fubjects whatever.

II. The

ready to break upon them. Mr. Lyttleton had
fcarce quitted their country, before they attempted to furprize Fort Prince George, where
the Indian hoftages were lodged, who, not being very ftrictly guarded, had found means to
form a confpiracy with their countrymen for
maffacreing the garrifon, and getting poffeffion of
the fort.

This attempt was conducted in the following
manner : On the 16th of February, two Indian
women

II. The articles of friendfhip and commerce concluded by
the lords commiffioners for trade and plantations, with the deputies of the Cherokees, by his majefty's command, at White-
hall, the 7th of September, 1730, fhall be ftrictly obferved for
the time to come.

III. Whereas the faid Cherokee Indians have at fundry
times and places, fince the 19th of Auguft 1758, flain divers of
his majefty's good fubjects of this province ; and his excellency
the governor having demanded that fatisfaction fhould be given
for the fame, according to the tenor of the faid articles of friendfhip and commerce aforementioned; in confequence whereof
two Cherokee Indians; of the number of thofe who have been
guilty of perpetrating the faid murders, have already been delivered up, to be put to death, or otherwife difpofed of, as his
excellency the governor fhall direct; it is hereby ftipulated
and agreed, that twenty-two other Cherokee Indians, guilty of
the faid murders, fhall as foon as poffible, after the conclufion
of the prefent treaty, be delivered up to fuch perfons as his excellency the governor, or the commander in chief of this province for the time being, fhall appoint to receive them, to be
put to death, or otherwife difpofed of, as the faid governor and
commander in chief fhall direct.

IV. The

women appearing on the other side of the river, Mr. Dogharty, one of the officers of the fort, went out to converse with them. While he was engaged in conversation, Ouconnostotah joining them, desired he would call the commanding officer, to whom, he said, he had something to propose. Accordingly, lieutenant Cotymore appearing, accompanied by enfign Bell, Dogharty, and Fofter, the interpreter, Ouconnostotah told him, he had something of consequence to impart to the governor,

whom

IV. The Cherokee Indians, whofe names are herein aftermentioned, viz. Chenohe, Qufanatanah, Tallichama, Tallitahe, Quarrafattahe, Connafaratah, Kataetoi, Otaffite of Watogo, Qufanoletah of Jore, Kataeletah of Cowetche, Chifquatalone, Skiagufta of Sticoe, Tannaefto, Wohatche, Wyejah, Oucahchiftanah, Nicholche, Tony, Toatiahoi, Shalliflofke, and Chiftie, fhall remain as hoftages for the due performance of the foregoing, articles, in the cuftody of fuch perfons as his excellency the governor fhall pleafe to nominate for that purpofe; and when any of the Cherokee Indians, guilty of the faid murders, fhall have been delivered up, as is expreffed in the faid articles, an equal number of the faid hoftages fhall forthwith be fet at liberty.

V. Immediately after the conclufion of this prefent treaty, the licenfed traders from this government, and all perfons employed by them, fhall have leave from his excellency the governor, to return to their refpective places of abode in the Cherokee nation; and to carry on their trade with the Cherokee Indians, in the ufual manner, according to law.

VI. During the continuance of the prefent war between his moft facred majefty and the French king, if any Frenchman fhall prefume to come into the Cherokee nation, the Cherokees fhall

T 2 ufe

he purpofed to vifit; and defired he might be attended by a white man as a fafeguard. The lieutenant affuring him that his requeft fhould be granted, the Indian faid, he would then go and catch a horfe for him; fwung a bridle thrice over his head, as a fignal, and immediately near thirty, mufkets, from different ambufcades, were difcharged at the Englifh officers. Mr. Cotymore received a fhot in his left breaft, which in a few days proved fatal; and Mr. Bell and the interpreter were both wounded. Enfign Mill, who remained

in

ufe their utmoft endeavours to put him to death, as one of his majefty's enemies; or, if taken alive, they fhall deliver him up to his excellency the governor, or the commander in chief of this province for the time being, to be difpofed of as he fhall direct; and if any perfon whatfoever, either white man or Indian, fhall, at any time, bring any meffage from the French into the Cherokee nation, or hold any difcourfes there in favour of the French, or tending to fet the Englifh and Cherokees at variance, or interrupt the peace and friendfhip eftablifhed by this prefent treaty, the Cherokees fhall ufe their utmoft endeavours to apprehend fuch perfon or perfons, and detain him or them, until they fhall have given notice thereof to his excellency the governor, or to the commander in chief for the time being, and have received his directions therein.

Given under my hand and feal, at Fort Prince George, in the province of South-Carolina, this 26th day of December, 1759, in the thirty-third year of his majefty's reign,

WILLIAM HENRY LYTTLETON, (L. S.)

By his excellency's command,

WILLIAM DRAYTON, Sec.

We

in the fort, directly ordered the soldiers to shackle
the hostages, in the execution of which order, one
man was killed upon the spot, and another wounded upon the forehead with a tomahawk ; so that it
was judged absolutely necessary to put all the hostages to death.   Ignorant of this catastrophe, in the
evening, a party of Indians approaching the fort,
and firing two signal pieces, cried loud, in the Cherokee language, " fight manfully, and you shall be
assisted," and continued firing all night upon the fort,
without doing the least execution : thus failing in
their scheme, they revenged themselves on the
open country, burning and ravaging all the plantations in these parts, and butchering all who fell into
their hands.   Soon after, they assaulted Fort Nine-
ty-six ; from whence, however, they were repulsed.
The Creek Indians, hearing of the Cherokee hostilities, took the field against the enemy, under one

We whose names are underwritten, do agree to all and every
of these articles ; and do engage for ourselves and our nation,
that the same shall be well and faithfully performed. In testi-
mony whereof, we have hereunto set our hands and seals, the
day and year above mentioned.

ATTAKULLAKULLA, (L. S.)
OUCONNOSTOTA, (L. S.)
OTASSITE, (L. S.)
KITAGUSTA, (L. S.)
OCONNOECA, (L. S.)
KILLCANNOKCA, (L. S.)

Joseph Axon, William Forster, sworn Interpreters.
Witness. *Henry Vane,* adjutant-general.

of

of their chiefs, called the Long Warrior. Seven
hundred rangers were raifed by the people of Carolina ; and the governor applied for affiftance to
general Amherft, commander in chief in America,
who forthwith detached twelve hundred chofen men
to South-Carolina, under the command of colonel
Montgomery. The colonel, immediately after his
arrival at Charles Town, proceeded to Twelve-mile
River, which he paffed in the beginning of June,
without oppofition ; and continued his rout by
forced marches, until he arrived in the neighbourhood of an Indian town, called Little Keowee, where
he encamped. Having reafon to believe the enemy
were not apprifed of his coming, he refolved to rufh
upon them in the night, by furprize. With this
view, leaving his tents ftanding, with a fufficient
guard for the camp, he marched through the
woods, towards the town of Eftatoe, at the diftance of twenty-five miles ; and, in his rout, detached a company of light infantry to deftroy Little Keowee, where they were received with a fmart
fire ; but rufhing in with their bayonets, the Indians were all flain. The main body reached Eftatoe in the morning ; but found the place deferted. Some few Indians, who had not time to
efcape, were killed ; and the town, confifting of two
hundred houfes, well ftored with provifions, ammunition, and all the neceffaries of life, was plundered, and reduced to afhes. It was neceffary to
ftrike a terror into thefe favages, by fome acts of
feverity ; and the foldiers became deaf to all the
fuggeftions

fuggeftions of mercy, when they found, in one of their towns, the body of an Englifhman, whom they had put to the torture that very morning. Colonel Montgomery followed his blow with fur-prizing rapidity ; in the fpace of a few hours he deftroyed Sugar Town, which was as large as Eftatoe, and every village and houfe in the Lower Nation.

The Indian villages were agreeably fituated, generally confifting of about one hundred houfes, neatly and commodioufly built ; and had large magazines of corn, which were confumed in the flames. All the men that were taken fuffered immediate death ; but the greater part of the nation had efcaped, with the utmoft precipitation. In many houfes the beds were yet warm, and the tables fpread with victuals ; the Indians not having time to fave their arms, and valuable effects. Having thus taken vengeance on the perfidious enemy, at the expence of five or fix men killed or wounded, he returned to Fort Prince George, with about forty Indian women and children, whom he had made prifoners.

As Attakullakulla, who had figned the laft treaty, difapproved of the proceedings of his countrymen, and had done many good offices to the Englifh fince the renovation of the war, he was now acquainted, by means of two of their warriors who were fet at liberty, that he might come down with fome of his chiefs, to treat of an accommodation, which would be granted on his account ; but that the negociation muft be begun in a

T 4 few

days, otherwise, all the towns in the Upper Nation would be ravaged, and reduced to ashes *.   Atta-kullakulla declaring, that he could not prevail on his countrymen to accept the offered mercy, colonel Montgomery resolved to make a second eruption into the middle settlements of the Cherokees, and began his march on the 24th of June.   On the 27th, captain Morrison, of the advanced party, was killed by a shot from a thicket, and the firing became so troublesome that his men gave way.   The grenadiers and light-infantry being detached to sustain them, continued advancing, notwithstanding the fire from the woods, until, from a rising ground, they discovered a body of the enemy, whom they immediately attacked, and obliged to retire into a swamp, which, when the rest of the troops came up, they were compelled to abandon, after a short resistance.   At length, the troops arrived at the town of Etchowee, which the inhabitants had abandoned.   Here, while the army encamped on a small plain surrounded with hills, it was incommoded by the enemy, who wounded some men, and killed several horses ; and were even so daring as to attack the piquet-guard, which repulsed them with difficulty ; but declined coming to an open engagement.   Colonel Montgomery, sensible, that as many horses were killed or disabled, he could not proceed further without leaving his provisions be-

* Attakullakulla, called the Little Carpenter, was one of the chiefs who had been brought when young to England, by Sir Alexander Cumming.

hind,

hind, or abandoning the wounded to the brutal revenge of a favage enemy, retreated in the night, that he might be the lefs disturbed by the Indians, and purfued his rout, for two days, without interruption; but afterwards fuftained fome ftraggling fires from the woods, though the Indians were put to flight as often as they appeared. In the beginning of July he arrived at Fort Prince George, having loft about feventy men in this expedition. In revenge, the Cherokees blockaded Fort Loudon, near the confines of Virginia, defended by an inconfiderable garrifon, ill fupplied with provifions and neceffaries. The garrifon, after a long fiege, being reduced to the utmoft diftrefs, having fubfifted for a confiderable time without bread, on horfe-flefh, and feeing no profpect of relief, their communication having been long cut off from all the Britifh fettlements, capitulated with the Indians, and obtained permiffion to retire*; the Indians desiring,

* Articles of capitulation agreed upon and affented to by captain Paul Demere, commanding his majefty's forces at Fort Loudon, and the head-men and warriors of the Overhill Cherokee towns.

Art. I. That the garrifon of Fort Loudon march out with their arms and drums; each foldier having as much powder and ball as their officer fhall think neceffary for the march, and what baggage he may chufe to carry.

II. That the garrifon be permitted to march for Virginia, or Fort Prince George, as the commanding officer fhall think proper, unmolefted; and that a number of Indians be appointed to efcort them, and to hunt for provifions on their march.

III. That

defiring, that when they arrived at Keowee, the Cherokees confined at that place fhould be releafed, a
lafting accommodation be eftablifhed, and a regulated trade be revived. In confequence of this
treaty, the garrifon evacuated the fort; but on
their march were furrounded and furprized by a
large body of Indians, who maffacred all the officers, except Captain Stewart, and alfo twenty five
foldiers: the reft were made prifoners. Captain
Stewart owed his life to the generous interceffion of
Attakullakulla, who ranfomed him, at the price of
all he could command, and conducted him fafe to
Holfton River, where he found major Lewis advanced with a body of Virginians. The Indians,
encouraged by their fuccefs, now undertook the
fiege of Fort Ninety-fix, and other fmall fortifications; but retired precipitately, at the approach of
a body of provincials. The people of Carolina,

III. That fuch foldiers as are lame, or by ficknefs difabled
fiom marching, be received into the Indian towns, and kindly
ufed until they recover, and then to be returned to Fort Prince
George.

IV. That the Indians do provide the garrifon with as many
horfes as they can conveniently, for their march, agreeing with
the foldiers or officers for payment.

V. That the fort, great guns, powder, ball, and fpare arms,
be delivered to the Indians, without any fraud, on the day appointed for the march of the troops.   Signed,

OUCONNOSTATA †, his mark.
PAUL DEMERE.
CUNIGACATGOAE †, his mark.

appre-

apprehenfive that the Creeks and Chactaws would join the Cherokees, addreffed their governor, to prevail with general Amherft to countermand the return of the regulars from thence, underftanding that colonel Montgomery's orders were, after hav_ing chaftifed the enemy, to return to New-York, with the troops under his command, and rejoin the grand army. The colonel was under a neceffity of obeying his orders ; but, at the earneft intreaties of the province, left four hundred men for its protection.

In the beginning of July the following year, colonel Grant, at the head of two thoufand fix hun_dred men, marched from Fort Prince George, to ravage the country of the Cherokees with fire and fword. On his march he was attacked by a body of Indians, who fired for fome time with great viva_city, but little effect, and were foon repulfed. Meeting with no oppofition in traverfing their country after this attempt, he reduced fifteen of their towns to afhes, befides villages, deftroyed all the ftanding corn, and drove the Indians to ftarve in the mountains. This fevere chaftifement pro-duced the defired effect : a deputation of the chiefs waited on the colonel, and fignified their defire to accept a peace, willingly agreeing to all the colo-nel's terms, except one, by which four Cherokees were to be put to death at the head of the army ; but this article being moderated, a new treaty was actually concluded, on the 10th of December, at Charles Town, in every other refpect, nearly the fame as that of 1759 ; and Sir William Johnfon made

a tour

a tour round the other Indian nations, in order to quiet the fears of the Indians, aroused at the conquests of Great-Britain; which the French emissaries had fomented, with their usual industry and success.

North-Carolina was at first governed by captain Hyde, Sir Richard Everard, and captain Barrington; but its history is so barren of events, as to afford nothing worth recording. The governors, indeed, received their salaries; but the police of the province was so neglected, that no provision was made for the clergy; even marriages being solemnized by justices of the peace. At present, the province seems emerging from its difficulties; and the government becoming more attentive to the colony in proportion as it has been more settled, by degrees, matters have been better regulated, and it now bids fair to become a valuable country.

The CLIMATE, SOIL, and NATURAL HISTORY of the two CAROLINAS.

These two provinces, lying between the 31st and 36th degrees of latitude, are together upwards of four hundred miles in length; and in breadth, to the Indian nations, near three hundred. The climate and soil do not differ considerably from those of Virginia; but where they differ, it is much to the advantage of Carolina, which, on the whole, is one of the finest climates in the world: the heat in sum-

mer

mer is, indeed, greater than in Virginia; but the winters are milder and shorter, and the year, in all respects, does not come to such violent extremities. However, the weather, though in general serene, and the air healthy; yet, like all American weather, is subject to such quick changes, and those so sharp, as to oblige the inhabitants to be more cautious in their dress and diet than Europeans generally are. Thunder and lightning happens frequently, and Carolina is the only English colony on the continent which is subject to hurricanes; but they are very rare, and nothing near so violent as those of the West-Indies. Part of March, all April, May, and the greatest part of June, are inexpressibly temperate and agreeable; but in July, August, and the greatest part of September, the heat is intense; and though the winters are sharp, especially when the north-west wind blows, yet they affect only the mornings and evenings, being seldom severe enough to freeze any considerable water; so that many tender plants, which do not stand the winter of Virginia, flourish in Carolina; oranges, both sweet and sour, being in great plenty near Charles Town, and both excellent in their kinds; and olives seem rather neglected by the planter, than denied by the climate. The vegetation of every kind of plant is incredibly quick; for there is something so kindly in the air and soil, that where the country wears the most barren and unpromising appearance, if neglected for a while, of itself, it shoots out an immense quantity of those

various

various beautiful flowering-fhrubs for which this country is fo famous. ·

Carolina is, in general a plain country, though every where interfperfed with gentle rifings ; the whole country is in a manner one foreft, where the planters have not cleared it. The trees are much the fame with thofe in Virginia, and by their different fpecies the quality of the foil is eafily difcovered ; for the grounds which bear the oak, the walnut, and the hickery, are extremely fertile : they confift of a dark fand, intermixed with loam ; and as here all the land abounds with nitre, it is a long time before it is exhaufted ; the planters never ufing any manure. The pine-barren is the worft of all, being an almoft perfectly white fand ; yet it bears naturally the pine-tree, which yields good profit in pitch, tar, and turpentine. When cleared, this kind of land, for two or three years together, produces tolerable crops of Indian corn and peafe, and, when flooded, anfwers well for rice ; befides, happily for the province, this worft fpecies of its land is favourable to one of the kinds of indigo, the moft valuable of its products. There is another fort of ground which lies low and wet, upon the banks of fome of the rivers, called fwamps, which though in fome places in a manner ufelefs, in others, is far the richeft of all their lands : thefe grounds confift of a black, fat earth ; and bear rice, the great ftaple of this province, which requires in general a rich moift foil, in the greateft plenty and perfection. The country near the fea is much the

worft ;

worſt,; moſt of the land thereabouts being a ſpecies of the pale, light, ſandy-coloured ground, what
is otherwiſe being little better than an unhealthy,
unprofitable, ſalt marſh : but the country, as one
advances further from the ſea, improves gradually, and an hundred miles beyond Charles Town,
where it begins to grow hilly, the ſoil is prodigiouſly fertile, the air pure and wholeſome, and the
ſummer heats much more temperate than in the flat
country ; for eighty miles from the ſea is all an
even plain, not a hill, a rock, ſcarce a pebble, being
to be met with. Wheat grows extremely well in
the back country, and yields an immenſe increaſe:
in the other parts of Carolina but little is raiſed,
it being apt to mildew, and ſpend itſelf in ſtraw ;
and theſe evils the planters take very little care to
redreſs, turning their attention to the culture of rice,
which is much more piofitable ; and are ſupplied
from New-York and Penſylvania with what wheat
they want, in exchange for this grain.

The land is every where very eaſily cleared, there
being little or no underwood ; their foreſts conſiſting chiefly of great trees, at a conſiderable distance aſunder ; ſo that a man could clear more land
in a week here, than in the foreſts of Europe he
could do in a month. The uſual method is to cut
the trees at about a foot from the ground, and then
ſaw them into boards, or convert them into ſtaves,
heading, or other ſpecies of lumber, according to
the nature of the wood, or the demands at the
market : if they lie too diſtant from a navigable
river,

river, they are heaped together; and left to rot.
The roots foon decay; and, before this happens,
little or no inconvenience is found from them, where
land is fo plenty.

The aboriginal animals of this country are, in
general, the fame with thofe of Virginia ; but
there is a ftill greater variety of beautiful fowls.
All European animals are in plenty here ; black
cattle have multiplied amazingly. It was a very
extraordinary thing, about fifty years ago, to have
above three or four cows; now, feveral planters
have a thoufand; and fome in North-Carolina, a
great many more. Thefe ramble all day in the
forefts ; but their calves being kept in fenced
paftures, the cows return every evening to them,
are then milked, kept all night, milked in the
morning again, and afterwards let loofe. The hogs,
which are vaftly numerous, range in the fame manner, and like them return, by having fhelter and
victuals provided for them at the plantation. Befides, the woods contain many wild cattle, horfes,
and fwine, though, at its firft fettlement, none of
thefe animals exifted in the country.

In the two provinces, there are ten navigable rivers, of a very long courfe, which receive
innumerable fmaller ones in their courfes, and
all abound in fifh. About fifty or fixty miles
from the fea, moft of the great rivers have
falls, which become more and more frequent in
proportion as one approaches nearer their fources ;
as is the cafe with almoft all the American rivers.

At thefe falls the traders land their goods, carry them beyond the cataract in horfes or waggons, and then refhip them, above or below the fall.

Charles Town, the capital of South-Carolina, is one of the firft cities in North-America, for fize, beauty, and commerce. Its fituation at the confluence of two navigable rivers, is admirably well chofen. The harbour is good in every refpect, except that of a bar, which prevents veffels of above two hundred tons from entering. The city is regularly and pretty ftrongly fortified, both by nature and art; the ftreets are well cut, the houfes large and well built, and let for high rents. The church is fpacious, and the architecture in good tafte, exceeding every thing of the kind in North-America. The town contains about eight hundred houfes, and is the feat of the governor, and the place where the affembly meets. The planters and merchants are rich and well bred, and feveral handfome equipages are kept in this city. Like the Virginians, the people here are vain, gay, and expenfive, in their drefs and way of living; fo that every thing confpires to render Charles Town the livelieft and politeft place, as well as the richeft, in all Britifh America.

NORTH-CAROLINA.

Port Royal, the beft harbour in this province, is far to the fouthward, on the borders of Georgia. It is capable of receiving the largeft fleets, both with refpect to number, bulk, and burthen, with the utmoſt ſafety; yet the town named Beaufort, built upon an iſland of the ſame name, is not yet conſiderable, though it bids fair for becoming, in time, the firſt trading town in this part of America.

The mouths of the rivers in North-Carolina form but indifferent harbours, and, except one at Cape Fear, do not admit veſſels of above fourſcore tons; ſo that larger ſhips are under a neceſſity of lying off in a ſound, called Ocacock, formed between ſome iſlands and the continent. This lays a weight upon their trade, by the expence of lighterage; upon which occaſion partly, though principally becauſe the firſt ſettlements were made as near as poſſible to the capital, which lies conſiderably to the ſouthward, North-Carolina was neglected, and for a long time was ill inhabited, and by an indolent and diſorderly people, who had hardly any law or government, to protect them in what little they had. As commodious land grew ſcarce in the other colonies, people in low circumſtances were induced to ſettle in this colony, where a great deal of excellent and convenient land remained yet to be patenteed; and the government becoming more attentive to the province as it became more valuable, by degrees, a better order was introduced; in conſequence of which, North-Carolina, though by no means ſo wealthy as its ſiſter province, has many more white people; things begin to wear a face of ſettlement, and, with proper management, the trade of this province, which even now is far from being contemptible, may become a flouriſhing

ing and useful branch of the British American commerce.

Edenton was formerly the capital of North-Carolina, if a trifling village can deserve that appellation; but the late governor, Mr. Dobbs, projected one further south, upon the river Neus, which, though more central, is by no means equally well situated for trade; a circumstance that ought always to be principally regarded in the colonies. However, none of the towns deserve notice; the conveniency of inland navigation, and the want of handicraftsmen, in all the southern provinces, is almost an insuperable obstacle to their ever having considerable ones.

TRADE, GENIUS of the INHABITANTS, &c.

The trade of Carolina, besides lumber, provisions, &c. in common with the rest of America, consists in three staple commodities, indigo, rice, and the produce of the pine tree, viz. turpentine, tar, and pitch. South-Carolina produces the two former commodities; the latter is the staple of North-Carolina.

Rice alone antiently formed the staple of South-Carolina: this wholesome grain makes a great part of the food of all ranks in the southern parts of the world. Whilst the act of navigation obliged the Carolinians to send all their rice first to England, there to be reshipped for the markets of

Spain

Spain and Portugal, the charges in confequence of this regulation lay fo heavy upon the trade, efpecially in time of war, when greatly aggravated by the rife of the freight and infurance, that rice hardly anfwered the charges of the planter; but the legiflature now permits them to fend their rice directly to any place to the fouthward of Cape Finifterre, which prudent indulgence has again revived the trade; and though the Carolinians have gone largely into the profitable article of indigo, they raife now above double the quantity of rice they raifed fome years ago; and this branch of their commerce alone is worth, at leaft, one hundred and fifty thoufand pounds fterling annually.

Indigo, probably fo called from India, where the plant was firft cultivated, and from whence, for a confiderable time, the Europeans had all that they confumed, is very like fern, when grown, and when young, fcarcely diftinguifhable from lucerne: the leaves in general are pennated, and terminated by a fingle lobe; the flower confifts of five leaves, and is of the papilionaceous kind, the uppermoft petal being larger and rounder than the reft, and lightly furrowed on the fide, the lower ones fhort, and end in a point; in the middle of the flower the ftile is fituated, which afterwards becomes a pod, containing the feeds.

Three forts of indigo are cultivated in Carolina: firft, the French or Hifpaniola indigo, which ftriking a long tap root, will only flourifh in a deep rich foil, and therefore, though an excellent fort, is

not

not fo much cultivated in the maritime parts of Carolina, which are generally fandy: the back counties are capable of producing it in perfection;
but the plant is fo tender, that it hardly bears the
winter of Carolina, on which account it is neglected.

The falfe Guatimala, or true Bahama kind, bears
the winter better, is a taller and more vigorous
plant, is raifed in greater quantities from the fame
extent of land, will grow in the worft foils in the
country, and is therefore more cultivated, though
inferior in the quality of its dye.

The wild indigo, being a native of the country,
anfwers the purpofes of the planter beft of all,
with refpect to its hardinefs, eafy culture, and the
quantity of its produce. The quality admits of
fome difpute; nor can the planters yet certainly
tell, whether to attribute the faults of their indigo
to the nature of the plant, to the feafons, which
have great influence upon it, or to fome defect in
the manufacture.

Indigo is generally planted after the firft rains
fucceeding the vernal equinox; the feed is fowed in
fmall ftrait trenches, about eighteen inches afunder,
at leaft; the plant, when full grown, is generally
eighteen inches in height, and is fit for cutting in
the beginning of July. Towards the end of Auguft it is cut a fecond time; and, if the autumn
proves mild, is cut a third time at Michaelmas.
The ground muft be weeded frequently, and the
plants cleared from worms every day; the planta-

tion

tion requiring the utmoſt care and diligence. A-
bout twenty-five negroes will manage a plantation
of fifty acres, and compleat the manufacture of the
indigo, befides providing their own neceſſary ſubſiſtence. If the land be very good, each acre yields
ſixty or ſeventy pounds weight of indigo ; at a medium, the produce is fifty pounds. The plant is fit
for cutting when it begins to bloſſom ; when cut,
the manufacturer muſt be extremely careful not to
preſs or ſhake it in carrying to the ſteeper, as the
beauty of the dye greatly depends upon the fine
farina that adheres to the leaves.

The apparatus for this manufacture is pretty conſiderable, though not very expenſive ; the whole
conſiſting only of a pump, vats, and tubs, of cypreſs, a wood both common and cheap in this province. The plant, when cut, is firſt laid to mace-
rate in a vat, about twelve feet long and four deep,
to the height of about fourteen inches. This veſſel, called the ſteeper, is then filled with water :
the plant having been thus macerated about twelve
or fourteen hours, according to the weather, begins
to ferment, riſe, and grow ſenſibly warm : at this
time ſpars of wood are run acroſs, to prevent its
riſing too much, and a pin is ſet to mark the higheſt pitch of its aſcent : when the liquor ſinks below
this mark, the fermentation having now attained
its due pitch, and beginning to abate, the operator
lets off the liquor, by a cock, into another vat,
called the beater ; the remaining groſs matter is
taken away to manure the ground, for which uſe

it

it is excellent, and new cuttings are put in, as long as the harveſt of this plant continues.

This liquor, ſtrongly impregnated with the particles of the indigo, is inceſſantly beat, and agitated with a ſort of bottomleſs buckets, with long handles, until it heats, froths, and riſes above the rim of the veſſel which contains it : to allay this violent fermentation, oil is thrown in, which inſtantly ſinks it. When this beating has continued from twenty to thirty-five minutes, according to the ſtate of the weather, (for in cool weather the longeſt beating is required) a ſmall muddy grain begins to be formed. To diſcover theſe particles the better, and in order to judge when the liquor is ſufficiently beaten, ſome of it is, from time to time, taken up in a glaſs. When it appears in a proper ſtate, ſome lime water is poured into it, and the whole gently ſtirred, which wonderfully facilitates the operation ; the liquor aſſumes a purple colour, the indigo granulates more fully, and the whole is troubled and muddy. It is now ſuffered to ſettle ; the clearer part is now left to run off into another ſucceſſion of veſſels, from whence the water is conveyed away as faſt as it clears at top, until nothing remains but a thick mud, which is put into coarſe linen bags, which are hung up, until the moiſture is entirely drained off. To compleat the drying, this mud is worked upon boards of ſome porous wood, with a wooden ſpatula, and is frequently expoſed to the morning and evening ſun, though but for a ſhort time only ; and then, being put into

boxes

boxes or frames, is again expofed to the fun, in the fame cautious manner, until the operation is finifhed, and that valuable drug called indigo fitted for the market. The greateft fkill and care is required in every part of the procefs, or there is great danger of fpoiling the whole ; nothing but experience can teach the exact medium to be obferved in every particular.

The goodnefs of indigo may be tried by fire, and by water. If it fwims, or if it wholly diffolves in water, it is good ; if it finks, it is bad ; the heavier the worfe : if it entirely burns away, it is good ; the adulterations remain unconfumed.

Perhaps in no branch of manufacture can. fo large profits be made, upon fo moderate a capital, as in that of indigo ; nor can the manufacture be carried on in any country with greater advantage than in Carolina, where the climate is healthy, provifions plentiful and cheap, and every thing neceffary for the purpofe procured with the greateft facility. The Carolinians have not neglected thefe advantages ; and if they go on with the fame fpirit, and attend diligently to the quality of their goods, they muft, of courfe, fupply the whole world with this commodity, and make their country the richeft, as it is already the moft fertile, part of the Britifh dominions.

Great quantities of turpentine, tar, and pitch, are made in North-Carolina : all are the produce of the pine tree. Turpentine is drawn from incifions made in the tree, from as great a height as a man can reach, with an hatchet, which meet at the bottom

tom

tom of the tree in a point, from whence the turpentine runs into a veſſel, placed to receive it: this is
the whole proceſs. Tar requires a more conſiderable apparatus, and great trouble: a circular floor
of clay, declining a little towards the center, is neceſſary, from which a pipe of wood is laid, the upper
part of which is even with the floor, and reaches ten
feet without the circumference; under the end
the earth is dug away, and barrels are placed to receive the tar. Upon this floor is built up a large
pile of pine wood, ſplit in pieces, and ſurrounded
with a wall of earth, a ſmall aperture being left
at the top, where the fire is firſt kindled. When
the fire begins to burn, this opening is likewiſe
covered, to prevent the fire from flaming out, and
to leave only ſufficient heat to force the tar downwards to the floor. The heat is tempered at pleaſure, by running a ſtick into the earthen wall, and
thus admitting air. Pitch is made by boiling tar
in large iron kettles, ſet in furnaces, or burning it
in round clay holes, made in the earth.

The import-trade of the Carolinas from Great-
Britain and the Weſt-India iſlands is very large, and
in every reſpect the ſame with that of the other colonies. Their trade with the Indians is likewiſe in a
very flouriſhing ſtate. The nature and prodigious
increaſe of the exports of South-Carolina may be diſ-
cerned from the following comparative view, which
ſhews what great improvements this colony has made
in a few years; indeed, from its natural advantages,
there is ſcarce any improvement of which this excellent province is not capable, if properly managed.

Ex-

Exported from CHARLES TOWN.

In 1731.

Rice,   41,957   barrels.
Indigo,
Deer-fkins,   300   hogfheads.
Pitch,   10,750   barrels.
Tar,   2,063   ditto.
Turpentine,   759   ditto.
Beef, pork, &c. not particularized.

In 1754.

Rice,   104,682   barrels.
Indigo,   216,924   pounds.
Deer-fkins,   460   hogfheads.
                   114   bundles.
                   508   loofe.

Pitch,   5,869   barrels.
Tar,   2,945   ditto.
Turpentine,   759   ditto.
Beef,   416   ditto.
Pork,   1,560   ditto.
Indian corn,   16,428   bufhels.
Peafe,   9,162   ditto.
Tanned leather, 4,196   barrels.
Hides in the hair, 1,200
Shingles,   1,114,000
Staves,   206,000
Lumber,   395,000   feet.

Befides a great many live cattle, horfes, cedar, cyprefs, and walnut plank, bees-wax, myrtle, and
fome raw filk and cotton.

North-

North-Carolina, reputed one of the leaft flourifhing of our colonies, certainly lay under great
difficulties; but is much improved within a few
years. The confequence of this inferior province
appears, by the following view of its exports,
which is fufficiently exact to enable the reader to
form a proper idea of the ftate of its commerce.

Exported from all the Ports of NORTH-CAROLINA,
in 1753.

Tar,	61,528	barrels.
Pitch,	12,055	ditto.
Turpentine,	10,429	ditto.
Staves,	762,330	in number.
Shingles,	2,500,000	in number.
Lumber,	2,600,647	feet.
Corn,	61,580	bufhels.
Peafe,	10,000	ditto.
Pork and beef,	3,300	barrels.
Tobacco, about	100	hogfheads.
Tanned leather, about	1,000	cwt.
Deer-fkins,	30,000	

Befides a very-confiderable quantity of wheat,
rice, bread, potatoes, bees-wax, tallow, candles,
bacon, hogs-lard, fome cotton, and a vaft deal of
fquared walnut and cedar timber, hoops, and
headings of all forts.

Some indigo alfo is raifed; but the quantity
cannot be afcertained, as it is all exported from
South-Carolina. A much greater quantity of tobacco

bacco than has been mentioned is also raised in this province; but being produced on the frontiers of, Virginia, is chiefly exported from thence. This province exports too, a considerable, quantity of beaver, racoon, otter, fox, mynx, and wild cats skins, and in every ship a good many live cattle, besides what are sold in Virginia.

Both the Carolinas have made frequent, but not sufficiently continued, efforts towards the cultivation of cotton and silk.. The excellent quality of their produce of this kind affords great encouragement to proceed in a project, which has not been prosecuted with that zeal which its importance certainly deserves, considering how well the climate is suited to these valuable productions. Silk indeed requires more trouble, and a closer attention, than even indigo; nor will a premium alone suffice to set on foot, with vigour, a manufacture in any country where the price of manual labour is dear; a circumstance which must long be an impediment to the growth of raw silk in Carolina, (though no part of the world is fitter for the business, and none could be so advantageous to England) unless some well contrived, and vigorously executed scheme be set on foot for that purpose; a matter worthy the most serious consideration of the British legislature.

The paper-currency of South Carolina amounted, some years ago, to two hundred and fifty thousand pounds sterling, and that of North-Carolina to fifty-two thousand pounds. A very inconsiderable

rable quantity of Englifh money circulates in either province; the current cafh confifting almoft wholly of Spanifh dollars and piftoles.

****

GEORGIA.

THE tract of land lying between the Savannah river and the river Alatamaha, which undoubtedly belonged to England, lying wafte and unfettled, a fcheme was formed for rendering it a barrier, to protect our fouthern colonies againft the Spaniards and Indians. The government alfo had in view to raife wine, oil, and filk; and to turn the induftry of thefe new colonifts from the timber and provifion trade, which the other colonies had gone into too largely, to channels more-advantageous to the public.

Accordingly, the whole country which lies between the rivers Savannah and Alatamaha, north and fouth, and from the Atlantic ocean on the eaft, to the Great South Sea on the weft, was, on the 9th of June 1732, vefted in truftees for twenty-one years, at the expiration of which period, the property, in chief, was to revert to the crown. This country extends about fixty miles from north to fouth, near the fea; but, in the inland parts, widens to above one hundred and fifty: from the

fea

I

sea to the Apalachian mountains, the distance is near three hundred miles.

The trustees being empowered to collect bene-factions for fitting out colonists, and supporting them till their houses could be built and their lands cleared, not only received large contributions for this purpose from the bank of England, the nobili-ty, gentry, &c. but the parliament also granted them ten thousand pounds. These liberalities ena-bled them to supply with working tools, stores, and small arms, above one hundred poor labouring people, who offered themselves by the beginning of November following, and were immediately sent over, under the care of Mr. Oglethorpe, one of the trustees, who generously bestowed his own time and pains, without the least reward, for the advance-ment of the settlement. The new settlers arrived, in good health, at Charles Town, the 15th of Janu-ary, 1733, where they were received by governor Johnson, and the Carolinians in general, with great marks of affection and humanity, and were presented by the assembly with an hundred breeding cattle, twenty-five hogs, and twenty barrels of rice; and being furnished with a party of horse-rangers and scout-boats, soon reached the river Savannah safe-ly, about ten miles up which river Mr. Ogle-thorpe fixed upon a spot for founding their new town, which he named, after the river, Savannah, originally inhabited by a nation called Yama-craw, of which Tomo Chichi was chief. The situ-ation of the town was pleasant and healthful; and

the

the new fettlers being generoufly affifted by the Carolinians, not only with their purfes but their labour, in raifing Savannah, great numbers of pines
were foon cut down, and the land cleared, and fown
with wheat.

The truftees reflecting, that many of our colonies, efpecially South-Carolina, had been much endan-
dangered, both internally and externally, by fuffering
the negroes to exceed the whites fo greatly in number, thought an error of this kind inexcufable in a
colony which was not only to defend itfelf, but intended to be a barrier to the others; and therefore
prohibited the importation of negroes into Georgia,
that the planters might be inured to an habit of induftry. Befides, the introduction of negroes fo near a
Spanifh garrifon, would have facilitated the defer-
tion of the Carolinian negroes to St. Auguftine.
In the next place, obferving what great mifchiefs
arofe in other fettlements from vaft grants of
land, which the grantees either jobbed out again,
to the difcouragement of fettlers, or, what was
worfe, fuffered to lie uncultivated; to avoid this,
mifchief, and prevent the people from becoming
wealthy, which, in their opinion, was inconfiftent
with the military plan upon which this colony was founded, they refolved, in laying out their
towns, to affign but twenty-five acres to each inhabitant; and none could come to poffefs more than
five hundred, by any means, according to the original fcheme. -Neither were thefe lands granted in
fee-fimple, or to the heirs-general of the fettlers, but

were

were inheritable only by their male iffue. The im-. portation of rum was alfo prohibited, to prevent the great diforders which were obferved to happen in other colonies, from the abufe of fpirituous liquors..

The Lower Creek nation, confifting of eight con-, federated tribes, hearing of this new colony, fent a numerous deputation, compofed of their kings and warriors, to treat of an alliance with it. Mr. Ogle-thorpe gave them audience in one of the new, houfes ; and at this meeting they gave fufficient proof, that they were far from being fo ignorant, of their natural rights as fome Europeans imagine. Oueekachumpa, in the name of the Lower Creek nation, claimed all the lands from the river Savan-nah as far as St. Auguftine, and up Flint river, which falls into the Bay of Mexico. He then ac-knowledged the fuperiority of the Englifh; and faid, that the great power, whofe immenfity he en-deavoured to exprefs by extending his hands and lengthening his words, had fent the Englifh thither for the good of his nation ; and that therefore they were welcome to all the land which they did not ufe themfelves. He confirmed this fpeech by laying eight buck-fkins, the beft things, he faid, his na-tion had to beftow, before Mr. Oglethorpe ; and thanked him for his kindnefs to Tomo Chichi, who, with fome of his friends, had been banifhed from his own nation; but, for his valour and wif-dom, had been chofen king by the Yamacraws, and had been relieved by the Englifh. As foon as he had done fpeaking, Tomo Chichi entered, and re-

turned

turned thanks in person for the favours he had received. The articles of agreement were then drawn up, and signed; which contained, as usual, stipulations for liberty of trade, reparations of injuries, and that the English should possess all the lands not used by them, though, at the laying out every town, a certain portion should be allotted for their use; and that all runaway negroes should be restored to the English, who agreed to pay a stipulated reward for each negroe. After having kindly entertained them, Mr. Oglethorpe presented each of the kings with a laced coat, a laced hat, and a shirt; each of their chiefs with a gun; and their attendants with a duffil blanket, and some other trifling things; and then dismissed them, highly satisfied with their treatment.

Soon after the conclusion of this treaty, Mr. Oglethorpe returned to Charles Town, in order to embark for England. During his absence, the fame of the new colony reached the Natchez, who likewise made an alliance with the inhabitants of Georgia. In the middle of May a ship arrived at Savannah with passengers and stores, the captain of which received the reward that had been promised for the first ship that should be unloaded at that town, and soon after another arrived with fifty families; so that the whole of this embarkation amounted to six hundred and eighteen, including women and children: and in March, 1734, from the general state of the trustees accounts, it appeared, that they had received towards settling the province, fourteen thousand eight hundred and twenty-two pounds,

twelve

twelve fhillings, and three-pence; and expended eight thoufand two hundred and two pounds, fix-teen fhillings, and fixpence.

In 1734, Mr. Oglethorpe arrived in England, and brought with him Tomo Chichi, his wife Le-nawki, his fon Tooanahowi, a war captain, and five chiefs of the Creek nation, with their interpreter, who were introduced to his majefty at Kenfington, by whom they were received gracioufly; and Tomo Chichi, prefenting him with fome eagle's feathers, made the following fpeech, which we infert as a fur-ther fpecimen of the Creek eloquence: " This day I behold the majefty of your face, the greatnefs of your houfe, and the numbers of your people. I am come for the good of the whole nation called the Creeks, to renew the peace they made long ago with the Englifh. I am come over, in my old days, though I cannot live to fee any advantage to myfelf: 1 am come for the good of the children of all the nations of the Upper and Lower Creeks, that they may be inftructed in the knowledge of the Englifh. Thefe are the feathers of the eagle, the fwifteft of birds, and who flies all round our nations: thefe feathers are, in our land, a fign of peace; and we have brought them over to leave them with you, O great king, as a fign of everlaft-ing peace. Great king! whatfoever words you fhall fpeak unto me, I will tell them faithfully unto all the kings of the Creek nation."

During their refidence in England, the govern-ment omitted nothing that feemed capable of ftriking them with the moft awful ideas of the

Englifh

Englifh power and magnificence; but from experience we find, that the Indians are but flightly impreffed with any ideas that are not familiar to them. However, Tomo Chichi gave uncommon proofs of his fagacity; and pointed out many particulars of great fervice to the Englifh, as well as the Indians. He requefted, that the weights, meafures, prices, and qualities of the Englifh goods, might be fettled; and, to prevent impofitions, that there fhould be but one ftorehoufe in every Indian town; which propofals the truftees thought fo reafonable, that they were immediately ratified, after having been referred to the board of trade for their approbation.

On the 30th of October, 1734, Tomo Chichi, and his chiefs, with their attendants, embarked at Gravefend for their own country, having had an allowance, during their refidence here, of twenty pounds a week, of which they fpent but little, being generally invited every day to the tables of perfons of the higheft diftinction. Befides this allowance, they received prefents to a very confiderable value upon their departure. The fhip in which they took their paffage, carried over likewife a number of German proteftants from Saltzburg, who, with others of their countrymen who afterwards arrived, were fettled at a fpot on the Savannah, where they built a town, called Ebenezer, which, by their induftry and fobriety, foon became a confiderable fettlement. About this time, the colony was alarmed with a report, that the Spaniards intended

X 2 tended

tended to attack it. Tomo Chichi profeffed a great defire to oppofe the enemy in perfon; but his affairs not permitting him, fent three of his chiefs. The rumour proving groundlefs, the planters of Georgia made a furprizing progrefs in clearing their lands; and the Englifh parliament granted them twenty-fix thoufand pounds, which, with very confiderable private donations, was expended upon ftrengthening their fouthern frontier. For this fervice, the truftees pitched upon the Scotch Highlanders, one hundred and fixty of whom, all able men, were fent over in 1735, and fettled upon Alatamaha river, fixteen miles, by water, from the ifland of St. Simon, where they built a fort, mounted with four pieces of cannon, which they named Darien, and a fmall town, called New Invernefs. In February, 1736, Mr. Oglethorpe arrived at Savannah, with about three hundred more fettlers; forty-feven of whom being Englifh, were fettled on the ifland of St. Simon, which was ceded to the Englifh, together with all the adjacent iflands, by the Creek Indians; the remainder built another town, called Frederica. Mr. Oglethorpe, in this voyage, forwarded the raifing the beacon of Tybee, and the building of a church, erected a wharf for landing goods, and provided men for cleaning the roads and compleating the fortifications.

In September, the fame year, it was ftipulated between Mr. Oglethorpe and the governor of St. Auguftine, that the Englifh fhould evacuate the

fort

fort built upon the ifland of St. George, forty miles north of St. Auguftine, near the influx of St. John's river; but that this evacuation fhould not injure his Britannic majefty's right to the faid ifland, or any other of his claims upon the American continent.

The inhabitants of Ebenezer, difliking its fituation, earneftly requefted to be fettled nearer the mouth of the river; and by their importunities, prevailed upon Mr. Oglethorpe, contrary to his opinion, to mark out a town for them on the fpot they defired. He next turned his attention towards compleating Fort Frederica, upon the ifland of St. Simon, near the northern mouth of the river Alamaha, which, with its outworks, forms a regular fquare, with four baftions, furrounded by a ditch. Mr. Oglethorpe then accompanied the Indians to furvey their country, principally with a view to prevent them from attacking the Spaniards, with whom England was then at peace. During this progrefs, he marked out another fort, on an ifland at the mouth of Jekell's found, which he named Cumberland ifland; and alfo vifited another ifland, about fixteen miles long, which produced naturally wild oranges, myrtles, and vines, to which he gave the name of Amelia ifland.

In 1737, the depredations daily committed by the Spaniards on the Englifh by fea, threatening a war betwixt the two powers, the Britifh government, in confequence of advice from South-Carolina, that the Spaniards at St. Auguftine and the

Ha-

Havannah, were making preparations for attacking the infant colony of Georgia, at the requeſt of the truſtees, ſent thither a regiment of ſix hundred men; and, for their encouragement, granted each ſoldier five acres of land, for his own uſe and benefit during his continuance there, with permiſſion to quit the ſervice at the end of ſeven years, if deſired, and a grant of twenty acres of land in the colony. The parliament of England, this year, granting the colony a freſh aid of twenty thouſand pounds, enabled the truſtees to ſend over another embarkation of foreign proteſtants. But it was now found by experience, that ſome fundamental errors had been committed in the original conſtitution of the colony: the regulations concerning inheritance, negroes, ſpirituous liquors, and ſmallneſs of the grants, though well intended, and ſeemingly likely to bring about very excellent purpoſes, appeared evidently made without ſufficiently conſulting the nature of the country, or the diſpoſition of the people. The tail-male grants were ſo grievous, as in a new colony, land muſt be for ſome time at leaſt, the only wealth of the family, that the truſtees ſoon corrected that error. The climate being exceſſively hot, and field-work very laborious, as in a new colony, the ground muſt be cleared, tilled, and ſowed, with vaſt and inceſſant toil, for a bare ſubſiſtence, the burthen was too heavy for white men, who had not been ſeaſoned to the country.

It is true, all the Engliſh colonies on the continent were originally ſettled without the help of negroes:

the

the whites were obliged to labour; they underwent it becaufe no other means prefented. But it is not the nature of man to fubmit to extraordinary hardfhips in one fpot, when they fee their neighbours on another, without any difference in the circumftances of things, in a much more eafy condition. Befides, no methods were taken to animate them in the hardfhips they underwent: the prohibition of rum, though fpecious in appearance, had a very bad effect; the waters in this unfettled country, running through fuch an extent of foreft, were unwholefome, and wanted the corrective of a little fpirit, as the fettlers themfelves wanted fomething to fupport their ftrength, in the exceffive heat of the climate; befides, its dampnefs, in feveral places, difpofed them to agues and fevers. This prohibition alfo deprived them of the only vent they had for their only marketable commodities, lumber and corn, which could fell no where but in the Sugar Iflands, from which, with this reftriction of negroes and rum, they could take very little in return. A levelling fcheme, in a new colony, is extremely unadvifeable: men are feldom induced to leave their native country but on fome extraordinary profpects: there ought always to be fomething of a vaftnefs in the view prefented to them, to ftrike the imagination powerfully; becaufe men never reafon well enough to fee, that the majority of mankind are not endued with difpofitions proper to make a fortune any where, be the propofed advantages ever fo great. The majority of mankind muft always

X 4 be

be indigent ; but in a new fettlement they muft all
be fo, unlefs there are fome perfons on fuch a comfortable and fubftantial footing, as to give direction
and vigour to the induftry of the reft.   People of
fubftance found themfelves difcouraged from attempting a fettlement, by the narrow bounds,
which no induftry could enable them to pafs ; and
the defign of confirming the inheritance to the male
line was an additional difcouragement : befides,
the grant, fmall as it was, after a fhort free tenure,
was clogged with a much greater quit-rent than is
paid in our beft and longeft fettled colonies.   Indeed, through the whole manner of granting land,
there appeared a low attention to the trifling profits
that might be derived to the truftees, or the crown,
by rents or efcheats, which clogged the deliberate
fcheme at firft laid down, and was in itfelf extremely injudicious.   In a flourifhing colony, with
extenfive fettlements, the crown receives a large revenue from the fmalleft quit-rents ; but, in an
ill-fettled province, the greateft quit-rents make
but a poor return, yet burthen and impoverifh the
people.

Thefe, and feveral other inconveniences in the
plan of fettlement, raifed a general difcontent : the
fettlers, finding themfelves not upon a par with the
other colonies, quarrelled with each other, and with
their magiftrates, complained, remonftrated, and
meeting with no fatisfaction, many of them quitted Georgia, and fettled in the other colonies,
where they deemed the encouragement better ; fo
that,

that, of above two thousand people, who had been sent from Europe in a little time, not above seven hundred remained in Georgia. The mischief grew worse and worse every day, till the government revoked the charter, took the province into its own hands, annulled all the particular regulations that had been made, and left the province exactly on the same footing with Carolina.

Though this step has probably saved the colony from ruin; yet, perhaps, it was wrong to neglect entirely the first views upon which it was founded, which were undoubtedly judicious; and if the methods taken to effect them were not so well directed, it was no argument against the views themselves, but a reason for some change in the means used to execute them. Nothing wants a regulation more than the dangerous inequality between the number of negroes and whites, in such English provinces where negroes are allowed. In Georgia, the first error of absolutely prohibiting negroes might have been turned to good account; for the settlers would have received the permission to employ them, under whatever restrictions, as an indulgence; and by executing whatever regulations were made in this point with strictness, by degrees, we might have seen a province fit to answer all the purposes of defence and commerce too; whereas they are permitted to use such a latitude in this respect, Georgia, instead of being a defence to Carolina, stands in need of a considerable force to defend itself.

In

In 1740, Mr. Oglethorpe made a progress of five hundred miles from Frederica fort; and at the town of Coweta held a conference with the deputies of that town, and likewise with those of the Chactaws and Chickesaws, Indian nations residing between the English and French settlements, who confirmed the grant they had already made of all the lands upon the Savannah river, as far as the river Ogeeche; and all the lands along the sea-coasts, as far as St. John's river, as high as the tide flows; and all the islands as far as that river, particularly, the islands of Frederica, Cumberland, and Amelia; reserving to the Creek nation, all the lands from Pipe-makers-bluff to Savannah, and the islands of St. Catharine, Offebaw, and Sappolo; declaring, that all the territory from Savannah river to St. John's river, and all the lands between them, and from St. John's river to the Bay of Apalachia, and from thence to the mountains, was, by antient right, the property of the Creek nation, who had maintained possession of it against all oppofers, and could shew the heaps of the bones of their enemies, by them slain in defence of their lands.

Upon the breaking out of the war between England and Spain in 1739, Georgia became one of the chief objects against which the Spaniards directed their hostilities. Accordingly, in 1742, they invaded Georgia from St. Augustine, with near six thousand men, including Indians; but were repulsed by general Oglethorpe, assisted by a small number of Indians, headed by Tomo Chichi's son.

From

From this period the colony drooped and languish-
ed, till Mr. Ellis was appointed governor, under
whose administration it again revived ; to whom
his majesty, upon his removal to another government, made a handsome present, as a mark
of his approbation of the judicious measures he
pursued for the good of the colony during his administration. James Wright, Esq; is the present
governor.

CLIMATE, and NATURAL HISTORY of GEORGIA.

The face of the country resembles Carolina, of
which it originally was a part, and though intensely
hot in summer, is, in general, a rich and delicious
country, its productions varying, indeed, according
to the different parts of the colony ; but in general
the soil produces rice, indico, cotton, Indian corn,
wheat, oats and barley, potatoes, pompions, melons, cucumbers, pease, beans, and sallading of all
kinds, throughout the whole year. Nectarines,
plumbs, and peaches grow naturally, in great
abundance, and by cultivation might be rendered
equal, if not superior, to those of Europe. Grapes
grow wild, and ripen in June. Apple and pear
trees, and apricot trees thrive well. The white
and black mulberry trees, which are met with in
the greatest plenty, afford excellent nourishment for
worms, the propagation of which was one of the
principal inducements for settling the colony.
Orange and olive trees arrive at the greatest perfection,

fection, efpecially in the fouthern parts of Georgia. The chief timber trees are oaks, of fix or feven fpecies, pines, hickery, cedar, cyprefs, walnut, faffafras, beech, and various other trees, unknown to Europeans, befides a great variety of flowering fhrubs.

This province produces variety of game, from the beginning of November to March; fuch as, a fmall kind of woodcocks and partridges, large wild turkies, turtle-doves, wild geefe, ducks, teals, and widgeons, with immenfe quantities of wild pigeons, and other birds peculiar to the country. During the fummer, the inhabitants kill deer and fummer-ducks. Tygers, bears, and the opoffum are common here; and the woods abound with cattle, wolves, racoons, and fnakes; but none are venomous, except the rattle-fnake. The rivers are full of alligators and fharks; but the coafts are plentifully ftored with trout, mullet, whitings, and a prodigious variety of other fifh. Oyfters are found in great plenty, though not fo well flavoured as thofe of England; as alfo clams, mufcles, and very large prawns.

TRADE and POPULATION.

Georgia has two towns already known in trade; Savannah, the capital, which ftands very well for traffic, about ten miles from the fea, upon a large river of the fame name, navigable for large boats two hundred miles farther, to the fecond town, Augufta, which ftands upon a moft fertile fpot, and is

fo

fo commodioufly fituated for the Indian trade, that, from the firft eftablifhment of the colony, it has been in a flourifhing ftate, and very early maintained fix hundred inhabitants in that trade alone. The bordering Indian nations are, the Upper and Lower Creeks, the Chickefaws, and the Cherokees; fome of the moft powerful tribes of America. The trade of fkins with this people is the largeft we have, comprehending that of Georgia, the two Carolinas, and Virginia. We deal with them a little for furs alfo, but they are of an inferior fort; all animals that bear the fur, by a wife providence, having it more thick, and of a fofter and finer fort, in proportion as they are found more to the north; the greater the cold, the better they are clad.

As for the fcheme of vines and filk, we were extremely eager in this refpect, at firft; and, in 1739, a fpecimen of Georgian filk was fent to London, and declared, by two very eminent merchants who dealt in that commodity, to be as good as any raw filk that came from Italy. But at the firft fettlement, fuch a defign was impracticable; becaufe a few people, fettled in an uncultivated country, muft provide every thing for the fupport of life, before they can think of manufactures; and muft grow numerous enough to fpare a multitude of hands from that moft neceffary employment, before they can fend fuch things either cheap, or in plenty to market. But now, though the province is grown more populous, and longer fettled, little is faid of either of thefe articles.

The

The misfortune is, though no people originally conceive things better than the Englifh do, we want the unremitting perfeverance neceffary to bring defigns of confequence to perfection.

At prefent Georgia is beginning to emerge, though flowly, out of the difficulties that attended its firft eftablifhment; being ftill but indifferently peopled, though now fettled above thirty-fix years. None of our other colonies were of fo flow a growth, though none had fo much the attention of the government, or of the people in general, or raifed fo great expectations in the beginning. The province exports fome corn and lumber to the Weft-Indies, raifes fome rice, and, of late, has cul-aivted indigo with fuccefs. Its imports from the mother-country are much the fame as the other colonies.

※※※※※※※※※※※※※※※※※※※※※※

F L O R I D A.

THE country round Georgia, between that and the river Miffiffippi, an extent of about fix hundred miles, ftill retains the name of Flori-da; tho' divided, fince its ceffion to England, into two diftinct provinces, viz. Eaft and Weft Florida.

England has had an undoubted right to this coun-try ever fince the reign of Henry VII. by whofe commiffion Sebaftian Cabot, in 1496, difcovered all this coaft, from north lat. 28 to 50, fixteen years
before

before it had been vifited by any Europeans. Then, indeed, the fouthern part of this continent, towards the Straits of Bahama, was vifited by the Spaniards, under Juan Ponce de Leon, in 1512; as it was, ten years after, by Vafquez Aillon; in 1527, by Pamphilo Navarez; and, in 1539, by Ferdinando Soto: but their cruelties fo exafperated the natives, that they expelled them all, one after another; nor did they leave a Spaniard in all Florida.

Florida remained entirely neglected by Europe, until the reign of Charles IX. king of France, when the celebrated leader of the Proteftants in that kingdom, admiral Chatillon, who was a man of too comprehenfive views not to fee the advantages of a fettlement in America, procured two veffels to be fitted out for difcoveries upon that coaft, in 1562; probably, with a view to retire thither with thofe of his perfuafion, if the fuccefs, which hitherto fuited fo ill with his great courage and conduct, fhould at laft entirely deftroy his caufe in France. Thefe fhips, in two months, arrived upon the coaft of America, near the river now called Albemarle, in the province of North-Carolina. The French gave the Indians to underftand, in the beft manner they were able, that they were enemies to the Spaniards, which fecured them a friendly reception, and the good offices of the inhabitants. They were, however, in no condition to make any fettlement.

On their return to France, the admiral, at this time, by the abominable policy of the court, apparently

parently in great favour, was so well satisfied with
the account they had given of the country, that, in
1564, he fitted out five or six ships, with as many
hundred men aboard, to begin a colony there. This
was accordingly done at the place of their landing
in the first expedition, where they built a fort about
two miles up the river May, now called St. John's,
which they named Fort Caroline. The Spaniards, in
1565, dispatched a considerable force to attack this
colony, under Don Pedro Menendez de Avilez, who
erected Fort St. Augustine, and once more took pof-
session of this country for Spain. Not satisfied with
reducing Fort Caroline, he put all the people to the
sword, after quarter given, changed the name of the
fort to that of St. Matheo, on whose day he became
master of it, and, committing great outrages upon
the natives, paved the way for the vengeance which
soon after fell upon them, for such an unnecessary
and unprovoked act of cruelty. For, though the
admiral and his party were by this time destroyed
in the infamous massacre of St. Bartholomew, and
though the design of a colony died with him, one

some ships, which sailed from that coast purely to
revenge the murder of his countrymen and his
friends. The Indians greedily embraced the opportunity of becoming associates in the punishment of the common enemy, joined in the siege of
two or three forts the Spaniards had built there,
took them, and in all put the garrison to the
sword, without mercy.

and

Satisfied with this action, the adventurers returned; and, happily for us, the French court did not understand, blinded as they were by their bigotry, the advantages which might have been derived from giving America to their Proteftant fubjects as a place of refuge.

The conftant wars between the Spaniards and Creek Indians, greatly prevented their enlarging their fettlements here; tho' by the evacuation of De Gorgues, they had for fome years no European competitors in Florida. They fortified and improved, indeed, their new fettlement at St. Auguftine; but as to St. Matheo, it was fuffered to go to decay, In 1585, fome private adventurers in England fitted out a fleet of twenty fail of fhips and pinnaces, under the command of Sir Francis Drake and Martin Forbifher, who attacked Fort Matheo, now called Fort St. Juan, which being very weak, was abandoned by the Spaniards; and Drake found in it fourteen pieces of brafs cannon, and about two thoufand pounds in cafh. This feems to be all the fruits of this expedition againft Florida; and the Spaniards conftantly maintained their garrifon at St. Auguftine, (though feveral attempts were made to reduce it by the Carolinians, and afterwards by general Oglethorpe) till the conclufion of the laft war, when the whole territory of Florida, including Louifiana, the town and ifland of New Orleans-excepted, was ceded to the crown of Great-Britain by the treaty of Paris, in 1762. His Britannic majefty, being fovereign of the foil, has the appointment of the governors in both the Floridas.

EAST-FLORIDA.

East Florida, the moſt ſouthern colony upon the continent of Britiſh America, lies between the 25th and 31ſt degrees of north latitude.

By the king's proclamation, dated the 7th of October, 1763, its boundaries were fixed, on the north, by the river St. Mary's ; on the eaſt, by the Atlantic Ocean, and the Gulph of Florida ; and, on the weſt, by the river Apalachicola, and the Gulph of Mexico.

Its length, from north to ſouth, is three hundred and fifty miles. Its breadth, from the mouth of St. Mary's river, its northern limits, to the river Apalachicola, is about two hundred and forty. At the mouth of St. Juan's river, forty miles ſouth of St. Mary's, where the peninſula begins, it is one hundred and eighty miles broad ; and grows narrower from thence to the capes of Florida, where its breadth may be between thirty and forty miles. It contains, upon the neareſt calculation, about twelve millions of acres, which is nearly as much as Ireland.

The ſea-coaſt of Eaſt-Florida is a low flat country, interſected by a great number of rivers. The country continues flat for about forty miles from the coaſt, and then grows a little hilly, and

in

in some parts rocky.   The soil in general is a light
sand.

Florida differs materially from the rest of America in this, that almost all the continent besides is
covered with a thick forest; whereas the trees in
Florida are at a distance from one another, and being clear of under-wood, this country has more the
appearance of an open grove than a forest.

In the interior parts the trees are larger, the
grass higher, and the cattle bigger, than towards
the sea, especially in that part of the peninsula which
lies betwixt the river St. Juan's, and the fort of St.
Mark d'Apalachie, which is about one hundred
and fifty miles to the north-west of this river.

To take a view of the eastern shore of Florida,
beginning from the north, we meet the river St.
Mary's, lying in 30 deg. 47 min. latitude.   It is a
mile broad at its mouth, where Amelia island is situated, has five fathom water upon the bar at low
water, and is navigable above sixty miles, where it
has three fathom water.   It is the best harbour from
the capes of Virginia to those of Florida : it takes
its rise out of the great swamp*, called by the Indians Owa-qua-phe-no-gaw.   The lands upon the
banks of this river are the richest in the northern.

* The word swamp is peculiar to America : it there signifies a tract of land that is sound and good, but by lying low is
covered with water.   All the forest trees, pines excepted, thrive
best in the swamps, where the soil is always rich, and when
cleared and drained, is proper for the growth of rice, hemp,
and indigo.

Y 2

parts

parts of the province; the abundance of cane-swamps fufficiently fhews the fertility thereof. The beft trees, that grow in the fwamps on this river, are the live oak and cedar, very ufeful for fhip-build-ing: their extraordinary fize is a ftrong mark of the goodnefs of the foil.

St. Juan's, now called St. John's river, lies forty miles fouthward of St. Mary's; the tract of land between them confifts of plains, covered with pines; thefe plains are called in America, pine-bar-rens, or highlands, in contradiftinction to the fwamps and lowlands.

From St. John's river fouthwards to St. Auguf-tine is forty-five miles: the country is much the fame as has been juft defcribed; but not quite fo good, the fwamps being neither fo frequent nor fo large.

The river St. John's, the principal river of this province, in point of utility and beauty, is not inferior to any in America. The fource of this river, which is not exactly afcertained, is in all probability near the capes of Florida: it paffes through five lakes, the loweft of them is called by the Indians the Great Lake: it is twenty miles long and fifteen broad, and has eight feet wa-ter; there are feveral iflands in it, and it is now called Lake George: this lake is one hundred and feventy miles from the mouth of the river. In going down from hence, the firft European ha-

ftore-
house:

I

house : fifteen miles lower is Mr. Rolle's settlement; the whole diftance from the lake to Mr. Rolle's is forty-five miles, and the country between is the beft yet difcovered upon the river. Mr. Rolle's plantation is well fituated on the eaftern banks, and is the moft confiderable upon this river, which is here very narrow : twenty-five miles from Mr. Rolle's, downward, is Piccolata, a fmall fort, with a garrifon. The river is here three miles broad.

The bar, at low water, is nine feet deep, its channel up to Lake George is much deeper; the breadth is very unequal, from a quarter of a mile to three miles. The tide rifes at the bar from five to eight feet, and two feet at Mr. Rolle's, though one hundred and twenty-five miles from the fea. There are neither fhallows nor any rapidity in the river; the current, owing to the flatnefs of the country, is very gentle, and veffels may go up the river almoft as eafy as down, for two hundred miles ; there is perhaps no river in the world more commodious for navigation.

St. Mark's river takes its rife near the mouth of St. John's river, runs from north to fouth, and parallel with the fea, till it empties itfelf into the harbour of St. Auguftine. From the flatnefs of the country, there are many falt-marfhes on both fides of the river, almoft up to its fource : thefe marfhes may be eafily defended from the tides, and will make very proper lands, either for rice, indigo, or hemp.

Y 3   We

We come now to the harbour of St. Auguſtine, which would be one of the beſt in America, were it not for its bar, which will not admit veſſels of great burthen, as it has but eight feet water*. The bar is ſurrounded by breakers, that have a formidable appearance when you enter it; but is not ſo dangerous as it appears, on account of the bar being very ſhort: ſince the government has appointed a good pilot, no veſſels have been loſt upon it. There is a road on the north ſide of the bar, with good anchorage for ſuch ſhips as draw too much water to go into the harbour.

A neck of main land to the north, and a point of Anaſtatia iſland to the ſouth, form the entrance of the port. Oppoſite to the entrance lies Fort St. Mark's, ſo called from the river it is ſituated upon. This fort is a regular quadrangle, with four baſtions, a ditch fifty feet wide, with a covert-way, place of arms, and a glacis: the entrance of the gate is defended by a raveline; it is caſe-mated all round, and bomb-proof: the works are entirely of hewn ſtone, and being finiſhed according to the modern taſte of military architecture, it makes a very handſome appearance, and may be juſtly deemed as pretty a fort as any in the king's dominions.

* It is neceſſary to obſerve, that the depth of the bars of the harbours on the eaſtern ſhore of Eaſt-Florida cannot be exactly aſcertained, as the tides there are chiefly regulated by the winds; a ſtrong weſterly wind will make but ſix feet, and an eaſterly wind twelve feet water upon the bar of St. Auguſtine, at low water.

The

The town of St. Auguftine is fituated near the glacis of the fort, on the weft fide of the harbour: it is an oblong fquare; the ftreets are regularly laid out, and interfect each other at right angles; they are built narrow on purpofe to afford fhade. The town is above half a mile in length, regularly fortified with baftions, half-baftions, and a ditch. Befides thefe works, it has another fort of fortification, very fingular, but well adapted againft the enemy the Spaniards had moft to fear. It confifts of feveral rows of palmetto-trees, planted very clofe along the ditch, up to the parapet; their pointed leaves are fo many cheveaux de frize, that make it entirely impenetrable; the two fouthern baftions are built of ftone. In the middle of the town is a fpacious fquare, called the Parade, open towards the harbour: at the bottom of this fquare is the governor's houfe, the apartments of which are fpacious and fuited to the climate, with high windows, a balcony in front, and galleries on both fides: to the back part of the houfe is joined a tower, called in America, a look-out, from which there is an extenfive profpect towards the fea, as well as inland. There are two churches within the walls of the town; the parifh-church, a plain building; and another belonging to the convent of Francifcan friars, which is converted into barracks for the garrifon. The houfes are built of free-ftone, commonly two ftories high, two rooms upon a floor, with large windows and balconies: before

the

the entry of moſt of the houſes runs a portico of ſtone arches ; the roofs are commonly flat. The Spaniards conſulted conveniency more than taſte in their buildings. The number of houſes in their time, in the town and within the lines, was above nine hundred : many of them, eſpecially in the ſuburbs, being built of wood or palmetto leaves, are now gone to decay. The inhabitants of all colours, whites, negroes, mulattoes, Indians, &c. at the evacuation of St. Auguſtine, amounted to five thouſand ſeven hundred, the garriſon included, which conſiſted of two thouſand five hundred men. Half a mile from the town, to the weſt, is a line, with a broad ditch and baſtions, running from St. Sebaſtian's creek to St. Mark's river : a mile further is another fortified line, with ſome redoubts, forming a ſecond communication between a ſtoccado fort upon St. Sebaſtian's river, and Fort Moza upon the river St. Mark's.

Within the firſt line, near the town, was a ſmall ſettlement of Germans, who had a church of their own. Upon St. Mark's river, within the ſame line, was alſo an Indian town, with a church built of free-ſtone. The ſteeple is of good workmanſhip and taſte, though built by the Indians. The lands belonging to this townſhip, the governor has given as glebe-land to the pariſh-church. The land about St. Auguſtine, in all appearance, is the worſt in the province.

Oppoſite to the town of St. Auguſtine lies the iſland of Anaſtaſia. This iſland is about twenty-
five

miles in length, and divided from the main land by a narrow channel, called Matanza river, though in reality an arm of the sea. The soil here is but indifferent: at present it is used for pasturage; but having some creeks and swamps in several parts, may in time be cultivated to advantage.

At the north end of this island is a watch-tower, or look-out, built of white stone, which serves also as a land-mark for vessels at sea. At the approach of any vessels, signals are made from this tower to the fort; a few soldiers do duty there on that account. A quarry of whitish stone is found opposite to St. Augustine, of which the fort and houses are built. Stone quarries are very rare in the southern parts of America, which makes this of Anastasia the more valuable: the stone is manifestly a concretion of small shells, petrified; it is soft under ground, but becomes very hard and durable by being exposed to the air.

Going southwards from Augustine, at the distance of a mile and a half, we come to St. Sebastian's creek. This stream takes its rise five miles north of Augustine, and, after making a sweep to the west, empties itself into the sea at this place: near the mouths of this creek are extensive saltwater marshes, overflown at high tides, which may be easily defended from the sea; higher inland are fine swamps.

We come next to Wood-cutters creek, which rises fifteen miles north of Augustine, and, after describing a semicircle to the west, much like Sebastian's creek, but with a larger sweep, empties itself

into

into the fea fix miles below Auguftine : the lands upon this creek confift of very good fwamps and highlands.

At the Matanzas, fifteen miles fouth of Wood-cutters creek, is a fmall fort, and harbour, fit for coafting veffels. The harbour is oppofite the fouth point of Anaftafia ifland, where there is a fecond watch-tower. The foil between Wood-cutters creek and the Matanzas, is tolerably good, on account of feveral creeks and fwamps.

From the Matanzas we come to Halifax river, which, like St. Mark's above-mentioned, runs parallel to the fea, and is feparated from it only by a fandy beach, in fome parts a mile, in others two miles broad. This beach, or bank, feems to be formed by the fands ; which, either by hurricanes or in a courfe of ages, have been wafhed up by the fea. The fource of this river, though certainly not very far from St. John's river, is not as yet well afcertained : before it reaches Mofquito inlet, Tomoko river falls into it. This river runs from weft to eaft ; and from it to St. John's is only four miles land-carriage.

From the Matanzas to Mufquito inlet is forty miles. At this place, Hilfborough river, coming from the fouth, and Halifax river from the north, meet, and are both difcharged here into the fea : the bar of this harbour has eight feet at low water.

About Mufquito inlet the country is low, and chiefly falt-marfh ; what highland there is, is covered with cabbage trees, papaw trees, and other tropi-

tropical plants, which fhew that Weft-India commodities may be raifed here. The weftern banks
of Halifax and Hillfborough rivers contain a great
deal of excellent land ; the many orange-groves,
which denote former Spanifh fettlements, and the
frequent remains of Indian towns, fhews that they
have been once well inhabited. We are as yet
unacquainted with the fources of moft of the rivers
in Eaft-Florida, and particularly that of Hillfborough river : it is generally believed to have a
communication with an Indian inlet, called by the
Spaniards Rio Days, fixty miles to the fouth, where
there is fuch another harbour as Mofquito, with
eight feet water ; it is faid to communicate with
St. John's river.

Between Indian River and the Capes of Florida,
are feveral rivers and harbours ; but they are not
yet actually furveyed.

In Eaft-Florida there is indeed a change of the
feafons, but it is a moderate one ; in November
and December many trees lofe their leaves, vegetation goes on flowly, and the winter is perceived.
The winters, however, are fo mild, that the tendereft plants of the Weft-Indies, fuch as the plantain,
the alligator pear-tree, the banana, the pine-apple
or ananas, the fugar-cane, &c. almoft conftantly
remain unhurt. Fogs and dark gloomy weather, are unknown in this country. At the
equinoxes, efpecially the autumnal, the rains fall
very heavy every day, betwixt eleven o'clock in
the morning, and four in the afternoon, for fome

weeks

weeks together; when a shower is over, the sky does not continue cloudy, but always clears up, and the sun appears again. The mildness of the seasons, and purity of the air, are probably the cause of the healthiness of this country, which the inhabitants of the Spanish settlements in America considered, with respect to its healthiness, in the same light that we do the south of France; the Spaniards, from the Havannah and elsewhere, frequently resorting thither for the benefit of their health; and since it came into the hands of Great-Britain, many gentlemen have experienced the happy effects of its climate.

By the best accounts of the first discovery of East-Florida, it appears to have been nearly as full of inhabitants as Peru and Mexico; and these accounts are, in some measure, verified, by the frequent remains we discover of Indian towns throughout the peninsula. The natives are described to have been larger, and of a stronger make than the Mexican Indians.

The peninsula of Florida is not broad, and as it lies betwixt two seas, the air is cooler, and oftener refreshed with rains, than on the continent: the entire absence of the sun for eleven hours, makes the dews heavy, and gives the earth time to cool; so that the nights in summer are less sultry here than in the north latitude, where the sun shines upon the earth for seventeen or eighteen hours out of the twenty-four. The heat, which in South-Carolina and Georgia is sometimes intolerable for want of wind,

wind, is alfo here mitigated, by a never-failing fea-breeze in the day-time, and a land-wind at night.

In no one part of the Britifh dominions is there found fo great a variety of trees, plants, and fhrubs, as in Eaft-Florida, where the productions of the northern and fouthern latitudes feem to flourifh together.

Without attempting to enumerate all the foreft-trees, I fhall only take notice of fuch as are moft ufeful, viz. the white and red pine, the fpruce fir, (different from that to the northward) the ever-green oak, the chefnut oak, the mahogany, red bay, walnut, hickery, black cherry, maple, afh, locuft, and logwood trees; the red and white mulberry tree, of which the forefts are full, and which grow to a larger fize than in any other part of America, fuftic and braziletto, faffafras and balfam of Tolu trees, the magnolia, tulip-laurel, and tupelow-trees, fo beautiful in gardens.

All the fruit trees (an indifferent fort of plumb, and a fmall black cherry, excepted) have been imported from Europe, and thrive exceeding well. A ftranger cannot help being ftruck with the lux-uriancy of the orange-tree; it is larger in fize, and produces greater abundance, and better flavoured fruit, than in Spain or Portugal: this tree is fo well adapted to the climate, that it has fpread itfelf every where. Lemons, limes, citrons, pomegra-nates, figs, apricots, peaches, &c. grow here in high perfection.

The

The myrtle wax fhrub, the moft ufeful and beneficial of the fpontaneous growth of America, is
found in all forts of foil, and in fuch plenty, in
Eaft-Florida, that, were there hands enough to
gather the berries, they could fupply all England
with wax : the procefs of making it is very fim-
ple ; they bruife the berries, boil them in water,
and fkim the wax off, which is naturally of a bright
green colour, but may be bleached like bees-wax,
and, on account of its hardnefs, is well adapted for
candles in hot countries. Of the opuntia, or prick-
ly-pear, there are different fpecies in Eaft-Florida ;
on one fort, with a fmooth leaf, the cochineal infect is found in incredible plenty : of the fruit of
the other fpecies is made a vegetable cochineal,
which may be ufed for ordinary purpofes inftead of
the true cochineal. The fenna fhrub, farfaparilla,
China-root, wild indigo, water and mufk melons,
are alfo indigenous plants of Eaft-Florida.

I cannot omit mentioning an herb of the growth
of Eaft-Florida, of which, as yet, very little notice
has been taken. This herb refembles entirely our
famphire in England, and is called barilla or kali :
it is the fame of which in Spain the pearl-afhes are
made. The fea-coaft, marfhes, and low-lands, overflown at high tides, are covered with it.

Eaft-Florida has a great plenty of all kinds of
game common to the climate. As to the domeftic
animals, they are, in general, the fame that we have
in Europe ; the horned cattle as big as in England,
efpecially in the inland parts.

It

It has alfo a great variety of birds; immenfe numbers migrate hither in winter, to avoid the cold of the northern latitudes. In the woods are plenty of wild turkies, better tafted, as well as larger, than our tame ones in England. The pheafant is in fize like the European; its plumage, like that of our partridge. The American partridge is not much bigger than a quail, and feems to be of that fpecies. The wild pigeons, for three months in the year, are in fuch plenty here, that an account of them would feem incredible; and all the different forts of water-fowls belonging to America, the fwan excepted, are found here in the greateft abundance.

The rivers of the fouthern provinces of North-America abound greatly with fifh, but thofe of Florida rather more than any other: thofe moftly made ufe of, are the bafs, mullet, different forts of rays, and flat-fifh, cat-fifh, fea-trout, and black-fifh; crabs, prawns, and fhrimps, of an extraordinary fize, oyfters, turtles, &c.

If one confiders the extent of Eaft-Florida, and the fmall number of inhabitants it has had thefe fixty years, fince the native Indians were exterminated by the Creeks, one would be apt to think, it muft of courfe be over-run with venomous infects and reptiles: feveral writers who mention Florida, have taken it for granted to be fo. The fact is quite otherwife; if we except the alligator, Eaft-Florida has fewer infects than any other province in America. Mr. Rolle, who for eighteen months lived conftantly in the woods,

woods, has feen but one rattle-fnake : for the hunting parties of the Creek Indians, who are difperfed
over the whole province; continually fet the grafs
on fire, for the conveniency of hunting ; by which
means not only the infects, but their eggs alfo, are
deftroyed.

There is an infect in Eaft-Florida, not known in
other parts of America, which is a large yellow
fpider :· the hind part of his body is bigger than a
pigeon's egg, and the reft in proportion ; its web is
a true yellow filk, fo ftrong as to catch fmall birds,
upon which it feeds : the bite of this fpider is attended with a fwelling of the part, and great pain,
but no danger of life. A great variety of lizards
are found here ; fome of them very beautiful,
changing their colour, like the cameleon : they are
quite harmlefs.

From the climate, and the great variety of tropical as well as northern productions, that are natives of this country, there is reafon to expect, that
cotton, rice, and indigo, not to mention fugar, will
grow here as well as in any part of the globe.

The cotton fhrub is known to thrive beft in a
light fandy foil, and in a climate that has frequent
rains : the pine-barrens, and worft parts of Florida, as well as its climate, are therefore fit for this
fhrub ; and Mr. Rolle has already planted it with
fuccefs. The quantity imported from the Weft-
Indies bears but a fmall proportion to the whole
confumption ; and the Manchefter manufactures
are greatly cramped by the fcarcity of this commodity.

modity. A small bounty upon the growth of it in Florida, might be attended with good effect, and be a wise encouragement of an infant colony.

With respect to the cultivation of silk in Florida, there is not the least doubt of the climate being better adapted to the silk-worm than any country in North-America.

In Carolina and Georgia, the worms are often injured by accidental frosts, and cold mornings ; in the spring, especially if it is a late one, they are sometimes actually destroyed, and at others benumbed and made sickly, for want of warmth : the southern situation of Florida has almost wholly exempted it from this disaster.

In Georgia there is often a great deal of thunder and lightning in the spring-season, which is apt to affect and injure the silk-worm ; whereas, in Florida, where frequent showers refresh the air, and the sea-breezes keep it in constant agitation, the thunder is neither so common nor so violent.

The sugar-cane is not a native of the West-Indies, nor will it grow there without art and cultivation ; and as both the soil and climate seem fit for sugar, one cannot reasonably doubt but the cultivation of it in Florida will be attended with success ; and if in some respects Florida be found inferior to the West-Indies, it has, in other respects, perhaps, the advantage of them *.

The

---

* This rather seems a visionary scheme, as the soil of East-Florida is in general sandy and poor, and the climate not always exempt from frosts, (vide Dickenson's voyage to Florida,

The ftock of a fugar-planter is not only procured, but fupported at a vaft expence : the exceffive price of labour in the Weft-Indies, arifing
from the unhealthinefs of the climate, and the
dearnefs of the neceffaries of life, virtually amounts
to a tax upon the fugar-planter ; for not only all
kind of cloathing, but provifion too, muft be imported from Europe and the northern plantations. The materials for building, all the lumber required to erect and repair the fugar-works,
muft be fetched from the continent. In Florida, they are found upon the fpot ; and the
overfeer, and other white fervants, will not only
be hired much cheaper in a plentiful and good
climate than in a fcarce and fickly one ; but
horfes, cows, and oxen, may be purchafed at lefs
than one fixth the price they bear in the Weft-Indies. It is not only the prime coft of the ftock
that differs fo much in the two countries, but the
expence of maintaining it bears the fame comparative difference ; fodder for the cattle, and corn
and flefh-meat for the fervants, are very fcarce in
the iflands, but plentiful in Florida.

In both the Floridas the lands are not fold, as in
the ceded iflands, but given upon conditions, which
intereft leads the grantee to perform ; and the re

p. 82 to 97) ; whereas, land can hardly be too rich for th
cane, which even in Cuba, and the north fide of Jamaica, fro
the north-weft winds, and fuch frequent and heavy rains as f
in Florida, will produce nothing but melaffes, though in tho
iflands there are no frofts to render the juice more four, if t
kill the cane.

fervatic

fervation made to the crown is only an halfpenny an acre, after the end of three, five, or ten years, which is regulated by the extent of the grants.

It often happens in the Weft-Indies, that when the ground is prepared, and the cane planted, the rains or feafons, as they are called, fail, and the crop is ruined by drought; a misfortune which is not to be apprehended in Florida.

Both the foil and climate of Eaft-Florida feem to fuit the indigo plant : the Spaniards planted fome of the Guatimala indigo in their gardens at St. Auguftine, where, in a poor fandy foil, the indigo plants were of a larger fize, and more luxuriant than in South-Carolina in the richeft and beft cultivated lands.

The vine grows almoft in all parts of America, fouth of Delaware, in great plenty; and it will, probably, not be owing to any defect either in foil or climate, but to the dearnefs of labour, or negligence of the inhabitants, if wine is not produced hereafter in fome plenty upon this continent; and currants, raifins, figs, and olives, will moft probably thrive here whenever they are planted. The prefent governor is James Grant, Efq;

Exports and Trade.

As the number of inhabitants, as yet, is but fmall, no great improvements and productions can at prefent be expected, though there are fome good fettlements already begun; the exports, therefore, of this province, of courfe, are but fmall, and confift chiefly of its trade with the

Indians.

Indians. The imports from the mother-country are the fame as thofe from the other colonies.

WEST-FLORIDA.

This province, bounded eaftward by Eaft-Florida, fouthward by the Gulph of Mexico, weftward by a line drawn through the middle of Lake Pontchartrain and the river Miffiffippi, and northward by the country of the Chactaws, makes a part of Louifiana, ceded by France to the crown of England, by the late peace : hence, a defcription of Weft-Florida, in fome meafure, includes that of Louifiana.

The face of the country is rather level, but extremely well watered. About twelve miles above the mouth of the river Miffiffippi, a branch of it runs, on the eaft fide, which, after a courfe of one hundred and fixty miles, falls into the north-weft end of the great bay of Spirito Santo. At firft, it is very narrow and fhallow ; but, by the acceffion of feveral rivers and rivulets, becomes navigable by the greateft boats and floops, and forms feveral pleafant lakes, particularly Lake Pontchartrain.

About fixty leagues higher up, on the eaft fide, is the river Yafoua, which comes into the Miffif-fippi, two or three hundred miles out of the country, and is inhabited by the nations of the Yafoues, Tonicas, Kowrouas, &c. Sixty leagues higher is the river and nation of Chongue, with fome others to the eaft of them. Thirty leagues higher the Miffif-fippi receives a river, that proceeds from a lake about

ten

ten miles.off, which is twenty miles long, and receives four large rivers. The Cafqui, the moft fouthern, being the river of the Cherokees, comes from the fouth-eaft, and its heads are among the mountains which feparate their country from Carolina, and is the great road of the traders from thence to the Miffiffippi, and the intermediate places. The river Ouefpere, which, about thirty leagues to the north-eaft of the lake, divides into two branches, whereof the moft fouthern is called the Black River; but there are very few inhabitants upon either, they having been deftroyed, or driven away by the Iroquois. The heads of this river are in that vaft ridge of mountains which runs on the back of Carolina, Virginia, and Maryland, through which there is a fhort paffage to the fources of the great river Potomack, on the eaft fide of them. The Ohio, more to the north, a vaft river, which comes from the back of New-York, Maryland, and Virginia, navigable fix hundred miles. It runs thro' the moft beautiful and fruitful countries in the world, and receives ten or twelve rivers, befides innumerable rivulets. Several nations formerly dwelt on this river, as the Chawanoes or Chouanons, a great people, who, with many other nations, were totally extirpated by the Iroquois, who made this river their ufual road, when they entered into a war with the nations either to the fouth or weft. The moft northerly, and which comes, like the reft, from the north-eaft, is the Ouabacha, or St. Jeremy's river. Twenty-five leagues above the Ohio is the great ifland of the Tamaroas, with

a naa nation over-againſt it of the name, and another named Cahokia, who dwell on the banks of the Chepuſſo. Thirty leagues higher is the river Checogou, or the River of the Illinouecks, corruptly called by the French Illinois ; which nation lived upon and near this river, in about ſixty towns, and conſiſted of twenty thouſand fighting men, before they were deſtroyed by the Iroquois, and driven to the weſt of the Miſſiſſippi. This is a large pleaſant river, and about two hundred and fifty miles above its entrance into the Miſſiſſippi, is divided into two branches : the leſſer comes from north and by eaſt, and it riſes within four or five miles of the weſt ſide of the lake of the Illinouecks or Michigan, as it is called in our map : the biggeſt comes directly from the eaſt, and proceeds from a moraſs within two miles of the river Miamiha, which runs into the ſame lake. On the ſouth-eaſt ſide there is a communication between theſe two rivers, by a land carriage of two leagues, about fifty miles to the ſouth-eaſt of the lake. The courſe of the river Checogou is above four hundred miles, navigable above half way by ſhips, and moſt of the reſt by ſloops and barges. It receives many ſmall rivers, and forms two or three lakes ; one eſpecially, called Pimeteovi, twenty miles long and three broad, which affords great quantities of good fiſh, as the adjacent country does game, both fowls and beaſts. Beſides the Illinouecks, are the nations Prouaria, Caſcaſquia, and Caracontannon ; and on the north branch inhabit part of the nation of the Maſcontans. On the ſouth-eaſt bank of the river Checogou, M.

de

de Sale, in 1680, erected a fort, which he named Crevecœur, or Heart-breaker, on account of the troubles he met with here. This fort ftands about half way betwixt the Gulph of Mexico and Canada, was the ufual road of the French to and from both, till they difcovered a fhorter and eafier paffage by the rivers Oubacha and Ohio, which rife at a fmall diftance from the lake Erie, or fome rivers which enter it. Eighty leagues higher, the river Miffiffippi receives the Mifconfing, a river refembling that of the Illinouecks, in breadth, depth, and courfe; and the country adjacent to its branches is alike pleafant and fruitful. Sixty miles before it falls into the Miffiffippi it is joined by the river Kikapouz, which is alfo navigable, and comes a great way from the north-eaft. Eighty miles farther, almoft directly eaft, there is a communication by a land-carriage of two leagues with the river Mifconqui, which runs to the north-eaft, and after a paffage of one hundred and fifty miles from the land-carriage, falls into the great bay of Poukeoutamis, or the Puans, which joins on the north-weft fide to the great lake of the Illinouecks. Higher up the Miffiffippi is the river Chabadeba; above which the Miffiffippi forms a fine lake twenty miles long, and eight or ten broad. Ten miles above that lake is the River of Tortoifes, a large fair river, which runs into the country a good way to the north-eaft, and is navigable forty miles by the greateft boats.

There are only two large rivers which do not communicate with the Miffiffippi, betwixt it and the peninfula of Florida; viz. the Coza, and the Apalache.

1. The

1. The Coza river, which the French call Mobile, is bigger, except the Mississippi and Ohio, than any river in this or the neighbouring provinces. It rises from the Apalachian mountains, with several heads, of which the most northern is at the town and province of Guaxala, at the foot of the said mountains; many rivulets uniting, after a course of eighty miles, form a river wider than the Thames at Kingston, with several delightful isles, some three or four miles long, and half a mile broad, in a country wonderfully pleasant and fruitful. The first considerable town or province is Chiaha, with a river of its own name, that helps to enlarge Coza, which is famous for its pearl-fishing; there being in the river and little lakes that are formed by it, a sort of shell-fish, which the antients named pinna, betwixt a muscle and an oyster. From thence the river grows larger and deeper, being reinforced by others from the mountains and vallies, till it enters the province of Coza, reckoned one of the most pleasant and fruitful parts of the country, and very populous. It consists of hills and vallies, rivulets, arable land, and lovely meadows. Prunes grow naturally in the fields, better than can be produced in Spain by culture; and though there are some vines that creep on the ground, there are others which mount, in almost all the places near the rivers, to the tops of the trees. The Coza river enters the Gulph of Mexico one hundred miles south of Mobile. One of the rivers that enters the Coza is the river of the Chactaws, which a collection of little streams renders a fine river. About the

the middle of it lies the mighty nation of the Chactaws, confifting of near three thoufand men, who
fpeak the fame language as their neighbours the
Chickefaws, juft now mentioned, to whom they
were lately, if they are not ftill, mortal enemies.
To the eaft of the Cozas are the Becues or Abecaes, who have thirteen towns, and dwell on divers
fmall rivers, which run into the Coza. It is a very
pleafant country, confifting of hills and vallies, and
its foil in general more marly, or fatter, than that
of the other provinces, which have moftly a
lighter mould. A little more to the fouth-weft,
between the Abecaes and Chactaws, the Ewemalas,
who are about five hundred fighting men, dwell
on a fair river of the fame name, which coming
from the north-eaft mixes with the Coza. Mr.
Coxe, whofe defcription of this country is our
guide, fays the river Coza falls into the Gulph
of Mexico, fifteen leagues weft of the great bay
of Naffau, or Spirito Santo. Near the mouth
of this river the French erected a fettlement, called
Fort Louis, twenty leagues north-eaft of the neareft
mouth of the Miffiffippi, which was the ufual refidence of the chief governor of Louifiana, who was
neverthelefs fubordinate to him of Canada. From
this garrifon the French ufed to fend detachments
to fecure their feveral ftations among the Indians
in the inland parts. The Alibamous, Chickefaws,
and Chactaws, the moft confiderable nations upon and
between the river Coza and the Miffiffippi, kindly
entertained the Englifh, who refided among them feveral years, and carried on a fafe and peaceable trade
with

with them, till about the year 1715, when by the intrigues of the French, they were either murdered, or obliged to make room for thefe new invaders, who unjuftly poffeffed and fortified the fame ftations, in order to curb the natives, and cut off their communication with the Englifh traders; whereby they engroffed a profitable trade for five hundred miles, of which the Englifh were a few years before the fole mafters.

The French had another fmall town and fort in the Ifle Dauphine, formerly called Slaughter Ifland, from the number of men's bones found there on its firft difcovery, the remains, as it is faid, of a bloody battle fought between two Indian nations. It is about nine leagues fouth of Fort Louis, and ten leagues weft of Penfacola; and was inhabited and fortified only on account of its harbour, being the firft place the French generally touched at on their arrival upon this coaft. The diftance between the river Coza and that of Apalache to the eaft, is about one hundred and ninety miles, and the coaft between them is very deep and bold.

The chief harbour betwixt thefe two rivers, and indeed the beft upon all this coaft, is Penfacola; it being a large port, fafe from all winds, with four fathom at the entrance, and deepens gradually to feven or eight. It lies eleven leagues eaft of Port Louis and Mobile.

On the weft fide of the harbour ftands the town of Penfacola, the capital. A fine river enters the Bay of Mexico on the eaft fide of this harbour, which

which comes about one hundred miles out of the country, after being formed by the junction of two other rivers. The land here is a barren fand ; but produces many pine-trees, fit for ship-masts. There is a communication from hence by land with Apalache.

Apalachy Cola is a good harbour, thirty leagues east of the former, and as much west from the river named by the Indians, Apalache. This river enters the Gulph of Mexico about one hundred miles from the cod of the Bay of Apalache, at the north-west end of the peninsula of Florida, in about north latitude 30. Here was a fort, called St. Mary de Apalache, which the Alibamous destroyed in 1705. It is not easy to find this place by reason of the isles and lakes before and about it ; and though a stately river, whose mouth makes a large harbour, yet it has not above three fathoms water at most on the bar ; but when that is passed, it is very deep and large, and the tide flows higher into it than into any river upon all the coast, some say no less than fifty miles. But this is not strange, the country being a perfect level, and the river having a double current, one from the west and the other from the south. On both sides of it, towards the sea-coast, live several nations, called by the name of the Apalache Indians ; and about the middle of it live the great nations of the Cushetaes, Tallibou-fies, and Adgebaches. This river proceeds chiefly from others, which have their origin on the south or south-west side of the great ridge of hills that runs

on

on the back of Carolina. There is a communication from hence by land to St. Augustine.

On the whole coast of this province, there are many vast beds of oysters, that produce pearls. Ambergrease is often found upon the coast; and also, especially after high winds, a sort of stone pitch, which the Spaniards soften with grease, and use for their vessels as pitch, than which they affirm it is better in hot countries, not being apt to melt with the heat of the sun. On both sides the river Mississippi there are many springs and lakes, that produce excellent salt. The country abounds in rich mines of copper, iron, lead, pitcoal, and quickfilver; and, in divers parts, there are great quantities of orpiment and fandarache.

The climate nearly resembles that of East-Florida; its natural products are also in general the same; and though the sea-coast is sandy and barren, the inland parts are capable of producing, in the greatest abundance, all the valuable commodities recommended as proper for cultivation in that province.

TRADE and POPULATION.

As many of the French who inhabited West-Florida before the late peace, have chose to become British subjects for the sake of keeping their estates, no doubt, considerable settlements will be soon made, especially as the land in the inland parts of this province is vastly preferable to East-Florida,

and

and its fituation for trade extremely good, having the river Miffiffippi for its weftern boundary.

There are at prefent about fix thoufand inhabitants in this province, who increafe faft, it being much more healthy and inviting than Eaft-Florida, efpecially the weftern parts, upon the banks of the Miffiffippi, which are faid to agree very well with Englifh conftitutions.

They already carry on a confiderable trade with the Indians, and export great quantities of deerfkins and furs. The French inhabitants here alfo raife confiderable quantities of rice, and build fome veffels. The imports from the mother-country are the fame as thofe of the other colonies.

A general Account of the INDIAN NATIONS.

THE Aborigines of America, amongft the infinite number of nations and tribes into which they are divided, differ very little from each other in their manners and cuftoms; and all form a ftriking picture of the moft diftant antiquity.

They are tall, and ftrait in their limbs, beyond the proportion of moft nations: their bodies are ftrong; but rather fitted to endure much hardfhip, than to continue long at any fervile work, by which they are quickly exhaufted. Their bodies and heads are flattifh, the effect of art; their features
tures

tures are regular, but their countenances fierce ; their hair long, black, lank, and as ftrong as that of a horfe ; they have no beards ; the colour of their fkin is a reddifh brown, improved by the constant ufe of bear's fat and paint.

When the Europeans firft came into America, they found the people quite naked, except thofe parts which it is common for the moft uncultivated people to conceal. Since that time they have generally a coarfe blanket to cover them, which they buy from us. The whole fafhion of their lives is of a piece ; hardy, poor, and fqualid : their education from their infancy is folely directed to fit their bodies for this mode of life, and to form their minds to inflict and endure the greateft evils. Their only occupations are hunting and war : agriculture is left to the women. When their hunting-feafon is paft, in which they exert great ingenuity, they pafs the reft of their time in an entire indolence, and obferve no bounds or decency in their eating and drinking. Before they were acquainted with the Europeans, they had no fpirituous liquors : but now this is the principal end they purfue in their treaties with us ; and from this they fuffer inexpreffible calamities ; for having once begun to drink, they continue a fucceffion of drunkennefs as long as their means of procuring liquor lafts. In this condition they lie expofed on the earth to all the inclemency of the feafons, which waftes them by a train of the moft fatal diforders : and, in fhort, excefs in drinking, amongft this uncivilized people, who have not art enough

enough to guard againft the confequence of their vices, is a public calamity. The few amongft them who live free from this evil, enjoy the reward of their temperance in a robuft and healthy old age.

Their character is ftriking. They are extremely grave in their deportment upon any ferious occafion; obfervant of thofe in company; refpectful to the old; cool and deliberate; never in hafte to fpeak before they have thought well upon the matter, and are fure the perfon who fpoke before them has finifhed all he had to fay. Nothing is more edifying than their behaviour in their public councils and affemblies. Every man there is heard in his turn, according as his years, his wifdom, or his fervices to his country have ranked him. Not a whifper is heard from the reft while he fpeaks; no indecent condemnation, no ill-timed applaufe. The younger fort attend for their inftruction.

There is no people amongft whom the laws of hofpitality are more facred; their houfes, their provifion, even their young women, are not enough to oblige a gueft. To thofe of their own nation they are likewife very humane and beneficent. But to the enemies of his country, or to thofe who have privately offended, the American is implacable. He conceals his fentiments, until he has an opportunity of executing an horrible revenge; but no length of time is fufficient to allay his refentment; no diftance of place great enough

to

to protect the object ; on whom, when in his power,
he exercises the moft fhocking barbarities, even to
the eating of his flefh.   To fuch extremes do the
Indians pufh their friendfhip or their enmity.

Notwithftanding this ferocity, no people have their
anger more under their command ; from their infancy, they are formed with care to endure every fort of
infult with a compofed countenance.   They efteem
nothing fo unworthy a man of fenfe and conftancy,
as a peevifh temper, and a pronenefs to fudden and
rafh anger.   And this fo far has an effect, that
quarrels happen as rarely amongft them, when they
are not intoxicated · with liquor, as abufive language.   But when their paffions are roufed, being
fhut up, as it were, and converging into a narrow
point, they become furious ; are dark, fullen,
treacherous, and implacable.

The Americans hold the exiftence of a Supreme
Being, eternal and incorruptible, who has power over
all.   Satisfied with owning this, which is tradition-
ary amongft them, they pay him no fort of worfhip.
There are indeed nations in America who feem
to pay fome religious homage to the fun and moon ;
and as moft of them have a notion of fome invifible
beings, who continually intermeddle in their affairs, they difcourfe much of demons, &c.   They
have ceremonies too, that feem to fhew they had
once a more regular form of religious worfhip ;
for they make a fort of oblation of their firft-
fruits, obferve certain ceremonies at the full moon,
and have in their feftivals many things that very

probably

probably came from a religious origin, though they perform them as things handed down to them from their anceftors, without knowing the reafon. They confider the other world as a place abounding with an inexhauftible plenty of every thing defirable; and that they fhall enjoy there the moft full and exquifite gratification of all their fenfes. Hence it is, no doubt, that they meet death with fuch indifference and compofure of mind; no Indian being in the leaft difmayed at the news, that he has only a few minutes to live, but, with the greateft intrepidity and compofure, harangues thofe around him; and thus a father leaves his dying advice to his children, and takes a formal leave of all his friends.

Great obfervers of omens and dreams, and eager pryers into futurity, they abound in diviners, augurs, and magicians, whom they rely much upon in all affairs; and believing that the whole hiftory of their future life may be collected from their dreams in their youth, they make dreaming a kind of religious ceremony when they come to fufficient years, which is thus performed: they befmear themfelves all over with black paint, and faft for feveral days, in expectation that their good genius will appear, or manifeft himfelf in fome fhape or other, in their dreams. The effect produced by this long faft in the brain of a young perfon, muft no doubt be confiderable; and the parents take care, during this operation, that the

VOL. II.   A a   dreams

dreams be faithfully reported the next morning; and this good genius, or propitious fpirit, being the fubject of the perfon's waking thoughts, becomes alfo the fubject of his dreams; and every phantom of his fleep is regarded as a figure of the genius, whether it be bird, beaft, fifh, a tree, or any thing elfe, and is particularly refpected by them all their lives after. When any perfon of diftinguifhed parts rifes up among them, they fuppofe him naturally infpired and actuated by this propitious fpirit, and have the utmoft regard and veneration for him on that account.

. Their phyfic is entirely in the hands of the priefts, who generally treat them, in whatever difor- der, in the fame way. That is, they firft inclofe them in a narrow cabbin, in the midft of which is a ftone red hot; on this they throw water, until the patient is well foaked with the warm vapour and his own fweat; then they hurry him from the bagnio, and plunge him fuddenly into the next river. This is repeated as often as they judge neceffary; and thus extraordinary cures are fome- times performed. But it frequently happens too, that this rude method kills the patient in the very operation; and it is partly owing to this practice, that the fmall-pox has proved fo fatal to them. However, they have the ufe of fome fpecifics of wonderful efficacy, the power of which they attri- bute to the magical ceremonies with which they are conftantly adminiftered; and purely by an appli- cation of herbs, they frequently cure wounds,

which

which with us refuse to yield to the moſt judicious methods.

Every nation has its diſtinguiſhing enſign, which is generally ſome beaſt, bird, or fiſh. Thoſe among the Five Nations are, the bear, otter, wolf, tortoiſe, and eagle ; and by theſe names the tribes are generally diſtinguiſhed They have the ſhapes of theſe animals curiouſly pricked and painted on ſeveral parts of their bodies ; and when they march through the woods, they commonly, at every encampment, cut the figure of their enſign on trees, eſpecially after a ſuccefsful campaign, that thoſe who paſs that way may know they have been there, recording alſo, in their manner, the number of ſcalps or priſoners they have taken.

Liberty, in its fulleſt extent, is their darling paſſion. To this they ſacrifice every thing. This makes a life of uncertainty and want ſup-portable to them ; and their education is directed in ſuch a manner as to cheriſh this diſpoſition to the utmoſt. Children are never, upon any ac-count, chaſtiſed with blows ; they are rarely even chidden. Reaſon, they ſay, will guide their children when they come to the uſe of it, and before that time their faults cannot be very great ; but blows might abate their free and martial ſpirit, and render the ſenſe of honour duller, by the habit of a ſlaviſh motive to action. When grown up, they experience nothing like command, depend-ence, or ſubordination ; even ſtrong perſuaſion is

in-

induftrioufly forborne by thofe who have influence amongft them.

On the fame principle, they know no punifh-ment but death.   They lày no fines, becaufe they have no way of exacting them from free men; and the death, which they fometimes inflict, is ra-ther a confequence of a fort of war declared againft a public enemy, than an act of judicial power exe-cuted on a citizen.   This free difpofition is gene-ral; and, though fome tribes are found in America with an head whom we call a king, his power is rather perfuafive than coercive, and he is reve-renced as a father, more than feared as a monarch. He has no guards, no prifons, no officers of juftice. The other forms, which may be confidered as a fort of ariftocracy, and are moft common in North-America, have no more power.   In fome tribes there are a kind of nobility, who, when they come to years of difcretion, are entitled to a place and vote in the councils of their nation : the reft are ex-cluded.   But amongft the Five Nations, or'Iro-quois, the moft celebrated commonwealth of North-America, and in fome other nations, there is no other qualification abfolutely neceffary for their head-men, but age, experience, and ability. However, there is generally in every tribe fome particular ftocks which they refpect, and who are confidered in fome fort as their chiefs, unlefs they fhew themfelves unworthy of that rank.

Their great council is compofed of thefe heads of tribes and families, with fuch whofe capacity

has

has elevated them to the fame degree of confideration. They meet in a houfe, which they have in
each of their towns for the purpofe, upon every fo-
femn occafion. Thefe councils are public. Here
all fuch matters concerning the ftate are propofed
as have already been digefted in the fecret councils,
at which none but the head-men affift. Here it is
that their orators are employed, and difplay thofe
talents which diftinguifh them for eloquence, and
knowledge of public bufinefs; for the chiefs
feldom fpeak much themfelves in public affemblies, thinking it beneath their dignity to ut-
ter their fentiments upon thefe occafions in an
audible manner : they therefore entruft them
with a perfon, who is ftiled their orator. None
elfe fpeak in their public councils; thefe are their
ambaffadors, and thefe are the commiffioners who
are appointed to treat of peace or alliance with
other nations. Their chief fkill confifts in giving
an artful turn to affairs, and in expreffing their
thoughts in a bold figurative manner, and with
geftures equally violent, but extremely natural and
expreffive.

When any bufinefs of confequence is tranfacted,
they appoint a feaft upon the occafion, of which almoft the whole nation partakes. At thefe feafts,
if they cannot confume all, what remains is thrown
into the fire ; for they look upon the fire as a thing
facred, and in all probability thefe feafts were antiently facrifices. Before the entertainment is ready,

the

the principal perfon begins a fong, the fubject of which is the fabulous or real hiftory of their nation, the remarkable events which have happened, and whatever matters may make for their honour or inftruction. The reft fing in their turn. They have dances too, with which they accompany their fongs, chiefly of a martial kind ; and no folemnity or public bufinefs is carried on without fuch fongs and dances. Every thing is tranfacted amongft them with much ceremony ; the ceremonies contributing to fix all tranfactions the better in their memory. Scarce any thing is undertaken with greater folemnity than hunting the bear ; and an alliance with a noted bear-hunter, who has killed feveral bears in one day, is more eagerly fought after than that of a celebrated warrior ; becaufe the chace fupplies the family both with food and raiment.

To help their memory, they have belts of fmall fhells, or beads, of different colours, which have all a different meaning, according to their colour or arrangement. At the end of every matter they difcourfe upon, when they treat with a foreign ftate, they deliver one of thefe belts. If they fhould omit this ceremony, what they fay paffes for nothing. Thefe belts are carefully treafured up in each town, and ferve for the public records of the nation ; and to thefe they occafionally have recourfe, when any contefts happen between them and their neighbours. Of late, as the matter of which thefe belts are made is

grown

grown fcarce, they often give fome fkin in place of the wampum, for fo they call thefe beads, and receive in return prefents of a more valuable nature; for they never confider what our commiffioners fay to be of any weight, unlefs a prefent accompanies each propofal.

Nor is the calumet, or pipe of peace, of lefs importance, or lefs revered, in many tranfactions relative both to war and peace. The ufe of the calumet is to fmoak either tobacco, or fome bark, leaf, or herb, which they often ufe in its ftead, when they enter into an alliance, or on any ferious occafion or folemn engagement: this being among them the moft facred oath that can be taken, the violation of which is efteemed moft infamous, and deferving of fevere punifhment from Heaven. When they treat of war, the whole pipe and all its ornaments are red; fometimes it is red only on one fide; and by the difpofition of the feathers, &c. one acquainted with their cuftoms will know, at firft fight, what the nation which prefents it intends or defires. Smoaking the calumet is alfo a religious ceremony, upon fome occafions; and, in all treaties, is confidered as a witnefs between the parties, or rather as an inftrument, by which they invoke the fun and moon to witnefs their fincerity, and to become guarantees of the treaty between them. The fize and decorations of the calumet are generally proportioned to the quality of the perfons they are prefented to, the efteem they have for them, and alfo the importance of the occafion.

A a 4

Their

Their fuits are few, and quickly decided; having neither property nor art enough to render them perplexed or tedious. Criminal matters come before the fame jurifdiction, when they are fo flagrant as to become a national concern. In ordinary cafes, the crime is either revenged or compromifed by the parties concerned. If a murder is committed, the family which has loft a relation prepares to retaliate on that of the offender. They often kill the murderer; and when this happens, the kindred of the laft perfon flain look upon themfelves to be as much injured, and think themfelves as much juftified in taking vengeance, as if the violence had not begun amongft themfelves. But, in general, the offender abfents himfelf; the friends fend a compliment of condolance to thofe of the party murdered; prefents are offered, which are rarely refufed; the head of the family appears, who in a formal fpeech delivers the prefents, which confift often of above fixty articles, every one of which is given to cancel fome part of the offence, and to affuage the grief of the fuffering party. With the firft he fays, " By this I remove the hatchet from the wound, and make it fall out of the hands of him that is prepared to revenge the injury :" with the fecond, " I dry up the blood of that wound ;" and fo on, in apt figures, taking away one by one all the ill confequences of the murder. As ufual, the whole ends in mutual feaftings, fongs, and dances. If the murder is committed by one of the fame family or cabbin, that cabbin has the full right of judgment, without appeal, within itfelf, either to punifh

the

the guilty with death, or pardon him, or to force him to give some recompence to the wife or children of the slain. All this while, the supreme authority of the nation looks on unconcerned, and never rouses its strength, nor exerts the fullness of a power more revered than felt, but upon some signal occasion. Then the power seems equal to the occasion. Every one hastens to execute the orders of their senate; nor was ever any instance of rebellion known among this people. Family-love, rare amongst us, is a national virtue amongst them, of which all partake; and there are friendships amongst them, fit to vie with those of fabulous antiquity.

The loss of any one, whether by a natural death or by war, is lamented by the whole town he belongs to. In such circumstances, no business is taken in hand, however important, nor any rejoicing permitted, however interesting the occasion, until all the pious ceremonies due to the dead are performed, which are always discharged with the greatest solemnity. The dead body is washed, anointed, and painted. Then the women lament the loss with the most bitter cries, and the most hideous howlings, intermixed with songs, which celebrate the great actions of the deceased, and those of his ancestors. The men mourn in a less extravagant manner. The whole village attends the body to the grave, which is interred habited in their most sumptuous ornaments. With the body of the deceased are placed his bows and arrows, with what he valued most in his life, and provisions for the long journey he is to take; for they hold

the

the immortality of the foul uhiverfally, though
their idea is grofs. · Feafting attends this, as it does ·
every folemnity. After the funeral, thofe who are
nearly allied to the deceafed conceal themfelves in
their huts for a confiderable time, to indulge their
grief. The compliments of condolance are never
omitted, nor are prefents wanting upon this occafion. After fome time they revifit the grave, re--
new their forrow, new cloath the remains of the
body, and act over again the folemnities of the
firft funeral.

Of all their inftances of regard to their deceafed
friends, none is fo ftriking as what they call the
feaft of the dead, or the feaft of fouls. The day
of ceremony is appointed in the council of their
chiefs, who give orders for every thing which may
enable them to celebrate it with pomp and magnificence. The neighbouring nations are invited to
partake of the feaft, and to be witneffes of the folemnity. At this time, all who have died fince the
laft folemn feaft of that kind, are taken out of their
graves. Thofe who have been interred at the
greateft diftance from the villages are diligently
fought for, and brought to this great rendezvous
of carcafes. The horror of this general difinter-
ment is beyond defcription.

This ftrange feftival is the moft magnificent and
folemn which they have ; not only on account of
the great concourfe of natives and ftrangers, and of
the pompous re-interment they give to their dead,
whom they drefs in the fineft fkins they can get,
                                                    after

after having expofed them for fome time in this pomp; but for the games of all kinds which they celebrate upon the occafion, in the fpirit of thofe which the antient Greeks and Romans celebrated upon fimilar occafions.

In this manner do they endeavour to foothe the calamities of life, by the honours they pay their dead; honours, which are the more chearfully beftowed, becaufe, in his turn, each man expects to receive them himfelf: and though amongft thefe favage nations, this cuftom is impreffed with ftrong marks of the ferocity of their nature; an honour for the dead, a tender feeling of their abfence, and a revival of their memory, are fome of the moft excellent inftruments for fmoothing our rugged nature into humanity; and it is certain a regard for the dead has been univerfal from the remoteft antiquity.

Though the women in America have generally the laborious part of domeftic œconomy, yet they are far from being the flaves they appear. On the contrary, all the honours of the nation are on the fide of the woman. They even hold their councils, and have their fhare in all deliberations which concern the ftate. Polygamy is practifed by fome nations, but it is not general. In moft, they content themfelves with one wife; but a divorce is admitted, for the fame caufes that it was allowed amongft the Jews, Greeks, and Romans. No nation of the Americans is without a regular marriage, in which there are many ceremonies; the principal of which

is,

is, the bride's prefenting the bridegroom with a plate of their corn.

Incontinent before wedlock, after marriage the chaftity of their women is remarkable. The punifh-ment of the adulterefs, as well as that of the adul-terer, is in the hands of the hufband-himfelf. Their marriages are not fruitful, feldom producing above two or three children; but they are brought forth with lefs pain than our women fuffer upon fuch oc-cafions, and with little confequent weaknefs. Pro-bably, the fevere life which both fexes lead is not favourable to procreation: and the habit unmar-ried women have of procuring abortions, in which they rarely fail, makes them more unfit for bearing children afterwards. This is one of the reafons of the depopulation of America; as whatever loffes they fuffer, are repaired flowly.

Almoft the fole occupation of the Indian is war, or fuch an exercife as qualifies him for it; and no man is at all confidered, until he has in-creafed the ftrength of his country with a captive, or adorned his houfe with a fcalp of one of its ene-mies. When the council refolve upon war, they do not declare what nation they are determined to attack, that the enemy may be off his guard. Nay, they even fometimes let years pafs over without any act of hoftility, that the vigilance of all may be unbent-by the long continuance of the watch, and the uncertainty of the danger. In the mean time, the war-kettle is fet on the fire; the

war-

war-fongs and dances commence; the tomohawk; painted red, is fent to all the villages of the fame nation, and its allies, with a belt of wampum: the meffenger throws the tomohawk on the ground, which is taken up by the moft expert warrior of the nation to which it is fent, if they chufe to join in the war; if not, is returned, with a belt of wampum fuitable to the occafion. The women add their cries to thofe of the men, lamenting thofe whom they have either loft in war, or by a natural death, and demanding their places to be fupplied from their enemies, ftimulating the young men by a fenfe of fhame.

When, by thefe means, the fury of the nation is raifed to the greateft height, the war-captain prepares the feaft, which confifts of dogs flefh. All that partake of this feaft receive little billets, which are fo many engagements which they take to be faithful to each other, and obedient to their commander. None are forced to the war; but when they have accepted this billet, it is death to recede. All the warriors in this affembly have their faces blackened with charcoal, intermixed with dafhes and ftreaks of vermillion, which give them a moft horrid appearance. Their hair is dreffed up in an odd manner, with feathers of various kinds. In this affembly, the chief begins the war-fong, which having continued for fome time, he raifes his voice to the higheft pitch, and turning off fuddenly to a fort of prayer, invokes the god of war, whom they
call

call Arefkoni, to be favourable to his enterprize,
and to pour deftruction upon the enemy. All the
warriors join him in this prayer with fhouts and ac-
clamations. The captain renews his fong, ftrikes
his tomohawk againft the ftakes of his cottage, and
begins the war dance, accompanied with the fhouts
of all his companions, which continue as long as
he dances.

The day appointed for their departure being arrived, they take leave of their friends, change their
cloaths, or whatever moveables they have, in token
of mutual friendfhip ; their wives and female rela-
tions go out before them, and attend at fome diftance from the town. The warriors march out
all dreft in their fineft apparel, and moft fhowy
ornaments, regularly one after another, for they never march in rank. The chief walks flowly before them, finging the war fong, whilft the reft obferve the moft profound filence. When they come
up to their women, they deliver up to them all
their finery, put on their worft cloaths, and proceed
on their expedition *.

Their

* Their military drefs is very romantic and terrible.
They cut off or pull out all their hair, except a fpot about
the breadth of two Englifh crown pieces, near the top of
their heads, and wholly deftroy their eyebrows. The lock left
upon their heads is divided into feveral parcels, each of which is
ftiffened, and adorned with wampum beads, and feathers of various fhapes and hues, and the whole twifted, turned, and connected together, till it acquires a form much refembling the modern

Their motives for engaging in a war are rarely the fame as ours. They have feldom any other end but the glory of the victory, or the benefit of the flaves which it enables them to add to their nation, or facrifice to their brutal fury; and it is rare that they take any pains to give their wars even the colour of juftice. It is not uncommon for the young men to make feafts of dogs flefh, and dances, in the midft of the moft profound peace; and fall fometimes on one nation, and fometimes on another, and furprize fome of their hunters, whom they fcalp, or bring home as prifoners. Their old men wink at this, as it tends to keep up the martial fpirit of their people, and inures them to watchfulnefs and hardfhip.

The qualities in an Indian war are vigilance and attention, to give and to avoid a furprize; and patience and ftrength, to endure the intolerable fatigues and hardfhips which always attend it: for the Indian nations are at an immenfe diftance from

dern pompoon. Their heads are painted red down to the eye-brows, and fprinkled over with white down. The griftles of their ears are fplit almoft quite round, and then diftended with wires or fplinters, fo as to meet, and tie together on the nape of the neck. Thefe alfo are hung with ornaments; and have generally the figure of fome bird or beaft drawn upon them. Their nofes are likewife bored, and hung with trinkets of beads, and their faces painted with divers colours, fo as to make an awful appearance. Their breafts are adorned with a gorget, or medal of brafs, copper, or fome other metal; and that horrid weapon the fcalping knife, hangs by a ftring from their necks.

each

each other, with a vaſt deſart frontier, and hid in
the boſom of almoſt boundleſs foreſts. Theſe muſt
be traverſed before they meet an enemy, who is
often at ſuch a diſtance as might be ſuppoſed to
prevent either quarrel or danger. But, notwithſtanding the ſecrecy of the deſtination of the party,
the enemy has frequent notice of it, and is prepared
for the attack, and ready to take advantage of the
leaſt want of vigilance in the aggreſſors. They never fight in the open field, but upon ſome very extraordinary occaſions : not from cowardice, for they
are brave ; but they deſpiſe this method, as unworthy of an able warrior, and as an affair which fortune
governs more than prudence. The principal things
which help them to diſcover their enemies, are the
ſmoak of their fires, which they ſmell at a diſtance
almoſt incredible ; and their tracks, in the diſcovery
and diſtinguiſhing of which, they are poſſeſſed of an
aſtoniſhing ſagacity; for they will tell, in the footſteps, which to us would ſeem moſt confuſed, the
number of men that have paſſed, and the length of
time ſince they paſſed, and are even able to find out
the ſeveral nations by the different marks of their
feet, and to perceive footſteps where an European
could diſtinguiſh nothing.

But as thoſe who are attacked have the ſame knowledge, their great addreſs is to baffle each other in
theſe points. On their expeditions therefore, they
light no fire to warm themſelves, or prepare their
victuals, but ſubſiſt merely on meal, mixed with
water ; lie cloſe to the ground all day, and march

only in night. As they march in their ufual order in files, he that clofes the rear diligently covers his own tracks, and thofe of all who preceded him, with leaves. If any ftream occurs in their route, they march into it for a confiderable way, to foil their purfuers. When they halt to reft and refrefh themfelves, fcouts are fent out on every fide to reconnoitre the country, and beat up every place where they fufpect an enemy may lie hid. In this manner they often enter a village, whilft the ftrength of the nation is employed in hunting, maffacre all the helplefs old men, women, and children, and make as many prifoners as they can manage. When they difcover an army of their enemies, their way is to throw themfelves flat on their faces amongft the withered leaves, the colour of which their bodies are painted to refemble exactly. They generally let a part pafs unmolefted; and then, rifing a little, take aim, being excellent markfmen; and fetting up a moft tremendous fhout, which they call the war-cry, pour a ftorm of mufket-balls upon the enemy; for thofe nations which have commerce with Europeans, have long fince laid afide the ufe of arrows. The party attacked returns the fame cry; every man in hafte covers himfelf behind a tree, and returns the fire of the enemy, as foon as they raife themfelves from the ground to give the fecond fire.

After fighting fome time in this manner, the party which has the advantage, rufhes out of its cover with fmall axes in their hands, which they dart

with great addrefs and dexterity ; they redouble
their cries, intimidating their enemies with menaces, and encouraging each other with a boaftful
difplay of their own brave actions. Being now
come hand to hand, the conteft is foon decided ;
and the conquerors fatiate their favage fury with
the moft fhocking infults and barbarities to the
dead.

The fate of their prifoners is terrible. During
the greateft part of their journey homewards,
they fuffer no injury ; but when they arrive at
the territories of the conquering ftate, or at
thofe of its allies, the people from every village
meet them, and think they fhew their attachment to their friends by their barbarous treatment of the unhappy prifoners ; fo that, when
they come to their ftation, they are wounded and
bruifed in a fhocking manner. The conquerors
manage their march fo as not to approach their village till towards evening. At day-break next
morning, they drefs their prifoners in new cloaths,
adorn their heads with feathers, paint their faces
with various colours, and put into their hands a
white ftaff, tofleled round with the tails of deer.
The commander of the expedition then gives as
many yells as he has taken fcalps or prifoners, and
the whole village affemble at the water-fide, if
fituated near a river. As foon as the warriors appear, four or five of their young men, well cloathed, get into a canoe, if they came by water, or
otherwife march by land ; the two firft carrying
each a calumet, and go finging to fearch the prifoners,

foners, whom they lead in triumph to the village. The war-captain then waits upon the head-men, and in a low voice gives them an account of every particular of the expedition, of the damage the enemy has fuffered, and his own loffes in it. This done; the public orator relates the whole to the people. Before they yield to the joy which the victory occafions, they lament the friends whom they have loft in the purfuit of it. The parties moft nearly concerned are afflicted apparently with a deep and real forrow ; but, as if they were difciplined in their grief, upon the fignal for rejoicing, in a moment, all tears are wiped from their eyes, and they rufh into an extravagance and phrenzy of joy.

In the mean time, the fate of the prifoners remains undecided, until the old men meet. It is ufual to offer a flave to each houfe that has loft a friend, giving the preference according to the greatnefs of the lofs. The perfon who has taken the captive attends him to the door of the cottage to which he is delivered, and with him gives a belt of wampum, to fhew that he has fulfilled the purpofe of the expedition, in fupplying the lofs of a citizen. They view the prefent which is made them for fome time ; and, according as they take a capricious liking or difpleafure to the countenance of the victim, or in proportion to their natural barbarity, or their refentment for their loffes, they either receive him into the family, or fentence him to death. If the latter, they throw away the belt with indigna-

tion.

tion. Then it is no longer in the power of any one to fave him. The nation is affembled, a fcaffold is raifed, and the prifoner tied to the frame, who opens his death-fong, and prepares for the enfuing fcene of cruelty with the moft undaunted courage. On the other fide, they prepare to put it to the utmoft proof, with every torment which the mind of man, ingenious in mifchief, can invent. They begin at the extremities of his body, and gradually approach the trunk. One plucks out his nails by the roots, one by one: another takes a finger in his mouth, and tears off the flefh with his teeth; a third thrufts the finger, mangled as it is, into the hole of a pipe made red hot, which he fmoaks like tobacco. Then they pound his toes and fingers to pieces between two ftones; they cut circles about his joints, and gafhes in the flefhy part of his limbs, which they fear immediately with red-hot irons, cutting and fearing alternately; they pull off this flefh thus mangled and roafted, bit by bit, devouring it with greedinefs, and befmearing their faces with the blood, in an enthufiafm of horror and fury. When they have thus torn off the flefh, they twift the bare nerves and tendons about an iron, tearing and fnapping them; while others are employed in pulling and extending the limbs themfelves, in every way that can increafe the torment. This continues often five or fix hours together. Then they frequently unbind him, to give a breathing to their fury, to invent new torments, and to refrefh the ftrength of the fufferer, who, wearied out with

2   fuch

such a variety of inhuman torments, often falls immediately into so profound a sleep, that they are obliged to apply fire to awaken him, and renew his sufferings.

He is again fastened to the frame, and again they renew their cruelty. They stick him all over with small matches of wood that easily takes fire, but burns slowly ; they continually run sharp reeds into every part of his body ; they drag out his teeth with pincers, and thrust out his eyes ; and, lastly, after having burned his flesh from the bones with slow fires, after having so mangled the body that it is all but one wound, after having mutilated his face in such a manner as to carry nothing human in it, after having peeled the skin from the head, and poured a heap of red-hot coals or boiling water on the naked skull, they once more unbind the wretch, who, blind and staggering with pain and weakness, assaulted and pelted on every side with clubs and stones, now up, now down, falling into their fires at every step, runs hither and thither, until one of the chiefs, whether out of compassion, or weary of cruelty, puts an end to his life with a club or dagger. The body is then put into the kettle, and this barbarous employment is succeeded by a feast as barbarous, and the following night is spent in rejoicings. But if none of the byestanders are inclinable to lengthen out his torments, he is either shot to death with arrows, or inclosed with dry bark, to which they set fire ; and in the evening, they run from cabbin to cabbin, and strike with small twigs their furniture,

the

the walls and roofs of their cabbins, to prevent his fpirit from remaining there, to take vengeance for the evils inflicted on his body.

The women, forgetting the human as well as female nature, act their parts, and even outdo the men, in this fcene of horror. The principal perfons of the country fit round the frame, fmoaking and looking on, without the leaft emotion. What is moft extraordinary, the fufferer himfelf, in the little intervals of his torments, fmoaks too, appears unconcerned, and converfes with his torturers about indifferent matters. Indeed, during the whole time of his execution, there feems a conteft between him and them which fhall exceed, they in inflicting the moft horrid pains, or he in enduring them, with a conftancy and firmnefs almoft above human. Not a groan, not a figh, not a diftortion of countenance, efcapes him; he poffeffes his mind entirely in the midft of his torments; he recounts his own exploits, informs them what cruelties he has inflicted on their countrymen, and threatens them with the revenge that will attend his death; and, though his reproaches exafperate them to a perfect madnefs of rage and fury, he continues his reproaches, even of their ignorance in the art of tormenting; pointing out himfelf the more exquifite methods, and more fenfible parts of the body. The women have this part of courage as well as the men; and it is as rare for an Indian to behave otherwife, as it would be for an European to fuffer as an Indian.

The

The prifoners who have the happinefs to pleafe thofe to whom they are offered, are immediately adopted into the family, are accepted in the place of the loft father, fon, or hufband, and have no other mark of their captivity, but that they are not fuffered to return to their own nation. To attempt this would be certain death. The principal pur-pofe of the war is to recruit in this manner; for which reafon a general who lofes many men, though he fhould conquer, is little better than difgraced at home. They therefore never chufe to attack but with a very undoubted fuperiority.

But if they have been unfuccefsful, things wear a quite different face, they then enter the village without ceremony by day, with grief and melancholy in their countenances, keeping a profound filence; or if they have fuftained any lofs, they enter in the evening, giving the death whoop, and naming thofe they have loft, either by ficknefs or the enemy. The village being affembled, they fit down with their heads covered, and all weep together, without fpeak-ing a fingle word, for fome confiderable time. When this filence is over, they lament aloud for their companions, and every thing wears the face of mourning for feveral days.

The fcalps, which they value fo much, are the trophies of their bravery; with thefe they adorn their houfes, which are efteemed in proportion as this fort of fpoils is more numerous. They have folemn days appointed, upon which the young

men

men gain a new name, or title of honour, from their head-men; and thefe titles are given according to the qualities of the perfon, and his performances, of which thefe fcalps are the evidence. This is all the reward they receive for the dangers of the war.

Such, in general, are the manners and cuftoms of the Six Nations, which in the main agree with thofe of all the North-Amerian Indians: tho' every tribe has fomething peculiar to itfelf. Among the Hurons and Natchez, the dignity of chief is hereditary, and the fucceffion is in the female line; and in cafe this whole line fhould be extinct, the moft noble matron of the tribe makes choice of any one fhe pleafes for a chief. If the perfon who fucceeds is not arrived to years fufficient to take the charge of the government, a regent is appointed, who has the whole authority, but acts in the name of the minor.

The Delawares and Shawanees are remarkable for their deceit and perfidy, paying little or no regard to their moft folemn engagements.

The Twightees and Yeahtanees, on the banks of the river St. Jofeph, that flows into Lake Mechigan, are remarkably mild and fedate, and feem to have fubdued their paffions beyond any other Indians on the continent. They have always been fteady friends to the Englifh, and might, no doubt, be made very ufeful fubjects, if proper fteps were taken to civilize them.

The

The Cherokees are governed by feveral fachems or chiefs, elected by the different villages. The Creeks and Chactaws are ruled in the fame manner. The Chickefaws have a king, and a council for his affiftance, and are efteemed a brave people. They are generally at war with all the other Indians eaft of the Miffiffippi: the Chactaws, Creeks, Cherokees, and the fouthern Indians, often fight pitched battles with them, on the plains of their country: having horfes in plenty, they ride to the field of battle, and there difmount, where the women fight, as well as the men, If they are hard preffed.

The Creeks and Chactaws punifh their women, when unfaithful to their hufbands, by cutting off their hair, which they will not fuffer to grow again till the corn is ripe the next feafon. The Chickefaws, their neighbours, are no-ways troubled with a fpirit of jealoufy; and fay, it is beneath a man to fufpect a woman's fidelity. They are tall, well-fhaped, and handfome featured, efpecially the women, who in beauty far excel any other nation to the fouthward: but even thefe are furpaffed by the Huron women, upon Lake Erie, who are allowed to be the moft beautiful favages upon the continent. They drefs much neater than any of the reft, and curioufly adorn their heads, necks, wrifts, &c. yet a jealous hufband is very rare, either among the Hurons or Iroquois.

The Ottawawas, or Souties, are lufty, fquare-built, and ftrait-limbed. The women, fhort, thick,

and

and ordinary ; yet their hufbands are very prone to jealoufy, and cut off the tip of the fufpected wife's nofe, that she may for ever after be diftinguifhed by a mark of infamy.

The Indians on the lakes are generally at peace with one another, poffeffing an extenfive and fruitful country. They are formed into a fort of empire, and the emperor is elected from the eldeft tribe, which is that of the Ottawawas, fome of whom are fettled near Detroit, but the major part further weftward, towards the Miffiffippi. Ponteack is the prefent emperor, who has certainly the faireft dominions, and greateft authority, of any Indian chief that has appeared on the continent fince our acquaintance with it. He not long fince formed a defign of uniting all the Indian nations under his authority; but mifcarried in the attempt. Were proper meafures taken, this chief might be rendered very ferviceable to the Britifh trade and fettlements in this country ; more extenfively fo, than any one that has ever been in alliance with us.

In travelling northward from Montreal, towards the Ottawawas river, you meet with fome few villages belonging to the Round-heads, fo called, from the fhape of their heads ; all poffible pains being taken by their mothers to make them round in their infancy, this being efteemed a great beauty.

The Efquimaux have been already defcribed, (Vol. I. p. 242.) Our acquaintance with the Sioux,

Nip-

Nippiffongs, and other northern Indians, is, as yet, but very flender. The Seguntacooks, or Abnaques, fettled in New-England, were formerly very numerous ; as were the Mimaux, in Nova-Scotia. Of the Penobfcots, Narigeewalks, St. John Indians, and many others to the eaft and fouth of the Gulph of St. Laurence, there are now fcarce any footfteps remaining, except a few families, difperfed up and down.

There have been many conjectures concerning the origin of the different nations of Indians in America ; it being taken for granted, that they are emigrants from fome other country. But as the Indians are very folicitous and careful to hand down their hiftory from father to fon, the account they give of themfelves feems moft deferving of credit. The Hurons, and fix confederated nations, and all the other tribes to the fouthward, except the Chickefaws, agree, that they came from the fetting of the fun into this country. The Chickefaws came from South-America, fince the Spaniards took poffeffion of it. The Indians on the great lakes north of the river St. Laurence, and thofe between that river and the Bay of Fundy, and quite to Hudfon's Bay, northward, except the Efquimaux, affert, that they came from the northward.

REFLEC-

REFLECTIONS on the prefent State of the North-American Colonies.

GReat-Britain, a country of manufactures, without materials; a trading nation, without commodities to trade upon; and a maritime power, without either naval ftores or fufficient materials for fhip-building, could not fubfift long, as an independent ftate, without her colonies. We need only mention what happened in 1718, when the Swedes and Ruffians entered into a combination to deprive England of naval ftores; and would fuffer none to be exported out of their dominions but in their own fhips, and at their own exorbitant prices, which muft foon have ruined the trade and navigation of this kingdom: but proper meafures being concerted for procuring thofe neceffary articles from the North-American colonies, they were immediately attended with the defired fuccefs; and Great-Britain had not only a fufficient fupply for her own ufe, but a large furplus for exportation. This nation alfo ftands in as great need of many other as neceffary and ufeful articles, which are or might be as eafily obtained from the colonies.

From hence we learn the ufe of colonies, and the intent of fettling them; which is to fupply the mother-country with fuch commodities as fhe has not of her own, and by that means to purchafe their neceffaries from it. By that means, they
would

would affift and fupport each other ; their connection and dependence would be mutual and reciprocal, and it is by fuch an eftablifhment alone, that Great-Britain can either reap the benefit of, or preferve the allegiance of her colonies. Many, indeed, think of nothing but keeping them in fubjection, by the rules and power of government ; but the firft thing to be confidered in governing any people whatever is, how they are to fubfift under that government. So long as the colonies produce nothing wanting in England, they can never live under her government, without great complaints on both fides : they cannot then vend their products in the mother-country, and muft depend on other powers for the chief part of their fupport, or manufacture their own commodities.

But colonies, as has been obferved, fhould live merely by agriculture, without either manufactures or trade, except what is confined to their mother country. To maintain a number of people merely by the produce of lands, requires ten times more land than many would allow them, while the North-American colonies are confined by chains of barren mountains, to a very narrow flip of land along the fea-coaft. It is found from daily experience in the tobacco-colonies, where they have hitherto fubfifted in that manner, that a planter fhould have forty or fifty acres of land for every labourer : where they are reduced to lefs, they are foon obliged to leave off that manner of living ; that quantity of land is required not only to produce

duce their ftaple commodities, and to fupply them
with frefh lands as they wear out, but to afford a
large range for their ftock, which fhould in a manner maintain themfelves, while the people beftow
their time and labour upon their ftaple commodities for Britain, otherwife they cannot live by
them. But it, appears, from a particular inquiry
into the number of people and quantity of land,
that in many of thefe colonies they have but ten
or twelve acres a-head, in others not above
twenty; and not a fufficient quantity in any of
them, to live merely by making tobacco, hemp, or
flax, if it be not in the fouthern or rice-colonies,
where the land will neither breed people, nor produce any thing. But if the colonies thus want land
to fubfift by their agriculture at prefent, that is,
to live by a dependance on their mother-country,
what can we expect from them in twenty or thirty
years, when their numbers may be double! It will
then be as impracticable for them to purchafe their
manufactures from their mother-country, as it
would be for Britain to purchafe all the manufactures fhe ufes, without making or felling any. To
confine them then to their prefent bounds, is to
oblige them to become independent of their mother-country, whether they will or not. And this
is the more to be regarded, as the people in the colonies muft increafe and multiply much fafter than
they do here; fince they live almoft entirely by
their agriculture, the only fource of population in
any part of the world.

All

All this abundantly appears, from a due account of the colonies, of the foil and climate of North-America, and of what they produce, or may be fit to yield for the benefit of the nation; of which we can only here give a general view, from which it will appear, that thefe colonies can never fubfift by that dependance upon her, by the prefent ftate of their agriculture. It is expected, they fhould do this by means of tobacco, indigo, hemp, and flax, which are the moft unfuitable to their foil, and the two laft to the climate, of any thing almoft that grows. Thefe commodities require the very beft and richeft lands, whereas their lands are very poor and mean. Tobacco is one of thofe rank and poifonous weeds which only grow on rotten foils and dunghills, fuch as frefh wood-lands, and will not thrive on any others. To make tobacco, indigo, hemp, or flax, efpecially on their lands, requires more manure than can poffibly be had for them in the foil and climate of North-America, which produce little or no grafs. The length and feverity of the winters in the northern colonies, and the badnefs of the pafturage in the fouthern, render it impracticable to maintain ftocks of cattle fufficient to manure lands for thefe commodities, which their lands will not produce without great quantities of manure. In the northern colonies, they are obliged to expend their manure on their corn and grafs grounds, and have none to fpare for hemp and flax; in the tobacco-colonies, that weed would require more manure than all the cattle and horfes in England

land yield; and in the fouthern colonies, their
fcorching fands will not take manure, much lefs
produce in perfection fuch commodities as thefe,
which many think fhould be their ftaple.   At the
fame time, they are obliged to plant Indian corn,
which, by its great fubftance, and fpreading root,
exhaufts the earth as much as thefe their ftaple
commodities.   Thus their lands do not produce
above a third part what they did formerly, when
they were frefh and fertile; while the people are
twice or thrice as numerous, and require the
produce of their lands for their own ufe, inftead
of being able to pay taxes, or even to purchafe abfolute neceffaries.

Hence in the colonies, corn is three or four
times as dear as it was only twenty years ago.   The
confequence of this is, it not only renders them unable to plant any thing for Britain, before the neceffaries of life; but as tobacco, hemp, and flax
exhauft their corn and grafs grounds, they hinder
the people to raife ftocks of cattle, either for their
fubfiftence, or to manure their lands for thefe
crops, and oblige them to keep ftocks of fheep;
thereby fupplying them with the materials both of
their hempen, linen, and woollen manufactures;
while they obftruct the growing of other commodities to purchafe thefe their neceffaries from
Britain.

This ftate of the colonies is more to be regarded, as their paftures will not maintain large cattle,
and

and are only fit to feed sheep and goats, on which they muft fubfift, as people do in the like foil and climate in all parts of the world. Their wool is likewife better than the Englifh, at leaft in the fouthern colonies; it is of the fame kind with the Spanifh wool, or curled and frizzled like that, and might be rendered as fine by the fame management. Sheep likewife maintain themfelves, in thefe fouthern colonies, throughout the whole year, without coft or trouble. Thus by the ftep which the colonies have lately taken, to raife all the fheep they can, they will foon have plenty of wool. With this they have already made cloth worth twelve fhillings a yard, which is as good as any made of Englifh wool. Some of their wool has been fent to England, where it fold for the price of the beft; although this was from a common tobacco plantation, where no care had been taken of it. This may perhaps be looked upon by fome as a lofs to England; but if fhe would ftudy to make a right and proper ufe of her colonies, might be of more fervice to her than any one thing they are capable of producing. They have already wool enough, which is as fit for their ufe as if it were finer; and the only way to hinder them to manufacture it, is to improve it fo as to make it fit to fend to England, and to fupply the place of Spanifh wool; and if that were rightly fet about, it might be eafily done.

In order to prevent this ftate of the colonies, and to fupply them with a proper ftaple commodity for

Vol. II.   C c   Britain,

Britain, nothing feems to be thought of but hemp
and flax ; but it fhews a great want of knowledge
to endeavour to improve lands with hemp and flax,
which are worn out with Indian corn and tobacco.
They are obliged to leave off planting tobacco, becaufe it requires manure once in three or
four years ; but hemp and flax require it every
year. It is contrary both to reafon and experience, to expect to get hemp and flax, which
require a ftrong, rich, and moift foil in a cool
climate, from the light, fandy, and parched
foil of North-America. They are as improper
for thefe fingular and peculiar climates, as for
the foil. The proper climate for hemp and flax
is from the middle of France to the middle of
Ruffia, that is, from the 45th to the 60th degree
of latitude, which in North-America extends from
Montreal to the northern parts of Hudfon's Bay,
where we have neither foil nor climate fit to produce any thing. If we would plant hemp and flax
to the fouthward of this latitude, in which all our
colonies lie, they fhould be fown in winter, like
wheat, that they may, in like manner, get ftrength
and fubftance before the heats of fummer come
on : this is the practice in fowing hemp and flax
from the fouthern parts of France to Egypt ; but
in North-America, on account of the long and
hard winters, and late and backward fprings, hemp
and flax cannot be fown in the proper feafon for
them any where to the northward of Carolina,
where the poor fandy foil is improper for thefe
crops.

crops. For this reafon, they fow hemp and flax in their fwamps, which are only the wafhings of the fand-banks which furround them ; in which hemp will fhoot up to a great height, it is true, but is as weak as the water it grows in. Hence, though they have had a bounty on hemp and flax in North-America fince the year 1693, which has been renewed from time to time, and they have as often tried to make thefe commodities, tney could never produce fuch quantities as to ferve for a ftaple commodity to fend to Britain ; but, on the contrary, are obliged to import confiderable quantities for their own ufe.

Since their lands will not produce thofe commodities which require a rich and fertile foil, it is propofed to plant them with cotton, which grows in the greateft plenty and perfection in all our colonies, from Maryland to South-Carolina and Georgia, and might even be made in the northern colonies, as it is in Ruffia, if they had the right fort. Cotton is as common, and as generally manufactured in many of them, as wool is in England. Thus it is as neceffary to get cotton from thefe colonies, to prevent their manufactures, as to fupply thofe of England. But cotton is a commodity of very fmall value, and a poor ftaple for any one colony, and much more for fo many : although the nation wants one million eight hundred thoufand pounds weight of cotton a-year, yet at a fhilling a pound, it is worth but ninety thoufand pounds ; and if they were to make it in any quantities, it would foon

C c 2

fall

fall to its usual price of nine-pence, and would not
clear them above fifty thousand pounds a-year,
which is not six-pence a-head for all the people in
North-America. It is for this reason that they are
obliged to manufacture their cotton; and we can
never expect to get either that, or hemp and flax,
from them, till they have many other commodities, that may enable them to live, and purchase
their necessaries with these.

The next commodity proposed for the staple
of the colonies is indigo, which thrives but very
indifferently either in the soil or climate. Indigo,
like tobacco, not only exhausts the substance of the
earth, but requires the very best and richest lands,
and such as have a natural moisture, in them;
whereas the lands in our southern colonies are
extremely poor and sandy; and have a barren dry-
ness in them, which renders them very unfit to
produce such a crop as this to any manner of advantage. Indigo is planted by the French on the
fresh wood-lands of St. Domingo, which are too
rich and moist even for sugar, to exhaust their
luxuriant fertility, in order to render them fit for
other crops. They likewise cut it every six weeks,
or eight times in a year, and for two years together; whereas, in Carolina it is cut but thrice,
and as the land has not substance and moisture to
make it shoot after cutting, and the summers are
too short, the third cutting is but of little value,
as even the second is in Virginia. The French and
Spaniards make great quantities of indigo, worth
eight

eight and ten fhillings a pound; but the little we make in Carolina is not, upon an average, worth above two fhillings, and a great deal has been fold for a fhilling, and lefs. This is therefore far from being fo rich and valuable a commodity in North-America, as many imagine; although it is of great fervice in the rice colonies, and helps them to keep up their plantations, by making a fmall quantity of indigo with their rice; and on fome few fpots of better lands, turns to more account.

From this brief account of thefe commodities, it muft appear, that they can never be the general and lafting ftaple of any colony we have in all North-America; which would be ftill much more evident, if at the fame time we confider the ftate of their agriculture, in other more neceffary and effential articles, the neceffaries of life. Wherever they have planted thefe commodities, their lands are fo exhaufted by them, that they will hardly produce the bare neceffaries of life, and much lefs fuch exhaufting weeds as thefe. It is for this reafon, that moft of our tobacco plantations are broke up; the people have been obliged to quit them many years ago, after all their charges and improvements upon them, and retire to the mountains, where they find fome frefh lands fit to produce that commodity, which are the fupport of the tobacco trade: but thefe will in a fhort time be worn out, as the reft have been; and when that happens, there muft be an end of the tobacco trade, without a fupply of frefh lands fit to produce that exhauft-

ing

ing weed, as well as to maintain cattle to manure
them, with convenient ports, and an inland navigation, to fhip off fuch a grofs and bulky commodity ;
of which there are none in all the Britifh dominions
in North-America, but the rich lands on the Miffiffippi and Ohio. Befides, light and fandy lands,
in hot climates, never bear good grafs, and much
lefs in North-America ; where they are generally,
covered with pines, which deftroy what little grafs
the earth might otherwife produce, and render every,
thing that grows upon it fo four, that no cattle will
tafte it, unlefs they are reduced to their laft fhift.
In a pine-barren, there is not a blade of grafs to be
feen ; and it is at the beft but very fcarce in all our
fouthern colonies. Their paftures are covered with
a tall-rank weed, more like bent than pafture-
grafs ; which is fo rank, hard, and dry, that they
make their brooms of it. Such is the produce of
their ftrongeft and beft lands. As for the poor and
fandy foils, which make nine-tenths of the whole in
our fouthern colonies, they are thinly covered with
a fmall fort of this grafs, and do not afford a bite
for a beaft for miles together. Their low grounds
and marfhes again are covered with nothing but
reeds, rufhes, and flags, which are their meadow-
grounds that fhould fupply the want of grafs on
their uplands. The hay they mow is nothing but
the three-fquare rufh, unlefs it is raifed by art, at
a greater expence than it is worth.

A foil and climate which produce fo little
grafs can never abound in corn, which requires
the

the same soil. Lands which abound with one, are always fruitful in the other, & *vice versa*. Such lands, therefore, are as improper for wheat, which requires a strong loamy soil, that is somewhat moist, as they are for hemp and flax, especially in a hot climate. Wheat thrives in this part of the world from Egypt to the middle of Russia, for thirty degrees of latitude; whereas in North-America, its growth is chiefly confined to seven degrees, and it cannot be said to thrive well but within four degrees, from New-York to the southern parts of Virginia, or from the 41st to the 37th degree of latitude. It was but very lately since they have sown some wheat in the inland parts of South-Carolina, with uncertain success: they never had a grain to the southward of the middle of North-Carolina; and to the northward of New-England, they have none but the French bled marsais. In the northern parts wheat is constantly subject to a blast, or smut, and in the southern to the rust. At the best, the grain is so small, that it yields at least a third less than the lands do in England. Hence they are obliged to quit their plantations as fast as they wear out, and to spread over a whole continent, in order to get a few patches of tobacco, or fields of Indian corn. And it is for these reasons, that corn has become so dear in the colonies, and more valuable to make than any thing for Britain; a certain sign, that they either want to extend their

set-

settlements, or to alter their staple commodities, if not both.

Since the acquisitions of Canada and Florida, indeed, the British dominions are so much enlarged, that no one seems to imagine, that the colonies can want land : and yet it is very certain, they have just lands enough to supply themselves and their manufacturers ; but they hardly produce any thing that will serve to purchase manufactures from Britain. Thus Britain, by the proclamation of October 7th, 1763, confines her colonies to bounds, in which they must necessarily interfere with her; and excludes them from all those territories which might be of service to her, and would keep them from falling into the state that we have represented. This must evidently appear to all who are acquainted with the countries which our colonies possess in North-America, with the nature of the soil and climate, or with their agriculture and staple commodities ; but as these are so little understood, they require a more particular consideration. Now all the colonies on the continent make three different countries, the state of which, with regard to their staple commodities, is in brief as follows :

The northern colonies produce nothing wanted in Britain, and are entirely unfit for that purpose; as appears from one hundred and fifty years experience. The length and severity of the winters, the late and backward springs; and shortness

of

of the summer season, are unavoidable obstacles to all such improvements in agriculture.

In Canada and Nova-Scotia, the snow lies six feet deep for six months in the year; and they have hard frosts and snows for a month or six weeks before this severe season, which they call winter: their winters are eight or nine months long, and they have little or no spring or autumn season. The spring does not begin before the month of June; and even in that month, our people who resided at Oswego, in the most southern part of all Canada, observed hard frosts, which destroyed every thing, at that time of year; and the like frosts, in the month of June, are sometimes felt on the warmer sea-coasts of New-England, to the southward of that. These frosts continue all over Canada during the whole summer. When they have not these frosts, they are subject to more pernicious cold winter fogs, which destroy the fruits of the earth in the middle of summer, particularly about the great lakes, and in Nova-Scotia, which is only the sea-coast of Canada; and they are not entirely free from them in a great part of New-England and New-York. Such countries must be very unfit for colonies, which should live merely by their agriculture, or become a prejudice to their mother-country.

Besides the climate, the best and fresh lands in all our northern colonies, which should produce staple commodities for Britain, are worn out by culture. They are obliged to expend their ma-

nure

--nure on their corn and grafs grounds ; their plantations are too fmall to make ftaple commodities ;
and they have many populous towns, which confume the produce of the lands, that fhould be fent
to Britain. Hence the produce of thefe colonies is
only the overplus of the corn and provifions, which
they make for their own ufe, and in a fhort time
will be little or none at all, as the people increafe
and multiply. There are nigh a million and an half
of people in thefe northern colonies, in a country
no larger than Ireland, and not by a fourth part fo
fruitful. What then can they poffibly have to
raife fterling cafh to pay taxes, when they have
neither ftaple commodities from their agriculture,
manufactures, nor a trade in them ? Or, how can it
be fuppofed, that they can ever purchafe their neceffaries from Britain ? Their only dependence is
upon a trade to the Weft-Indies, the fifhery, or the
fur-trade ; the laft of which is very inconfiderable ;
the firft has been long ago infufficient to maintain
fuch a number of people, and is reduced to little
or nothing by the great increafe of the people, the
addition of more northern colonies, and by the
fouthern engaging in it : and the fifhery is the
ftaple of New-England, and fource of all their
remittances to England, in which Nova-Scotia
muft now interfere. If thefe things are confidered,
it will be impoffible for the colonies to take almoft any thing from Britain, or to have any connection with her, when they become more populous,

I   unlefs

unlefs they extend their fettlements to the fouth-ward.

The tobacco colonies enjoy a better foil and climate, and have by that means hitherto had a good ftaple commodity, which has been of more fervice to the nation than all the other products of North-America put together, fo long as their lands were frefh and fertile; but moft of them are worn out with that exhaufting weed, and will no longer bear it : they are then turned into corn and pafture grounds, which produce nothing but corn, cattle, and wool, as in the northern colonies; and we fhall foon want a fupply of lands for tobacco, as much as for any thing that North-America will produce. Thefe colonies likewife want fome other ftaple as much as all the reft, if not more. Formerly they made three hogfheads of tobacco a-head, where they cannot now make one, while the people are four times as numerous.

The next divifion contains the fouthern or rice-colonies, which make the great extent of the Britifh dominions on this fide of the Apalachian Mountains ; but it is the great misfortune of the nation, that this extenfive part of her dominions, which lies in a climate that might otherwife produce every thing we want from North-America, is as barren as it is unhealthful, and unfit to raife any confiderable colonies.

The whole fea-coaft of North-America, from the Bay of New-York to the Gulph of Mexico, is a low, flat, fandy beach; the foil for a great diftance

from

from it is fandy and barren ; the climate is very
rainy, and as thefe rains have no drain from the
land, but ftagnate all over a low flat country, they
form innumerable fwamps and marfhes, which render it very unhealthful. It is a common opinion,
that all this part of the continent, which ftretches
into the ocean at a confiderable diftance from the reft,
has been recovered from the fea, and is nothing but
a drained marfh or fand-bank. Accordingly, in all
this fpace, nothing is to be found, either on the
furface or in the bowels of the earth, but beds of
fea-fhells, in place of ftones, metals, and other minerals. Many other caufes likewife confpire to
render thefe fouthern coafts of North-America unhealthful ; and as they are barren, and the heats
fo fultry, that people are not able to undergo
the toils of planters in them, they are abandoned
almoft by all. Thefe fouthern colonies are from
one hundred and fifty to two hundred miles broad,
between the fea and mountains, of which about one
half is thus low, flat, and unhealthful.

Thus all thefe extenfive fouthern parts of North-
America produce little or nothing, and the lands
are hardly worth cultivating, if it be not in the
unhealthful and deftructive fwamps and marfhes ;
which they are obliged to be at the immenfe toil
and fatigue of clearing, draining, and cultivating,
at the rifk of their lives, in order to get rice to fupply the place of wheat, and to have pafturage on
the low grounds, neither of which the uplands afford.

ford *. Out of an hundred and odd thoufand barrels of rice which they make in a year, Britain confumes but four thoufand; hence they want markets for this, as all our other colonies do for other forts of corn, which is become the chief produce of them all; they thereby interfere with one another, depreciate their ftaple, cannot vend any quantities of it, and are on thefe accounts unable to make remittances to Britain, to pay their debts, or to purchafe their neceffaries from hence, which obliges them to enter into manufactures. To fettle any more fuch colonies then as Florida, is only to ruin thefe, and the intereft of Britain in them; unlefs we get fome other ftaple for them, which the country will hardly admit of, if it be not filk, and that requires more hands than thefe unhealthful fea-coafts will breed.

Thefe are the reafons why we have fo few people in our fouthern colonies, and are never likely to have any number by our prefent proceedings. We think of nothing but extending our fettlements ftill farther on thofe peftiferous fea-coafts, even to the funken lagunes of Eaft-Florida, and the barren fands of Mobile and Penfacola; and to add more drains of people to the many we already have.

None of the fouthern parts of that continent can ever be planted, without a very great lofs of people, but at the diftance of an hundred,

* See a Defcription of South-Carolina in 1710.

or

or an hundred and fifty miles from the sea-
coaſt *.

Beſides ſtaple commodities there is another more
material point to be conſidered in the colonies;
which is their great and daily increaſe; and for
which, unleſs we make proviſion in time, they can
never ſubſiſt by a dependence on Britain.   There
are at preſent nigh three millions of people in them,
who may in twenty or thirty years increaſe to ſix
millions, as many as there are in England, if they
have room in that continent to extend their bounds.

It will indeed be very difficult for the people in
the colonies to ſubſiſt, or become very numerous, in
the countries they now poſſeſs; but it will be as
difficult, if not impracticable, to confine them to
thoſe bounds. So ſoon as planters want land they
ſtarve; and to avoid that, people will do any thing.
It is for this reaſon, that although they are confined in their bounds by the proclamation of
October 7th, 1763, yet they pay no regard to
it.   Thus the uſe the nation has for new ſettlements and acquiſitions in North-America, is for
the great increaſe of the people who are already

---

* The acute diſeaſes in theſe unhealthful parts of North-
America generally turn to intermittents, which are not mortal, even in twenty months; but in a few months more bring
on that cachexy, with an emaciated habit, a ſwelled belly, and
pale ſallow complexion, which is the characteriſtic of the bad
ſtate of health in all the ſouthern and maritime parts of North-
America; after which acute diſeaſes are mortal, and chronic diſeaſes incurable, without a change of air and climate.

there,

there, and to enable them to fubfift by a dependence upon her ; which they can never do, unlefs they extend their fettlements. The teft therefore of all our acquifitions is, whether will the people in the colonies, who want lands to make ftaple commodities for Britain, remove to them ? It is only by this rule, that we can judge of the utility of any acquifitions or new fettlements to Britain. But will any planter in North-America remove either to Canada or Florida ? Is it not obvious to every one, that fuch a removal would be from bad to worfe, if it may not perhaps be to get a rice plantation or two, in the deftructive fwamps and marfhes ? We already have but too many fuch poor and barren lands, and inhofpitable climates, and thefe are much worfe than what we had before.

The only advantage of thefe acquifitions proceeds from the expulfion of our enemies from them, and not from the fettling of colonies, for which they are totally unfit. By the reduction of Canada and Florida, the colonies have fuch a fecurity from the enemy, by which they were before furrounded, that they may extend their fettlements with fafety, and cultivate thofe lands which may both enrich them and the whole nation : but of fuch lands, there are none either in Canada or Florida ; and to exclude the colonies from all others, for the fake of thefe deferts, is to deprive the nation of all the advantages which might otherwife be reaped from the reduction of them, and of the very object for which the nation engaged in fuch an expenfive war.

The

The fruitful part of the Britifh dominions is di-vided into three different countries by the moun-tains, which run through the middle of them, from north to fouth ; and from their fouthern extremity, they run weft to the Miffiffippi, forming two ridges, in fhape of the letter L. On the eaft fide of thefe mountains lie the territories poffeffed by our fouth-ern colonies ; on the weft are the territories of the Ohio ; and on the fouth are what we call the terri-tories of the Miffiffippi ; the two laft being divided from one another by the Weftern or Chickefaw mountains, which run through them from Caro-lina to the Miffiffippi. Thus the fruitful parts of the Britifh dominions are divided into three, which we may call the eaft, weft, and fouth divifions ; each of which contains, at moft, about fifty thou-fand fquare miles of good and fertile land, and forms a country about the fize of England, in cli-mates that are fit to produce every thing the na-tion wants.

Now, it is the fouthern divifion which we ought to fettle in the firft place. This extends from the fea-coaft of Georgia to the Miffiffippi, and is bound-ed on the north by the Weftern or Chickefaw moun-tains, and on the fouth by the Gulph of Mexico : the whole of this country is about five hundred miles in length, from eaft to weft ; and four de-grees of latitude, or two hundred and forty miles broad, of which one half, on the fea-coaft, is the barren defert of Florida above defcribed ; the reft is the fruitful part of the country, which
we

we would propose to settle. This makes about sixty thousand square miles, of which we possess about ten thousand in Georgia and Carolina, and have fifty thousand to settle from thence to the Mississippi.

This country may be divided into two parts, the eastern division in Carolina and Georgia, and the western on the Mississippi; which would make two good colonies. The last of these, known by the name of the country of the Natches, on the Mississippi, which extends from the island of New Orleans to the Chickesaw mountains, is well known to be by far the best and most fruitful country in all these southern parts of North-America; and extends from the Mississippi to the river Cousfa, which falls into the Bay of Mobile; making a rich and fertile country, about two hundred miles square, which would perhaps produce more than all these southern parts of the continent put together, from hence to Virginia. In all that distance, we do not meet with a good and fruitful country of any extent, if it be not in the inland parts of North-Carolina, which is but very narrow, and has neither a convenient water-carriage from it, nor a good port belonging to it. The only other fruitful country in these southern parts of the continent, is in the inland parts of Georgia, on the heads of the rivers Alatamaha and St. Mary's, with Flint river adjoining; which was recommended by the Spaniards as the most proper place for a settlement, after they had searched the whole country, from the Cape of Florida to the Mississippi; and some

peo-

people who lived in the country, at the forks of the Alatamaha, have given us the same account of it, and of the countries adjacent.

If this country in Georgia was annexed to South-Carolina, as far as the river Chatahoochè, it would foon be fettled, and would make that a very refpectable colony on our fouthern frontiers, which would foon join to the other on the Miffiffippi, and they might thereby fupport one another, without any charge to the nation *. It is well known, that Georgia was only feparated from Carolina to pleafe the Indians, who would not fuffer the Carolinians to fettle to the fouthward of the river, after their quarrel with them in the year 1715; but that is now rather a reafon for enlarging and ftrengthening that colony, which, in

one

* The only obftacle to this junction of Carolina with the Miffiffippi, proceeds from the Creek and Chactaw Indians, who lie in the way; but that obftacle might be removed, by proper management. We got poffeffion of Carolina by two powerful nations of Indians who held it engaging in war with one another; in which moft of them were extirpated, and the reft afterwards fled to the peninfula of Florida. If thefe Indians were fettled there again, they might be out of the way both of harm and mifchief, which they will ever be in where they are. A great part of them left that country, only in the year 1715, where they might get their living by fifhing and hunting better than where they are, or nigh our plantations, which extirpate them.

If thefe and all the other Indians in the Britifh dominions, were at the fame time deprived of fire-arms, we might be rid of all future trouble from them; and that might now eafily be done,

when

one hundred years, is hardly able to defend itself against its inteftine foes, the negroes and Indians. This ftate it has been reduced to by difmembering it, and erecting a feparate colony, which has no people hardly in it to this day, and is not able to fupport its own government, notwithftanding the vaft charges it has coft, amounting to two hundred thoufand pounds, at leaft, more than was ever before expended on all the colonies we have. For thefe reafons, it is propofed to annex Georgia to South-Carolina, to which it properly belongs, and which it might ftrengthen; and, in lieu of this, North-Carolina fhould be extended to Wineau, as that is the only port to all the inland and fruitful parts of that country, which hardly produces any thing for want of fuch a port, although,

in

when they have none to fupply them. It is only by this means that their infurrections are to be prevented, and with more humanity than by endeavouring to extirpate them. If ever Florida is peopled and cultivated, it will only be by the Indians, who are a vaft advantage to Spain, and might be rendered as ferviceable to Britain, inftead of a perpetual annoyance, by fupplying them with implements of hufbandry.

Another caufe of thefe infurrections of the Indians, proceeds from the banditti of Indian traders who go among them, and are worfe than the Indians themfelves. They are there out of reach of the law, and obferve no one law of civil fociety. The fending of fuch people among the Indians begets that familiarity which gives them a contempt of the whole nation; but by keeping them more in awe, and at a diftance, without fuch parley and talks with them, they would have a greater refpect for it. For thefe reafons, their trade fhould

be

in point of fertility, it is of more value than all the reft of Carolina and Georgia put together.

Now, if this were done, and all the ftraggling and unprofitable fettlements of Canada, Nova-Scotia, Eaft and Weft Florida, were united in one on the Miffiffippi, the nation might be rid of an enormous expence in " defending, protecting, and fecuring them ;" they would fecure thefe more va-luable parts of the Britifh dominions, and by be-ing united together might be able to defend them-felves; the nation would thereby have lands for all the planters we have, inftead of obliging them to enter into manufactures for want of lands to culti-vate; and we fhould thus have two good and pro-fitable colonies in the fouthern parts of America, which might fupply the nation with the many valuable commodities that are fo much want-ed, and would produce more for Britain than all

be confined to one or two places, where juftice might be done, and good order preferved. For this purpofe, Ofwego in the north, and Augufta in the fouth, would be fufficient for all the Indian trade in North-America; if it be not what New-England has fo well eftablifhed and regulated in the eaft, by the fame means. If their trade were confined to thefe two places, the northern Indians would be drawn to Canada, and the great lakes, where the furs are to be had, and where they could only find a vent for them; and the fouthern Indians would find it as convenient to fettle in their former country of Florida; by which the nation would reap the benefit of both thefe acquifi-tions, much better than by being at fuch an expence, both of men and money, to fettle and protect them; and the Indians would, at the fame time, leave all the fruitful parts here men-tioned for us to cultivate.

our colonies in North-America. Had Carolina been a fruitful and healthful country, it would long ago have been the moft confiderable and profitable colony the nation has; and the only way to render both that country and Florida of fervice to the nation, is, to fettle the inland and weftern parts, which are as fruitful and healthful as the eaftern and maritime parts, to which we are confined, are the reverfe of both: and when thefe are peopled and fecured, it will be eafy to extend our fettlements up the Miffiffippi, and acrofs both the Apalachian and Chickefaw mountains to the territories of the Ohio, by which we may fecure, people, and cultivate every part of the Britifh dominions that can be of any fervice to the nation.

The Inland Parts of LOUISIANA defcribed.

THE whole country, from the ifland of New-Orleans to the rivers Ohio and Illinois, is the richeft and moft fruitful of any in the Britifh dominions, and extends upwards of a thoufand miles, containing more fruitful lands than are in all our colonies put together. There are no good lands in all North-America but upon the fides of rivers, and as the Miffiffippi is fo much larger than all the other rivers in that continent, the lands upon it are as much more extenfive and fertile. This we are are affured of, by thofe who were fent from Vir-

ginia,

ginia, in 1742, on purpofe to furvey thofe countries, who reported, " they faw more land on the
Miffiffippi, and its many large branches, than
they judged was in all the Englifh colonies, as
far as they are inhabited." The fame is confirmed by the French, who tell us from experience of
them, " the lands on both fides of the Miffiffippi
are excellent for culture, and produce Indian corn,
tobacco, indigo, &c. and all kinds of provifions,
with little or no care or labour, and almoft without
culture ; the foil being a black mould, of an excellent quality *". More particularly in the country of the Natches above-mentioned, we are told
by a planter of fixteen years experience in that
country, the foil is a fertile mould, three feet deep
on the hills, and five or fix feet deep in the vallies,
with a ftrong clayey foundation † ; the like of which
is certainly not to be feen any where elfe, in all
thefe fouthern parts of North-America. Even
the hill-fides are covered with canes, which in
our colonies only grow in the deepeft and richeft
fwamps.

Such lands have a natural moifture in them,
which is the very foil that both hemp, flax, and indigo delight in ; and thefe are the three firft commodities that the nation wants from the colonies.
Upon fuch lands, hemp and flax might be made in
quantities, as a ftaple commodity, to fend to Britain ; whereas, on the poor lands in our colonies,
and their fmall plantations, they can only make a

* Du Mont, Memoires de la Louifiane, tom. i. p. 16.
† Du Pratz Hift. Louifiana, tom. i. p. 263.

little

little for their own ufe. The one would be of the greateft fervice, when the other is a prejudice to the nation. The climate likewife is as fit for thefe commodities. Here hemp and flax might be fown in winter, which is the only proper feafon for them in any part of North-America. This would afford time for making another crop in fummer, which fhould be indigo. Every labourer might cultivate two acres, or more, in hemp, and one or two in indigo, the produce of which would be worth from thirty to forty pounds a-year. This would enable them to purchafe negroes, and to enlarge the Britifh plantations, beyond what they are otherwife capable of. Such plant-ations would be more profitable than even fu-gar-colonies, and fupply the nation with more valuable and-neceffary articles. A hundred thou-fand labourers, which might be eafily found in all our colonies, taken together, would at the rate of twenty pounds a head, make two millions a year; but fuppofe they make only one half of this, it is as much as all our colonies in North-America now produce. If we compare this with the barren deferts of Canada and Florida, what a wide difference is there!

By this means, the nation might get the trade, both of indigo, hemp, and flax, and fupply all Eu-rope with thofe commodities, as we now do with tobacco; which laft thefe lands are fit to produce, in much greater plenty and perfection than any other part of North-America: and when our to-

D d 4   bacco

bacco plantations are worn out, there are no lands to fupply their place in all the Britifh dominions, but thofe on the Miffiffippi. There are three things neceffary for a tobacco plantation ; to wit, rich and fertile lands, good pafturage for maintaining ftocks of cattle for manure, and an inland navigation, with convenient ports, to fhip off fuch a grofs and bulky commodity from every plantation ; which three conveniences are only found in the tobacco plantations, and on the Miffiffippi. Our tobacco planters, therefore, may find others there, when their old plantations are worn out, as moft of them already are, and will all be in time. It is but five hundred miles, in a ftraight line, from the fea-coaft of Carolina and Georgia, which is no great way to go for good lands in North-America.

Thus we fee, that the territories of the Ohio and Miffiffippi are very fit to produce tobacco, indigo, hemp, and flax, which are the grand ftaple commodities of North-America ; and it is to produce thefe, that lands are wanted there. Thefe are likewife the proper crops for frefh wood-lands, or new fettlements. Lands which will not produce thefe at firft, are not worth poffeffing. In a few years they are worn out, and will hardly yield the neceffaries of life. It is for this reafon, that on our poor plantations, frefh lands will always be wanted for thefe commodities, which no other part of the Britifh dominions will produce. Here likewife planters have the neceffaries of life, with little or no coft or labour, which is as neceffary to make ftaple commo-

diti es

dities for Britain. The paſtures are covered with green grafs knee-high, the like of which is not to be ſeen in any other part of North-America ; ſuch lands yield three and fourſcore buſhels of corn to an acre, and the cattle maintain themſelves the whole year, without the charge of feeding them *. Hence the country abounds with wild kine, a large creature, like an ox, with a fleece like a ſheep, the wool, hides, and tallow of which are of great value.; but in our colonies the paſturage is ſo poor, that there are none to be ſeen.

At the ſame time, theſe countries are as healthful as they are fruitful. The whole country above the iſland of New-Orleans to the river Ohio, is high, dry, and hilly, refreſhed with cooling breezes from the adjacent mountains, which aſſuage the heat of the climate, and render it healthful. The banks of the Miſſiſſippi, on the eaſt ſide, are from one hundred to two and three hundred feet high, without a marſh near them. It is likewiſe obſerved, throughout all theſe countries on the Miſſiſſippi, that it ſeldom rains. The Apalachian mountains intercept the clouds brought up from the ocean. How different this, from the low, flat, ſandy, marſhy and rainy ſea-coaſts of all our ſouthern colonies. If the nation would people the ſouthern parts of North-America, or expect any indemnity for her expences in the late war, it can only be obtained from theſe countries, which were the immediate objects of the war.

* See Du Pratz, ibid.

When

When thefe lands are cleared, and exhaufted
with tobacco, indigo, hemp, and flax, they will
produce filk, cotton, wine and oil, for ever, which
are the great commodities that this nation wants.
It is fuch commodities as thefe that we fhould call
acquifitions : thefe are the proper produce of North-
America, and render colonies there fo beneficial to
Britain, but of much lefs confequence either to
France or Spain. They make thefe commodities
at home, and would be lofers by making them in
North-America. Colonies.there, whofe ftaple muft
foon be filk, wine, and oil, could not depend upon
France or Spain : hence, it is the greateft folly in
them, to endeavour to raife colonies in North-America ; fuch a falfe policy can only be equalled
by Britain's confining her colonies to countries
whofe ftaple is corn and wool. The ifland of
Hifpaniola is of more fervice to France than North-
America ; and if we are excluded from the Miffiffippi, Britain will lofe by her fucceffes, what France
has gained by her defeats—profitable colonies in
America.

The true Means of improving the NORTH-AMERICAN COLONIES.

THE fingular and peculiar climate of North-
America hardly agrees with any one thing that
is commonly propofed to be planted in it, and the

foil is as unfuitable to many others. The productions of Europe are there either deftroyed by
the long and intenfe colds in the north, or burnt
up by the fun in the fouth, efpecially on their
fcorching fands. Hence there is hardly any of
them that will thrive in our colonies, as the ftaple
of a country ought to do : the caufes of this would
abundantly appear from a due account of the climate of North-America. From certain obferva-
tions in both Europe and America, for thirty years
together, we are well affured, that there is a difference of at leaft fourteen or fifteen degrees of latitude between the refpective climates in thefe two
continents ; it being fo much colder there than
here *, confequently, we can expect nothing to grow
there

---

* This coldnefs of the climate, which is felt all over North-
America, appears to proceed, chiefly and principally, from the
three following caufes, befides others which confpire with them,
particularly the nature of the foil.

I. America extends farther north than any other part of the
world, and by that means is fo much colder, Europe is-fur-
rounded by the warmer ocean, which is always open ; Afia, by
an icy fea, (the *mare glaciale*) ; and America by a frozen continent, which occafions the diverfity of climates in thefe three
continents.

II. That continent, which is thus extenfive in the northern
parts, is one entire groupe of high mountains, covered with
fnow, or rather with ice, throughout the whole year. Thefe
mountains rife in the moft northern parts of the continent that
have been difcovered in Baffin's Bay, and fpread all over it to
New-England. Hence the coaft of Labrador is the higheft-
of any in the world, and may be defcried at the diftance of forty leagues ; and in the weftern parts, difcovered by the Ruffians,

2

there as it does here. It is for this reason, that the nation is disappointed, and every one is so much deceived about North-America.

In such singular climates, few or no products of the earth will thrive, as the staple of a country should do, but the natural productions of the soil and climate; and we must plant and improve these, if we would have proper staple commodities for our colonies, of which many might be found. Of this we have a remarkable instance, in the very first commodities the nation wants from North-America, which are hemp and flax: the European hemp or flax neither agrees with the soil or climate; but you may there have at least five or six sorts of these commodities, which are natural

to

fians, they tell us, " the country had terrible high mountains, covered with snow in the month of July." This was in latitude 58 degrees, and the country to the southward of that, in 40 degrees, is by the Spaniards called *fierras nevados*, snowy mountains. So a ridge of mountains rise at Cape Tourmente, by Quebec, and run four or five hundred leagues, forming the greatest ridge of mountains in the universe, which spread over all the northern parts of the continent. These are what we call the Northern snowy mountains.

III. All the countries which lie within the verge of these mountains, or north of New-England, are perpetually involved in frosts, snows, or thick fogs; and the colds which are felt in the south, proceed from these frozen regions in the north, by violent north-west winds. These are the peculiar winds of that continent, and blow with a fury which no wind exceeds. It appears from many observations, that they blow quite across the Atlantic Ocean to Europe. The great lakes of Canada, which are inland seas, extending north-west for twelve or

thirteen

to both. You may find much better and ftronger hemp there, on the mereft barren fands, than the richeft lands in Europe will produce. It is from fuch a production of their colonies, which is as common in them as hemp or flax are in Europe, and as generally manufactured, that the Spaniards make many manufactures preferable to any of the kind that we have feen; they have three or four different forts of it, and we might have five or fix more forts from our colonies, as well as many other valuable commodities. But they have been at the pains to explore the productions of their plantations, and by that means get fo many valuable returns from them, which we have entirely neglected, and thereby get fo little from ours. We do not ufe any productions of the country, and others will not thrive in it. The only rule we feem

to

thirteen hundred miles, give force and direction to thefe winds, which blow from the northern frozen regions, and bring the climate of Hudfon's Bay to the moft fouthern parts of that continent, whenever they blow for any time.

Many imagine, that thefe colds proceed from the fnows lying in the woods; but that is the effect, and not the caufe of the cold. They who attribute this to the woods do not diftinguifh between wet and cold, or the damps of wood-lands and frofts, which are very different things. Thefe colds are fo far from being occafioned by the woods, that one half of that continent, which is the coldeft, and from which they proceed, has not a wood in it; and is fo barren, that it does not bear a tree or a bufh. It is from this want of woods in the northern parts, and the great lakes, that thefe furious winds proceed; which are very much abated by the woods. In the woods, thefe cold

winds

to have for improving our colonies, is to make
fuch commodities in them as the merchants and
ttradefmen want, whether they will produce them
or not.

The ftaple commodities commonly propofed for
the colonies will not maintain them, and for that
reafon they are obliged to manufacture them.   To
maintain fuch a number of people, and whole
countries, by fuch employments, they fhould have
a variety and number of them, and fuch as are more
profitable.   By doing things only by halves, we
obftruct the defign altogether.   We fhould either
promote thefe defigns to fome purpofe, or let them
alone.   Every thing that has been done in them,
to promote the intereft of Britain, has only ferved
to eftablifh the manufactures of the colonies, from
the making of iron, to hemp and flax.   Unlefs they
have

winds may be endured ; but in the open fields, they are infuf-
ferable either to man or beaft, and that even in our fouthern
colonies.   Hence, if all the woods in that continent were cleared, Canada and Nova-Scotia would be as uninhabitable as Hudfon's Bay, our northern colonies as cold as Canada, and the adjacent fouthern colonies in the fituation of the northern.   Let
us not deceive ourfelves, therefore, with the vain hopes of mend-
ing nature, and abating the rigor of thefe inhofpitable climes ;
that is not to be done, but by cutting off, at leaft, twenty degrees of that continent in the north, and levelling the innumerable fnowy mountains.

No part of the world can be compared to this in point of climate but the eaftern parts of Afia, which are almoft contiguous
to America in the north; and are expofed to the like cold wind
from the continent.   Hence it appears, from comparing man
obferv

have fome other more valuable commodities, they can never fend thefe to Britain.

By being all employed in planting one or two commodities, as tobacco and rice, the people ftarve one another, when they become numerous, and are obliged to leave off planting altogether. Thefe two, indeed, afford employment for labourers throughout the whole year, for which reafon they are fo generally planted; but other commodities are very different in this refpect. The making either of filk, wine, or oil, alone, does not employ the labourers above two or three months in the year, and for that reafon will not maintain them; and as they have no other employments, they cannot follow any one of thefe. This is the great obftacle to all thefe improvements in the colonies. Thus they complain, for example, they cannot live by making filk, as they make but a pound or two in a feafon; but as this requires only fix weeks in the fpring of the year, if they had a crop to fucceed this in fummer, and a vintage after both in autumn, as they have in all countries where thefe commodities are

observations in both, that our colonies enjoy the fame climate with Eaft-Tartary, China, Corea, and Japan, the products of which are fo rich and valuable. Here then we might have many of the moft valuable commodities for the colonies; and as thefe are fo totally different from any thing that Britain produces, they might for ever keep the colonies from interfering with their mother-country, and preferve a lafting connection and correfpondence between them. Moft of the ftaple commodities of America came from the Eaft, as fugar, rice, cotton, coffee, indigo, &c.

made,

made, they might from them all get a better living
than by manufactures, which they cannot do by
any one of them alone. It is only by thefe means
that whole countries can ever be maintained, merely by their agriculture, without manufactures. .

✱✱✱✱✱✱✱✱✱✱✱✱✱✱✱✱✱✱✱✱✱✱✱✱✱✱✱✱

REMARKS on the TRADE and late REGULA-
TIONS of the COLONIES.

BY the cuftom-houfe accompts, from the year
1756 to 1765, inclufive, the following is the
ftate of the trade between Great-Britain and North-
America, on an average :

	£.	
Exports from Britain	2,037,577	
Imports into Britain	857,056	
Balance due to Britain	1,180,521	
Total Exports in thefe nine years	£. 18,338,199	
Total Imports	7,713,506	
Total Balance due to Britain in nine years	10,624,693	

Now, as the colonies exported to the value of
eighteen millions, and owe five or fix millions to
Britain, they cannot have paid more than thirteen
millions in thefe nine years, which is one million
four hundred and forty-four thoufand pounds per
annum ; and as people who are fo much in debt
are

are obliged to pay their all, this muft be their annual income, and agrees with the above account of
their produce.

Now, as their enumerated commodities amount to £. 767,000
The value of their non-enumerated commodities
   muft be   677,000
                                                              _____
                                                       Total 1,444,000

But as the entries at the cuftom-houfe are well
known to exceed the real value of the exports, this
income of the colonies cannot be fo much as thefe
accounts make it; and cannot exceed one million
four hundred thoufand pounds per annum.

Befides this, they owe a public debt of feven
hundred and fixty-feven thoufand pounds. Thus
their public and private debts amount to more than
fix millions of money; the intereft of which alone,
at five per cent, comes to three hundred and fifty
thoufand pounds; but as many of them pay eight
per cent. according to the cuftom of the trade, the
intereft of their debts may be reckoned half a million a-year; efpecially, if we add the lofs they fuftain in the exchange by making remittances of
money, which has of late been thirty and forty
per cent. and the ten per cent. they pay on protefted bills, with fix per cent. per annum till they are
difcharged. If we add this to the balance of trade
they owe to Britain, the two amount to their whole
income.

If we deduct this intereft of their debts, lofs of
exchange, and protefted bills, from their income

VOL. II.   E e   above-

above-mentioned, their net income is but nine hundred thoufand pounds a-year; which is the whole
of what all the colonies in North-America have to
purchafe their neceffaries from Britain. This fum,
divided among three millions of people, is but fix
fhillings a-head per annum. Even if we allow
their income to be a million and a half a-year, it
is but ten fhillings a head.

Thus the colonies have to difcharge a debt of
fix or feven millions, to pay an annual balance
of nigh one million, and to maintain three millions
of people, out of an income of a million and a half
a-year, at moft, which is certainly impracticable.
How then does it appear, " they can certainly
bear more, they ought to pay more?" as we are
told by the author of the late Regulations concerning the colonies.

To fupply them with neceffaries from Britain, not
to mention many other articles, would require at leaft
three pounds a-head. At this rate, three millions
of people would fpend nine millions a-year; but
as their income is only a million and a half, the
difference of feven millions and a half muft be
looked upon as a national lofs, which we render irreparable by taxes, duties, confinement of their fettlements, &c. all which oblige them to fupply
themfelves: and, by thefe proceedings, we deprive the nation of the advantages which might
be reaped from the colonies, for the impracticable
attempt of raifing one hundred thoufand pounds,
to maintain Canada and Florida.

Their

Their expences in the war have involved them in great part of this debt. It appears from the certificate of the commander in chief, that he had twenty thousand provincial troops under his command, besides what they had in other services: to pay these troops, they raised about six millions, and owe that sum to Britain.

In these circumstances, it is impossible that they should have any money. The balance of trade they owe to Britain would, in one year, drain them of all the money they have, were it five times more than it is. They have no way to get money but by a trade to the West-Indies, the balance of which is against them. Hence, in all these colonies, you hardly meet with any thing but paper money. This paper occasions a trade and circulation, it is true; but as the balance of that trade is so much against them, it drains them of their current cash.

Thus their trade and paper-currency drain them of that money which their agriculture brings in; and obliges them to make their own necessaries, instead of purchasing them here.

But if this is the case of the most fruitful countries, what can we ever expect from North-America? or from the produce of the poor and mean lands there, the greatest part of which will hardly yield the bare necessaries of life? What could any one ever expect from a little tobacco, rice, pitch and tar, or fish, the chief products of North-America, to maintain two or three millions of people. The advantages of the North-American trade seem not to be considered in a public light. If

E e 2

they

they are of fmall value, they are, on that account,
more profitable to the public ; becaufe they are
grofs and bulky, by which they are fources of
navigation, and fupport the maritime power of the
nation.   If you calculate the freight, commiffion,
and charges, on the products of North-America,
they amount to half their value ; which is all clear
gain to Britain, but is fo much deducted from the
income of the colonies.

Thus the colonies, which produce ftaple commodities for Britain, are a much greater advantage to the nation than feems to be apprehended.
They pay, one with another, one half of all that
they make, for tranfporting and vending the reft,
which is all expended in Britain.   By that means,
you get their all, and cannot poffibly have any
more.   Were they to have the profits only of tranfporting and vending their own products, their income would be double of what it is ; but as thefe
are now all reaped by Britain, to deprive it of this,
is to rob the nation of its beft income.   This is
the advantage of the colonies, and the tax which
they pay for their protection ; which is much more
advantageous to the nation than a petty revenue.

Befides this deduction on their products, and the
heavy duties upon them, the colonies pay all the
taxes of Britain on every thing they confume ; as
it is well known, all taxes fall on the confumers,
whoever may firft pay them.   Now, as thefe
taxes on Britifh goods amount at leaft to fifty or fixty per cent. is not this much more advantageous

vantageous to the nation than a petty revenue ? Were they to pay one hundred thousand pounds in taxes, they must supply themselves with manu-factures to that value : the public would lose the taxes and duties on these goods, the merchants their profits, and the nation the benefit of the trade and navigation; which losses would amount to twice or thrice as much as the tax. "We would therefore humbly recommend it to such gentlemen as are guardians of the trade of the nation, (says Mr. Gee) that our own interest is not mistaken for that of the planters." Instead of taking mo-ney from them, he, who was a very good judge, thinks it necessary to lend them money, to improve their plantations, for the benefit of Britain. With-out such improvements on their lands, it will be impossible for them to purchase a tenth part of their manufactures from Britain.

But we are told, " they do not plead poverty, but privilege." It appears, by many letters from the colonies, that their great objection against in-ternal taxes was, the being taxed by those who were unacquainted with their condition and cir-cumstances, and the proper ways of levying such taxes among them, or the consequences of them; and that the proposed taxes and regulations would be highly detrimental to the mother-country : but as these were not regarded, it put them upon making the plea of privilege.

But it is urged, " the whole sum expected to be raised by the stamp-duty was one hundred thou-

fand

fand pounds a-year; the repartition of this upon one million five hundred thoufand people, at which the loweft computation eftimates the prefent inhabitants of that country, would not draw from each perfon more than half the value of a day's labour in North-America *.

If their circumftances are bad, it is alledged, " England has even furnifhed them with refources to raife the revenue fhe has required ; the bounties given to them on flax, hemp, and timber, would enable them to fupport the new impofitions." But thefe bounties have proved ineffectual. Timber will not bear the charge of tranfportation from North-America, and if they make

hemp

---

* We are told by the author of the Regulations, p. 61 " they can earn three fhillings and fixpence per diem by their agriculture ;" to wit, by making tobacco at a penny a pound; or corn at two or three fhillings a bufhel, by which, it is certain, they do not earn as many pence a day. In the tobacco-colonies they make more by their agriculture than in any others ; and although they are or have been all employed in it, yet eight hundred thoufand people make but about three hundred thoufand pounds a-year by their tobacco, which is but feven fhillings and fixpence a-head per annum ; and not above ten or twelve fhillings, including all the other branches of their agriculture. The labourers, who are about a fifth or fixth part, make about fifty fhillings a-head per annum, or three pounds at moft, which is but two-pence a day ; and that appears to be the value of labour on plantations in North-America. They who eftimate the price of labour in the colonies, by the day, do not know what their labour is, and much lefs the value of it. There is no fuch thing as day-labourers on plantations, and it is inconfiftent with the defign of them, to admit of any.

On

hemp or flax, it is only for their own manufactures, which will not furnish them with sterling cash to pay taxes, unless they vend their manufactures, which such an imposition must have forced them to do. It must indeed be owned, that the granting of this bounty was a very just and commendable measure, and intended for the benefit of the nation ; but the misfortune is, this, with all the others, are more likely to prove a loss and detriment, than any benefit, either to Great-Britain or the colonies.

Besides these pretended resources, it is alledged, " the increase of the establishments there furnishes them with another fund, which alone would more than balance the account. These establishments are in Canada, Nova-Scotia, Georgia, East and West Florida, with which the colonies have nothing to do. All that they can expect from these new set-tlements

---

On plantations, every one is employed by the year, in order to make a crop, which lasts for a twelvemonth. Now, the wages of such labourers are four or five pounds a year for men, and forty shillings for women, who are the chief manufacturers ; this brings the price of labour, at a medium, to three pounds a-year, which is but two-pence a day, for every day in the year.

The dearness of day-labour in the colonies proceeds from two causes ; first, the labourers who are thus employed by the year, in order to make a crop of staple commodities for Britain, and their provisions with it, may lose their whole crop by neglecting it for a few days, and cannot spare a day's work, without losing ten times as much as it is worth, and perhaps their whole year's subsistence.

Secondly, If there are any common labourers to be found, who are not engaged by the year, as there seldom are, they can-

not

tlements is, to interfere with them; and cut off so much of their refources in remittances to Britain, which muft prove equally prejudicial to both.

It is a very fallacious argument to fay, " the expenditure was reftrained to that country ;" becaufe it was ordered, " that all the produce of the American duties fhould be paid to the deputy-paymafter, in America, to defray the fubfiftence of the troops;" for thefe troops were kept in the new governments, Canada, Nova-Scotia, and Florida, and not in the colonies which were to have paid this money for their fubfiftence.

It was propofed to have raifed one hundred thoufand pounds annually by the ftamps, and nigh as much more by the cuftoms and duties on their trade, which appears, by all accounts, to be as much money as is in all the North-American co-

not find employment for above a few days in a month perhaps; and for that reafon, they muft have as much for two or three days work, as will maintain them for as many weeks ; but at the year's end, they have not perhaps earned two-pence a day for all the wages they may get, which is generally a fhilling a day, fterling cafh.

About populous towns the cafe is very different, and labour much dearer : they do not there make the neceffaries of life, which enhances the price of labour ; they have likewife a variety of employments, and a demand for labourers, who are employed on plantations in the country, and by that means are fcarce and dear. Thus we are not to eftimate the price of labour from a few towns, as Bofton, New-York, or Philadelphia, which we only hear of in Britain. Thefe are not plantations, but trading or manufacturing towns.

lonies :

lonies: this they were fo fenfible of, that though
we are told here, " they did not plead poverty,
but privilege ;" yet the faculty of lawyers, in New-
Jerfey in particular, gave it as their opinion to the
chief juftice, " there was not as much money in
the country as would pay the ftamp-duties alone
for one year ;" and the fame was generally believed
in all the other colonies, including the other taxes.
Hence, the execution of the ftamp-act muft at any
rate have been impracticable, and as ruinous in its
confequence, efpecially to Britain, as it was, by all
true friends of liberty, deemed in itfelf to be arbitrary and unjuft.

The plaufible pretence, indeed, that is ufed for
all thefe meafures, is, that " this expence is neceffary for their own defence and protection." Can
it be fuppofed, that thefe colonies, which are now
fo much more populous and powerful than ever,
and are entirely free from an enemy, by which they
were before furrounded, can now want any fuch
defence and protection ? They never before had
above four, or at moft fix, independent companies in all North-America ; and can they now want
fifteen regiments ?

Befides, the colonies are defended by their militia, which they are at great expence to raife and
train : every perfon in them, capable of the fervice, is obliged to bear arms, and to be provided
with them at their own expence ; and fuch an expence of a ftanding army, with their militia, is the
more

more grievous, as they have no manner of ufe nor occafion for it. They who would make that ex_pence neceffary for their protection, do not under_ftand what their fafety and fecurity confift in. The colonies muft defend themfelves with their hands, and not with their purfes. If any fervice of this kind is expected from them, it muft be a *fervitium in capite,* a perfonal fervice, and not a pecuniary fervice, in fterling cafh. In the laft war but one, the colonies were repaid the money they expended in defending themfelves, and protecting his majefty's dominions, as it was thought they could not well bear the burden of one or two hundred thoufand pounds; but now, the authors of the ftamp-act and regulations, would have exacted money from them, when they had raifed fix millions, and had quite exhaufted themfelves by thefe public fervices.

The protection of all the Britifh dominions, both at home and abroad, depends upon the fleets and maritime powers of Great-Britain; and not on a few troops difperfed up and down in the deferts of Canada and Florida, at fuch a diftance from all the colonies on that continent, as well as every other part of the king's dominions, that they can neither defend them, nor be defended by them. This protection, which the colonies both want and get from the mother-country, they fupport and maintain by the trade and navigation to them, and by paying the charges of all the Britifh fhips

and

I

and mariners, numerous as they are, which are con-cerned in that trade: for this they pay at leaft one half of their whole income, which is the tax they pay for their protection; and is as great a one, if not greater, than is paid by any Britifh fubjects; and ten times more advantageous to this nation than all the taxes that were impofed upon them could ever have been *.

It is upon this trade to the plantations, that the fafety of the whole nation depends, and more parti-

---

* Total amount of Britifh fhips and feamen employed in the trade between Great-Britain and her colonies on the continent of America, of the va-lue of goods exported from Great-Britain to thefe colonies, and of their produce exported to Great-Britain and elfewhere; on an average of three years.

Colonies	Ships	Seamen	Exp. from G. Brit.	Exp. from Colonies.
Hudfon's Bay	4	130	£. 16,000	£. 29,340
Labrador American veffels, 120				49,050
Newfoundland (2000 boats)	380	20,560	273,400	345,000
Canada	34	408	105,000	105,500
Nova-Scotia	6	72	26,500	38,000
New-England	46	552	395,000	370,000
Rhode-Ifland, Connecticut, and New-Hampfhire	3	36	12,000	114,500
New-York	30	330	531,000	526,000
Pennfylvania	35	390	611,000	705,500
Virginia and Maryland	330	3,960	865,000	1,040,000
North-Carolina	34	408	18,000	68,350
South-Carolina	140	1,680	365,000	395,666
Georgia	24	240	49,000	74,200
St. Auguftine	2	24	7,000	
Penfacola	10	120	97,000	63,300
	1,078	28,910	3,370,900	3,924,606

cularly

cularly of Great-Britain itfelf. It ought never to
be forgot, for the fafety of Great-Britain, what was
fo very remarkable in the fpring of the year 1756,
when England was threatened with an invafion,
and could not man a fleet for fix weeks, on account
of an eafterly wind which blew during the whole
time of that imminent danger, till a wefterly wind
brought our fhips home from America, after which
our fleet was manned in a week or two. To
ruin this trade to the colonies, therefore, as it muft
have been, for the fake of a petty revenue, which
could neither be paid nor collected, was the certain
way to deprive the whole nation, both at home and
abroad, of the only fafety and fecurity it enjoys.
Of this we have another moft convincing proof,
during the very fhort time that thefe regulations
lafted in America; when we are told, by a very
good judge, and credible eye-witnefs on the fpot,
that "twenty thoufand feamen and fifhermen were
turned out of employ, and the fhipping they
ufed to navigate and improve, were hauled up,
and laid by as ufelefs."

This lofs of trade by the late regulations is the
more to be regarded, as they feem to have been calculated on purpofe to ruin the colonies of New-England; which are, and always have been, the bul-
wark of all the Britifh dominions in America, to
whom this nation owes both the fifhery of Newfoundland, the only thing in Britifh America that
wants protection, and all her other poffeffions in
the northern parts of that continent.

How

How infufficient the troops kept in North-America are to protect the colonies, abundantly appeared upon the late infurrection of the Indians. The troops were difperfed in the deferts of Canada and Florida, from Quebec to Penfacola, Mobile, and St. Auguftine, at fuch a diftance from the colonies, that they could give them no relief: they could not be drawn out of garrifon there, left thofe acquifitions fhould be left entirely defencelefs ; and by that means the colonies, waiting for their affiftance, were over-run and maffacred by a few Indians, for a year or two together ; till fome volunteers from Virginia and Penfylvania joined a fmall party of the troops, and fubdued them. Now, if the colonies fhould be invaded by a foreign enemy, what protection could they expect from thefe troops, who could not defend them from a handful of Indians ?

Hence it clearly appears, that this expence, which is fo burdehfome to the nation, is entirely needlefs. All the conquefts made by the glorious fucceffes of the war, amounting in value to fix or feven millions a-year, were given up for thefe deferts of Canada and Florida ; and for that reafon they muft be fupported as valuable acquifitions, although at a great expence, and to the ruin of the nation. This was the defign, and only ufe, of taxing the colonies, or of keeping fuch a force in North-America, after both Canada and Cape Breton are reduced.

As for the defence and fecurity of our colonies, Crown-Point and Niagara would have fecured

cured them, both from the Indians and French, even when they were in poffeffion of Canada, and much more now, when they are drove out of it; but Quebec and Montreal will do neither. Thefe, or Florida, are no greater feeurity to our colonies, than a fort in the Orkneys would be to England. The fecurity we obtain is from the expulfion of our enemies, and not from maintaining them in the country, to put the nation again to all the expences which have been fo lately incurred on their account. The only object in all thefe northern parts of America is the fifhery, for which Canada is of no ufe nor fervice.; Canada can be nothing but a factory for the fur trade, and Nova-Scotia only a fifhing fettlement, of both which this nation already has too many.

It has indeed been given out, that thefe taxes on the colonies were to relieve the fubject at home; but even if the colonies had paid their taxes, Britain would have been involved in an additional debt, for the fupport of Canada and Florida, over and above that aid. The whole of the intended taxes on the colonies amount to one hundred and fixty thoufand pounds a-year, when the expence incurred is nigh five hundred thoufand pounds; wherefore, Great-Britain muft ftill have been burdened with a charge of three hundred thoufand pounds per annum, over and above what the colonies were to have paid; by which laft, fhe muft have loft twice or thrice as much. Thus the whole charge and lofs to Great-Britain would have been

between

between fix hundred thoufand pounds and feven hundred thoufand pounds, a-year, with the probable lofs of her intereft in the colonies to the bargain. Thus the nation is doubly indebted to the colonies, for faving her this needlefs and ruinous expence.

As for the making of a profitable colony of Canada and Nova-Scotia, that is contrary to nature itfelf. Unlefs they live by their agriculture, they can be of no ufe or fervice to this nation ; but that is certainly not to be expected, either in Canada or Nova-Scotia. Their agriculture would not even maintain the colonies of New-England, which could not fubfift without the fifhery. In thefe northern parts of America, nature has provided that plentiful fource of fubfiftence for mankind in the feas, which fhe has denied to the land.

The only object, therefore, in all thefe northern parts of America, as we have faid, is the fifhery, and unlefs we have that, we get nothing by the fettling of the country, but a burden and charge, which they will not defray. There is not even the leaft profpect, that any of thefe northern fettlements will ever be able to defend themfelves; and for that reafon, they put the nation to fuch an expence for their defence and protection, and muft expofe it to perpetual infults, if not to new wars and troubles, on their account.

Many may perhaps think, that this may be done by fettlements in the country adjacent to the fifhery ; but we are well fatisfied, that fuch fettlements

are

are more likely to prove a means of loſing the
fiſhery. St. John's, in Newfoundland, is the old-
eſt ſettlement in all North-America, but is not yet
able to defend itſelf againſt two or three ſhips;
and all the reſt of theſe paltry fiſhing ſettlements,
north of New-England, are, and are ever likely
to be, in the ſame defencelefs condition. We ſhall
never raiſe a force in theſe, or any other countries,
ſufficient to defend them, where the people cannot
ſubſiſt by their agriculture, or rather have no ſoil or
climate fit to cultivate. Yet, notwithſtanding it
is ſo difficult to raiſe a force ſufficient to defend
and ſecure theſe countries, there are more ports
and harbours in them to be defended, than are
perhaps in all Europe, excluſive of Great-Britain
and Ireland. The whole coaſt, both of Newfoundland and Nova-Scotia, is one continued harbour,
and expoſed to every fiſhing veſſel; while there is
but here and there a ſpot fit for ſettlers to inhabit,
and thoſe at ſuch diſtances from one another, that
they can neither ſupport, nor be ſupported by, each
other. It is for theſe reaſons, that ſuch ſettlements
can never be in a poſture of defence, although
they are expoſed to every invader, who may hold
the country, and command the fiſhery, by that
means, which they could not otherwiſe do. Britain muſt ſecure both theſe and all her other dominions, by her fleets, which theſe ſettlements will
rather weaken, by interfering with the Britiſh
fiſhery; and muſt thereby deprive the whole nation of that ſecurity which they are intended to

4　　　　　　　　　give,

give, if they do not again involve it in another war.

Thus the only advantage the nation can expect from the reduction of Canada and Cape Breton, is a security for the fishery ; and if that were rightly improved, it might, no doubt, be rendered a very great national benefit ; but by settling those countries, it is to be feared, we shall deprive the nation of all the advantages which might otherwise be reaped from them.

If the nation, in the prosecution of the war, exerted itself at home, the colonies did the same abroad, and bore even a greater share of the burden, in proportion to their abilities, than Great-Britain herself : and altho' this was no more than their duty to do, yet it was not certainly all done for themselves. Nova Scotia gives Britain a command of the fishery, and the advantages reaped from it ; whereas, it can only interfere with the colonies, and may deprive them of that which in New-England is the chief, if not the only, means of their support. How then does it appear, " whatever may be the value of the acquisitions in America, the immediate benefit of them is to the colonies ?" or that " they profited so much by the war ?" All our acquisitions are not worth one groat to them. The sole acquisition is the fur trade, which is still enjoyed by Canada ; and the colonies only have their former share, which is no object either to them or to Great-Britain *.

The

* By the custom-house account of the importation of furs, since the reduction of Canada, the whole fur trade of North-

The only object for the immediate benefit of the colonies, or for the interest of Great-Britain in them, are fruitful lands to cultivate, that will pro-duce staple commodities ; of which they have not got one foot since the peace, though this was the other great and principal object of the war ; be-ing excluded from the Ohio and Mississippi, by the proclamation issued for that purpose. Thus if they were at such expences, or gained any advan-tages in the war, they have been deprived of them since the peace. But if they were even possessed of them, they would not so soon raise sterling cash, to pay taxes. The making of new settlements is a matter of expence, and not of immediate benefit or profit ; and the colonies should rather be re-lieved from taxes, and supported with credit, to enable them to be at that expence, than burdened with such impositions to maintain Canada and Florida. They have formerly been in debt to Bri-tain, by the settling of new plantations, which paid their debts ; but now they are in debt, for want of such fresh lands, and have no way to pay even their just debts, or to purchase absolute neces-saries : if we would enable them to do either of these, proper regulations should be thought of for this purpose ; by which alone either Great-Britain or the colonies, can indemnify themselves for their expences in the war, or recruit their circumstances after it. But instead of these, nothing seems to be

America, south of Hudson's Bay, cannot be estimated, on an average, at above forty thousand pounds per annum.

thought

thought of but trade, which at the beſt is a very improper, buſineſs for colonies, who ſhould only trade with their mother-country ; and for want of commodities to trade in, which they can only have from their agriculture, the North-American colonies are very conſiderable loſers by their trade, as we have ſhewn above. If they would gain any thing by their trade, they ſhould ſupply themſelves with their own neceſſaries from the produce of their lands, and ſhould make their imports, which they now conſume, articles of commerce : this is the firſt regulation wanted in the colonies, and might very eaſily be complied with. By that they might make, with their gains, and the ſavings of what they now expend, at leaſt half a million a year ; and Great-Britain might ſave nigh as much in Canada and Florida, which, with the return of ſo much from the colonies, are articles amounting to a million a-year, and highly worthy of conſideration.

Next to theſe, the regulations moſt wanted in the colonies are ſuch as concern the improvements of their plantations in ſtaple commodities for Britain, which are equally intereſting to them and to their mother-country. If we would expect any thing from them, we ſhould firſt put them in a way of making it. This is to be done by two ways, as we have ſaid, either by extending their ſettlements to new and freſh lands, and more favourable climates, or by improving their old plantations ; the firſt of which depends upon Great-Britain, and the laſt is more particularly the buſineſs of the colonies ; although there is little hopes of ſeeing it done without the

encou-

encouragement and affiftance of their mother country. A little laid out upon fuch an occafion,
would be the beft harveft they ever reaped? It is
in this manner that the colonies fhould be taxed,
both for their own benefit and the intereft of the
whole nation. Such taxes may be paid in the commodities propofed, when they cannot poffibly pay
others, till they are enabled by the produce of their
lands. This would likewife enable them to pay
their debts, and to purchafe their neceffaries from
Britain; whereas, all other taxes deprive them of
the means of both.

For this purpofe, fome encouragement has been
given to the growing of hemp and flax, and the
getting of timber; but thefe are never likely to be
a lafting ftaple of any of our colonies, and are at
the beft but very infignificant refources for fupport-
ing fo many countries, and maintaining fuch a number of people. Since thefe therefore are fo infufficient to anfwer the purpofe, fome other methods
fhould be thought of, to promote fuch a fignal intereft of the nation, of which any one or two that
can be propofed would not be fufficient.

Thus the repeal of the taxes impofed upon the
colonies is fo far from being a facrifice of the higheft permanent interefts, and of the whole majefty,
power, and reputation of government, as many
feem to think, that it appears to be the only way
to fecure them *.

By

* The dignity and power of government was fecured by the
wife and juft law enacted, " to bind the colonies fubjects of
Great-

' By taxes, you firſt oblige the people to ſupply themſelves, independent of Great-Britain, and
then to carry on a trade with other nations, in order to raiſe money, both of which are equally oppoſite to the " higheſt permanent intereſts and government of Great Britain." The daily and great
increaſe of the people in North-America muſt
render their income and abilities either to purchaſe neceſſaries or to pay taxes, ſtill leſs than at
preſent, unleſs they have both manufactures and a
trade in them. Even if they were to make all the
improvements in ſtaple commodities that could
well be propoſed or thought of, they would never
pay taxes. Before they can make theſe, the people
will be twice as numerous as they are, and their
income, if it were ten times as great as at preſent,
would hardly be ſufficient to purchaſe their neceſſaries from Britain.

Thus it ſignifies nothing, whether Great-Britain has
a right to tax her colonies, or not, ſince it would be
the greateſt loſs and detriment to the nation ever to
exerciſe that right. The nation gets both their money,
if they have any, and their effects, by trade ; and can
expect none by a revenue. Upon theſe accounts, it
is abſolutely neceſſary to repeal totally the taxes im-
poſed upon them, as it was equally contrary to the
very nature of things, and the intereſt of Great Bri-

Great-Britain, in all caſes whatſoever," as they ought to be ; but
that cannot extend to impoſſible caſes, ſuch as the taking of money from them, when it is impoſſible they ſhould have any.

tain, that they fhould ever be able to pay them, till they enjoy all the profits of their own labour, and of a trade in the produce of it, which is to make them independent.

Many indeed feem apprehenfive, that the total repeal of the late acts may make the colonies more inclinable to affert an independence. The inhabitants of the colonies, like all other Englifhmen, have ever had a firm attachment to their mother country, and her government, on account of the invaluable bleffings they enjoy from her happy conftitution and form of government : this has hitherto fecured to them thofe liberties and privileges, which they derive from her, and are as tenacious of as all other Englifhmen ; this is the great band of union between the colonies and their mother country, which we fhould diffolve, by depriving them of the liberties and privileges of their fellow-fubjects, which they have hitherto enjoyed, and think they are entitled to by their birth-right, in common with all other fubjects of the realm. They know very well, if they were to throw off the mild and aufpicious government of Great-Britain, they muft be fubject to tyrants of their own, and expofed to invafions from their enemies. Their liberties, fafety and fecurity, are a certain pledge for their allegiance and dependence, which is above all others. This is a band of union between them and their mother-country, founded on the nature and reafon of things, and the rights of mankind, which are as lafting as the world itfelf, if not counter-acted.

Befides

Befides this, there is as great a tie of union from their interefts, which are mutual, and naturally connected together. The colonies which produce ftaple commodities for Britain could not find fuch another market for them; and even thofe which produce nothing of that kind, have the liberty of vending their products in other parts of the world, and the advantage of a trade with Great-Britain at the fame time. To cement their union, therefore, and to make it lafting, nothing is wanting but totally to repeal the late acts, and fecure their property by fuch a trade, both in public and private tranfactions, under the prefent happy conftitution.

F f 4 BRITISH

BRITISH ISLANDS

IN THE

AMERICAN WEST-INDIES.

❧❧❧❧❧❧❧❧❧❧❧❧❧❧❧❧❧❧❧❧❧❧❧❧❧❧

JAMAICA.

THIS ifland, one of the Great Antilles, was difcovered by Columbus, in his fecond voyage to America; but it does not appear that he made any fettlement there, upon its firft difcovery: however, it is pretty certain, that he entertained fo favourable an opinion of Jamaica, that he marked it out as an eftate for himfelf. On his fourth expedition to America, a violent ftorm obliged him to run into this ifland a fecond time, where he was relieved from the greateft dangers and diftreffes. His fhips being rendered, by the ftorm, fo abfolutely unfit for fervice as to admit of no repair, Columbus prevailed upon fome of the failors to pafs over in a canoe to Hifpaniola, to reprefent his calamitous fituation to the governor, and to requeft veffels to carry his peo-

ple,

ple. Eight months elapfing without the leaft intelligence from his meffengers, or affiftance from the governor, the natives were incenfed at the delay of the Spaniards, (the fubfifting them being a heavy burthen upon their poverty) and brought in provifions very fparingly; whereupon the feamen mutinied in great numbers. This mutiny confiderably weakened the admiral's authority and ftrength, whilft the natives were further exafperated at the diforders committed by the mutineers; but Columbus found means to recover his authority among the natives. Forefeeing a vifible eclipfe of the moon, he fummoned the Indian chiefs, and, by means of an interpreter, acquainted them, " That the God whom he ferved, provoked at their refufing to fupport his fervants, intended a fevere judgment upon them, of which they fhould fhortly fee a manifeft fign in the heavens; for that the moon, on fuch a particular night, would appear bloody, an emblem of their fpeedy deftruction." His prediction, though ridiculed at firft, when accomplifhed, terrified the barbarians exceedingly. They fell at his feet, and befought him, in the moft moving manner, to avert the judgments which threatened them, and brought him plenty of provifions, which he accepted, charging them to atone for their paft faults by their future generofity. This ftratagem afforded him a temporary relief; but he faw no profpect of getting out of the ifland, and the mutiny of his men was in danger of growing general, when a

fhip

fhip appeared in the offing, fent by Obando, the governor of Hifpaniola, who had refolved not only to abandon, but to infult that great man in his misfortunes. The captain of the veffel was a mortal enemy to Columbus, and the defign of this voyage was only to be a witnefs of his diftrefs; for he forbade his crew all manner of communication with the admiral or his men, and after delivering him a complimentary letter, embarked, without even flattering him with the leaft hope of relief.

Thus abandoned, his firmnefs and prefence of mind did not forfake him; without betraying the leaft fign of difappointment or grief, he told his men, in a chearful manner, that he was promifed an immediate fupply; that he had refufed to depart in this fhip, becaufe fhe was too fmall to carry them all; and that he was determined not to quit the ifland, until every one of his crew might enjoy the fame conveniency. His eafy and compofed air, and the care he fhewed for his people, far beyond his own prefervation, reconciled their minds, and made them, in general, await their fate with patience. But fenfible that his ftay might be very tedious in the ifland, and that his affairs would grow worfe every day, he came to a refolution of taking vigorous meafures with the refractory: he accordingly fent his brother with a proper force, well armed, to treat with them, and, if neceffary, to compel them to obedience. The captain of the mutineers, grown infolent with a long courfe of licentioufnefs, not only rejected the admiral's terms, but offered violence to

his

his brother; who attacked the rebels with so much resolution, that ten, with their chief, were slain in a moment; the rest fled, and were soon after obliged to submit.

The admiral might have spent his whole life in this miserable exile, if a private person, actuated by esteem for his merit, and compassion for his misfortunes, had not fitted out a ship for his relief, which brought him safe to the island of Hispaniola, where he refreshed himself and his men for some days, and then sailed for Spain; but did not live long after his arrival.

Some authors are of opinion, that Columbus, during his residence upon Jamaica, founded the town of Metilla; no improbable circumstance, when we reflect, that the natives were fully reconciled to the Spaniards before they quitted the island. His son and family built St. Jago de la Vega, and several other towns, which were abandoned, on account of the advantageous situation of St. Jago, which in a short time contained one thousand seven hundred houses, two churches, two chapels, and an abbey. The court of Spain, notwithstanding its ingratitude to Columbus, having granted both the government and property of Jamaica to his family, his son was the first European governor, with the title of duke de la Vega. But the descendants of the great Columbus degenerated from his virtues; and having no idea of any West-Indian acquisition that did not produce gold and silver, neglected improving Jamaica, studying only to
raise

raife their rents, and opprefs the planters. Columbus had preferred this iſland on account of its ſitu-
ation·and populoufnefs ; but his defcendants,, or
their fubftitutes, murdered ſixty thouſand of the
natives, under the moſt exquifite tortures.

We are but little acquainted with the particulars
of the Spanifh commerce.while they poſſeſſed Jamaica. In 1596, Sir Anthony Shirley, who commanded an Englifh fquadron, took and plundered
the town of St. Jago. In 1635, colonel Jackfon,
in his paſſage from the Leeward Iſlands, landed
five hundred men, and, after driving two thouſand
of the ·enemy from· their works at Paſſage Fort,
made himſelf maſter·of the town of St. Jago,
with the loſs of forty men, and received a confiderable ſum by way of ranſom for the town.

The iſland came into our poſſeſſion during the
ufurpation of Cromwell, by means of a formidable
armament fitted out with a view to reduce the iſland
of Hifpaniola, under the command of colonel Venables and admiral Penn, who ſailed from England
with feven thouſand land forces, moſtly veteran
troops. The army was greatly reinforced by the
inhabitants of Barbadoes and the other Leeward
Iſlands, and, on the 13th of April, the fleet arrived off Hifpaniola. The place of their landing was ill chofen ; the army had near forty
miles to march before it could act, and the
foldiers difheartened, fainting and dying with
the exceſſive heat of the climate, and the want
of proviſions, and difcouraged yet more by the
cowardice

cowardice and difcontent of their officers, yielded
an eafy victory to a handful of Spaniards, and reimbarked ignominioufly, with great lofs.

The principal commanders, a little reconciled by
this misfortune, and afraid to return back to England without ftriking fome decifive ftroke, refolved to
attempt Jamaica, before the inhabitants could receive news of their repulfe from Hifpaniola, knowing the ifland was in no good pofture of defence.
They accordingly exerted themfelves vigoroufly, to
avoid the miftakes which had proved fo fatal in the
former expedition; the officers who had fhewn an
ill example by their cowardice were feverely punifhed, and orders were given to fhoot any foldier
who fhould turn his back to the enemy.

On the 2d of May the troops were landed on
Jamaica, and laid fiege to St. Jago, the capital.
The inhabitants being in no condition to oppofe
fo ftrong a force, would have furrendered immediately, but for the ftrange delays of our generals and their commiffioners. The town however, at laft, capitulated; but not until the inhabitants had fecreted their moft valuable effects in
the mountains. The whole ifland fhared the fate
of its capital; for though Spanifh parties fometimes attempted to furprize the Englifh from the
woods, yet they never appeared in a body, and at
laft found means to convey themfelves and their
effects to Cuba.

The viceroy of Mexico, underftanding that
the mulattoes and negroes had been left in the
woods,

woods, fent orders to the governor of Cuba to fupply the exiles with whatever was neceffary for retaking the ifland, and promifed to fupport them with a proper land force. They accordingly returned thither; but lived difperfed in the weods in fo miferable a manner, that the five hundred regulars, who were fent to their affiftance, refufed to affociate with them, and fortified themfelves at St. Chereras, in the northern part of the ifland, where they foon received confiderable reinforcements. In the mean while, the Englifh began planting the fouth and fouth eaft parts of the ifland, of which colonel D'Oyley was left governor, with three thoufand men; and Penn and Venables returned to England, leaving a large fquadron for the protection of the ifland, under the command of vice-admiral Godfon.

Cromwell refolving to truft no officer recommended by Venables, whom he fufpected of favouring the royal caufe, fent major Sedgwick, with a reinforcement of one thoufand men, to fuperfede D'Oyley. In the mean while, the Spaniards, at St. Chereras, having been reinforced with thirty companies, befides artillery and provifions, from Cuba and the continent, had thrown up feveral formidable works at Rio Nuebo, in the precinct of St. Mary's. D'Oyley attacked them, drove them from their works in a few days, with great lofs, and demolifhed their intrenchments. They next attempted to make a ftand at Point Pedro, from which they were likewife driven, and were obliged,

at

at laft, to return to Cuba; leaving the Englifh in quiet poffeffion of Jamaica.

The Spanifh negroes and mulattoes, however, ftill kept in the woods and mountains, where they fubfifted by game and plunder. Part, perceiving themfelves abandoned by the Spanifh regulars, murdered their governor, chofe one of their own number, fent a deputation to D'Oyley, and delivered up their arms : but another party of them ftill remained, headed by fome of the old Spanifh inhabitants. The negroes who fubmitted were very ufeful in clearing the ifland of the remains of the Spaniards, who were entirely rooted out, and not above twenty or thirty of their negroes left upon the ifland in a year's time ; but they knew the inland parts of it fo well, that they could not be diflodged, and afterwards proved very dangerous enemies. Major Sedgwick having died a few days after his arrival, D'Oyley ftill continued governor, and acted with equal wifdom and refolution. But while the colony was improving beyond all example, a fpirit of mutiny infected the army. The ringleaders, colonel Raymond and lieutenant-colonel Tyfon, were probably encouraged, by their knowing how difagreeable D'Oyley was to Cromwell ; but he had the courage to bring them both to a court-martial, where they were fentenced to be fhot, which was accordingly executed. By this time, Cromwell had ordered colonel Brayne, in Scotland, to embark with a thoufand men, from Port Patrick, for Jamaica, to fuperfede perſede D'Oyley ; but that gentleman likewiſe died ſoon after his arrival : and it is very remarkable, that D'Oyley remained governor at the time of the Reſtoration.

Soon after the Reſtoration, colonel D'Oyley was ſucceeded by lord Windſor as governor of Jamaica, who, in 1663, was ſucceeded by Sir Thomas Modiford, who, having a great eſtate at Barbadoes, had retired to Jamaica to aggrandize himſelf, as ſeveral other wealthy planters had alſo done. The Engliſh inhabitants at Jamaica had, by this time, increaſed in number to between ſeventeen and eighteen thouſand ; but its chief trade conſiſted in their depredations upon the Spaniards, which, in all probability, were winked at by the governor.

Modiford, who knew better than any man of his time the intereſt of the Engliſh Weſt-India iſlands, introduced into Jamaica the art of making ſugar, of planting cocoa groves, and erected ſalt-works ; ſo that the arts of induſtry began to prevail over the old habits of the planters, and the iſland wore a new face. However, many of the old planters were too much attached to their former cuſtoms to abandon them ; and hence ſprung up the buccaneers, whoſe proceedings make ſo great a figure in the hiſtory of the Weſt-Indies. They conſiſted of adventurers of all nations, who reſorted to Jamaica, on account of the vaſt conveniency of its ſituation for plundering the Spaniards, and, when aſſembled, bound themſelves down to certain regulations, that would have done honour to a more virtuous inſtitution.

A

A Portuguefe pirate founded the fraternity; but being drowned as he was conducting a prize to Jamaica, was fucceeded by a Dutchman of Brazil, nicknamed Braziliano, who, when but a private man, being chofen ringleader of a mutiny, ran away with the fhip, and intercepted a rich Spanifh veffel, homeward-bound, the cargo of which, confifting chiefly of ready money, he and his companions fquandered at Jamaica, in the moft abfurd and tafteless extravagance. When their money was fpent, they again went to fea, and took another prize; but being taken upon the coaft of Campeachy, were condemned to be hanged: however, their fentence was mitigated to their ferving in the gallies, from whence they efcaped, and returned to Jamaica, where they continued to follow their former piratical practices. In this depredatory war, one Scott, a Welfhman, who plundered Campeachy, and Mansfield, an Englifhman, diftinguifhed themfelves; and another Englifhman, Davis, brought from the Sack of Nicaraqua above fifty thoufand dollars for his own fhare of the plunder. He afterwards formed an expedition againft St. Auguftine, and fucceeded, though the caftle was garrifoned by two hundred men. But the moft diftinguifhed of all was Henry Morgan, a Welfhman, who, being of a roving difpofition, went when young to Barbadoes, from whence he removed to Jamaica, commenced pirate, and ferved as Mansfield's lieutenant in the expedition againft St. Catharine's, which they attacked and took, with fifteen ships and five hundred men, leaving one Simon as governor on the island, with a garrison of one hundred men. The buccaneers were so elevated by this conquest, that they would have proceeded against Panama itself, had they not received intelligence that the Spaniards were prepared to receive them; upon which, they retired to the island of Tortuga, in the Gulph of Mexico, about fifteen miles from the continent.

In confequence of the complaints made by the court of Spain against the buccaneers, Modiford was fent for home in custody, and Sir Thomas Lynch, who fucceeded him, received orders to check them. But they, not conceiving that any practices could be illegal that brought in money to themselves and the Jamaicans, had the confidence to propose to Lynch to make a settlement upon the isle of St. Catharine's; which demand he refufed. Mansfield retired in discontent to Tortuga, where he died; and Simon was obliged to surrender his government, by capitulation, to the governor of Costa Rica. Morgan now became head of the buccaneers, and behaved with unparalleled boldness. His first expedition was against Puerto del Principe, which he took, and shared fifty thousand dollars among his crew; which being composed of different nations, the French here abandoned him, on account of the death of one of their countrymen.

It is difficult to reconcile the behaviour of the court of England at this time, towards that of

Spain,

Spain, to the principles of good faith. It is true, the Spaniards laid claim to places, and exclusive rights of commerce in America, which the English had never allowed; but still both crowns had always kept up a good correspondence, and had mutually promised a redress of grievances. Morgan's next enterprize was against Puerto Velo, a rich city in the district of Panama, which he plundered of two hundred and fifty thousand dollars, besides other rich merchandize; all which centered in Jamaica. After this successful expedition, he, in a little time, had under his command fifteen ships and nine hundred men, with which force he made an unsuccessful attempt upon Hispaniola; but afterwards attacked and took Macaraibo, upon the Terra-Firma, where the booty he made was equal to what he got at Puerto Velo, besides destroying three Spanish men of war off the harbour.

Morgan, with all the vices of a pirate, was no spendthrift; he more than once endangered his life by depriving his men of what they judged their just due. Notwithstanding this, the fame of his successes was such, that at his rendezvous next year at Tortuga, he found himself at the head of two thousand men, and thirty-seven sail of ships. He now projected the conquest of Panama itself. To facilitate this enterprize, he took possession of St. Catharine's island, while Brodely made himself master of Fort Chagre, where he remained with a garrison of five hundred men, to secure a

G g 2   retreat.

retreat. With the remainder, Morgan then marched against Panama, the inhabitants of which
oppofed him with more fpirit than was expected. Nothing could equal the difcouragements which he encountered in this expedition.
Finding the river that led towards the city impaffable by large fhips, he was obliged to leave a detachment to take care of his fleet and artillery, and to
embark part of his men on board canoes, while
others marched by land, for fix days, under moft
inconceivable miferies, from the heat of the climate
and want of provifions. They had fcarcely made
a junction, before they were attacked by the governor of Panama, with four regiments of foot,
and two fquadrons of horfe, whom they defeated,
with the lofs of fix hundred men. The victors
immediately pufhed on to the city, mounted the
walls, without the affiftance of artillery or fcaling
ladders, and, after fome difpute, became mafters
of Panama.

Morgan made ufe of his fuccefs with no great
moderation; and ftands accufed of fetting the
town on fire, without confulting any of his companions, the better to conceal the true account of the
plunder he had fecured for himfelf. He remained
four or five months in Panama, during which time
he laid the adjacent country under contribution,
and iffued his orders with the utmoft coolnefs, in
which he was punctually obeyed by his men.
When he left Panama, it is faid, that the gold,

silver,

silver, and precious spoils of the city, loaded one hundred and seventy-five beasts of burthen; and his prisoners amounted to six hundred, whom he obliged to ransom themselves. In his retreat, he plundered the town of Cruz, and demolished the fortifications of Chagre. Upon the division of this immense booty, each share did not amount to above fifty pounds; which exasperated his men afresh against their commander, whom they accused of defrauding them. Morgan, apprehensive their discontents might end in a mutiny, sailed with four ships, whose crews he had gained over to his interest, to Jamaica; and is said to have carried with him four hundred thousand dollars, on his own account, leaving the rest of his companions at Chagre.

In 1670, the Spanish and English crowns signed a treaty, the articles of which were confined to America only. At the time this treaty was concluded, Charles II. was resolved to put a stop to the depredations of the buccaneers; and John lord Vaughan succeeded Sir Thomas Lynch in this government, who was sent home to answer for his conduct in encouraging them. There is reason to suppose that Morgan, when upon his expedition against Panama, got intelligence of what had passed between the courts of England and Spain; for he declared, he would give over buccaneering the moment he arrived at Jamaica.

Though Vaughan had strict orders to put a stop to the piracies against the Spaniards, yet he seems

to

to have brought over a pardon for paſt offences of this kind, which had been accepted by Morgan; for about this time he was knighted, on account of his valour, and was made one of the commiſſioners of the admiralty at Jamaica, where he had purchaſed a large eſtate, and was making very conſiderable improvements. Jamaica, at this time, laboured under the ſame misfortune as Barbadoes, by the inſtitution of the Royal African company of England, whoſe ſhips, aſſiſted by thoſe of the crown, ſeized all Jamaica veſſels which they found trading to any part of Guinea, and, under pretence of their charter, committed terrible depredations upon the Jamaica trade; and, as the importation of negroes is ſo capital a point with all the Sugar Iſlands, muſt have ruined them, had not the trade been laid open by parliament.

An incident which happened at this time was of great ſervice to Jamaica, though judged prejudicial to our Weſt-India trade in general. England ceded to Holland Surinam, a very flouriſhing ſettlement, in conſideration of certain ceſſions made by the Dutch in North-America; a ſcheme dictated by the duke of York, for the benefit of his North-American friends. The Surinam Engliſh were ſettled at Jamaica, in St. Elizabeth's precinct, to the number of fifteen hundred planters, beſides their families, where lands were aſſigned them to cultivate.

Lord Vaughan was ſucceeded, in 1678, by Charles, earl of Carliſle, during whoſe adminiſtration,

tion, the people of Jamaica entertained the fame apprehenfions that then filled all England, as if the French, Irifh, and Englifh papifts had entered into a confpiracy to exterminate the proteftants. Their alarms were not a little increafed by the neighbourhood of Monf. d'Eftrees, with a ftrong fquadron; and Lord Carlifle's time, during his government, was almoft wholly fpent in making preparations to receive the enemy, or in ufing endeavours to remove the apprehenfions of the people. The climate difagreeing with his conftitution, he returned to England in 1680, leaving Sir Henry Morgan deputy-governor; who, to make amends for his former conduct, was extremely vigilant againft pirates, and furprized, in Cow bay, a pirate floop, commanded by one Everfon, a Dutchman, but manned by Englifh. Everfon was killed in the engagement; but the crew, as no proof of their depredations on the Spaniards could be obtained in Jamaica, were fent to Carthagena, to be tried and punifhed by the Spanifh government.

In 1682, Sir Thomas Lynch, a warm loyalift, was again appointed governor of Jamaica; and, to wipe off the fufpicion he had formerly incurred of encouraging pirates, exerted himfelf the more remarkably in fuppreffing them. Sir Henry Morgan, notwithftanding his great fervices, was fent prifoner to England. He pleaded the commiffion of the governor and council of Jamaica, and the public thanks they had given him, in defence of his actions; but this did not prevent his fuffering a

G g 4 long

long minifterial profecution, without being brought
to a trial, to the ruin of his health and private
fortune. The affembly, about this time, gave a
fubflantial proof of their loyalty, by continuing
his majefty's revenue in the ifland for twenty-one
years.

Under Sir Thomas Lynch, feveral excellent laws
were paffed for the good of the ifland. Notwithftanding all his care, the French, Dutch, and fome
Englifh pirates ftill continued to infeft thofe
feas; many of them having French commif-
ons, that crown being then at war with Spain.
The king's fhips, the Ruby and Guernfey, were
perpetually cruizing to. windward againft them;
and the governor fitted out a galley, which
was of great fervice in fcouring the coaft. The
Englifh commanders, however, were greatly puz-
zled how to behave towards fuch pirates as carried
French commiffions, and who never offered any
violence to the fubjects of England. The king of
France, however, foon found that no benefit accrued to himfelf, or his fubjects, by his granting commiffions to pirates, who, when opportunity offered, plundered all nations equally; and
therefore difpatched orders to his governors in
America to recall all French commiffions that had
been granted to thofe free-booters, who were hence-
forward to be deemed common pirates.

Colonel Hender Molefworth fucceeded Sir Thomas Lynch, and proclaimed king James the Second's acceffion in the ifland, with great folemnity,

ty, and transmitted home a most loyal congratu-
latory addrefs. A post-office was foon after erected in Jamaica; and, in 1687, the duke of Albermarle, fon of him who had fo great a fhare in the
reftoration of Charles II. having impaired his fi-
nances, was fent governor to this ifland, where he
might retrieve his fortune, as to a kind of honourable banifhment, for his zeal againft popery. On
Sunday, the 19th of February, this year, a moft
dreadful earthquake was felt all over the ifland,
which damaged a vaft number of houfes, and ruined many fugar-works. The fad confequences of thefe
earthquakes had been frequently felt by the Englifh
fince they had been in poffeffion of the ifland, having neglected the precautions of the Spaniards, who
built their houfes very low, with light roofs, and
piles driven deep into the ground. The duke did
not long enjoy his new government; the climate,
and hard drinking, haftened his death. Little
worth notice occurred during his government. A
proclamation indeed was publifhed, for the more
effectually fuppreffing pirates in America; but this
was little elfe than mere matter of form, they being quite rooted out before this time. Upon the
duke's death, colonel Hender Molefworth was, by
the council and affembly, again appointed governor.
About this time the Revolution happened, and a
convention was entered into between Spain and
England for fupplying the Spanifh Weft-Indies
with negroes; whereupon Don St. Jago del
Caftillo, afterwards knighted by king William,
was appointed Spanifh commiffary at Jamaica.

In

In 1690, the earl of Inchiquin was appointed governor. On the 29th of June following, a dangerous conspiracy broke out among the negroes. In 1691, the French attempting a settlement upon Hispaniola, lord Inchiquin had orders to dislodge them, if possible. Accordingly, he dispatched the Swan and Guernsey men of war, the Quaker ketch, and a large transport, with nine hundred men, to Hispaniola. This armament raised great expectations ; but only took a few small vessels at sea, and destroyed a few inconsiderable works by land.

On the 27th of June, 1692, Jamaica was visited with another most dreadful earthquake. Port Royal, the finest and most populous town in the West-Indies, was totally destroyed. The wharfs sunk down at once, and water to the depth of several fathoms filled the place where the street had stood : the earth, in opening, swallowed up people, and threw out their bodies in other parts of the town, and with such rapidity, that some of them lived many years after. Northward of the town, a thousand acres were sunk, mountains were split ; and no fewer than two thousand souls perished in the town. The ships in the harbour shared this disaster ; several were lost, and the motion of the sea carried the Swan frigate over the tops of houses, without oversetting. The rest of the island suffered in proportion. In short, its horrors were so great as to exceed all description.

But the earthquake itself was far less ruinous to the island than its consequences. At least three

thou-

thoufand white inhabitants died of peftilential difeafes, caufed by the putrid effluvia that iffued from
the apertures. The lofs which the planters and merchants fuftained was immenfe ; but the affembly
humanely exempted the fufferers from paying large
fums as duty upon wine that had been deftroyed.
Before the Jamaicans had time to recover themfelves, the French invaded the north fide of the
ifland with three hundred men ; but the Guernfey
man of war, and fome other floops, burnt their fhips,
and deftroyed or made prifoners all who had landed, excepting eighteen, who made their efcape in a
floop. An annual faft was inftituted in commemoration of this dreadful judgment.

Lord Inchiquin dying in Jamaica, in 1692, was
fucceeded by colonel William Beefton, who on this
occafion was knighted ; and, upon his arrival,
remedied a number of abufes that prevailed
during the former government*. In 1694, Sir
William Beefton receiving information, that three
fifty-gun fhips had arrived at Petit-Guaves, from
France, put the ifland into a proper ftate of defence.
His intelligence proved true : On the 17th of June,
the three French men of war, in company with
about feventeen privateer-floops and tranfports,
commanded by Monf. du Caffe, the French governor of Hifpaniola, appeared off the ifland, and
landing their troops at Cow Bay, about feven

* In 1693, agents were firft appointed for fettling the colony's affairs in England, with a falary of four hundred and fifty
pounds per annum.

leagues

leagues eaft of Port Royal, plundered the plantations, and after committing a great many barbarities retired, upon the approach of fome Englifh
forces. They next landed fifteen hundred men in
Carlifle Bay, in Vere parifh, to the weftward of
Port Royal, and attacked a breaftwork defended by
two hundred Englifh, whom they compelled to retreat, after a very fmart engagement. In the mean
time five companies of foot, and fome horfe, advancing againft the enemy, made them retreat precipitately, with confiderable lofs. The two following days were fpent in continued fkirmifhes, in
which the French loft a great many men, and fome
of their beft officers. This difcouraged them from
proceeding in the enterprize : under the cover of
night they reimbarked their men, and fet the prifoners afhore, having loft in this expedition above
feven hundred men.

The next year a fquadron was fent to Jamaica,
under the command of captain Wilmot, with twelve
hundred land forces on board, to make an attempt
upon the French fettlements in Hifpaniola, in concert with the Spanifh governor of St. Domingo.
Colonel Lillingfton, who commanded the land-
forces, landed his men within three leagues of Cape
Francois, the principal French fettlement in Hifpaniola, on the 18th of June, amidft a brifk fire
from the enemy, while Wilmot bore up within cannon-fhot of the fort. Wilmot, in fearching for a
place to land, narrowly efcaped falling into an ambufcade ; however, next night he returned with an
addi-

additional force, which fo daunted the French, that they immediately blew up their fort, fired the town, and retreated in the night with the utmoft precipitation, leaving behind them forty. pieces of cannon, unfpiked, which fell into the hands of the Englifh, who next morning plundered the town.

Port au Paix, the ftrongeft French fettlement in Hifpaniola, was next attacked. Wilmot waited fome days in expectation of the arrival of the land-forces; but being difappointed, landed a party of feamen about five miles eaft of Port au Paix, and deftroyed the plantations to the walls of the fort, which was built in the form of a quadrangle, and landing his heavy artillery, in a few days, opened fome batteries to the weft of the fort, which the feamen ferved fo furioufly, that the French foon abandoned the place; but were intercepted in their retreat, and almoft all their officers flain, or taken prifoners. Such in general is the account of this expedition, which might have been ftill more beneficial, had Wilmot followed his inftructions literally, which were to act againft Petit Guaves, and to deftroy in his return the French fifheries on the banks of Newfoundland. Wilmot died on his paffage to England, where the fleet arrived in a miferable condition.

In 1696, Monf. de Pointis, with a powerful French fquadron, made a feint of attacking this ifland; but though he had on board two thoufand buccaneers, the Jamaicans made fo good a fhew, that he fheered off without making any attempt

on

againſt it. By this time, admiral Nevil, in conjunction with a Dutch ſquadron, had ſailed in queſt of him; but De Pointis receiving intelligence of his being in thoſe ſeas, bore away for the Bahama iſlands; but at laſt fell in with the Engliſh ſquadron; from which he eſcaped, tho' one of his richeſt ſhips, valued at two hundred thouſand pounds, was taken, and carried into Jamaica. Admiral Nevil, in concert with the Dutch admiral, Meeſe, attacked and burnt Petit Guaves; but died of a broken heart on his paſſage to Virginia, having been refuſed admittance into the harbour of the Havannah. De Pointis more fortunate, eſcaped a ſecond time from an Engliſh ſquadron, which he found lying at anchor in the Bay of St. John's, in Newfoundland, and a third time from a ſquadron commanded by captain Harlow, which he outſailed.

One Paterſon, a Scotchman, learning from Dampier, and other Weſt-Indian adventurers in London, that the iſthmus of Darien was inhabited by an independent people, who would willingly permit any European nation to ſettle in their country, on condition of aſſiſting them againſt the Spaniards, formed a project for peopling this ſpot with his countrymen; and for raiſing in Holland, Hamburgh, &c. ſubſcriptions towards carrying it into execution. Upon this project was grafted another, for a trade between Scotland and Africa, notwithſtanding the charter of the Royal African company. The ſcheme met with prodigious encouragement; and an act was paſſed in Scotland

for

for erecting a company, called, the company of Scotland trading to Africa and the Weft-Indies; with great immunities, which occafioned an univerfal ferment in England ; petitions and remonftrances were prefented to the king by the Eaft-India company, France, Spain, and Holland, who all complained of the Scotch project, as utterly inconfiftent with their commercial rights : even both houfes of parliament remonftrated, that the late Scotch act, if carried into execution, muft abfolutely deftroy the moft valuable branches of the Englifh commerce.

The Scotch, however, continued raifing fubfcriptions, with uncommon fuccefs, particularly in Hamburgh, where an hundred thoufand pounds were fubfcribed ; upon which his majefty ordered the Englifh refident at Hamburgh, to threaten the fenate with his higheft difpleafure, if they entered into any treaty with the Scotch. Thus they were difappointed in their great expectations at Hamburgh, as well as in England. Repeated addreffes from the company, and even from the parliament of Scotland, were prefented to the king, without their receiving any fatisfactory anfwers ; yet their difappointment was far from damping their zeal : four hundred thoufand pounds were fubfcribed, noble offices and warehoufes were erected, and four fixty-gun fhips, befides tranfports and tenders, were built for the fervice of the colony.

At length, three of their fhips, and two tenders, with two hundred men on board, failed from the

Frith,

Frith, in 1698, and arrived safe in the Bay of Darien, and immediately took poffeffion of St. Catharine's ifland, which they fortified, its port being
fecure and capacious enough for fhips of the greateft burthen. Orders were now fent to the feveral governors of the American provinces and Weft-India iflands, ftrictly prohibiting them to give the
Scotch any fupply. In the mean while, the Spanifh
governor of Santa Maria attacked the new fettlement; but was defeated, with the lofs of an hundred men, and taken prifoner. Great part of their
provifions having been confumed during their
voyage, they were foon threatened with famine,
being unable to comply with the exorbitant demands of thofe who would have carried on a
'clandeftine trade with them; and thus were forced
to abandon the fpot which had feemed to promife
fuch immenfe riches. Their miferies after quitting
Darien were inexpreffible: thofe who arrived at
Jamaica were confidered as little better than pirates,
and received no other relief than what they paid
for with their few remaining goods. Scarcely
had the firft colony abandoned Darien, before a
frefh recruit arrived; but their principal victual-
ling tranfport having been burnt by accident, they
too were obliged to quit the colony. A third
embarkation, better provided than either of the
former, landed foon after, but mifcarried, through
the divifions of thofe who had the management
of it; fo that, unable to refift the Spaniards, they
alfo abandoned the fettlement, by capitulation.

In-

In 1699 admiral Benbow arrived at Jamaica, with a confiderable fquadron; but during his paffage, a peftilential diftemper carried off an incredible number of feamen, which difabled this active commander from undertaking any expedition againft the enemy this year. Two Englifh men of war were caft away near Hifpaniola; and Fort Charles, in Port Royal, was blown up by accident. In the courfe of the following year, Sir William Beefton died, and was fucceeded, in April 1701, by major-general Selwyn, who died foon after his arrival. Upon his death, Peter Beckford, Efq; was appointed lieutenant-governor by the council. A war now breaking out between England and France, on account of the duke of Anjou's fucceffion to the Spanifh crown, admiral Benbow exerted his utmoft endeavours to intercept the French fleet under Monf. du Caffe, whom he indeed defeated; but through the cowardice and difobedience of four of his captains, after a running fight that lafted two or three days, was obliged to defift, before he had effected the total deftruction of the French fquadron. In this engagement, the admiral had his leg broke by a chain fhot, of which wound he died foon after. The two captains, Kirby and Wade, were fhot for cowardice; Hudfon died before his trial; and Conftable was cafhiered from her majefty's fervice, for breach of orders, and neglect of duty. Upon the admiral's deceafe, rear-admiral Whetftone took upon him the command of the fquadron at Jamaica, where the

fpirit

spirit of privateering was now very strong. A small squadron from thence plundered and burnt a town called Toulon, about twelve miles from Carthagena. The fleet then sailed up the river Darien, and being joined by the Indians, attacked the fort of Santa Maria, got possession of the mines, and, in three weeks time, gained fourscore pounds weight of gold dust, besides discovering some plate that had been buried by the inhabitants ; and afterwards burnt the town, and carried off the negroes. Some vessels went farther up the river, in search of another mine, but without success ; and two sloops landed near Trinidada, which they plundered and burnt.

Lord Peterborough, who upon the death of Mr. Selwyn had been appointed governor, never went to the island ; but, in 1703, colonel Handasyde was appointed lieutenant-governor by the crown, soon after whose arrival, the town of Port Royal was burnt to the ground : however, the two royal forts, and magazines, were not damaged ; nor any of the ships in the harbour burnt, except one brigantine and a sloop. The assembly voted, that Port Royal should not be rebuilt; and that the inhabitants should remove to Kingston. Port Royal continued a long time a mere heap of rubbish ; but a small handsome town has been since built on the same spot.

In 1704, vice-admiral Graydon arrived with a squadron. On his passage, he fell in with Du Caffe's fleet, which had just escaped from admiral Ben-

bow,

bow, and was very foul and leaky. Captain Cle-land, of the Montague, attacked the sternmost ship; but was instantly called off by Graydon, who pretended the urgency of his orders, in excuse for this shameful conduct. Having collected what force he could at Jamaica, and the other West-Indian islands, he sailed for Placentia, in Newfoundland, and held a council of war, where it was determined, that the French were too well prepared to justify an attack, and accordingly returned to England. On his arrival, he was dismissed the service, for his misbehaviour.

In the mean while, admiral Whetstone destroyed a great many French and Spanish ships, in their harbours, and brought off an hundred and twenty prisoners, with a very considerable booty. Among the ships he destroyed, were four French privateers, that were intended to plunder the island. The privateers were equally successful. Captain Kerr, who commanded the squadron during Whetstone's return to England, behaved with the utmost tyranny, and was suspected of holding a correspondence with the French. The Jamaicans, however, prosecuted him in England with such effect, that he lost his commission, and the instruments of his tyranny were punished. At this time, the Jamaicans were dissatisfied with the conduct of their governor, who had suffered one Rigby to monopolize several of the most lucrative employments in the island. The assembly passed a bill against such engrossments, which, after some alterations, was at

last

laft allowed in England. The differences between
the governor and affembly ftill continuing, lord
Archibald Hamilton was fent over as governor,
who arriving in July, 1711, deferred the meeting of the affembly, by the advice of Rigby, Bro-
derick, the attorney-general, and one Stuart, a phy-
fician, all violent Tories. Hoftilities ftill continued
between France and England, in the Weft-Indies ; ·
and the French admiral Coffart, after making a
defcent on Montferrat, threatened Jamaica. The
univerfal confternation for fome time fufpended
party heats ; and an embargo was laid on the fhipping, which proved fatal to many of them, through
a terrible hurricane, that deftroyed the canes all
over the ifland, and did incredible damage, though
it lafted but fix hours.

The great numbers of Scotch and Irifh who attended lord Archibald to Jamaica, difgufted the inhabitants ; as feveral arbitrary acts of government
were committed to fupply thefe hungry adventurers, particularly, lands were feized, under pretence of being efcheated to the crown. Thefe practices were at laft fo flagrant, that the affembly
paffed three acts ; the firft, for preventing any perfon from holding two offices or pofts in the ifland ;
the fecond, for regulating exorbitant fees ; and the
third, for quieting men's poffeffions, and preventing
vexatious fuits at law. The ifland, at this time,
was in a moft deplorable fituation. Its governors,
bred up either in the army or navy, refided in
chancery, where their will was their law ; the chief
                                        juftice

justice had a few years before been a cabbin-boy, but marrying a planter's widow, had become a judge; and all the other judges and justices in the island were of the same stamp.

After the peace of Utrecht, the ships of war which had been stationed here being recalled, the merchants and principal inhabitants applied to the governor to grant letters of marque, for the security of the island against free-booters. Some of these commissions being abused, a great clamour was raised against lord Archibald; which increased, when sloops were fitted out from Jamaica for fishing upon the wrecks of some rich Spanish ships, lost near the Bahama islands, of which the governor of Cuba complained, as an infraction of the treaties between the two crowns. At the accession of George I. the Jamaicans raised a purse of a thousand pounds, for the encouragement of their agents in England, employed to obtain redress of their grievances; and lord Archibald was recalled, and sent prisoner to England, upon a charge of encouraging piracy, of which he was afterwards acquitted, and Peter Haywood, Esq; appointed in his room, who was almost immediately succeeded by Sir Nicholas Lawes, an eminent planter. Sir Nicholas repaired the fortifications of Port Royal; and observing, that the remains of the buccaneers and pirates, who did infinite prejudice to the English trade, always found a ready asylum in the Spanish settlements by embracing the Roman catholic religion, requested commodore

H h 3   Vernon,

Vernon, to demand satisfaction of the governor of Trinidada for the depredations of the Spaniards; to demand Nicholas Brown and Christopher Winter, as traitors and pirates; and to threaten reprisals, in case of a refusal. But his menaces were in vain; and Sir Nicholas, not chusing to proceed to the execution of his threats, published a proclamation for apprehending Brown and Winter, with five hundred pounds reward for each. These rough proceedings against the Spaniards were far from being agreeable to the people in general, on account of their lucrative trade with the Spanish West-Indies, and produced a breach between the assembly and the governor, who threatened, that if they did not comply, the government would take advantage of the precariousness of their tenures, and secure his majesty's interest, without their assistance. But all political differences were suspended for a time by a most terrible hurricane, which happened on the 30th of August, 1722, and did incredible damage. In the beginning of May this year, the Launceston took a Spanish guarda costa, with fifty-eight men, which had taken a Jamaica snow, six leagues off Hispaniola. As such captures were infractions of the treaties subsisting between the two kingdoms, the governor, council, and captains of his majesty's ships, held a council of war for trying them; and forty-three being convicted of piracy and robbery, were executed. This severity was far from closing the breach between the governor and the assembly, so that he desired to be
recalled;

recalled; but not before the militia had been formed into a regiment of horfe, and eight regiments of infantry; a regulation the more neceffary, as the runaway negroes were grown formidable, and made excurfions as far as Spanifh Town.

Such was the fituation of affairs, when the Jamaicans employed in their defence the Mofquitos, an Indian nation on the continent, inhabiting a fandy bay between Truxillo and Honduras, where they were driven by the Spaniards, from Honduras. During the government of the duke of Albermarle, thefe Indians put themfelves under the protection of England. Ever fince, upon the death of their king, the next heir repairs to Jamaica, where he proves his title to the crown, and receives his commiffion from the governor. They are a quiet, inoffenfive people, except to the Spaniards, who drove them from their native country, for whom they have an invincible averfion; and are fo well defended by mountains and moraffes, that the Spaniards have never been able to conquer them. About the year 1690, they obtained a confiderable victory over the Spanifh Indians, and were fince invited to refide in Jamaica; but their love of independency made them refufe this offer. No American Indians are more expert hunters and fifhers; and they are fo ufeful at fea, that moft Jamaica traders engage fome of them in their fervice. Their king, or fome of their chiefs, always compliment a new governor on his arrival, and are treated with great civility. Their manners and cuftoms greatly

refemble thofe of the other Indian nations. Two
hundred of thefe Indians were formed into two
companies, under their own officers, with regular
pay; who, during their ftay upon the ifland, which
was but a few months, did very confiderable fervice
againft the negroes.

The differences between tne governor and affembly, who feem to have affumed an independency
incompatible with the principles of the Englifh government, ftill continuing, the duke of Portland, a
great fufferer by the South-fea fcheme, was appointed to fucceeed Sir Nicholas Lawes; and colonel Dubourgay was made lieutenant-governor,
who had been nominated to the fame place under
Sir Nicholas, but had never exercifed his office.
His grace, with his dutchefs, after touching at Barbadoes, where they were magnificently entertained,
arrived at Jamaica the 22d of December, 1722.

The duke was far more affable, and eafy of ac-
cefs than any of their former governors; and the
iflanders, on the other hand, fettled five thoufand
a-year upon his grace, being double what had been
allowed to any former governor. Great inteftine
divifions fubfifting among the iflanders, fome of
whom were upon very bad terms with the affembly
and council, his grace exerted himfelf to the utmoft
to reconcile their differences. But one of the moft
difficult parts of his adminiftration had relation to
an old claim which had been fet up by the Jamaicans, of having their laws rendered perpetual,
though it had been always difcouraged by their governors;

vernors; but they were in hopes, that the generous provision which they had made for the duke would induce him to comply with their requeſt; and accordingly, foon after his arrival, paſſed a law to that effect; to which his grace gave a negative, acquainting the aſſembly, " That the affair had been conſidered at home; and that the objections to it were of ſuch weight; as not to leave the leaſt room to expect that the bill would meet with his majeſty's approbation." His grace met with another great difficulty, the ſettling of the ſilver coin, the value of which had been fixed, by proclamation, in the reign of queen Anne*; but had been diſregarded ſo far by the Jamaicans, that they had raiſed their money threepence upon each dollar; which produced a repreſentation from the principal Weſt-India merchants, both at Jamaica and London, to the then ſecretary of ſtate, in conſequence of whoſe advice his grace undertook to remedy the evil, and ſucceeded.

	£.	s.	d.
* Seville pieces of eight, old plate	0	6	0
Ditto, new plate	0	4	$9\frac{1}{2}$
Mexico pieces of eight	0	6	0
Pillar pieces of eight	0	6	0
Peru pieces of eight	0	5	$10\frac{1}{2}$
Croſs dollars	0	5	$10\frac{1}{2}$
Ducatoons of Flanders	0	6	7
French crowns, or grand ecu.	0	6	0
Cruſados of Portugal	0	3	$9\frac{1}{2}$
Rixdollars of Germany	0	6	0
Dutch three guilder pieces	0	6	$10\frac{3}{4}$

The

The great quantity of uncultivated land, contrary to the tenor and fpirit of the original grants, had long been a fubject of complaint in England ; becaufe, had they been properly improved, the fugar trade muft have been extended, and the French checked in their vaft fale for thofe commodities in the European markets : an evil apparently owing to the felfifh views of the great planters, who, though poffeffed of vaft tracts of improveable fugar lands, did not chufe to cultivate them ; the fcarcity of fugars keeping their price high enough to anfwer their end, without being at farther expence. His grace ftrongly recommended the removal of this abufe to the council and affembly; but to little effect. The bad ftate of the high roads, occafioned by the vaft conveniences of water-carriage, was another object which he recommended to the legiflature of the ifland, who removed the grievance ; fo that at prefent there are convenient communications between all the principal parts of the ifland. The want of clergymen of piety, morals, and reputation, being alfo a third matter of complaint, owing chiefly to the uncertain provifion made for them, an ample provifion was now fettled for the clergy. The endowment of the minifter of St. Catharine's was fixed at three hundred pounds per annum ; that of Port Royal at two hundred and fifty pounds ; three others, at two hundred pounds per annum ; and all the reft at one hundred and fifty pounds per annum, which, with the large perquifites, might be juftly confidered a comfortable provifion.

In

In 1726, the growing connections between the Imperial and Spanish courts having given umbrage to the English ministry, admiral Hosier was sent with a squadron to prevent the arrival of the Spanish treasures in Europe for that year, in order to disable the court of Madrid from executing the schemes it had formed in favour of the pretender. The duke of Portland did not live to see the event of this expedition; dying of a fever on the 4th of July, 1726, sincerely lamented by the whole island.

Hosier arrived with his squadron before Porto-bello, and demanded the South-Sea company's ship, the Royal George, which was instantly delivered to him. The secrets of the British councils, at this time, were very ill kept; for ten days before his arrival at Porto-bello, an advice-boat, from Old Spain, brought an account of his intention, upon which the treasure was relanded, and carried back to Panama; otherwise, he must have met at sea the Spanish galleons, on board which were above six millions sterling. Hosier being tied up from committing any other hostilities than merely preventing the galleons from sailing for Europe, was obliged to lie off that sickly coast till diseases swept away such numbers of his seamen, that he became an object of ridicule to the Spaniards, and of compassion to his countrymen at Jamaica, who generously afforded him succours of all kinds.

After the death of the duke of Portland, the government devolved upon John Ayscough, Esq; as president of the council; a gentleman of unexceptionable

tionable character, who held the administration till
the arrival of major-general Hunter, appointed
governor by his majesty, for his great knowledge of
American affairs. Governor Hunter arrived in the
Lark man of war, on the 29th of January, 1728,
and issued writs for the meeting of the assembly, on
the 21st of March following, who made him a present of six thousand pounds, which he accepted,
notwithstanding the general instructions given to
the West-Indian governors; but refused to grant
him a salary of more than two thousand five hundred pounds per annum.

To enumerate all the Spanish depredations during
his administration, would be endless. The passive
behaviour of the English court rendered the nation
every where contemptible. But the people of Jamaica were not wanting to themselves: they transmitted to England particulars of all their losses, in
the most aggravating terms; which excited so uni-
versal a spirit of detestation against the Spaniards,
that at last a war broke out between the two
crowns, to the great mortification of the English
ministry. Governor Hunter, upon some surmise of
the designs of the Spaniards, laid an embargo upon
the shipping, which was considered as an oppressive
measure, and detrimental to the trade of the island;
and imputing the dissatisfaction of the islanders to
concealed papists, procured an act of assembly; by
which all persons, from sixteen to sixty, were obliged
to abjure the church of Rome. The bill met with
a warm, and perhaps indiscreet opposition; but
the

the governor's intereſt prevailed. He died in March, 1734. Among many other plans for the benefit of the Weſt-India iſlands, Governor Hunter laid one before the government for ſending ſix independent companies, for the protection of the iſland ; a meaſure the more neceſſary, as the rebellious negroes were now very numerous, had inveigled great numbers of their countrymen to join them, and had fortified a paſs in the mountains, called Nawny ; being ſupplied with powder and fire arms by certain Jews, probably employed by the French and Spaniards, who threatened a deſcent.

Mr. Ayſcough now, a ſecond time, ſucceeded to the government, till his majeſty's pleaſure ſhould be known. Senſible of the neceſſity of immediately ſuppreſſing the negroes, martial law took place, by which every man was to become a ſoldier. Captain Stoddart, at the head of a ſtrong party, with three field-pieces, undertook to diſlodge them from Nawny. He accordingly got, before night, to the foot of the hill, and obſerving the utmoſt caution and ſilence, mounted the narrow paſſage leading to it in the dark, without being perceived ; and having got the field-pieces mounted upon the eminence, began to play upon the negroe town with cartridge ſhot and muſket bullets, which killing and wounding great numbers, the whole fled with the utmoſt precipitation. Their town was demoliſhed, their proviſions deſtroyed, and they ſuffered more that day than they had done for twenty years before,

fore, with little or no lofs on the fide of the Englifh; and, after a few other fkirmifhes, were entirely difabled from rebelling again, for many years. By this time, the fix independent companies arrived from England, to whom the affembly gave an additional pay, finding them very ufeful in garrifoning the different pofts of the ifland.

Henry Cunningham, Efq; a Scotch member of parliament, next fucceeded to the government of Jamaica; who owed his preferment entirely to the partiality of the then minifter of ftate, Sir Robert Walpole. Before his arrival, Mr. Ayfcough was dead, and the adminiftration had devolved on Mr. Gregory, who had been chief juftice. Cunningham had feveral altercations with the planters, being inftructed to endeavour to allay the fpirit of refentment againft the Spaniards; and being naturally intemperate, died of a fever, contracted at an entertainment, fix weeks after his arrival. Upon his death, Sir Orlando Bridgman was nominated to the government; but never vifited the ifland. Mr. Gregory, therefore, as prefident of the council, reaffumed the adminiftration of the ifland; but the clamours againft Spain became fo outrageous in England, that the minifter found himfelf under a neceffity of appointing fome man of character and refolution; and accordingly, Edward Trelawney, Efq; was made governor. Mr. Trelawney's firft care was to put the ifland in a proper ftate of defence, and to heal its inteftine divifions. The rebellious negroes, though defeated,

were

far from being fubdued ; and not only kept poffeffion of the woods, and lurking places in the
mountains, but were a terror to all who lived near ;
fo that great tracts of the beft land in the ifland lay
uncultivated. To have attempted to reduce them
by arms, at this time, would have been highly im-
politic, as the Spaniards would have certainly fupplied them with ftores of all kinds. Mr. Trelawney, therefore, offered them pardon and fecurity, which they readily embraced, on condition of
being governed by one of their own number,
fubject to the controul of the governor of Jamaica,
and to the infpection of certain whites, who were to
refide among them.

In 1739, the Shoreham man of war was difpatched to the Weft-Indies, with orders for making
reprifals on Spain, which were received with
the greateft joy ; more efpecially at Jamaica,
from whence great numbers of privateers were in-
ftantaneoufly fitted out. Commodore Brown, who
commanded the fquadron lying there, put to fea
with five fhips of war, and proceeded directly to the
Havannah ; but the officers of the navy not thinking thefe orders fufficiently authorized them to attack the Spanifh fettlements, commodore Brown,
through fear of exceeding his orders, loft feveral
opportunities of diftreffing the enemy.

The arts and influence of the minifter would
have continued to defeat the voice of the nation,
had not the court of Spain baffled all his complying meafures, difdaining even to fave common ap-
pearances ;

3

pearances; fo that at laft his majefty was convinced
how abfolutely neceffary it was to purfue vigorous
meafures. Accordingly, captain Vernon was pitched on to command an expedition againft the Spanifh Weft-Indies, with which he was perfectly acquainted.

Vernon, immediately upon his arrival, attacked
Porto-bello, with only fix fhips of the line, made
himfelf mafter of the town and forts, and entirely demolifhed the fortifications. His next attempt
was againft the town of Chagre, in which he was
equally fuccefsful.

The eftablifhment of the South-Sea company,
and the affiento-contract, gave a fevere blow to the
profperity of the ifland; for its trade with the Spaniards was not only difcouraged at home, as incompatible with the interefts of that company, but the
company alfo complained in fuch terms to the court
of Spain, of the illicit trade carried on by the Jamaicans, that the Spaniards, under pretence of fuppreffing it, had committed all the depredations
which gave rife to the war. The court of Verfailles declaring, that they would not fuffer the
Englifh to make any conquefts in the Weft-Indies, and having fent fquadrons to affift the
Spaniards in bringing home their treafure, the miniftry refolved to fend fuch a naval and land force,
under the command of Sir Chaloner Ogle and
lord Cathcart, as, when joined with the fhips already in the Spanifh Weft-Indies, might be equal
to the conqueft both of French and Spanifh America.

rica. This greatly hurt the trade of Jamaica, by the vast number of hands that were pressed in England for the manning of so large a fleet; so that seamen's wages rose upon that island to the extravagant rate of twenty guineas per man, besides other advantages, for the run home; and few were to be procured even at that rate. This scarcity of hands was the more fatal to Jamaica, as the inhabitants were both able and ready to have fitted out squadrons of privateers, for making attempts and settlements upon Cuba, and other parts of Spanish America; which must have turned out extremely advantageous to the adventurers, and have saved the public vast sums.

Lord Cathcart dying on his passage, the command of the land-forces devolved on general Wentworth, who entertained as great a contempt for the sea service as Vernon did for the army. Thus, from the dissentions that prevailed between the two principal commanders, Carthagena and St. Jago, the capital of Cuba, were attacked in vain; and this expedition, the most expensive ever attempted by England, ended unhappily, though the damage sustained by the Spaniards was estimated at a million sterling.

Notwithstanding the immense national loss sustained by these two expeditions, in which, at least, twenty thousand English subjects perished, though few were killed by the enemy, the Jamaicans were very considerable gainers by the Spanish prizes that were brought into the island, which rendered them very alert in promoting any expedition against the Spanish West-Indies. The reinforcement from England, confisting of near three thousand troops, arriving at Jamaica, on the 15th of January, in a general council of war, at which governor Trelawney was present, it was resolved to surprize Panama, in consequence of a plan laid down for that purpose, by one lieutenant Lowther. An expedition against Panama being a favourite scheme of Trelawney's, he embarked in this as a colonel; but the Spaniards being alarmed, and reinforced by the garrison of Porto-bello, through the negligence of Vernon and Wentworth, the attempt was judged impracticable, at that time, in a council of war, and the forces returned to Jamaica.

Upon their return, lieutenant Hodgson was now sent to the Mosquito coast, to settle at Rattan, in the Gulph of Honduras, one hundred and fifty leagues south-west of Jamaica, and fourteen to the north-west of Truxillo bay, on the Spanish main; a healthy well watered island, about thirty miles long, and thirteen broad. From this step, the Jamaicans promised themselves, exclusive of the logwood-trade, an opening for a commerce with the Spanish inhabitants of Guatimala. Hodgson carried out with him a captain's commission for one Pitts, a logwood cutter, who having been long settled in those parts, had great interest with the Indians; and two hundred of the American regiment, with fifty marines, were sent, under convoy of the Litchfield and Bonetta sloops, to Rattan, with an engineer, stores of

3 all

all kinds, and six-months provision. The settlement was effected without opposition, a town, and fortifications for its defence, were erected, and Pitts appointed governor. Vernon and Wentworth, on their return to England, were graciously received, and both preferred, notwithstanding their mutual recriminations; and Sir Chaloner Ogle remained at Jamaica with the fleet. The spirit of discord, which had possessed Vernon and Wentworth, seems now to have entered into Sir Chaloner Ogle and governor Trelawney; and even swords were drawn in their disputes. Ogle, though brave, was ignorant of every thing but his own profession; and Trelawney, who was of a hasty unforgiving temper, could by no means be brought to a reconciliation with him, which proved very detrimental to the island. Little occurs with regard to the history of Jamaica during the remaining part of the war.

Trelawney was succeeded by Charles Knowles, Esq; Under him the island enjoyed a tolerable share of tranquillity; but the seat of war being transferred elsewhere, the inhabitants no longer partook of the benefits which their situation heretofore threw in their way, and several bickerings arose between them and their governor. The administration at home was now daily troubled with complaints against the planters of Jamaica, from the sugar-refiners and grocers, on account of the high price of sugars; and the affair, at last, was brought before the parliament, where the cause of the Jamaicans

was

was vigoroufly fupported by alderman Beckford,
On the 8th of March, 1753, the committee of the
houfe of commons, to whofe confideration the matter had been referred, reported, that the peopling
of the ifland of Jamaica with white inhabitants,
and cultivating the lands thereof, was the moft proper meafure for the fecurity of that ifland, and for
increafing the trade and navigation between that
ifland and Great Britain, as well as to and from feveral other parts of his majefty's dominions ; and
that the endeavours hitherto ufed by the legiflature
of Jamaica, to increafe the number of white inhabitants, and to enforce the cultivation of lands, in
the manner which may conduce beft to the fecurity
and defence of the ifland, have hot been effectual
for thefe purpofes. A bill was accordingly ordered
in, for the better peopling the ifland of Jamaica
with white inhabitants ; for encouraging the cultivation of lands, at prefent uncultivated in that
ifland ; and for making a proper diftribution of
fuch lands, which was read a firft time ; but the reprefentatives of the council and affembly of Jamaica had fo much weight, that the houfe thought proper not to proceed on the bill till further information was received concerning the ftate of the
ifland.

Mean while, the Jamaicans were peftered with
Spanifh depredations, and in vain fent repeated
complaints on that head to England. The miniftry,
not thinking them of fufficient importance to rifk
a war with Spain, acquainted them, that they
might

might proceed with their own admiralty powers against the delinquents ; the principal of whom were Simon and Domingo de Cuenca, who, after committing the moſt flagrant acts of piracy, coming to trade on the iſland, were apprehended. Their defence on their trial was, that they acted under a commiſſion from the king of Spain ; but as ſuch a plea was ridiculous in a time of peace, they were both condemned ; and orders were ſent from England for their execution; though the Spaniſh ambaſſador had intereſted himſelf greatly in their favour.

The ſeat of government had always hitherto been fixed at St. Jago de la Vega, commonly called Spaniſh Town. As the iſland increaſed in commerce and population, St. Jago, being an inland town, was found to be extremely inconvenient for the merchants, who generally reſided at Kingſton, and complained of the expence that attended their taking out clearances at Spaniſh Town, and the great trouble they were put to in going thither to attend the aſſembly, and the courts of law ; and therefore requeſted the governor to remove the ſeat of government to Kingſton, which he accordingly did. This raiſed him a great many enemies among the planters whoſe eſtates and properties lay near Spaniſh Town ; and nineteen members of the aſſembly ſent over repreſentations againſt him to his majeſty. But a difference of a ſtill more important nature aroſe between the governor and aſſembly. It had always been cuſtomary at Jamaica, for the laws that were paffed to be in force until they obtained the royal affent; but as the government had found very bad effects from the execution of thofe laws in the intermediate time, the governor had been directed not to give his affent to any bill wherein his majefty's prerogative, or the property of his fubjects, might be prejudiced, or the trade or fhipping of the kingdom any ways effected, unlefs a claufe was inferted fufpending the execution of fuch bill until his majefty's pleafure fhould be known. The governor, in adhering to thefe inftructions, embroiled himfelf with the affembly, who, on the 29th of October, 1753, refolved, that they had a right to raife, and to apply public money, without the confent of the government and council, alledging the antient practice, in juftification of this refolution; and feveral other votes were paffed, highly derogatory to the royal prerogative.

Matters now came to fuch an extremity, that the governor was obliged to diffolve the affembly, whom he accufed of invading the royal prerogative, of attempting to alter the eftablifhed conftitution of their country, of having entered into a combination to govern independently, and of endeavouring to fubvert the government, and wreft it out of the hands of the fovereign ; of having fquandered, for years paft, upwards of ninety thoufand pounds of the public money, in gratifications to particular favourites, and in making jobs of their fortifications, and other public buildings, to the great

grievance

grievance of the public, who ought to have another
opportuity of chufing more faithful reprefentatives,
as the whole power of the affembly centered in a
decemvirate. Thefe charges, though perhaps
overftrained, were not groundlefs ; for a very
powerful faction had actually formed an affociation,
which, under a pretext of preferving the tranquillity of the ifland, obliged the members to be
determined in all their proceedings by three fourths
of their own number : this affociation was to fupport the governor in his meafures, as long as he
appeared to have at heart the public fervice ; but
were to join in oppofing him, if it was thought
he acted otherwife, firft giving notice to the other
members.   An extraordinary paper, as it was called, was alfo drawn up, allotting the feveral fub-
fcribers their particular fhares of bufinefs, which
engagements were undoubtedly unconftitutional.
The next affembly did not prove more agreeable
in its complexion, and was likewife diffolved.
Knowles, in his turn, was accufed of arbitrary proceedings, and bad practices. However, the parliament of England, by their refolutions, condemned thofe of the affembly, concerning the raifing and application of money ; and juftified the
governor in the feveral checks he had given to
their proceedings, but were filent with refpect to
the propriety of his removing the feat of government. Upon the return of Knowles to England,
brigadier Háldane was appointed governor, who
died before he entered upon the exercife of his

govern-

government: he was fucceeded by William Lyttleton, Efq; governor of South Carolina ; and the
inteſtine diviſions of the iſland feemed now entirely
at an end.

In 1760, a dangerous confpiracy among the negroe-ſlaves broke out on Eaſter Monday, which
for fome time filled the whole iſland with terrible
apprehenſions. Two Coromantic negroes, belonging to Ballard Beckford, Efq; named Tacky and
Jamaica, had long been concerting a rebellion
with three other chiefs of their country, who were
each to have an eſtate for his good fervices ; but by
the affiſtance of the free negroes fettled at Nawny,
after a few ſkirmiſhes, in one of which captain
Cudjoe loſt his fon, the rebels were entirely defeated, few efcaping, their commanders, Tacky and
Jamaica, ſlain, and the ringleaders being tried,
and found guilty of rebellion, were executed by
various tortures.

In order to prevent fuch infurrections for the
future, the juſtices aſſembled at the feſſions of peace
eſtabliſhed the following regulations : That no negroe ſlave ſhould be allowed to quit his plantation,
without a white conductor, or a ticket of leave :
that every negroe, playing at any fort of game,
ſhould be fcourged through the public ſtreets :
that every publican fuffering fuch gaming in his
houfe ſhould forfeit forty ſhillings : that every proprietor fuffering his negroes to blow a horn, or
make any other noife in his plantation, ſhould be
fined in ten pounds ; and every overfeer allowing

                                              thefe

thefe irregularities fhould pay half that fum, to be demanded, or diftrained for, by any civil or military officer: that every free negro, or mulatto, fhould wear a blue crofs on his right fhoulder, on pain of imprifonment : that no mulatto, or negroe, fhould hawk or fell any thing, except frefh fifh and milk, on pain of being fcourged : that rum and punch houfes fhould be fhut up during divine fervice on Sundays, under the penalty of twenty fhillings ; and on other nights at nine o'clock. Notwithftanding thefe regulations, the remains of the rebellious negroes made nocturnal irruptions into the neareft plantations, where they acted with all the wantonnefs of barbarity ; fo that the people of Jamaica were obliged to ufe the utmoft vigilance and circumfpection, while rear-admiral Holmes took every precaution to fecure the ifland from infults and invafion.

The admiral having received intelligence, that five French frigates were equipped at Cape-Francois, on the ifland of Hifpaniola, in order to convoy a fleet of merchant-fhips to Europe, ftationed the fhips under his command in fuch a manner as was moft likely to intercept them ; and by the gallantry of captains Norbury, Uvedale, and Maitland, who fell in with the French fleet, two of the frigates were taken, and the other three deftroyed. Immediately after the capture of the frigates, eight French privateers were deftroyed, or brought into Jamaica, where every day numbers of rich prizes arrived. Thus this ifland remained in a more flourifhing

rifhing condition, during the latter end of the late war than it had known for almoft a century before ; and by the treaty of Paris, in 1763, was left in full enjoyment of the fugar-trade, free from the rival- fhip of Guadaloupe or Martinique. The magazines, fortifications, &c. are in excellent condition, its commerce fecured by a fquadron ftationed there for its protection, and the ftipulations obtained from Spain in favour of the logwood trade, have now confirmed our right to that important branch, which, no longer precarious, is now fixed on a folid bafis.

Soon after the conclufion of the late peace, the powder magazine of Augufta, the beft fortrefs in the ifland, blew up by lightning ; all the buildings in the fort were fhattered in pieces, and about thirty whites, among whom were feveral officers, one lady, and eleven negroes, were killed by the explofion. Great numbers were wounded, at the diftance of a mile from the place where it hap- pened, and the concuffion felt above ten miles in circumference. The lofs fuftained, exclufive of two thoufand eight hundred and fifty barrels of gunpowder, amounted to upwards of fifteen thou- fand pounds fterling.

The CLIMATE, NATURAL HISTORY, and PRO-DUCTS of JAMAICA, and the other Weft-Indian Iflands.

Jamaica lies between the 75th and 79th degrees of weft longitude from London, and is between

seven-

feventeen and nineteen degrees diftant from the equi-
noctial. It is in length, from eaft to weft, upwards
of one hundred and forty Englifh miles, in breadth
about fixty, and of an oval form ; divided by a
ridge of rocky mountains, which give rife to a vaft
number of fine rivulets, well ftored with fifh of various kinds, though they contain none of the European fpecies, except eels and crawfifh. The
mullet is very palatable, and the colipever little inferior to falmon. None of thefe rivers are navigable, or indeed could be made fo without vaft expence ; yet fome of thefe are fo large, that canoes
loaded with fugars, pafs from very remote plantations to the fea-fide. The foil, in general, is excellent, efpecially in the northern parts of the ifland,
and prodigioufly fertile.

The longeft day is little above thirteen hours,
and the night proportionably long. About nine in
the forenoon the heat is intenfe, and could fcarce be
endured, was it not tempered by the fea-breeze,
which generally begins to blow about that time,
and continues till five in the afternoon. The nights
are fometimes pretty cool ; and every night there
falls a piercing dew, which is extremely unwholefome. Twilight continues not above three quarters of an hour. The feafons are only diftinguifhed
by the denomination of wet and dry. On the whole,
if the ifland was not fubject to violent ftorms, hurricanes, and earthquakes, and if the air was not
violently hot, damp, and extremely unwholefome
in moft parts, the fertility and beauty of the country,

try, would make it as defirable a fituation for pleafure as it is for profit.   The fouth and north parts
of the ifland are the moft wholefome, agreeable,
and leaft fubject to hurricanes.

The river waters are many of them unwholefome, and tafte of copper, though there are fome
excellent fprings.   In the plains are feveral
fprings, of which falt is made ; and in the mountains, not far from Spanifh Town, is a hot bath of
extraordinary medicinal virtues, which relieves in
the dry belly-ach, an endemial diftemper of Jamaica.

The natural products of this ifland are as numerous as perhaps thofe of any fpot in the world of
the fame fize.   The tree which bears pimento, or
all-fpice, commonly called Jamaica pepper, rifes to
the height of above thirty feet, is ftreight, of a
moderate thicknefs, and covered with a very
fmooth, fhining, grey bark.   It fhoots out a vaft
number of branches on every fide, which bears a
plentiful foliage of very large beautiful leaves, of
a fhining green, like thofe of the bay tree.   The
bunches of flowers are formed at the very ends of
the twigs, each ftalk bearing a flower that bends
back, within which are to be difcerned fome fta-
mina of a pale green colour ; to which fucceed a
bunch of berries, rather larger than juniper-berries,
like which, when ripe, they become black and
fmooth ; but before they are quite ripe, are picked
off the tree, and dried in the fun. This tree grows
moftly upon the mountains. The ifland alfo pro-
                                                    duces

duces the wild cinnamon tree, whose bark is so useful in medicine ; the manchineal, which bears a
moft beautiful apple, and affords a moft ornamental
wood for cabinet-makers, though the apple and
juice, in every part of the tree, are deadly poifons ;
the mahogony tree ; the cedar ; the cabbage tree,
about an hundred feet high, which bears a fubftance on the top which looks and taftes like cabbage, and no lefs remarkable for the extreme hardnefs of its wood, which, when dry, is incorruptible,
and fcarcely penetrable by any tool ; the palm,
from which an oil is drawn, much efteemed by the
negroes ; the white wood, which is never affected
by the worm with which thefe feas abound ; the
foap-tree, whofe berries anfwer all the purpofes of
wafhing ; the mangrove and olive bark, ufeful to
tanners ; the fuftick red-wood ; and, lately, the
logwood, employed in dying ; and the forefts fupply the druggifts with guaicum, farfaparilla, china-
root, caffia, and tamarinds. The ifland alfo produces aloes, and the cochineal plant, though the
Jamaicans are ignorant of the method of managing
it. The maftick-tree, iron-wood, and bulley-tree,
are hard woods, fit for the millwright.

The ifland of Jamaica is divided into nineteen
parifhes, which fend each two members to the affembly. Port Royal, the antient capital, ftood
upon the point of a peninfula, which formed a
part of the fhore of a noble harbour of the fame
name, in which a thoufand fail of the largeft fhips
may anchor, with the greateft conveniency and fafety ;

ty; there being depth of water at the key of Port Royal for veffels of the greateft burthen to lie clofe to the wharfs. This conveniency, and the refort of the buccaneers, (though the foil is only a hot, dry fand, which produces none of the neceffaries of life, not even frefh water) foon rendered it a very confiderable place, in about thirty years time containing two thoufand houfes, which rented as high as in London. In fhort, few places in the world could be compared to it for trade, wealth, and an entire corruption of manners. Port Royal continued in this flourifhing ftate until the 9th of June, 1692, when it was overwhelmed by an earthquake. It was rebuilt, and a fecond time deftroyed by fire. The extraordinary conveniency of its harbour tempted the inhabitants to rebuild it once more; but, in 1722, an hurricane reduced it, a third time, to an heap of rubbifh. Warned by thefe repeated calamities, the affembly removed the cuftom-houfe, public offices, and market from thence; and the principal inhabitants removed to the oppofite fide of the bay, to a town called Kingfton, now the feat of government, advantageoufly fituated for frefh water, and all manner of accommodations. The ftreets are of a commodious width, regularly drawn, and intercept each other at equal diftances, and right angles. It contains upwards of a thoufand houfes, many of them handfomely built, tho' low, with porticos, and fuitable conveniences for the climate. The harbour, by the care of governor Knowles, is now ftrongly fortified; its entrance being

being defended by Fort Charles, one of the strong-
eft in the Britifh iflands, and a battery of fixty
pieces of cannon, befides additional works. Kingfton fends three members to the affembly.

St. Jago de la Vega, or Spanifh Town, fituated
on the river Cobre, a confiderable, though not navigable ftream, that falls into the fea near Kingfton,
formerly the feat of government, and the place
where the courts of juftice were held, though inferior in fize and refort to Kingfton, and a town of
lefs bufinefs, is equal in gaiety to many European
cities, which it feems to rival in all polite diverfions.
This town fends three reprefentatives to the affembly.

In St. Catherine's parifh ftands a fort, mounted
with ten or twelve carriage guns, called Paffage
Fort, being the greateft thoroughfare in the ifland.
Port Negril has a good fafe harbour, and lies conveniently for intercepting the Spanifh trade to and
from the Havannah. Port Antonio, in St. Ann's
parifh, would be the beft harbour in the ifland,
were it not for its difficult entrance; however, it is defended by a regular fort, and a fmall
garrifon. There is likewife a fort at the bay of
Port Morant, on the fouth-eaft part of the ifland,
where are excellent plantations, both of fugar and
cotton, and a falt work.

The government of Jamaica is the beft in the
gift of the crown, that of Ireland excepted. The
ftanding falary is two thoufand five hundred pounds
per annum; the affembly vote the governor as

much more; and this, with the great perquifites annexed to his office, make the whole near ten thoufand pounds per annum.

TRADE.

The principal exports of the ifland are fugars, of which they export about twenty thoufand hogf-heads per annum, fome of which weigh a ton. Moft of this is fent to the mother-country, though a fmall part of it goes to North-America, in exchange for beef, pork, cheefe, corn, peafe, ftaves, plank, pitch, and tar. Rum, of which they export about four thoufand puncheons, efteemed better than that of the other Weft-India iflands: molaffes, in which they make the greateft part of their returns for New England, where there are vaft diftilleries: cotton, of which they export two thoufand bags. Indigo was formerly much cultivated; but the quantity now made is inconfiderable. Some cacao and coffee are alfo exported; but the latter is not much efteemed. The Jamaicans alfo fend to England a confiderable quantity of pimento, ginger, drugs, fweetmeats, and mahogony and manchineal plank.

The logwood-trade is alfo confiderable. We formerly cut logwood in the Bay of Campeachy, on the northern fide of the peninfula of Jucatan; but being expelled from thence by the Spaniards, the logwood-cutters fettled upon the Gulph of Honduras, on the fouthern fide of the fame penin-

fula,

fula, where they were protected by a fort, now demolished, agreeable to an article of the late peace. These logwood-cutters are mostly fugitives from all parts of North-America, who live in a lawlefs manner, though they elect one of their number king, to whom they pay very little obedience. They amount in number to about five hundred, and go always well armed. The country they inhabit is extremely marſhy, the air prodigiouſly infeſted with muſkettoes, and the water full of alligators; yet a life of licentiouſneſs and large gains, have perfectly reconciled them to the hardſhips of their employment, and the unwholeſomeneſs of the climate.

In the dry feaſon, when they cut logwood, they advance a conſiderable way into the country in ſearch of the logwood. In the wet ſeaſon, when the whole country is overflowed, they know the marks where the logwood lies, which being a heavy wood, ſinks in the water, but is ſo eaſily buoyed up, that a ſingle diver is capable of lifting very large pieces. The logwood is thus carried by the favour of the land-floods into the river, to the port where the ſhips lie that come upon this trade, which in ſome years employs near ſix thouſand tons of ſhipping, conſumes a large quantity of Engliſh manufactures, and is of conſiderable uſe in fabricating many others; the whole value of the returns being not leſs than ſixty thouſand pounds ſterling per annum. It is generally carried on by veſſels from North-America, which purchaſe their goods in Jamaica.

VOL. II. K k The

The trade which is carried on between Jamaica
and the Spanish main is still more profitable than
that of the logwood, efpecially in time of war. It
is carried on in the following manner: The veſſel
from Jamaica being furnifhed with negroes, and a
proper aſſortment of other goods, proceeds to a
place called Monkey Key, within four miles of
Portobello. On its arrival, a perſon underſtanding
the Spanifh tongue is immediately ſent aſhore, to
give notice to the merchants of that town. Information is likewiſe given, with all poſſible expedition, to the merchants of Panama. Without loſs
of time, the traders ſet out, difguiſed like peaſants,
and carrying their ſilver in earthen jars, covered
with flour, in order to deceive the officers of the
revenue. They generally repair on board, where
they are handſomely entertained, and at their departure take their purchaſes along with them, either negroe-ſlaves, or dry goods packed up in ſuch
a manner as to be carried by one perſon, leaving
behind them the price agreeed on in dollars. They
are likewiſe furniſhed with proviſions ſufficient to
ſerve them during their return. This traffic commonly laſts for about five or ſix weeks. If the
whole cargo is not difpoſed of at this place, they
ſhape their courſe then for an harbour called the
Brew, about five miles diſtant from Carthagena,
where they quickly find a vent for the reſt of their
goods. Theſe are the two principal places where
this trade is carried on, but they are not the only
ones; the Caraccas, and many other parts upon
that

that coaft, have alfo their fhare. ' Nor are the Englifh the only nation concerned in it; the French
from Hifpaniola, and the Dutch from Curaffow,
likewife interfere, and have, within thefe few years,
almoft entirely cut out the Englifh, owing chiefly
to the injudicious regulations of a late minifter. There was, however, when it flourifhed, no
trade more profitable than this; the payments being not only all in ready money, but the goods felling at an higher price than in any other market.
But it is prohibited by the Spaniards, under fevere
penalties; and the guarda coftas, when they catch
any of thefe interlopers, treat them little better than
if they were pirates. Befides, they frequently feize,
and otherwife maltreat, the fair traders, under pretence of their being concerned in this contraband
traffick. This practice has given rife to numberlefs difputes between the courts of Great-Britain
and Spain, and particularly was the occafion of the
firft Spanifh war.

This commerce at all times, and the prizes which
in great numbers are carried into Jamaica in time
of war, for of all our iflands it is the beft fituated
for making captures, occafion a vaft influx of treafure into it; fo that great fortunes are made as ra-
pidly here as any where elfe in the world, whilft the
people appear to live in fuch a ftate of profu-
fion and luxury in their equipages, their cloaths,
furniture, and tables, as in any other place would
bring on beggary and bankruptcy. On this account their treafure makes but a very fhort ftay

K k 2 amongft

amongft them, but is immediately tranfmitted to North-America, or Europe, to purchafe the different articles of luxury and conveniency, as well as to fupply their extraordinary demand for flaves, which is annually for above fix thoufand head, both to fupply their own deficiency and the Spanifh market.

BARBADOES.

BArbadoes was the firft fettled, and is ftill the beft peopled, confidering its fize, of any of the Englifh Weft-India iflands.   It is uncertain by whom it was firft difcovered; moft probably by the Portuguefe, in their voyages between Europe and Brazil, for it lies nearly in that tract: the name it ftill bears feems to warrant this conjecture.   The firft Englifhmen who landed here are faid to be fome failors belonging to Sir William Courteen's fleet, which was cruizing againft the Spaniards, about the end of king James's reign. On their return to England, the favourable report they made of the foil, induced feveral adventurers to go over and fettle there.   But the ifland being entirely covered with wood, and no animals found upon it except hogs (a proof that it had been difcovered before, either by the Spaniards or Portuguefe) their attempts were far from being attended with fuccefs at firft.

Charles

Charles I. in the beginning of his reign, made a grant of this ifland to the earl of Carlifle. It does not appear that this nobleman endeavoured to fettle it on his own account ; but he difpofed of part of it in fhares to others, who fell to planting tobacco. This culture by no means anfwered expectation, and they turned their views to raifing cotton and indico, which fucceeded better ; but it was not till the year 1647 that fugar, their prefent ftaple, became the principal object of cultivation. At that time, the king's affairs being entirely ruined in England, many gentlemen of rank and fortune, his adherents, flying from the perfecutions of their enemies, took refuge in this ifland. From this period, its advance in produce and population is perfectly amazing. In the year 1650, thirty thoufand whites, and above double the number of Indian or negroe flaves, are computed to have been living on that fmall ifland. The trade was then in the hands of the Dutch ; but foon after, under Cromwell's government, it was confined to the mother-country by the act of navigation. The colony ftill continued to improve, and in the year 1676, reached its higheft pitch. The inhabitants, at that time, amounted to fifty thoufand whites, and one hundred thoufand flaves ; a degree of population not to be paralleled in China itfelf. Four hundred fail of fhips, at an average of one hundred and fifty tons each, were employed in the trade, and their annual exports were reckoned to amount to three hundred and fifty thoufand pounds ; but fince that time

K k 3

the

the trade and population of. the iḷland have been
rather in a declining way, for which various caufeṣ
may be aſſigned. The firſt is the fudden increaſe
oḟ the French iſlands, and the ſettlement of our
own, particularly Jamaica, which naturally drew
away many of the inhabitants, from Barbadoes.
The next is a contagious diſtemper, imported,
ſome ſay, from England, others from Afṛica,
which broke out in the year 1692, and carried off vaſt numbers of people; no leſs than twenty dying in a day in Bridgetown, the capital, and
in the ſame proportion through the reſt of the
iſland. This diſtemper continued for ſome years,
and made great havock. To this was added the
war, which raged all that time, and was another
inſtrument of depopulating the iſland; great numbers being carried off by ill-concerted and unfuc-
ceſsful expeditions againſt the French colonies.
To theſe cauſes may be added the running out and
impoveriſhment of the lands; ſo that in later
times, with extreme culture and manure, they are
not able to raiſe ſo much produce as the land before
brought, in a manner, ſpontaneouſly forth: but it
is ſtill a very conſiderable and a very valuable ſettlement. It is computed that there are above
twenty-five thouſand whites, and above treble
that, number of negroes on the iſland; a moſt
amazing population, if it be compared with
the reſt of the iſlands, and if it be conſidered, that it does not contain above one hundred
thouſand acres. Beſides rum, molaſſes, cotton, ginger,

ger, and aloes, it exports about twenty-five thoufand hogſheads of ſugar every year, eſtimated to
be worth three hundred thouſand pounds ; ſo that,
by the increaſe of the price of ſugars, the returns of
this iſland have diminiſhed little from what they
were at its moſt flouriſhing period.

Soon after the Reſtoration, king Charles II.
having purchaſed the property of the iſland from
the earl of Kinnoul, heir to lord Carliſle, it became
henceforth a royal and a regular government ; for
the ſupport of which, and of the fortifications, the
colony has granted a duty of four and a half per
cent. on their produce, amounting, one year with
another, to above ten thouſand pounds. The militia of this iſland is reckoned at five thouſand men,
and it has been known to ſend out nearly that number againſt the French ſettlements : beſides which,
there is generally a regiment of regular troops
quartered here, though ſeldom compleat. The
ſalary of the governor, perquiſites included, is
never leſs than five thouſand pounds ; and all the
other officers of the civil eſtabliſhment, which is
ſupported with great credit, have very handſome
appointments. The clergy of the church of England, which is the religion eſtabliſhed here, as in
the other iſlands, (and there are but few diſſenters)
have likewiſe very liberal proviſions aſſigned them.
On the whole, it is ſaid, that there appears in this
iſland ſomething more of order and decency, and
of a regular ſettled people, than in any other
iſland in the Weſt-Indies.

Bar-

Barbadoes lies in the Atlantic Ocean, in the latitude of 13 north, and the longitude of 59 weſt. It is nearly of a triangular form, being in length twenty-five miles, from ſouth to north, and fifteen in breadth, from eaſt to weſt, where broadeſt. It is, for the moſt part, a plain level country, ſave a few hills, here and there, of an eaſy aſcent. Tho' originally quite overſpread with woods, there is little now remaining, being moſtly cut down to make room for ſugar and other plantations. The whole iſland, indeed, appears like one continued plantation ; and it is ſo thick ſown with gentlemen's houſes, that there ſeems to be hardly one but what is within call of ſome other. The air is pretty healthy, and rather cooler than that of the large Weſt-India iſlands ; the reaſon of which ſeems to be, it is ſo ſmall and level that it generates no land wind, and the ſea-breeze, or trade-wind, perpetually blows. It is, like the other iſlands, ſubject to tornadoes and hurricanes in the ſummer months, which are very terrible and dangerous to the ſhipping ; for they have no harbours to ſhelter themſelves in, but only bays, where they lie at anchor, and in the principal one, Carliſle Bay, ſo called from the original proprietor, there is no good anchoring ground, it being foul, and apt to cut the cables. At the bottom of this bay, where there are very commodious wharfs, for the ſhipping and landing of goods, the principal town ſtands, called Bridgetown, which was once a very flouriſhing place, conſiſting of above twelve hundred houſes ; but it

has

has been lately almoft entirely deftroyed by two dreadful fires, which committed vaft devafta-tion, on account of the buildings being all of wood, which, in a hot and dry feafon, takes fire like tinder. But fuch difafters will be prevented for the future; an act of affembly having paffed prohibiting fuch buildings in the town hereafter, and ordering that they fhall henceforth be of brick. There is a college in this place, the only inftitution of that nature in the Weft-Indies. Its founder was colonel Codrington, who endowed it in a very li-beral manner; but it has not fully anfwered the benevolent intentions of the generous donor. We have already mentioned the principal articles which this ifland exports; but their imports are in far greater number, being almoft every neceffary con-venience and luxury of life, even to their very houfes, which are brought over framed in wood, and ready to be put up, from North-America.

This is all we think needful to fay of the ifland of Barbadoes; for to give a hiftory of its fucceffive governors, with the dates of their commiffions, and other things of that fort, would be as little entertaining as the mufter-roll of a regiment; and it would be equally uninterefting to enter into a detail of the difputes between the inhabitants of the colony and their governors, of their appeals to the government here, with other trifling affairs. For the fame reafon, we fhall obferve a fimilar conduct in our account of the other iflands.

3

SAINT

SAINT CHRISTOPHER's, NEVIS, MONTSERRAT, and ANTIGUA.

THE ifland of St. Chriftopher's, vulgarly called St. Kitt's, is the colony that was fettled next in order of time. By an uncommon accident, the Englifh, under Sir Thomes Warner, and the French, under M. Defnambue, arrived on this ifland in the fame day, in the year 1626. They made an amicable divifion of it between them; agreeing, however, that the fifhing and hunting, the mines, falt-ponds, and moft-valuable timber, fhould remain in common to both nations. After this they fell to planting, in which the Englifh (being more regularly fupplied from home) fucceeded fafter, and throve better than the French; infomuch, that they fettled likewife the little ifland of St. Nevis, feparated from St. Kitt's by a fmall ftreight, hardly navigable for canoes. Three years after the firft fettlement, they were diflodged by the Spaniards, who beheld with jealoufy their progrefs in the Caribbee iflands. After their departure, both nations returned back, and took poffeffion of their former habitations. The Englifh built for themfelves elegant and convenient houfes, whilft the French were contented to refide in huts, after the manner of the native Caribbeans. However, they feem to have lived in harmony together till the war in queen Anne's time, when the French part was conquered by the Englifh, and

the

the whole was finally ceded to them by the treaty of Utrecht.

St. Kitt's is about seventy-five miles in circumference. Its principal and almost sole commodities are sugar and rum, the former of which is said to be the best in quality of any that our islands produce. There is one very remarkable mountain in this island, the head of which constantly overtops the clouds. At a distance, it has the appearance of a man, with another on his back; which was the reason that Columbus, its first discoverer, gave it the name of St. Christopher's, which it still bears. There are two towns of some note in this island, the principal of which is Basse-terre, formerly the capital of the French part; the other is called Sandy Point, and always belonged to the English. There is no such thing as a harbour, or any thing that has the smallest appearance of it in this island: on the contrary, at the few landing places that there are, there is a continual surf beating on the shore, which is sandy, and prevents any key or wharf being erected upon it, and also makes landing always inconvenient, sometimes dangerous. Owing to this, they are obliged to adopt a very peculiar method of getting heavy and bulky goods, such as rum and sugar hogsheads, either shipped or landed. They use for this purpose a small boat, of a particular construction, called a *moses*. This comes from the ship, manned with the most expert rowers. When they see what they call a lull, or any abatement in the violence of the surge, they push ashore, and lay the broadside

of

of the *mofes* on the beach, on which the hogfhead
is rolled in, and then they fet off on board the fhip.
In this tedious and inconvenient manner, the fugar
is caried on board by fingle hogfheads, though accidents frequently happen, by which they are loft.
Rum, cotton, and other commodities which will
bear the water, are generally fwam off, or afhore.
The fame method of loading and unloading is, for
the fame caufes, ufed at Nevis and Montferrat.

The air at St. Kitt's is accounted wholefome,
and not fo hot as at Jamaica; the fea-breeze always
prevailing there, for the fame reafon as at Barbadoes. The inhabitants are computed to be feven
thoufand whites, and twenty thoufand negroes.
On account of its being extremely mountainous
in the middle, it is faid to contain not more than
twenty-four thoufand acres fit for fugar, of which
it produces ten thoufand hogfheads annually, and
rum in the ufual proportion, which is reckoned that
of three to five.

We have already mentioned the date of our fettlement made on the ifland of Nevis, which is little
more than fix miles long, and appears to be one
continued mountain, the top of which reaches far
above the clouds, the fugar plantations lying on the
fides of it, near the bottom. Small as it is, it was
once in a moft flourifhing condition, containing about
ten thoufand white and twenty thoufand black inhabitants, which, however, are now reduced to half
the number. It produces fix thoufand hogfheads
of fugar, with rum in proportion.

The

The island of Montserrat, so called by the Spaniards from the resemblance it bears to a mountain of that name near Barcelona, lies in the 17th deg. of north latitude ; and is about nine miles in length, and as much in breadth, being nearly of a circular form. Its inhabitants and produce are much the same with those of Nevis. It was settled by Sir Thomas Warner. The original colonists were Irish, and the present inhabitants are chiefly composed of their descendants, or the natives of Ireland. The use of the Irish tongue is common, even amongst the negroes.

Antigua, which in the Spanish tongue signifies a place without water, received its name from that circumstance ; there being no rivers in it, and but few springs, and those brackish, so that the inhabitants are obliged to preserve the rain water in cisterns. This island lies in 16 deg. 11 min. north latitude, and 63 deg. west. It is of a circular form, twenty miles in length and breadth, and near sixty in circumference. The air is not so wholesome as at Barbadoes, and it is more subject to hurricanes ; but then it has excellent harbours, particularly English Harbour, which is capable of receiving the largest man of war in the navy. Here also is a dock-yard, with stores, and all other materials and conveniences for repairing, heaving down, and careening ships. But the principal trade is carried on at the harbour of St. John's, where the capital stands, and which has water sufficiently deep for merchant vessels. The town of St. John's was

once

once in a very flourishing state, as may be judged by the loss sustained at the late fire, which was computed at the amazing sum of four hundred thousand pounds. But in all probability it will rise, in process of time, out of its ashes, better built and more flourishing than ever.

This island was first attempted to be settled by Sir Thomas Warner, much about the same time that St. Christopher's, Nevis, and Montserrat were planted ; but that establishment did not take place. It was afterwards granted by Charles II. to lord Willoughby, then governor of Barbadoes, who, some years after receiving the grant, effectuated an establishment upon it. Soon after, but by what means is not known, it became again the public property. It raises, at present, about sixteen thousand hogsheads of sugar, which was at first of a very bad quality, unfit for the English market, and was therefore disposed of among the Dutch and Hamburghers : but the planters have greatly improved their staple since, and it is now as good as in any of the other islands.

These four islands, Antigua, St. Christopher's, Nevis, and Montserrat, are all under the government of one captain-general, who had a very considerable appointment, amounting to three thousand five hundred pounds sterling a year. His residence is now generally at Antigua. Each of these islands has its distinct governor, whose salary is about two hundred pounds a year, and a separate council and assembly.

There

There are two other iflands under this jurifdiction, thofe of Barbuda and Anguilla ; but they have no direct communication with England; on account of their having no commodities for that market. The inhabitants are more in the nature of farmers than planters ; and content themfelves with raifing ftock and provifions, which they difpofe of to the other iflands.

The VIRGIN ISLANDS.

THERE is a clufter of fmall iflands a little to the windward of Porto Rico, called the Virgins, which are divided between the Danes and Englifh, and are indeed the only fettlements which the former enjoy in the Weft-Indies. The principal of thofe in the Englifh poffeffion is called Tortola. This ifland is very unhealthy, and its chief production is cotton, faid to be of the beft quality that is raifed in thefe parts of the world.

GRENADA, TOBAGO, SAINT VINCENT, DOMINICA.

WE have already mentioned 'the reduction' of Grenada, by the fame fleet and army which conquered Martinico. This was the only
French

French ifland which the Englifh retained at the treaty of peace. It was foon after erected into a government, to which were annexed the iflands of Tobago, Dominica, and St. Vincent, formerly neutral, but now ceded to Great-Britain alfo. We fhall give fome account of thefe in the firft place, and then return to Grenada.

The ifland of Tobago lies the fartheft to the fouthward of any belonging to the Englifh, being in the latitude of 11 deg. 45 min. north. It is about twelve leagues in length, four in breadth, and thirty in circumference. King Charles I. in the year 1628, granted it away to the earl of Pembroke and Montgomery; but we do not hear that any fettlement was attempted, far lefs made, in confequence of this grant. Therefore, during the time of the civil wars, the Dutch took poffeffion of it, and began to plant, and clear the woods, and were in a fair way of thriving, when the Spaniards from the ifland of Trinity, and the favages from St. Vincent's, fell upon them, and cut them off to a man. After which it continued a defert, till the year 1664, when it was again fettled by other Dutch adventurers, who, for the firft fourteen years, were exceeding-fuccefsful, and had made it one of the moft flourifhing of the iflands : but, in the year 1678, they were totally expelled by the French, and their plantations entirely ruined ; and though it was reftored at the treaty of Nimeguen, yet the Dutch never after made any attempts to refettle it. After this, it came to be confidered as a

neutral

ncutral ifland, between the French and Englifh, till
it was adjudged to the latter by the laft treaty of
peace. It is juft now beginning to be fettled, the
land having been previoufly fold for the benefit of
the public, by commiffioners appointed for that
purpofe. Befides the commodities common to
the Weft-Indian iflands, it is faid to furnifh the
following, peculiar to itfelf: an excellent kind of
faffafras, a fpecies of mace and nutmegs, and gum
copal, in great quantities. It is likewife fuppofed
to poffefs another advantage, of very great moment; it lies out of the tract of thofe hurricanes
which are fo much dreaded in the other iflands.

The ifland of St. Vincent is twenty-four miles
in length, and half as much in breadth. The
warmth of the climate is fo well tempered with the
fea-breezes, that it is accounted extremely healthful and agreeable, and on the mountains it is rather
cool. The foil in general is extraordinary fertile,
though the country is every where hilly, and in
fome places mountainous. Amongft the hills
there are feveral pleafant vallies, and at the bottom
of the mountains very large and extenfive plains.
No ifland in the world is better watered than St.
Vincent's; many rivulets taking their rife in the
mountains, and fhaping their courfe from both
fides into the fea. There are alfo feveral fine
fprings at a fmall diftance from the fea, the flope
to which is fo eafy and regular, that there are hardly any marfhes, or ftanding water, on the ifland.
It has, however, one difadvantage; it has no har-

bours, and but one good bay, called St. Antonio, which is deep and fandy, and where ſhips may lie fafely and commodiouſly. The fugar-cane feems to be a native of this iſland, for it grows wild here. When the French were ſettled here, they raiſed no fugar at all, but every other commodity peculiar to the Weſt-Indies ; by the help of which they car-ried on a conſiderable trade with their other iſlands. Since it has been in poſſeſſion of the Engliſh, large fugar-works have been erected, and conſiderable quantities imported. This iſland is at preſent much farther advanced in ſettlement and cultivation than Tobago.   It enjoys a lieutenant-governor, and a council and aſſembly of its own.

Dominica lies almoſt exactly in the middle, between the two principal French iſlands, Martinico and Guadeloupe ; lying eight leagues north-weſt from the former, and at the ſame diſtance ſoutheaſt from the latter.   It is at leaſt twenty-eight miles in length, and about half that in breadth ; and being nearly of a rectangular form, and not interſected by deep bays, contains more ground in proportion to its circumference than moſt of the other iſlands.   It is thought by ſome to be almoſt twice as large as Barbadoes ; and the French reckon it half as large as Martinico.   The climate is reputed to be very wholeſome, and it is watered by above thirty rivers, many of which are ſaid to be navigable ſome miles from the ſea, the reſt very commodious for plantations, and abounding in fiſh. The country has a mountainous appearance, eſpecially

tially towards the sea, but the declivities are commonly gentle, so that the cultivation is not difficult; and the soil being a deep black mould, of exceeding fertility, it largely and speedily rewards the toils of the planter. In the interior part of the island there are many rich and fine vallies, and several large and spacious plains.

It bears, in great plenty, all the woods which are common in the West-Indies ; and produces what are called ground provisions in great abundance, such as bananas, potatoes, and manoul, of which cassada is made, which serves as bread to the Indians and negroes, and even to many of the Europeans. The pine apples of this island are said to excel most others in size and flavour. Wild and tame hogs, as likewise all sorts of fowls, are here extremely plentiful. There are, properly speaking, no harbours in this island ; but there is good and safe anchorage all along the coast. There is, besides, Rupert's Bay, so called from the famous prince Rupert's anchoring there, which is one of the largest, safest, and most commodious in the whole world, and capable of containing the whole royal navy of Great-Britain. In fact, our fleets destined for the West-Indies generally come to anchor in this bay, for the sake of supplying themselves with wood and water, for which there are here excellent conveniencies. On the whole, this island is a most important acquisition to Great-Britain, whether we consider it on account of itself, or its situation : the vast quantities which, when fully

L l 2

fettled, it will produce of fugar, rum, cotton, coffee, and other valuable Weft-India commodities,
and the manufactures and other goods which it will
take in return, muft be a great improvement to the
riches, trade, and navigation of the mother-country. Then by its fituation, lying in the center of
the French iflands, in cafe of a rupture with that
people, it will be of infinite advantage to the Britifh nation, by totally ftopping all intercourfe between them, and greatly interrupting their commerce with France. There are likewife faid to be
rich mines of precious metals in the bowels of the
mountains in this ifland; but, indeed, the moft valuable mines are what are raifed on the furface of the
ground, by the labour of hands. A free port, under certain reftrictions, has, about five years ago,
been erected here by act of parliament. It was
originally a member of the government of Grenada; but it has lately been made a feparate government, very judicioufly, in our opinion, both on
account of its own importance, and its remote fituation from all the other iflands in the Grenada diftrict.

Grenada, and the clufter of fmall iflands near it,
called the Grenadines, is now, excepting Jamaica,
by far the moft valuable colony which Great-Britain poffeffes. It exports no lefs than twenty thoufand hogfheads of fugar, and a proportionable
quantity of rum, efteemed to be the next in goodnefs to that made in Jamaica, and by many thought
equal to it. Befides, it produces coffee and cotton

in

in greater abundance than all the reft of our iflands taken together; its produce in thefe two latter articles being efteemed equal in value to one half of its fugars. Hence, it is evident that its annual exports cannot amount to lefs than half a million fterling; and when it is confidered, that this is paid for by the produce and manufactures of Great-Britain, and by negroe-flaves, the property of Britifh merchants, it may be eafily conceived, what a mighty acceffion this new acquifition has made to the riches and trade of the mother-country.

We fhall now give a defcription of this ifland, and the other fmaller ones adjacent to it. Grenada lies in 11 deg. 13 min. north latitude, being the foutbernmoft of all the Antilles, and diftant only thirty leagues from the Spanifh main. It is about thirty Englifh miles in length, and where broadeft about fixteen; but its breadth is unequal. It is computed to be twice as large as Barbadoes, and to contain in fugar-land more than one third of what is in Martinico; but thefe are points which cannot be determined with any precifion. From its fituation, the climate muft be naturally very hot; but, as in all the other fmall iflands, this heat is greatly tempered by a continual fea-breeze. Befides, its climate has fome advantages peculiar to itfelf; the dry and rainy feafons are remarkably regular in their periods, the blaft has not been hitherto known in the ifland, and, what is the happieft cir-cumftance of all, it lies out of the tract of hurri-canes, which, with refpect to the fecurity of the fet-

tlements

tlements on fhore, and the fafety of the navigation, is an ineftimable benefit in this part of the world.

There are very high mountains in Grenada ; but they are few in number.   The reft of the country is divided into plains and gentle eminences, which are capable of cultivation to the very top. This ifland is extremely well watered, and, which is re- markable, its principal ftreams proceed from a large lake at the top of an high mountain, fituated in the center of the ifland, and flow down the fides of the mountain, in different directions, to the fea. Moft of the hills furnifh fmaller brooks ; and there are almoft every where very fine fprings near the fea.   River and fea fifh, turtles, and wild fowl, are here in abundance.

But the principal excellence of Grenada con- fifts in its convenience for anchorage, and in its harbours.   There is good anchoring ground all along the coaft, and on the eaft and weft feveral fmall bays and creeks, commodious for veffels, and for landing and fhipping goods.   But there are two of the fineft harbours in the world in Grenada.   The firft of thefe lies at the fouth- eaft extremity of the ifland, and is divided in- to the outward and the inner port : the entrance into the former is three quarters of a mile broad, but becomes gradually wider, and is above a mile extent within : the entrance into the inner port is about a quarter of a mile in breadth; and grows alfo wider as you advance further ; it is, for the moft part, about feven fathom deep, and is excel- lent holding-ground, being every where a foft ouzy
bottom.

bottom. The ships here may lye alongside of the warehouses, and take in their loading with great ease and convenience; after which they can, with very little trouble, be towed into the outer harbour, which enjoys this peculiar advantage, that ships can sail either in or out with the common trade wind.

The other harbour is situated at the north-west end of the island; and is a full quarter of a mile broad at the entrance, and so capacious within, that it is capable of holding, in the utmost safety, a large fleet of line of battle ships.

The Grenadilloes are a cluster of small islands, which lie between Grenada and St. Vincent, in a north-and-by-east direction. Their number is not well known, as many of them are little better than rocks: however, there are said to be twenty three which are capable of cultivation, and of producing cotton, coffee, and indigo, some say sugar; but that seems doubtful, as the cane is a very delicate plant, and requires a more distant situation from the sea than can be found in such small islands. The chief of them still retains the Indian name of Couriacou. It is of a circular form, and is about seven miles in length and breadth. Here is an excellent harbour. It is now tolerably well settled; its produce is coffee and cotton, and it sends three members to the assembly of Grenada. The island of Bequia is likewise reckoned among the Grenadilloes, though only two leagues southwest of St. Vincent. It is the largest of them all, being above twelve leagues in

L l 4 circum-

circumference : it is likewife faid to be the moft fruitful, and to have a good port, in which the French veffels navigating between Grenada and Martinico ufed to take fhelter during the late war.

Grenada, excepting Jamaica, is the only Weft-India colony which the Englifh poffefs by the right of conqueft. In Jamaica, the Spaniards, to a man, abandoned their fettlements. In Grenada it was quite otherwife ; by the treaty of peace, the French fettlers were allowed a certain time to confider whether they fhould retain their eftates, and become Britifh fubjects, or depart the ifland, and fell their eftates, provided it was to Britifh fubjects. Some have chofen the former, others the latter. Accordingly, purchafes have been made in the iflands of Grenada and Curiacou, to the amount of confiderably more than a million fterling ; and as near one half of the ifland ftill remains in the hands of the French, and as it may be eafily believed, that what was fold was difpofed of at an under price, fome judgment may be formed of the immenfe value of the whole.

From the conqueft till the peace, and for fome time after, Grenada remained a military government. During all that time, the greateft harmony fubfifted between the Englifh and the French, or, as they chufe to call themfelves, the New Subjects. But on its being made a civil government, and an affembly being called, difputes and diffentions arofe, in which, it muft be confeffed, a party amongft the old fubjects were the aggreffors. They difputed with the French their right of voting for

members

members of the affembly ; they branded them with
the name of aliens, and made religion the pretence.
This is certainly the firft time that ever a religious
difpute was heard of in a Weft-India colony, where
all men, from the nature of the lives they lead, and
perhaps from that of the climate, feem to be alike
ignorant of and indifferent about religion. In Grenada it would appear they are only ignorant. But it
would be doing the Britifh fettlers injuftice to fay,
they were unanimous in this attack upon their fellow-fubjects the French ; on the contrary, thofe of
the greateft fortune and confideration amongft them
were their moft ftrenuous friends and advocates.
But Mr. Melvill, the governor, was fuppofed to
be at the bottom of it, which does not feem to be
deftitute of foundation from what has paffed here,
where this matter has been violently agitated in the
public papers. The adminiftration, however, have
been far from adopting the narrow and confined
prejudices which have given rife to thofe animofi-
ties ; on the contrary, two French fubjects have
been permitted to take their feats in the council,
and three in the affembly, without being obliged
to fubfcribe to the teft, which, upon the whole, is
certainly a prudent and healing meafure. At all
events, it is undoubtedly of the utmoft importance
(both for the well-being of the colony itfelf, and
the confequence it may be attended with in cafe of
a future war) that fome mode of adminiftration
fhould be laid down and fteadily purfued, which
may unite and confolidate together both the nations

tions inhabiting thofe iflands as firmly and fpeedily as poffible.

BERMUDAS.

THE only two infular governments belonging to Britain that remain undefcribed, are thofe of Bermudas and the Bahama iflands. We fhall begin with the former.

The Bermudas are a clufter of fmall iflands in the 32d deg. of north latitude, and 67th of weft longitude. They are above two hundred leagues from any land whatfoever, and lie in the midft of a vaft tempeftuous ocean, as plainly appears from the innumerable holes and cavities, which the waves, beating upon the rocks with which they are furrounded, have cut into them. The American navigators never pafs between the Bermudas and Cape Hatteras, which is in 35 deg. of north latitude, without terror. They call them the horfe latitudes, becaufe, on account of the violent gales of wind they meet in traverfing them, they are frequently obliged to throw the horfes overboard, which they are carrying to the Weft-India iflands, and to the Dutch fettlements at Surinam.

Thefe iflands are faid to be in number four-hundred; but by far the greater number are uninhabited rocks, and thofe which are inhabited do not

contain

contain above twenty thoufand acres. The principal ifland is called St. George, and is in length fixteen miles, and in breadth three, where broadeft. Though by nature extremely well fortified, the inhabitants have taken the precaution to ftrengthen it farther, by erecting fortifications at the moft acceffible places. The Englifh fettlers here are about ten thoufand : but there are many of the natives difperfed in the continent and iflands, in the character of traders and feamen ; for being extremely prolific, and their iflands fupplying but few materials for commerce, and none for manufactures, both ambition and neceffity oblige them to go elfewhere to feek their fortunes. They are perhaps as handfome and well-looking a people, both men and women, as any in the world, owing to the temperance of their living and the excellence of their climate, and are extremely kind and hofpitable to thofe few ftrangers who come amongft them. The negroe-flaves upon thefe iflands are not fo many in proportion as on the others, and being almoft all born there, as well as better ufed than is cuftomary elfewhere, they are in general as ferviceable and intelligent as white fervants.

The principal and moft profitable employment of thefe iflanders, is building floops, and fmall brigantines and fnows, of an excellent and moft durable cedar wood, which they had once growing among them in vaft plenty ; but from the great confumption, it is now faid to be on the decreafe. It is incorruptible, and never touched by the

worms :

worms : veffels built of it run for a long time, perhaps fix or feven years, without requiring the
leaft repair, not even calking. They are of a peculiar conftruction, and all of them very faft failors,
and on that account in great requeft amongft all
nations, efpecially in time of war, for privateers.
A fmall floop, not much above one hundred tons,
has been known to fetch twelve hundred pounds.
There are quarries of a foft white ftone, which,
however, hardens afterwards in the air, much in the
nature of Bath ftone, of which they carry cargoes
to the continent, and this feems to be, properly
fpeaking, the only produce they have. They had
once a manufacture of a particular kind of chip
hats, which were, for a time, in great requeft
amongft the ladies in England ; but the fafhion
ceafing, the manufacture ceafed alfo. The iflands
of Bermudas abound in great variety of wild-fowl,
efpecially of the aquatic kind. Their founds, and
furrounding feas, are well ftored with fifh, and the
Bermudians are moft dextrous fifhermen, efpecially
with the harpoon. They are faid to truft fo much
in this dexterity, as frequently to go to fea very
flenderly ftored with provifions, expecting to catch
fufficient during the voyage, and they are never
known to be difappointed. There are a great
many whales about thefe iflands, many of the fper-
maceti kind, and they are not unfrequently driven
afhore. An incident of this nature afforded a
fubject for an excellent poem, by the polite and
elegant Waller, the firft great refiner of Englifh
poetry.

poetry. The inhabitants once attempted a whale fishery; but it did not meet with success. Ambergrease, that drug of such immense value, but whose composition is so utterly unknown, is sometimes met with among the rocks, in lumps of a considerable bignefs. Three feamen, who were by some accident left ashore on these islands before they were settled, found, in the course of their rambles among the rocks, a lump of that commodity, weighing above eighty pounds, with several other pieces of a smaller size.

Mulberry-trees thrive extremely well in the Bermudas; and, considering their populousness, it might be expected, that raw silk could be made a considerable article of produce, for the main obstruction to the raising of that commodity in the continent, is the dearnefs of labour and the scarcity of hands. Some authors propose attempting to raise cochineal here; but this appears to be a project which has no probability of succeeding. A much more feasible scheme, in our opinion, would be the culture of vines, for which both the climate and foil seem admirably calculated; and they could not fail of a constant market for them in the neighbouring continent.

There is one capital town here, called St. George, after the name of the principal island, in which it stands. It is one of the finest towns in our plantations, containing above a thousand houses, built of a beautiful white free-stone, peculiar to these islands. It is, besides, extremely strong, both by

nature

nature and art. The harbour, before which ·it ſtands, is inacceſſible to ſtrangers, without the aſ- ·ſiſtance of pilots, and is at all times extremely dangerous : it is, beſides, defended by ſeven forts, upon which ſeventy great guns are mounted, all which could be brought to bear upon any veſſel which ſhould attempt to force an entrance.

' There have been diſputes about the origin of the name of theſe iſlands ; ſome alledging, that they are called Bermudas from the great ·quantity of black hogs found upon them, for it ſeems that is the Spaniſh name for thoſe animals. But it is more probable that they were called ſo from one John Bermudas, a Spaniard, ſhipwrecked upon them. They are alſo called the Summer Iſlands, from an accident of the ſame nature, which happened to Sir George Summer, one of the firſt ſettlers of· Virginia. It was owing to this that they were firſt ſettled by the Engliſh. The Virginia company hearing a favourable report of the ſoil and temperature of the air, and indeed they are ſaid to be the pleaſanteſt and healthieſt ſpot on the face of the earth, ſent a colony thither, which in a ſhort time throve exceedingly. They now conſtitute a diſtinct royal government ; the governor and council being appointed ·by the crown, and the aſſembly choſen by the people.

The

The BAHAMA or LUCAYO ISLANDS.

THESE iflands were the firft land difcovered by Columbus. They were at that time
very populous, and the inhabitants were a moft
innocent and harmlefs race of men ; but they
were all, in a few years after the difcovery,
butchered and totally extirpated by the mer-
cilefs Spaniards, who feem to have had no
other incitement to that act of barbarity but a
cruel difpofition, and an innate thirft for human
blood ; for the Spaniards never attempted any fettlement upon them, as they did not produce the
precious metals ; but, after having depopulated,
left them to be occupied by the firft Europeans
who fhould think it worth while to form an eftablifhment there. Thefe were the Englifh : King
Charles II. granted them to the proprietors of Carolina, who fent out feveral governors, and built
the town of Naffau, on the ifland of New Providence, which is the feat of government. They were
more than once expelled by the French and Spaniards, and the fettlement was entirely diflodged in
the year 1708, and continued in a depopulated condition, entirely neglected by the Britifh government, till 1718, when meafures were taken to refettle thefe iflands, upon the following occafion :
After the peace of Utrecht, great numbers of feamen, either thrown out of employment or loath to
difcontinue the privateering life, fo nearly allied to
the piratical, which they had been accuftomed to
during

during the war, commenced pirates, and boldly declared war againſt all mankind. They reigned for
ſome years in the American and Weſt-Indian ſeas,
and they took a great many ſhips from all nations.
The harbour of Providence, which they fortified,
and where they built huts or houſes, was their
principal rendezvous; and they grew to ſuch a
height as at laſt to attract the notice of government. Captain Woodes Rogers, the famous cir-
cum-navigator, was ſent out at the time above-
mentioned, with a commiſſion to be governor, with
three men of war, and orders to diſlodge them.
This he effected with little oppoſition; and on his
publiſhing a proclamation promiſing a pardon and
indemnity, moſt of the pirates came in and ſub-
mitted. Their poſterity continue there to this day,
and ſeem ſtill to retain ſome of the habits of their
anceſtors. During the time of war, their great
and favourite occupation is privateering, in which
they are not over-ſcrupulous, either in ſeizing neutral veſſels, or getting them condemned afterwards. In time of peace, many of them follow
wrecking as a buſineſs, fitting out ſmall veſſels to
look for ſhips which have been caſt away on the
Florida ſhore, or on the ſhoals and keys of the Bahama bank. They ſometimes meet with very rich
prizes; and it is alledged, how truly we cannot
ſay, that they will ſometimes decoy thoſe whom
they perceive to be ſtrangers, into places where
they are ſhipwrecked, and plunder them afterwards.

Ever

Ever since the government of captain Rogers, the Bahama islands have continued to be the acknowledged property, and have remained in the possession of the English. They lie to the northward of Cuba, and east and south-east of East-Florida, between the 21st and 28th deg. of north latitude, and the 71st and 82d of west longitude. Their number is very uncertain, amounting, without doubt, to some hundreds; but by far the greatest part are small rocks and keys, that is, little hillocks, just emerging out of the water. Some, however, are of a very considerable bigness. The principal are, first, the island of Bahama, from which the rest take their general name, which lies in 26 deg. 45 min. latitude, and is distant from the peninsula of Florida about twenty leagues. It is in length about fifty miles, and where broadest sixteen. It enjoys a temperate air, and is reported to be a very fruitful and pleasant country; but it is uninhabited. The next is Lucayo, which has also given its name to these islands: this, as well as Andros and Long-Island, runs out much more in length than breadth. They are all narrow slips, and five or six times longer than broad. But the most eligible of all those islands for a settlement, is that of Exuma; not only on account of the fertility of the soil and temperature of the climate, but the excellence of the harbour, or as it is commonly called, the sound, which is capable of containing the whole navy of England in safety. A plantation was attempted on this island before the late

war; but was afterwards deferted, out of appre-
henfion of the enemies privateers.

There are only three of thefe iflands fettled, and
thofe neither the largeft nor the moft fertile; Providence, already mentioned, Harbour-Ifland, and
Eleuthera. They are all, however, remarkably
healthful; it being no uncommon thing to fee perfons, efpecially in Eleuthera, aged above an hundred years. The foil of Providence is hard, dry,
and rocky; it does not feem capable of rearing any
produce except cotton, which has been lately attempted with a tolerable profpect of fuccefs.
There grow great plenty of limes in Providence;
and inconfiderable as this article may feem, it con-
ftitutes the chief part of their exportation to North-
America. They alfo carry thither pine-apples,
which are moftly raifed in Harbour-Ifland and
Eleuthera. Green turtle, in great numbers, are
catched on the Bahama banks, the greater part of
which are now brought to London. They cut
dying woods, lignum vitæ, and an inferior fort of
mahogony, on their own iflands and the Florida
keys, of which their chief returns to England confift. In fhort, this eftablifhment is at prefent of
little confequence, except on account of its fituation in time of war; but were all the beft iflands
to be once fully fettled by induftrious inhabitants,
as they are capable of producing cotton, indigo,
and fugar, they would foon become of very great
confequence to the mother-country.

Of

Of the MANUFACTURE of SUGAR.

IT will appear from this account we have given of the trade and commerce of America and the West-India islands, that all their imports into Great-Britain, as well as other parts of the world, or their returns for the manufactures received from thence, consist of simple unmanufactured produce, except the three following articles, rum, sugar, and indigo. We shall therefore say something of the manner in which the two latter are prepared for the European market; for the first, being by the common process of distillation, is already sufficiently understood.

The best situation for a sugar plantation is on the banks of a navigable stream, for the convenience of water, both for the mills and carriage. A situation near the sea, on the windward part of an island, is not eligible; for the cane is a tender plant, and liable to be blasted: therefore, it is evident, that very small islands, however fertile their soil, are not proper for sugar plantations. After the spot is pitched upon, it must be cleared of all the wood, the roots grubbed up, and then diligently hoed. Then, in the planting season, which is the month of August, small trenches are dug in the ground, about half a foot deep, and at proper distances. In each of these a cane is laid, lengthwise, and then covered with earth. In a short time, a young cane sprouts up from every joint of the

buried

buried plant, and becomes tall and vigorous in about a fortnight; it, however, requires to ſtand ſixteen months before it is ready for cutting. Cane grounds, for the ſake of diſpatch and ſaving time, are generally divided into three parts: one is of the canes that are to be cut in the approaching ſeaſon, the other is of the canes that are new planted, and the third of fallow ground, and preparing to be planted. By this means, there are annual crops; but in ſome places, where the ground is fertile or newly broken up, the ſame roots ſupply three or four ſucceſſive cuttings. The tops of the canes, and the leaves, are excellent fodder for the cattle; and the refuſe, after the juice is preſſed out, ſerves for the purpoſe of firing.

The canes being cut, which is done near the root with a billet, are tied into bundles, and carried to the mill, which is either worked with water, wind, or cattle. By means of the wheel, three great cylinders, or rollers plated with iron and ſet perpendicular, are ſet in motion. The middle roller moves the ſide ones, each in an oppoſite direction. The canes are firſt put in between the middle and one of the ſide rollers, and ſqueezed through, where they are received, and again thruſt in between the middle and the other roller, and again ſqueezed through in an oppoſite direction. The juice thus obtained, runs through a hole into a vat, placed under the rollers for its reception; from whence it is conveyed by pipes into a great reſervoir, where, however, it is not ſuffered to ſtand long,

long, for fear of turning four, but is by other pipes conveyed into a large cauldron, where it is boiled until no more fcum rifes; from this it is fuccef-fively conveyed through five or fix boilers more, all which gradually diminifh in fize, till it comes to the laft, when, being now greatly reduced in quantity, it becomes of a very thick and clammy confiftence; and now, to procure the granula-tion, fome lime water is poured in, which occafions a very violent fermentation, which, when it has continued a fufficient time, is made all at once to fubfide, by throwing in a fmall bit of butter. It is now taken out, and placed in a cooler, where it dries, granulates, and becomes fit for being placed in the pots, which is the laft part of the operation. The pots are conical, or fhaped like a fugar-loaf; there is a hole at the point, which muft be confi-dered as the bottom, over which a ftrainer is put. The fugar now purges itfelf of its remaining im-purity; the molaffes, or treacly part, drains thro' the aperture into veffels placed for its reception. It is now called mufcavado fugar, is of a yellowifh brown colour, and in that condition is commonly put into the hogfheads, and fhipped off. But when a greater degree of finenefs is wanted, and a far-ther purgation of the fugar from the molaffes, the pots juft mentioned are covered with a fort of white clay, like that ufed in making tobacco-pipes, di-luted with water. This penetrates the fugar, and uniting with the molaffes, and carrying them off with it, leaves the fugar of a whitifh colour, but

whiteft

whiteſt at top. They are now called clayed ſugars; and though this operation is ſometimes repeated three or four times, by which, at every time, the ſugar is diminiſhed in quantity but increaſed in value, it ſtill goes under that name ; refining ſugar being in a manner prohibited in the iſlands, by the impoſition of an heavy duty of ſixteen ſhillings the hundred weight.

Of the molaſſes rum is made, and ſometimes of the juice of thoſe poor canes which will not produce ſugar. It is computed, that when things are well managed, the rum and molaſſes defray the annual expence of the plantation, and that all the ſugars are clear gain. A compleat ſugar-work, with land in proportion, and from two hundred and fifty to three hundred ſlaves, may manufacture about five hundred hogſheads of ſugar, producing, one with another, and clear of all charges, fourteen or fifteen pounds ſterling each. From whence the immenſe profits of a ſugar-plantation, though the expences at the firſt ſetting out muſt be great, may be eaſily conceived.

Of the MANUFACTURE of INDIGO.

THERE is no commodity from which a planter, with a ſmall capital, raiſes ſo great a profit as from the culture and manufacture of indigo. This dye uſed to be produced in great quanti-
tities

tities in our Weft-India iflands ; but it has been of late greatly neglected there, and the preference given to fugar. South-Carolina and Georgia are the two colonies where its culture is moft attended to, and where it is raifed in the greateft quantities.

The plant, or rather weed, from which this dye is made, when young, is hardly to be diftingtiished from lucerne-grafs; but, when come to maturity, has much the appearance of fern. It generally grows to the height of about two feet, the leaves round, of a green colour, inclining towards brown on the upper fide of the leaf, filver coloured underneath, and pretty thick ; the flowers are almoft like thofe of peafe, and of a reddifh colour, from whence proceed long crooked pods, refembling a fickle, which contains a little feed in them like radifh feed, of an olive colour. The manner of planting it is as follows : the ground fet apart for that being firft diligently cleared of all other vegetables, holes are made in it about a foot diftance from each other, in every one of which ten or twelve feeds are thrown, and then lightly covered with earth. In three or four days, efpecially if there has been rain, the plant will appear; and in fix weeks, or two months, be ready for cutting, and making indigo. The time of fowing is commonly after the firft rains which fucceed the vernal equinox ; confequently the firft cutting, for there are fometimes three, muft be about the beginning of July ; the fecond is towards the end of Auguft, and at Michaelmas, if the feafon has been favoura-

ble, the third and laft cutting is obtained. During all this time the plantation muſt be attended
with the utmoſt care; the land muſt be weeded
every day, and the plants carefully cleanſed from
the worms. To a plantation of fifty acres about
twenty-five negroes are allotted. Every acre, if
the land be very good, produces ſixty or ſeventy
pounds weight of indigo; the medium is computed at fifty. When the plant begins to bloſſom
it ought to be cut, after which, and in carrying it
to the place where it is manufactured, great care
muſt be taken to preſs or ſhake the leaves as little
as poſſible; for much of the beauty and value of
the indigo depends on the fine farina or meal which
adheres to them.

Indigo works, though large, are not very expenſive; the whole conſiſting of a pump and vats
or tubs of cypreſs wood. The firſt vat is called
the ſteeper, which is from twelve to fourteen feet
ſquare, and about four feet deep. In this the
indigo weed is laid to the height of fourteen inches;
and in about twelve or ſixteen hours, according to
the heat or coolneſs of the weather, after the water
has been let into the vat, it begins to ferment,
ſwell, riſe, and grow ſenſibly warm; upon this
ſpars of wood are laid acroſs to prevent its riſing
too much. When it is judged that the fermentation has attained its due pitch, and is beginning to
abate by its falling below a certain mark, placed
on purpoſe on the ſide of the vat, the liquor is
made to run off by a cock into another vat, called
the

the beater.   The grofs matter remaining in the
fteeper is ufed for manuring the ground, and new
cuttings are put in as long as the harveft continues.

The liquor now in the fecond vat being ftrongly
impregnated with the particles of indigo, next un-
dergoes the operation of what is called the beating,
which is performed with a fort of bottomlefs
buckets, having long handles : with thefe, for the
fpace of twenty, thirty, or thirty-five minutes, according to the temperature of the air, this liquor is
continually and ftrongly wrought and agitated till
it heats, froths, ferments, and rifes above the rim of
the veffel containing it.   Should the fermentation
be too violent it is inftantly allayed by throwing
in a fmall quantity of oil.   By this means a fmall
muddy grain begins to be formed ; for the falts,
and other parts of the plant, now incorpora-
ed with, and diffolved in the water, are feparated from it, and a granulation enfues.   When it
is fufficiently beaten, of which a judgment is
formed by taking up fome of it, and viewing it in
a glafs, in order to haften the granulation, a certain
quantity of lime water is let in from an adjacent
veffel, the workmen gently ftirring it all the time.
The liquor now affumes a purplifh colour, and
the whole becomes turbid and muddy ; it is then
fuffered to fettle, and the clear water is gradually
drained off, till nothing remains at bottom but a
thick mud, which is put into bags of coarfe linen.   Thefe are hung up, and left hanging till all
the

the moifture is entirely drained off.   To finifh the drying, this mud is turned out of the bags, and worked upon boards of fome porous timber, with a wooden fpatula; with the fame view it is frequently expofed to the morning and evening fun, though for a fhort time only.   The laft operation is the curing, which is performed by cutting it into little fquare pieces, and putting it into boxes and frames, where it is again expofed to the fun in the fame cautious manner.   After indigo is ready for the market there are two ways of proving its goodnefs; the firft is by throwing it into water; if it finks, it is worth little, and the heavier the worfe; if it fwims it is good ; if it diffolves entirely it is likewife good.   The fecond is by fire; if it confumes entirely away, it is good, for the adulterations remain untouched.

There are three forts of Indigo cultivated in Carolina and Georgia, which owe their difference to the nature of the feed.   The firft is the French, or Hifpaniola indigo, which ftriking a long tap root, requires a deep rich foil, and is therefore but little cultivated in the maritime parts, which are generally fandy.   The fecond is the falfe guatimala, or true Bahama; and the third is the indigenous indigo, a native of the country.   Both thefe are content with any foil; and for eafinefs of the culture, and quantity of the produce, though not for the quality of the dye, anfwer the purpofes of the planter better.

THOUGHTS

Thoughts on the Slave-Trade, and the Number and Management of Negroes in the Plantations.

ALL the field-work in the West-Indies, and in Virginia, and the colonies to the southward, except in some of the back settlements, is performed by negroes, brought from the coast of Africa, or born of those who have originally come from thence. This trade is carried on by ships fitted out and furnished with proper cargoes at the ports of London, Bristol, or Liverpool. They repair to the African coast, and having got on board their intended number, or nearly so of Blacks, who are generally prisoners taken in the wars, which the petty nations on that coast carry on amongst one another for that very purpose, they sail to the West-Indies, or to the southern continental colonies, where the slaves are either consigned to the correspondents of the British merchants, or disposed of by the masters of the respective ships, which then return to Britain, loaded with the produce of the colonies where they have left their cargoes.

This is the manner in which this famous commerce is managed, to which there are innumerable objections on the side of humanity, and which indeed can only be justified by necessity; but which must ever continue as long as men prefer their interest to all other considerations.

The

The foundation of this trade lies in the want of hands to cultivate the fouthern plantations, the unfitnefs of Europeans for that purpofe, and, laftly, in the barbarifm of thofe nations where the flaves are procured. Hence it appears that this trade, againft which many well-meaning men have fo loudly exclaimed, whilft there are civilized nations who want flaves, and whilft there are bar- barians who will fell them, muft ever remain. Should thofe regions which now fupply America with that fpecies of commodity, as it may be called, ever come to be inhabited by a wife, civi- lized, and well policied people, this commerce would, no doubt, from that æra be at an end; and our adventurers in that bufinefs would be conftrained to feek out fome other quarter of the world inhabited by uncultivated nations. This has ever been the cafe. The Greeks and Romans were fupplied with the greateft number of their flaves from Thrace, and other barbarous countries in Europe, Afia, and Africa.

Slavery is a very ancient inftitution, coeval with our knowledge of human affairs. The laws relat- ing to it conftituted a great part of the Roman code. Thefe were originally exceffively fevere, but were afterwards mollified by the emperors. The behaviour of the ancients to their flaves was likewife extremely cruel, and quite in the fpirit of their laws. By degrees, however, as the minds of men grew more humanized, and as the old fero- city of manners began to abate, flavery was infen-

fibly

fibly abolifhed among all the European Chriftian nations, except the Poles and Ruffians. But the nature, fituation, and climate of their American fettlements revived it amongft them in thofe countries. It is a neceffary but unfortunate circumftance. Neceffary, becaufe fuch is the nature of the climate, and of the labour to be performed, that no European conftitution is able to undergo it, or at leaft to perform fo much as to be any fort of equivalent to the expence. By the original fettlement of the colony of Georgia, negroe-flaves were totally excluded from it; but a very fhort experience made it appear, that this was an impracticable meafure; that inftitution was obliged to be repealed, and blacks are now as numerous there as in any other of the colonies. It is certain that Africans, or their defcendants, are better able to fupport fevere labour in hot countries than any of European blood. But it is an unfortunate circumftance, becaufe no inftitution is fo apt as flavery to extirpate the milder and more amiable virtues of compaffion and humanity, and to render men cruel, hardhearted, and remorfelefs. Men who are furrounded with great numbers of their fellow-creatures, who are their own abfolute property, come foon to confider them in the light of animals and beafts of burthen, and by degrees extend that confideration to all the reft of the fpecies. A remarkable inftance of this in South-Carolina we have heard well attefted. The moft laborious drudgery in that colony is clearing the rice of its hufk. This

is

is now generally performed by machines; but formerly it was done by the hand-labour of the slaves, who ufed for that purpofe a wooden trough, in which the rice is put, and then beat it with a mallet, much of the fame nature with that ufed by paviors. An eminent planter in that colony, whenever there happened a fudden demand for rice, ufed commonly to deftroy five or fix of his flaves in a feafon, by over-tafking them at that drudgery, and coolly juftified this fhocking barbarity, by alledging, that he found the extraordinary profit he made by this means of his rice, more than compenfated the value of the flaves he loft. We are afraid that fuch barbarians are too often to be met with in all our colonies.

It is certain that the treatment of the negroes in our plantations is very hard and fevere; and the punifhment inflicted upon them for faults and neglects very cruel and inadequate. In capital cafes it is generally attended with torture: they are often burnt; frequently hanged up alive, in which fituation they are generally eight or nine days a dying. This, befides the natural inhumanity of thofe who have been long converfant among the flaves, is likewife owing to the vaft difproportion of numbers between the whites and the blacks, which obliges the former to obferve the latter with a ftricter eye, and to chaftife them with a feverer hand. This is moft evidently proved from the very different treatment which negro flaves ex-

perience

perience in the northern provinces from what they meet with in the fouthern, and in the Weft-Indies. In the former, namely, Penfylvania, the Jerfeys, New-York, New-England, and Nova-Scotia, where their numbers are but fmall, compared with the whites, and where the wealth of their mafters does not confift in them; they are treated much in the fame manner as if they were whites; they are neither punifhed more feverely, nor obliged to labour harder. It muft be confeffed it will ever be impracticable to treat them in the fame manner in the fouthern colonies and iflands. The nature of things will not permit it, but ftill a mea-fure is to be obferved.

Another bad confequence of the fevere treat-ment and hard labour thefe poor creatures undergo is, the prodigious annual decreafe of their num-bers, which is fo great that in the ifland of Bar-badoes, where there are computed to be about feventy-five thoufand blacks, an annual impor-tation of no lefs than five thoufand is required barely to keep up the ftock. A circumftance which is perfectly amazing, efpecially when we confider the difproportion between the blacks and whites is not fo great as the other iflands; and confequently it may be fuppofed the treatment the former meet with is not fo rigid; and likewife that Barbadoes is a very healthy climate, quite friendly to their conftitutions, as much at leaft as their na-tive country, where they are fo wonderfully prolific

lific that, notwithstanding the immense drains annually made by the slave-trade, and the losses occasioned by their perpetual wars, their numbers
have not sensibly decreased.   If such be the yearly
excess of deaths above births in Barbadoes, it
must at least be proportionable in the other islands,
from whence the sum of the whole may be easily
computed.   That it is solely occasioned by the
severity of their masters, is evident from the
following circumstance.   There are some excepti-
ons to this habitual severity of planters, and those
who are so, find their advantages in it; for instead
of being obliged to purchase supplies of new negroes to keep up their stock, they are known to
turn out into their fields an additional number of
working hands every year, born and bred upon
their own estates.   These instances are, however,
at present so extremely rare, that it is to be feared
they can never serve as an example.

But it is of the highest importance both to the
interests of humanity, and what will be more
attended to by some, to those of commerce, that
a stop should be put to this daily waste and destruction of the human species, especially when
the means of doing it, which have been already
pointed out, are so easy and agreeable.   But when
men have once got into a certain tract, or bias,
they are not easily driven out of it.   For that
purpose, some force or change of circumstances
are often necessary.   Were the laws now subsisting which oblige every planter to have a certain
pro-

proportion of white fervants to his negroe flaves, to be ftrictly enforced it would be attended with many good confequences. But, perhaps, the moft effectual meafure would be to lay a pretty heavy duty per head upon all new negroes imported from Africa for the ufe of the plantations; we do not mean fuch a duty as would amount to a prohibition, but only fuch as would make the planter perceive it was for his intereft rather to breed from his prefent ftock of old negroes, than to keep up that ftock by a conftant purchafe of new ones. Were this meafure to take place, and to be purfued to its full extent and effects, it would not be in the leaft detrimental to commerce, or to the confumption of our manufactures, as fome at firft view might be apt to imagine. It is true, it might fomewhat leffen the number of fhipping now employed in the flaving-trade; but this would be more than compenfated by a greater confumption of our manufactures. For the number of flaves continuing by fuppofition ftill the fame, and thofe being all or at leaft for the moft part creolians or natives, and confequently as is the cafe now, more valuable and induftrious; both the habits of the flaves and the intereft of the planters would require them to be better cloathed; all which is done from our manufactures. It is a wife difpenfation of Providence, that a courfe of virtue, humanity, and benevolence, as it is moft agree-

VOL. II.   N n   able

able to human nature, so in the matter of temporal concerns, it is likewise most profitable and advantageous. To induce one man, or set of men, to excel others in virtue, nothing is required but the possessing more enlightened understandings.

F I N I S.

Lightning Source UK Ltd.
Milton Keynes UK
UKHW021630081118
331957UK00011B/1384/P